Content and Commerce Driven Strategies in Global Networks

Building the Network Economy in Europe

European Commission
Directorate General XIII/E
Luxembourg

www.echo.lu/info2000/
info2000@echo.lu

Legal Notice

By the COMMISSION OF THE EUROPEAN COMMUNITIES, Directorate General XIII/E, Telecommunications, Information and Exploitation of Research

Disclaimer

Neither the Commission of the European Communities nor any person acting on behalf of the Commission is responsible for the use which might be made of the following information. The views expressed in this report are those of the authors and do not necessarily reflect those of the Commission of the European Communities.

Rights Restrictions

 Nothing in this report implies or expresses a warranty of any kind. Results from this report should only be used as guidelines as part of an overall strategy. For detailed advice on corporate planning, business process management, technology integration, and legal or tax issues, the services of a professional should be obtained.

A great deal of additional information on the European Union is available on the Internet. It can be accessed through the Europa server (http://europa.eu.int).

Cataloguing data can be found at the end of this publication.

Luxembourg: Office for Official Publications of the European Communities, 1998

ISBN 92-828-4289-4

Printed in Belgium

PRINTED ON WHITE CHLORINE-FREE-PAPER

Table of Contents

List of Exhibits

Preface

The economies of the European Union Member States and many other nations of the world are in the earliest stages of a revolution. At the request of the European Union's Directorate General XIII/E, Gemini Consulting has undertaken to describe this transformation and examine its complex dynamics.

Having begun in North America and Scandinavia, the network economy is now spreading to the rest of the developed world. Faced with this phenomenon, the European Union stands to profit significantly by examining innovative network commerce efforts occurring across Europe as well as in markets where the network economy is already established and beginning to flourish. Comparisons between these markets will reveal key drivers and constraints to the development of the network economy.

The network revolution will reach all sectors of the economy and society with the content industry playing a central role. The more far-reaching economic and social implications are only now becoming apparent. Business and government leaders must consider these matters today to prepare for the future.

Earlier studies (Consulting Trust's "New Opportunities for Publishers in the Information Services Market" in 1993; IEPRC's "The Future of Media and Advertising" in 1995; and Andersen Consulting's "Strategic Developments for the European Publishing Industry towards the Year 2000" in 1996) focused primarily on market opportunities created for publishers by new electronic media. In this decade, the Internet has emerged as a significant new market and a tool for transforming business operations. Operating a Web site and employing network technologies to build stronger, more manageable connections with employees, partners, and customers are no longer potential sources of competitive advantage but fundamental to doing business.

In this study, we analyse how a broad range of businesses have benefited from network commerce. We also examine the critical roles of content and the content industry within the network economy. Finally, we review the larger financial, social, and political issues helping to shape the network economy, recognising that for European content firms to prosper in the new economy, many factors beyond their control (e.g. government policies, telecom costs, consumer attitudes) may have to change.

We hope this effort will be useful to businesses, governments, other organisations, and individuals attempting to navigate the swiftly-moving currents of the new economy.

The CONDRINET Team

Acknowledgements

Several individuals and organisations have contributed to the success of the CONDRINET study. We want to acknowledge some of the key contributors and thank them for their assistance. We especially wish to thank the many individuals who consented to interviews or participated in the two Round Table discussions in Paris. In addition, we owe a debt of gratitude to our Project Officer, Dr. Massimo Garribba of DGXIII/E, and the members of the CONDRINET Steering Committee. Interviewees and Round Table participants are individually identified in an appendix to this report.

A CD-ROM to accompany this document was produced by Cap Gemini Innovation, Paris, under the direction of Bertrand Maigné. For information on ordering copies of the Executive Summary, Full Report, or CD-ROM, see page 56, or visit the CONDRINET Web site at www.echo.lu/condrinet/.

CONDRINET Team

Jean-Dominique Abrial, Project Co-Director
Gemini Consulting
Jean-Dominique.Abrial@gemcon.com

Randall S. Hancock, Project Co-Director
Gemini Strategic Research Group
Rshancock@mindspring.com

Jean Haguet, Project Manager
Gemini Consulting
Jean.Haguet@gemcon.com

Charles Gerlach, Principal Author
Gemini Strategic Research Group
Cgerlach@ix.netcom.com

David Kohn, Principal Author
Gemini Strategic Research Group
Dkohn@gemconsult.com

Emanuel Michau, Author — Legal Expert
Michau & Associés
Emanuel.Michau@wanadoo.fr

Jean-Christophe Hua, Contributor
Gemini Consulting
Jean-Christophe.Hua@gemcon.com

John Webster, Editor
Gemini Consulting
John.Webster@gemcon.com

Tristram Oakley, Editor
Gemini Strategic Research Group
Toakley@gemconsult.com

Lana Langlois, Graphic Design & Layout
Gemini Strategic Research Group
Langlois@gemconsult.com

Anne Fessler, Graphic Design & Layout
Gemini Strategic Research Group
Afessler@gemconsult.com

Special thanks also to Ishreen Markar, Philip Blackwell, John Kavanagh, Pierre Tegner, Maria Linde, Maria Lion, Jane Whiting, and Catherine Cointet.

Introduction

The scope of CONDRINET is as broad as the concept of network commerce. This study covers a wide range of topics and addresses critical issues having to do with the emerging network economy. In this introduction, we provide this report's contents and how it can be put to use most effectively.

Using this Study

This report has been designed to meet the needs of a variety of individual users. Brief chapter descriptions are provided on the title page of each chapter and a summary of the chapter is provided at the end of the chapter. Each chapter includes examples supporting the concepts and issues under discussion. Finally, in order to help create a more useful tool for managers and business strategists, chapters four through ten conclude with a list of related recommendations specifically targeting businesses, content firms, and governments.

Organisation

We have divided this report into ten chapters. In addition, there are six appendices, a glossary, and a bibliography. The study focuses primarily on the interactive content industry from its roots in traditional media through its expansion into a digital interactive environment in which media and commerce converge. We examine all aspects of the digital media industry — consumers, producers, the business environment, and regulatory, technological, and financial issues. Our objective throughout has been to deliver pragmatic recommendations and advice for conducting commerce in a network environment.

Chapter 1 may be read as a stand-alone executive summary, describing the study's key findings and providing a detailed overview of the analysis supporting those findings. Chapter 2 provides context for discussion of the evolution of the digital media industry and of the trends occurring in specific industries and markets.

In Chapter 3, we frame our discussion of the interactive content industry, introducing our concept of the interactive content value web, based on an industry value chain, but incorporating the increasingly complex relationships among content, commerce, and network connectivity.

Chapter 4 examines how a new digital content and communications industry structure is emerging as a result of technological advancements and macro-economic changes. These changes are affecting the relationship between content supply and demand on an industry-wide basis, as well as the dynamics of vertical and horizontal integration in the media and telecommunications sectors.

In Chapter 5, we look at network commerce and its potential to address a series of business needs, ranging from additional distribution channels, cost reduction, efficiency, flexibility, and innovation, to the creation of competitive advantage through customer lock-in.

In Chapter 6, we examine how end-user needs translate to market demand for network commerce and content. Ultimately, market demand will determine the success of the many new media platforms and products that are becoming available.

Chapter 7 explores how technology (in combination with consumer demand) has enabled the network revolution, and how it will continue to profoundly shape its evolution.

In Chapter 8, we examine how legal and regulatory frameworks provide both preconditions and constraints in terms of the evolution of network commerce.

In Chapter 9, we examine key financial drivers and constraints to the evolution of network commerce. Tax policy and the venture capital environment are central in determining where the money to fund the emerging network economy will come from. European Monetary Union is also likely to have a significant impact on the evolution of network commerce in Europe.

In Chapter 10, we study the broader implications of network commerce, considering in particular its potential impact on employment, education, European competitiveness, and society in general.

Methodology

The CONDRINET study draws heavily upon the experience of the Cap Gemini family of companies and their day-to-day efforts partnering with businesses and other organisations to develop real-world strategies. Many of the recommendations and analyses contained in this report are distilled from our experience helping clients develop strategies to address the issues discussed in this report. Further, we have drawn heavily on the latest research, including many reports produced by world governments and multilateral bodies. Extensive interviews with industry participants, primarily in Europe, have also helped validate our analyses. CONDRINET team members have attended a number of industry conferences and benefited from regular discussions with the project Steering Committee sponsored by DG XIII/E. Finally, two Round Table sessions were held in Paris to refine our understanding of the relative roles of television and the Internet in the evolution of the network economy, and of the specific issues confronting European network commerce entrepreneurs.

Living Document

Please visit our CONDRINET Web site at http://www.echo.lu/condrinet/ and share your point of view and impression of CONDRINET with us. We view this report as a "beta version" and invite your critical comments to help refine the product.

Executive Summary

We are at the beginning of a "network revolution," a technology-enabled change that is poised to transform the content industry as well as much of business and society. This study covers the evolution of the interactive content industry from its roots in traditional media through its growth into a digital interactive environment in which media and commerce converge. This chapter highlights the key findings of the study.

We are at the beginning of a "network revolution" — an economic and social transition comparable to the Industrial Revolution. This revolution reflects the migration of significant amounts of commercial and social activity from the physical world to interactive, digital networks built upon open standards[1] (e.g. the Internet, some online services, some interactive television systems). This revolution is creating a new economy and presents momentous challenges and opportunities for businesses, governments, and individuals. It may be one of the most important changes facing Europeans today.

The measurable impact of the network revolution is likely to be significant over the next five years, while its impact on the European economy as a percentage of total gross domestic product and in terms of total jobs created or lost will still appear relatively small. However, within that five-year time frame some industries (e.g. publishing, financial services, automotive retailing) will be fundamentally altered. The longer-term viability of many individual firms, and even the competitiveness of nations, may be determined by the strategies they choose to pursue. Within the next five years, we estimate that more than 80 million Europeans will become regular network users and that 500 billion euro in annual sales will be either directly transacted or indirectly affected by the use of these networks (Exhibit 1.1). More than 100,000 jobs directly related to the network economy are already unfilled in Europe; an estimated 500,000 more are likely to be created by 2002. Many jobs will be lost as well, and the near-term net impact of the network revolution on job creation will depend on the responses of individuals, businesses, and governments to training and job mobility issues.

Exhibit 1.1 **Measuring the Network Revolution**

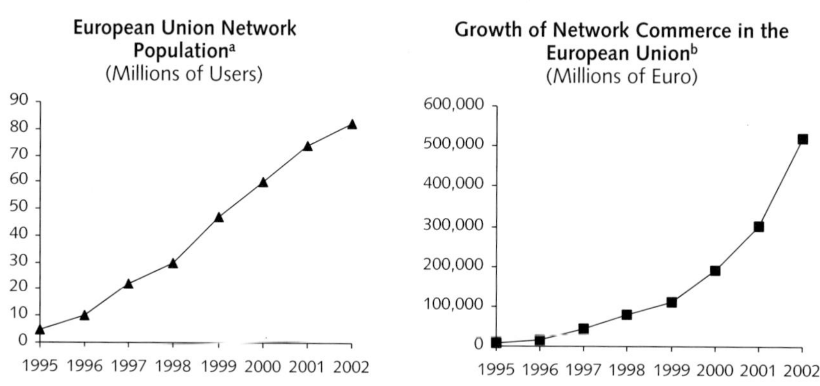

Note: Gemini Strategic Research Group Estimates.

a. Estimated growth of Internet users in EU15 nations based on observed growth rates in individual nations and historic growth rates in advanced markets.

b. Includes direct network-based transactions in all categories of goods and services (business-to-consumer and business-to-business) and transactions consummated offline but directly affected by use of the network (e.g. offline automobile purchase facilitated by Web-based research).

The network revolution has special implications for Europe's traditional content industries (e.g. publishers, broadcasters). The critical role of content (text, music, graphics, video, data, etc.) in the network economy creates new opportunities for traditional content firms to sell their products and content expertise. A recent study by the US Department of Commerce found that publishers are at the forefront of consumer interest in the World Wide Web with 90 percent of Web users going online primarily for news and information. Around the globe, thousands of newspapers and broadcasters have already established significant Web presences. Despite the quick response to the changing landscape, however, the fundamental impact of digital networks on content creation and distribution also places considerable pressure on those traditional content industries. The proliferation of content and blurring of markets enabled by computing and network technologies is already devaluing content that is not highly differentiated in terms of quality, timeliness, customisation, and originality. Some firms will capture the opportunities presented by this historic change. Tens of thousands of new businesses will launch; some will join the ranks of Europe's leading firms. Inevitably, however, many European content firms will be heavily buffeted by the emergence of this new economy; some will fail to adjust and disappear.

European businesses, governments, and individuals must proactively foster change to realise the opportunities inherent in this emerging economy. To stay at the forefront of competition, they must commit to building adequate market and business infrastructures and encouraging a general shift in mindset toward network usage — no small order, admittedly. A sufficient market infrastructure (e.g. inexpensive and ubiquitous network access and services coupled with inexpensive and easy-to-use access devices) has to be available to allow all participants — especially consumers — to operate easily in the network world. Equally, a supportive business infrastructure (e.g. sufficient capital, flexible regulations, a skilled and motivated workforce, policies encouraging competition) must exist to promote growth and success in the network economy. Participants must adjust to the changes that are occurring and act now to capture opportunities rather than simply wait for and react to the outcome.

We have identified four key priorities for European businesses:

- Pursue a comprehensive approach to the use of networks to transform business processes.
- Create fast, flexible "learning" organisations with motivated, empowered, and IT-literate workers at all levels.
- Work effectively with other businesses and governments on matters such as self-regulation and standardisation.
- Focus on capturing and nurturing customers' attention and trust by delivering personalised products and services and building strong communities of interest.

Many governments are already recognising the intrinsically decentralised nature of the network economy and have refrained from unnecessary legislation, which has often proven both ineffective and counterproductive. Governments can prove most effective as facilitators of development and leading adopters. In this context, we have identified five key priorities for the public sector:

- Ensure that telecommunications competition brings inexpensive, open-standards-based broadband network access to a substantial portion of the population.
- Facilitate business-led self-regulation efforts to develop basic business rules and standards on a world-wide basis.
- Ensure that educational and human resources policies will provide sufficient numbers of skilled workers and stimulate employee mobility.
- Improve access to capital by promoting the development of pan-European small-cap markets, removing barriers to new venture creation (e.g. excessive regulation of new businesses, high taxes on capital gains, draconian bankruptcy codes), and helping to link venture capitalists with entrepreneurs.
- Become visible users of network technologies in an effort to improve the responsiveness and quality of services that are delivered to citizens.

Our discussion in this executive summary of the emerging network economy and its implications for European content firms and governments is divided into three parts (Exhibit 1.2). First, we describe the enablers of the network revolution and the factors shaping its development. Second, we examine the six fundamental characteristics of business in the network economy (network commerce). Finally, we look at the broader social and political implications of the network economy. Throughout the discussion, we provide both examples and recommendations for European businesses and governments.

Exhibit 1.2 **Executive Summary Structure**

1.1 Network Revolution

A new economy is emerging

- **1.1.1** Enabled by technology
- **1.1.2** Underpinned by market needs
- **1.1.3** Reaching critical mass of users and services
- **1.1.4** Guided by regulatory and financial realities

1.2 Network Business Characteristics

Industries and markets are changing

- **1.2.1** Lowers transaction costs
- **1.2.2** Makes content more critical
- **1.2.3** Blurs boundaries
- **1.2.4** Shifts power
- **1.2.5** Speeds competition
- **1.2.6** Requires new models for success

1.3 Broader Implications of Network Commerce

Societies and politics are evolving

- **1.3.1** Requires adjustments in the workforce
- **1.3.2** Demands more from education
- **1.3.3** Alters levers of regional competitiveness
- **1.3.4** Changes culture
- **1.3.5** Redefines roles of government
- **1.3.6** Requires global approaches to legal and regulatory policies

1.1 The Network Revolution

The explosive growth of the world-wide network economy will create unprecedented opportunities and threats for European firms, governments, and individuals. European content firms, in particular, will be challenged to compete with many new content creators and purveyors, adopt new economic models, and incorporate new technologies into their operations — all within a short time. In fact, many established content businesses throughout the developed world are already addressing these challenges (e.g. more than 2,700 newspapers around the world offer services on the Internet; more than 800 local television stations in the US alone have Internet sites).

This network revolution reflects the migration of a significant portion of economic and social activity from the physical world to digital networks — primarily those based on Internet Protocol (an open networking protocol defining the transport of packets of data over disparate networks). This migration leads to the convergence[2] of many formerly separate types of devices, networks, content, and industries. Such familiar indicators as usage growth rates, changing end-user attitudes, and business investment decisions suggest that the network economy is already spreading rapidly throughout the developed world, significantly altering the way firms and individuals conduct business and obtain and communicate information. Technology, end-user needs, market trends, and financial and regulatory factors all play a part in enabling and shaping the revolution.

1.1.1 Enabled by Technology

Technology is an essential enabler of the network revolution. Technology exists — or will soon exist — to enable most of the key applications and services associated with the network economy. Moore's Law is the technological principle at the heart of the network revolution. Gordon Moore, co-founder of Intel Corporation, observed in 1964 that the amount of processing power one can purchase for a given amount of money doubles about every eighteen months (Exhibit 1.3). As a consequence, the cost of almost any product or service based on digital technologies has decreased dramatically. Manufacturers now build inexpensive microprocessing chips into a wide selection of products ranging from automobiles to telephones. Today, 15 billion microchips are in use, and soon manufacturers will embed them in almost every product. Moore's Law is considered likely to hold true for at least the next quarter century; however, many of the critical developments required to realise the promise of the network economy may reside in improved standards and software, and in network organisational refinements — rather than further increases in processing speed.

Exhibit 1.3 **Moore's Law**

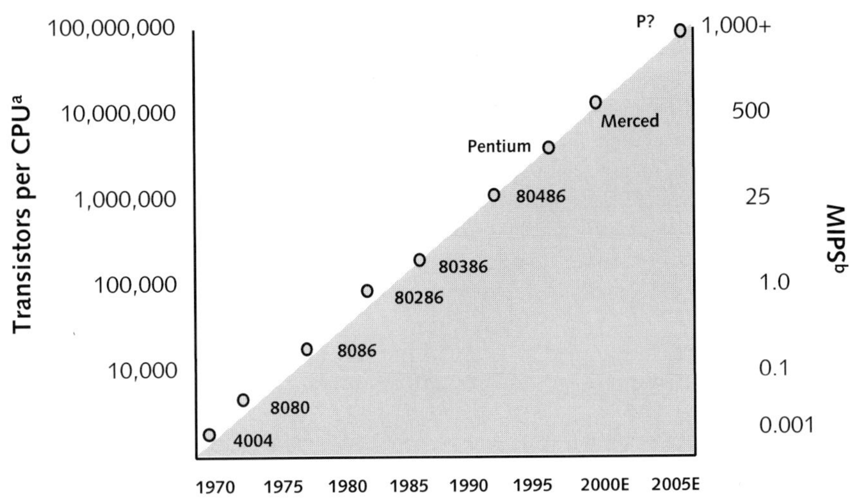

Source: Intel Corporation; *BYTE*; Gemini Strategic Research Group.

a. Central processing unit.

b. Millions of instructions per second.

Four other critical technical developments are supporting the network revolution. First, analogue content of all types is being converted into digital format, making it easier to copy, manipulate, store, and transmit. Second, the amount of bandwidth (network capacity measured in bits per second) available for transport of digital data is increasing rapidly. Construction of new networks and the use of new technologies such as cable modems, digital subscriber line (DSL), and dense wave division multiplexing (DWDM) point to the continued exponential growth of network capacity, greatly increasing network capabilities and decreasing transmission costs. Third, packet-switched networks, such as the global Internet, will soon carry most telecommunications traffic, rapidly surpassing the volume of traffic carried by public-switched telecommunications networks and making media-rich yet inexpensive new telecommunications services available to much of the population. Finally, hardware and software developers are increasingly building products and services based on open standards, ensuring greater interoperability and competition — once again resulting in less expensive yet superior products and services.

For content firms, technology lowers the costs of creating, duplicating, and distributing many products, reducing these costs as barriers to entry. Anyone who wishes can use an inexpensive PC and the network to produce and distribute content that would otherwise never be created or made available.

RECOMMENDATIONS

Businesses

- Develop a thorough understanding of the capabilities and limitations of the key technologies used in the network economy (e.g. create an internal group dedicated to following technology development). Actively experiment with new technologies to truly understand their capabilities.
- Count on the continued improvement of network-related hardware and software capabilities. Many current technological constraints will be minimised as software and hardware rapidly continue to develop.
- Use technologies based on open standards. Do not try to lock in customers or partners through proprietary technology; open standards eventually prevail.

Content Firms

- Digitise content and treat it as the primary product rather than a secondary product.
- Explore how interactivity enhances content and changes its nature and value (e.g. experiment with a wide range of interactive products and continuously track how technology can enhance these products).
- Continue leveraging the power of technology to improve content creation, replication, and distribution.

Governments

- Support businesses in the creation of open and common technological standards, without restricting the development of technology (e.g. by legislating narrow, inflexible standards).
- Improve processes for commercialisation of government-funded research (e.g. through public-private partnerships).

1.1.2 Underpinned by Market Needs

The network revolution is underpinned by market needs — both expressed and latent. While observers often debate whether "market pull" or "technology push" triggers innovation, the reality is that markets and technology evolve together as part of a "co-evolutionary" system. Expressed needs create market pull — end users demand that their product and service needs be fulfilled more effectively, more conveniently, less expensively, and faster. For example, mobile telephones were developed in response to a need to make and receive telephone calls anywhere, anytime. In contrast, technology push occurs where technology fulfils expressed needs in unexpected ways or fulfils latent needs (needs for goods or services that the end user would value but has never experienced or would never think to ask for). A classic example is the use of the French Minitel service (originally created as an electronic telephone directory and information service) for adult-oriented "chat."

Many approaches to product and service development do not anticipate customer needs so much as reflect customer reactions to existing services. What is missing with these approaches is an ability to tap into latent needs. Simply "listening to the customer" and responding is no longer sufficient because customers may not be able to articulate what they really want. We did not grow up needing a Walkman, for instance, but Sony discovered a latent need for a small personal stereo and capitalised on that need. Many successful businesses are capable of envisioning new customer needs before customers can articulate the needs themselves. To tap into these latent needs, firms must be able to listen to the tacit — to the implicit — as well as the expressed needs. If a firm listens only to the expressed needs, it will provide what its competitors are providing. But if a firm really wants to probe latent needs, it must adopt a different strategy.

Today, firms have a revolutionary opportunity to build flexible technology platforms that they can begin to evolve in co-operation with lead users. By tapping into customer practices, innovative firms can discover a wide range of opportunities. Firms can go beyond observing customers to actually working with customers, understanding latent needs and gaining tacit knowledge to develop more effective customer solutions. Here, the Internet provides a fundamentally new way to link to customers. It can be used, for example, to create a "virtual community" of product users, which a manufacturer can access to understand user perspectives and concerns.

Innovation in telecommunications has traditionally been slow. While technology has provided many incremental improvements, it has neither changed telecommunications fundamentally, nor led to radically new product or service development. The Internet changed all this, unleashing a competitive frenzy of service development that is unprecedented. What economist F. A. Hayek called "competition as a discovery procedure" has allowed thousands of firms to find new ideas through decentralised trial and error, through adaptation and improvisation. This has allowed marketers to explore what customers know but cannot articulate.

The most successful Web-based news, entertainment, and retail sites are constantly innovating in response both to the expressed desires of their customers and to latent needs discovered through observations of the behaviour of visitors to their sites. In addition, the relatively low cost and openness of Web-based platforms allows almost anyone with an interesting idea for a service or product to market it. Many — even most — of these ideas prove unsuccessful, but entrepreneurs learn through this experimentation and go on to develop other products and services. Other entrepreneurs, their imaginations sparked by the lessons of these failed products and services, go on to build on them, fuelling a cycle of innovation.

Finally, many needs are well understood, and we can observe today how entrepreneurs have successfully exploited network technologies to address them. Many people want to communicate with others, to share their ideas and interests with the world, to be entertained, and to be empowered as consumers. Many want to communicate in real-time with others. The success of AOL's chat rooms and instant messaging service; the success of the ICQ instant messaging service; and the Vocaltec Internet telephone directories of users, all provide dramatic evidence of this need. Many people also want to share their hobbies and interests with others by creating personal Web sites. The millions of people who have set up Web sites on GeoCities, Tripod, and other sites demonstrate the importance of this need. As consumers, people also seek greater selection, better information, better prices, and so forth. The most successful Web retailers owe much of their success to their ability to empower customers. Auto-by-Tel places detailed information in the hands of automobile purchasers, empowering them to make better deals. Amazon.com combines a huge selection of books for sale at reasonable prices with the ability to easily navigate that selection.

RECOMMENDATIONS

Businesses

- Investigate end-user needs using interactive technologies to capture, store, and analyse data to understand those needs and better address them. Identify and focus on lead users to better understand how the market is likely to evolve.
- Seek intersections between what customers want, such as ability to communicate, access information, be entertained, or be empowered as consumers, and what is possible to deliver.

Content Firms

- Recognise that traditional forms of content have evolved to meet certain consumer needs. Do not abandon them without good reason (e.g. printed books and newspapers will not go away for a very long time, if ever).

Governments

- Like businesses, governments may also investigate the needs of their citizens using new interactive technologies to capture, store, and analyse data to understand those needs and better address them.

1.1.3 Reaching Critical Mass of Users and Services

The network economy "takes off" when a significant portion of potential users perceives that a "critical mass" of valuable products and services has become accessible over a given network. The need for this critical mass creates a dilemma: potential users want products before investing in the service, but potential service providers need demand. Once critical mass is reached, adoption takes place through a viral uptake in commercial activity, rising along a steep growth curve. The rapid growth of network commerce has actually occurred in a series of markets "exploding" in succession — the first occurring in the North American and Nordic markets, followed by a number of markets in Europe, and more recently in Japan. These market explosions appear to bear out Metcalfe's Law (named after Robert Metcalfe, inventor of the Ethernet networking protocol and founder of 3Com Corporation), which holds that the utility of a network is equal to the square of its number of users (e.g. one fax machine is useless; two connected fax machines are somewhat useful; a million connected fax machines are far more valuable than the sum of the parts — Exhibit 1.4). The differences in the timing of these explosions are attributable to several factors — the cost of network access and market fragmentation caused by language differences being among the most important.

Exhibit 1.4 **Metcalfe's Law and the Succession of Market "Explosions"**

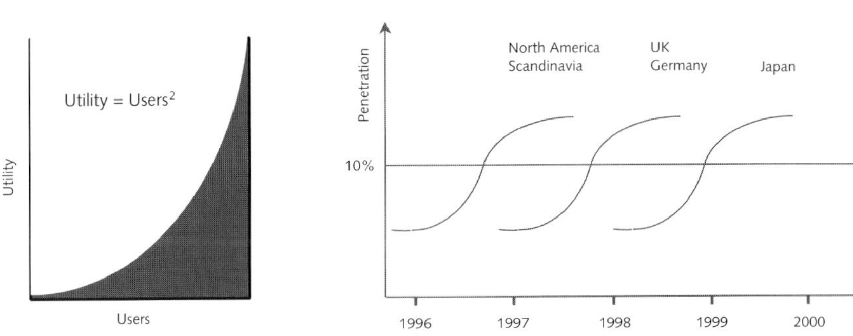

Source: Adapted from Mui & Downes, *Unleashing the Killer App*, 1998, and Jupiter Communications.

The Internet is the ultimate exemplar of Metcalfe's Law, since the Internet, by definition, allows the connection of disparate networks and devices. As such, the Internet has emerged as the most rapidly adopted technology in history. Radio existed for thirty-eight years before it reached a penetration of 50 million listeners; television took thirteen years to reach 50 million viewers. It was not until sixteen years after the introduction of the Altair PC kit that 50 million people were using personal computers. In contrast to these other successful technologies, after becoming available to the public, the Internet required only four years to reach 50 million users.

A competitive environment that can satisfy the need for low-cost, high-bandwidth, ubiquitous connections to the network is imperative in order to reach the critical mass of users necessary to spark the market "explosions." There is a correlation between access fees and Internet penetration (Exhibit 1.5). Another example of cost's importance as a factor in enabling the creation of a critical mass of activity is seen in the impact of online service AOL's decision to alter its pricing policy from metered charges to a flat rate. This move prompted an influx of subscribers and an increase in time spent online. AOL's flat rate, together with a flat rate for most local telephone calls in the US, meant that users stayed online as long as they liked without incurring additional costs. This resulted in a vast increase in commercial activity and interaction between subscribers on the service. In turn, supply of, and demand for, services increased, leading to even more people joining AOL.

Exhibit 1.5 **Comparison of Internet Penetration and Access Costs, Selected OECD Nations[a]**

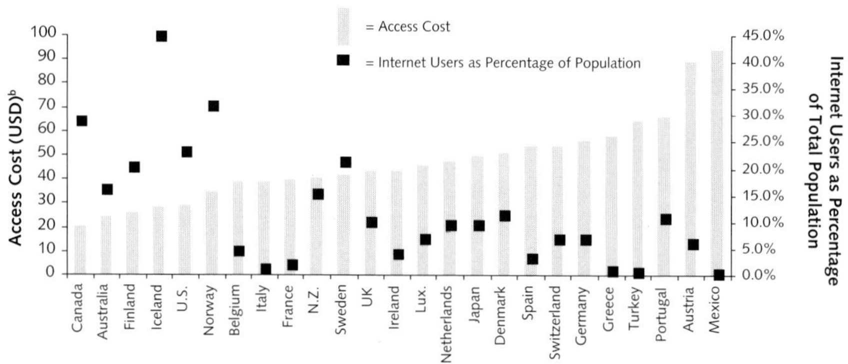

Source: NUA Internet; OECD; Gemini Strategic Research Group.

a. Internet user and penetration data for first quarter 1998.

b. Internet and PSTN tariffs for off-peak usage from August 1996, based on twenty hours per month of usage.

Language has also played an important role in the development of network markets. The Internet originated in the English-speaking world and achieved a critical mass there first. Much of the early success of the Internet in Scandinavia may be attributed to the high level of English proficiency there and the relative acceptance of English-language information. Users in those nations were also quick to develop services in Swedish, Finnish, Norwegian, and Icelandic, fuelling an even broader interest among potential users in those markets. As more users go online and more services develop, markets reach critical mass. This has already happened in Germany and Japan, with the Spanish-speaking and Portuguese-speaking populations on the Internet likely to be the next big markets to take off.

Exhibit 1.6 **Distribution of Global Internet Users by Language, OECD Nations, First Quarter 1998**

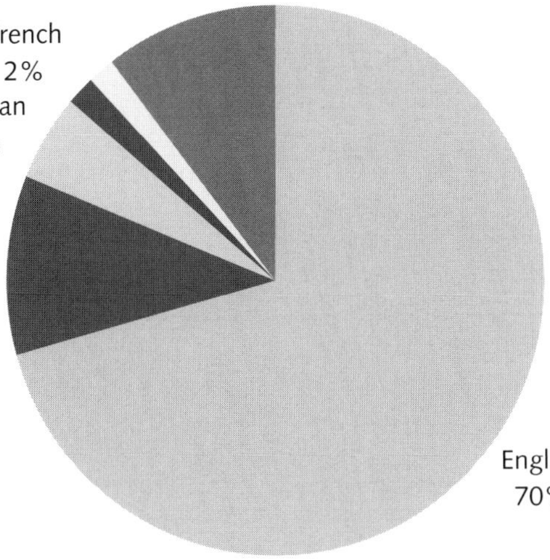

Source: NUA Internet; OECD; Gemini Strategic Research Group.

RECOMMENDATIONS

Businesses

- Become leaders in establishing a network presence, focusing on learning more than your competitors or potential competitors.
- Be prepared for rapid growth.
- Personalise content and services and develop the relevant technology partnerships to do so.

Content Firms

- Promote and link network products with traditional content products.
- Reengineer content development processes (e.g. create common databases of digital content for print, broadcast, and network channels).

Governments

- Ensure competition in the telecommunications services industry. The availability of inexpensive, easy, and ubiquitous access to the network — in particular the cost of local phone service — is essential to the success of the network economy.
- Place public information and services on the network. Adding content to the network will help it reach a critical mass of users and services.

1.1.4 Guided by Regulatory and Financial Realities

Naturally, regulatory and financial realities influence the growth of network commerce. Some of the most important laws and regulations affecting network business are those relating to telecommunications competition. Inexpensive communications costs will ensure inexpensive network access and therefore promote its use.

Taxation is one of the most far-reaching financial factors affecting where and whether businesses are established. The Irish economy's tremendous growth over the last five years is in part due to its low corporate tax rates, intended (along with its excellent educational and worker training programs) to attract manufacturers, investors, and entrepreneurial enterprises.

A strong capital market infrastructure is essential to network commerce success, providing capital, expertise, and a positive attitude toward risk-taking. The Silicon Valley in the US has become the "hot spot" of network commerce innovation due to a financial infrastructure that channels money and management know-how into promising ideas. In the Silicon Valley, innovators, investors, managers, and educators have come together to create firms, technologies, and business models of the future. Venture capital firms (e.g. Kleiner, Perkins, Caulfield & Byers; Hummer Winblad Venture Partners; Flatiron Partners; thousands more) provide capital, expertise, and a web of relationships to thousands of new and growing ventures. The NASDAQ stock exchange provides a dynamic source of capital and a means of making these investments liquid for stakeholders. Without this business infrastructure, many of the network commerce products available today would never have come to market.

Fortunately, the European venture capital industry is growing and placing more emphasis on funding start-ups (e.g. venture capital funding in Europe doubled between 1996 and 1997); new small-cap markets are emerging (e.g. Neuer Markt; EASDAQ, Nouveau Marché); and European successes (e.g. Intershop, SAP, Baan) are beginning to foster further innovation. The European Monetary Union also is likely to play an important role in consolidating venture capital and small-cap market activities in Europe, leading to larger capital pools and a more efficient venture capital infrastructure. Finally, some major European firms are setting up corporate venture funds to develop internal and external start-up activities. For example, the French telecommunications firm Cégétel has created a 60-million-euro venture fund to be invested within four years (half in Europe and half in the US), and dedicated 60 percent of this amount to start-ups. Cégétel's objective is to identify new technologies, thereby fostering internal innovation.

RECOMMENDATIONS

Businesses

- Press governments to reform regulations (e.g. lower taxes; streamlined regulations; capital gains tax reform).
- Self-regulate where practical, with an eye toward developing broad, transparent guidelines that can be "enforced" in a meaningful way. Create guidelines for businesses on the network so that government is not compelled to intervene.
- Combine preparation for EMU and Year-2000 with network commerce development; use these IT issues as catalysts for developing a business-wide network commerce strategy and infrastructure.
- Create internal corporate venture funds.

Governments

- Support the development of a pan-European small-cap market.
- Aid entrepreneurial ventures. Help educate entrepreneurs and match them with venture capitalists.

1.2 Network Business Characteristics

Industries and markets are changing. Businesses in the network economy face reduced transaction costs, an increased reliance on content, blurring industry and market boundaries, a shift in power from producer to consumer, accelerated competition, and new business models (Exhibit 1.7).

Exhibit 1.7 **Shifting Levers of Competitive Advantage in the Network Economy**

Industrial Economy	Characteristics	Network Economy
• Cost saving through vertical integration (e.g. traditional newspaper publishers)	Reduced Costs	• Flexibility through outsourcing or "componentisation" (e.g. Intuit financial services Web site)
• Customers can visit physical location and inspect goods (e.g. grocer, clothing store)	Role of Content	• Customer chooses goods based on description found online
• Clear distinction among producers of content (e.g. newspapers versus business magazines)	Blurred Boundaries	• All firms become content firms (e.g. Expedia travel services provides travel-related content)
• Limited choices for consumers through pre-determined channels (e.g. movie theaters)	Shift in Power	• Many choices for consumers through variety of channels (e.g. video-on-demand or radio "webcasting")
• Business and market infrastructures that constrain ability to change quickly (e.g. print encyclopedia takes time and expense to change)	Accelerated Competition	• Business and market infrastructure enabling ability to change quickly (e.g. Yahoo! constantly revises product based on real-time market information)
• Business builds distribution network and signs up customers as subscribers (e.g. newspaper)	New Business Models	• Business places content on network and attempts to attract as many users as possible.

Source: Gemini Strategic Research Group.

Industry structures in the network economy differ from those in the industrial economy and can best be represented by a "value web" which places the end user in the centre of an "ecosystem" of component firms (i.e. firms organised around discrete competencies and able to easily "plug into" the operations of other firms) that join through the network to create and deliver products and services. The value web (Exhibit 1.8) is meant to represent a dynamic system and to emphasise competitive processes going on within marketplaces, rather than a static structure of industries, as it might appear. The segments in the web should not be thought of as rigidly divided, but as constantly shifting "clusters" of activity, with the clusters that are closest together having the strongest influence over one another.

Exhibit 1.8 **Interactive Content Value Web**

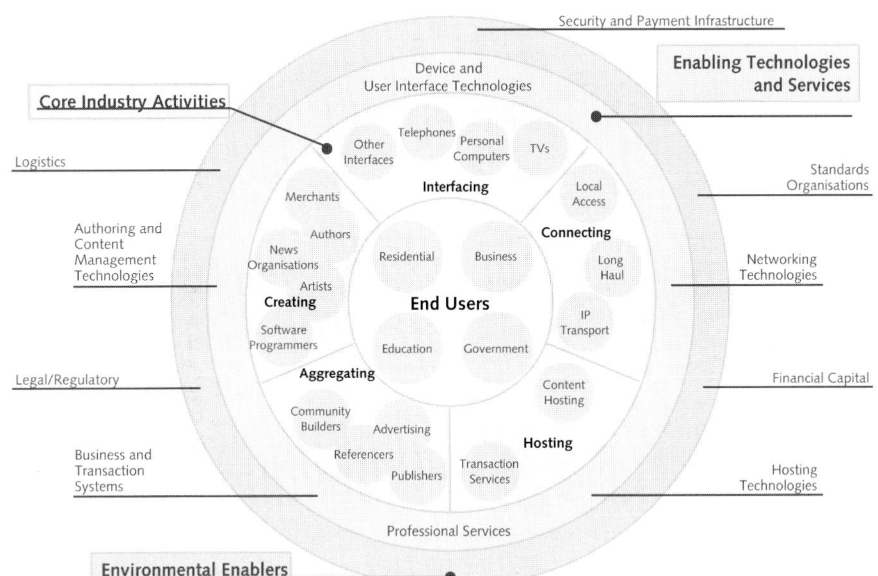

Source: Gemini Strategic Research Group; Gemini Consulting.

Value is created and flows through the web in a series of transactions. For example, an individual interested in British comedy troupe Monty Python might create a Web site on the subject as part of a "neighbourhood" section of one of the online community sites such as GeoCities, Tripod, or Angelfire. These communities might be hosted on servers operated by a commercial hosting service such as USWeb. The content creator might use local telephone lines to access a local Internet service provider, such as Demon Internet in the United Kingdom. Visitors to the site might consist of hundreds of thousands of Monty Python fans from around the world, connected to the Internet using their own local telephone carriers and any of maybe 10,000 Internet service providers. These visitors may have discovered the site through "portal" services such as Yahoo! or AOL. GeoCities creates "value" by providing services that attract users, and aggregates them to sell targeted advertising on the site. The advertising is typically placed by a firm like Doubleclick, which purchases advertising space for companies. Telephone carriers and Internet service providers generate value through the sale of network connectivity. Commercial hosting services derive value from the sale of hosting services to firms like the community organiser. Portals also generate revenues through the aggregation of users, only on a larger scale than the community organiser in our example. The value to content creators in this instance is purely psychological.

Because the global network is so pervasive, blurring traditional market and industry categories, traditional segmentation and measurement schemes are no longer effective. End users are, in effect, at the centre of their own value webs and uniquely capable of satisfying their own needs.

The dynamics of the value web are based on six business characteristics of the network economy; in concert, they bring network commerce to life. In effect, network commerce:

- Lowers transaction costs,
- Makes content more critical,
- Blurs boundaries,
- Shifts power,
- Speeds competition, and
- Creates the need for new models for success.

1.2.1 Lowers Transaction Costs

Open, ubiquitous, interactive networks can significantly increase market efficiency, enabling all participants in the market to reduce transaction costs. As Nobel Prize-winning economist Ronald Coase observed, firms tend to organise to perform internally only those functions that cannot be performed less expensively in the market. Reduced transaction costs decrease the cost of outsourcing non-core functions to specialised firms. This will especially help small firms to become more competitive and extend their markets. Information-intensive industries, such as financial services, publishing, and entertainment, are aggregating component functions provided by specialised firms, rather than building these capabilities in-house. For example, a brokerage site like E*Trade provides a wide range of news sources acquired from specialists in financial information. Another example of this process is a manufacturing firm hiring Federal Express or DHL to operate its entire warehousing and shipping function by seamlessly integrating information systems. In the content realm, numerous Web-based news, marketing, and entertainment sites integrate content provided by specialists such as Reuters (general and business news), Bloomberg (financial data), and MapQuest (maps).

Given these possibilities, players are connecting all functions, both within and outside the firm, in order to fully capture the advantages of network commerce. Dell Computer sells products to customers in more than thirty countries through the Internet, reaching customers in many of these countries from localised Web sites. Customers are able to pick from a selection of features and design the computer that best meets their needs and budget. Dell also manages inventory, accounting, production, and shipping functions through network technologies, and co-ordinates purchase and receipt of materials through direct network connections to suppliers. In effect, network technologies allow Dell to let its customers control production, avoiding inventory swings, overstocks, obsolescence, and repricing. Currently, Dell manages forty-plus inventory turns per year and is constantly working to increase this number.

This comprehensive adoption of network technologies has delivered significant, measurable results. Dell not only sells $1 billion worth of computers over the Web per year, but also saves $9 million per year in customer support and sales costs plus an amount in inventory and supplier transactions which likely exceed 10 percent of its operating costs compared to the methods used by more traditional firms. In addition, major corporate customers (1,200 of which now have customised service and support intranet sites set up by Dell) report savings of several million dollars in procurement and customer support costs directly attributable to the use of Dell's services. The company's comprehensive approach to network commerce benefits every aspect of its business.

Governments are also learning to capture the efficiencies enabled by network commerce. The Netherlands government, for example, reports that it has saved 4 billion euro through the use of online purchasing and transaction capabilities.

RECOMMENDATIONS

Businesses

- Become more flexible by outsourcing many non-core functions.
- Be comprehensive: where practical, migrate transactions, both internal and external, to the network.
- All employees, especially top management, should have Internet access and use it.

Content Firms

- Create products that can be easily customised and integrated into other firms' network content products. License other firms' content and integrate into your network content products.

Governments

- Use the network for transactions with citizens (tax collection, automobile registration, etc.) as well as with suppliers (bidding and collaboration on contracts, payments, and collections).
- Migrate political processes to the network (e.g. voting, interaction with citizens and businesses on policy issues).

1.2.2 Makes Content More Critical

Content drives commerce in the network world. Digital networks cannot deliver products to the consumer in physical form — they can only deliver digital images, sound, or text — in effect, content (Exhibit 1.9). For some firms, content is the primary product. Other firms offer merely a digital representation of their primary product, a complementary content product, or an unrelated content product used to attract attention. In every case, content plays a central role for companies conducting network commerce. This presents a huge challenge to traditional content firms. *All businesses become content businesses as they move to the network world.* Content proliferates in the network environment; anyone, especially end users, can become a content creator.

Exhibit 1.9 **Role of Content In Network Commerce Buying Process**

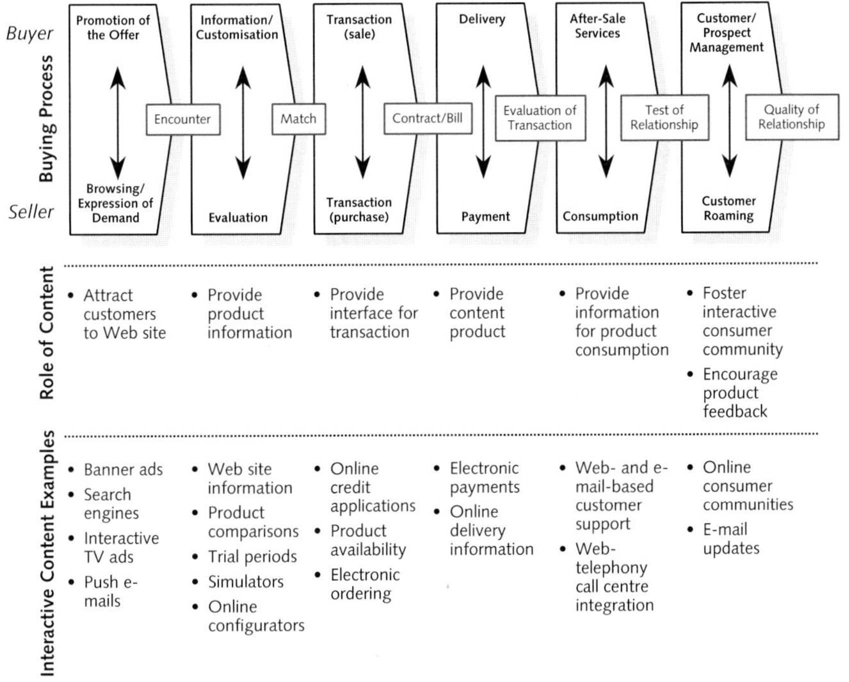

Source: Gemini Strategic Research Group; Gemini Consulting.

Further, digital networks dramatically alter the cost of content creation and distribution. Digital content can be reproduced and distributed at a fraction of the cost of physical content. Ever-increasing computing power continues to reduce the cost of creating and manipulating digital content. Over the network, digital products, such as software, music, and video, can be delivered to consumers at no additional cost to the creator (beyond the costs of payment processing). Moreover, as technology evolves, legal protection alone is insufficient to protect intellectual property rights, and commercial and technical means must be adopted to enforce or derive value from intellectual property rights.

Numerous technical means of protecting intellectual property rights have been developed (e.g. digital watermarks, Intertrust, IBM Cryptolope), although no one simple, widely-deployed method has yet emerged. Many firms are also recognising that there are ways to derive value from intellectual property even with imperfect intellectual property protection. For example, Microsoft chairman Bill Gates recently noted that most of the copies of Microsoft operating systems used on computers in China are pirated, but noted that "[a]s long as they are going to steal it, we want them to steal ours. They'll get sort of addicted, and then we'll somehow figure out how to collect sometime in the next decade."[3] Microsoft may find that it eventually "collects" not by convincing them to pay, but by deriving revenues from transactions driven by the placement of links on the Windows desktop.

In this environment, undifferentiated content becomes worthless, and even differentiated content loses some of its value. Content firms are challenged to create highly customised products or to leverage their content development expertise to assist non-content firms in the network environment.

RECOMMENDATIONS

Businesses

- Uncover knowledge or information that can be leveraged to develop or strengthen customer relationships.

Content Firms

- Explore the potential value of content to a variety of firms doing business on the network.
- Market content development and management expertise to other companies on the network (e.g. experiment and grow consulting and development capabilities).
- Explore how technologies such as Intertrust and digital watermarks can be used to protect intellectual property rights.

1.2.3 Blurs Boundaries

Networks blur long-standing boundaries — within the value chain and across geographies — between markets and industries and between businesses and consumers. In the hypercompetitive network economy, incumbents reposition, unexpected outsiders appear, new partnerships emerge, and markets are radically redefined as diverse industries merge. In addition, consumers participate actively in the creation of products and services and even become major content producers. Firms like the G7 taxi service in Paris (data on the movement of its taxis is used to create real-time traffic flow information that is sold to subscribers) reposition their data to generate new revenues. Many Web-based news and entertainment services (e.g. My Yahoo!, MSNBC) allow users to customise the content they receive extensively. The US's National Aeronautical and Space Agency (NASA) publishes information aimed at educating children. If a child wants to find out how hurricanes form, he or she can research the NASA Web site instead of referencing a traditional publication. On a service like Firefly Network, fellow users recommend music purchases. ICQ's Internet-based instant messaging service brings together 14 million users who are able to communicate with each other — they create the content.

Amazon.com is a competitor to retail book outlets, but because the company offers so much content to promote book sales, including editorial content created by an in-house staff, it also competes with publishers (e.g. an article in a library journal recommends using the free Amazon.com database to search for information about books rather than buying the higher-priced Books in Print CD-ROMs).

RECOMMENDATIONS

Businesses

- Implement a continuous process of competitor analysis to track who your competitors and potential partners are (e.g. a content firm's strongest competitors may not be other content firms).
- Be prepared to partner on a limited basis with a firm that is a competitor.
- Evaluate in-house content and explore ways to leverage it.

Content Firms

- Differentiate content as much as possible to compete with traditional and non-traditional firms (e.g. manufacturers, governments, professional services) that are also developing and distributing content.
- Market content creation and aggregation competencies to non-content firms.

Governments

- Adjust market definitions and statistical categories to reflect changes in markets and industry structure, since many categories based on outmoded definitions may distort market statistics.

1.2.4 Shifts Power

Networks shift power from producer to consumer by dramatically increasing the quantity and quality of available information and by increasing the supply of goods, services, and content. This new dynamic changes the structure of content industries and firms. The Internet provides consumers with access to the widest possible range of products and services. Consumers gain a comprehensive view of the market. Nobel Prize-winning economist Herbert Simon has noted that in an economy of plenty, attention becomes the scarcest resource. Companies and industries are organising themselves to most effectively capture and maintain end users' attention. Disney has focused on attracting the attention of families with small children by deploying a variety of products (films, music, toys) through many channels (movies, home video, CD-ROM, television, Broadway, Internet, theme parks). The company leverages the captured attention continually to promote new products. Other businesses also retain customer attention and build loyalty through such communities. For example, UFB-Locabail, a French bank, has tried to capitalise on its customer base by developing Business Village, a cluster of communities dedicated to specific professions.

As competition for attention develops, end users gain bargaining power, which translates into lower prices, more services, special offers, loyalty programs, and the power to choose from an abundance of products. New partnerships emerge, for example in the form of content aggregation. Portals (e.g. Yahoo!, Voilà, Scandinavia Online) are being created to provide unique entry sites for the network. Once end users are "locked in," attention grows in value as customer relationships strengthen and can be fully exploited. As end users become loyal, it is possible to market more products and services to them, and to extract more revenues per capita. In addition, gaining an existing customer's loyalty is much less expensive than acquiring a new one. Using the network, businesses can manage customer relationships much more effectively and efficiently. Therefore, for businesses in the network economy, retaining customer attention and building loyalty are the keys to competitive advantage.

To respond to the power of consumers, businesses are personalising their offerings on a cost-efficient yet scaleable basis. Network commerce allows for new marketing approaches, such as one-to-one marketing and the "mass customisation" of goods. Dell Computer's ability to deliver customised PCs to its customers in almost real time is an excellent example of this process.

RECOMMENDATIONS

Businesses

- Decide where to place brand emphasis and develop strong branding strategies to generate trust.
- Focus on the customer relationship as a key source of competitive advantage.
- Create active customer communities. Create facilities for easy and meaningful customer interactions with each other (e.g. discussion groups, chat servers). Over time, this may become the only source of competitive advantage.
- Personalise services and invest or partner to improve the level and quality of this personalisation.

Content Firms

- Develop products and partnerships to attract and retain customer attention to create competitive advantage in the network economy.

Governments

- Ensure that data privacy regulation protects the privacy of citizens while remaining flexible enough to accommodate personalisation of services.

1.2.5 Speeds Competition

Networks enable immediate dissemination of information and interactive capture of feedback. Increasingly, businesses — not just technology firms — are competing in Internet time.[4] Players' frequency, boldness, and aggressiveness of dynamic movement create disequillibrium and change. Short product life cycles and short product design cycles threaten market stability (Exhibit 1.10).

Players are developing and organising their core competencies to sense changing conditions and adapt quickly in a network economy. As companies like Amazon.com and Barnes & Noble have ventured online, German publishing giant Bertelsmann has adjusted its strategy to include a competing online outlet. Eliminating the middleman and selling directly to consumers through the Internet, Bertelsmann aims to take advantage of a network economy opportunity. Equally, firms like Netscape, Yahoo!, and Microsoft have perfected flexible design processes that allow them to constantly innovate in collaboration with their customers.

Exhibit 1.10 **Comparison of Development of Microsoft Windows and Netscape Navigator**

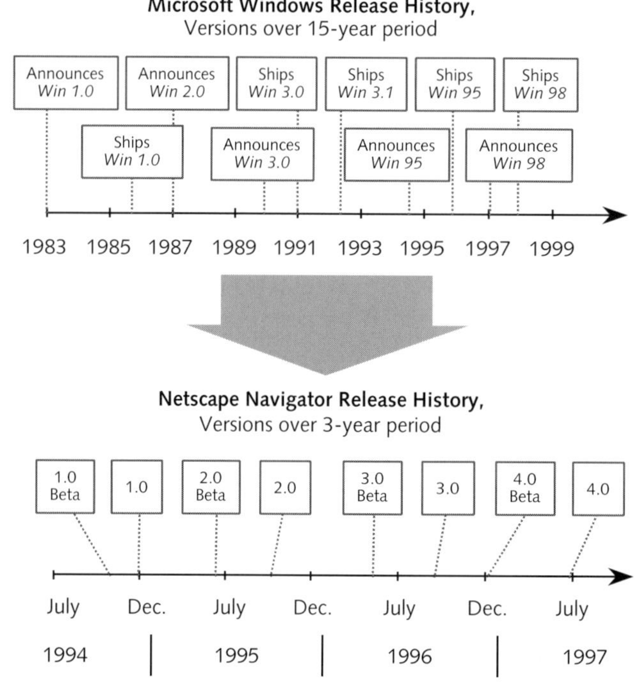

Source: Microsoft Corporation; Netscape Communications Corporation.

Competition is so fast that firms must constantly re-evaluate their competitive advantages. Firms must "stay ahead of themselves" by actively working to disrupt their own advantages and those of competitors. While Netscape Communications Corporation jumped to an early lead and continued to innovate in the browser software market, Microsoft changed the rules of the game by offering its browser for free. Netscape has responded by opening its source code to developers to encourage further innovation, and has focused on its Web site to drive revenues.

Content firms are also learning to compete in Internet time. As might be expected, news sites like CNN Interactive or one operated by the leading French financial daily *Les Echos*, continually update information on their sites in "real time." They also constantly analyse consumer-response data to determine which are their most effective features and strategies. Like most Internet-based services, Yahoo! has built a flexible system architecture that the company can use to quickly and easily test and roll out new services. Yahoo! distributes a new service on a limited number of servers, compares the results to other servers running different services at the same time, then analyses the results. Many of the most successful network services (e.g. Travelocity, Amazon.Com, AOL) have been through dozens (even hundreds) of evolutionary revisions in their brief histories, taking a significant lead over competitors who have not had the opportunity to so thoroughly hone their offerings.

RECOMMENDATIONS

Businesses

- Build a more flexible organisation, capable of responding readily to change (e.g. lean management, culture of innovation and experimentation, telecommunications technologies effectively leveraged).
- Anticipate, prepare for, and embrace fast change. Constantly re-evaluate what value you are adding for the consumer.
- Implement a scenario-driven strategic planning process which allows the firm to identify key market developments and respond appropriately.

Content Firms

- Constantly re-evaluate how you derive revenues from content products. Be prepared to use all network delivery channels as well as traditional formats.
- Develop acquisition and partnering strategies to address the need for rapid change.

Governments

- Reduce bureaucracies and regulations that limit industry change (e.g. limitations on employment flexibility).

1.2.6 Requires New Models for Success

Business models for successfully capturing network commerce opportunities are beginning to appear. While every successful business model is unique, all have two sets of components: the revenue model and the organisational model (Exhibit 1.11). Many firms look to networks only as new distribution channels or new product platforms (e.g. electronic publishing). Successful network firms have recognised that they must comprehensively integrate the network into their business, using it not only to generate revenue and improve the reach and richness of their customer relationships, but also to reinvent their business processes, linking with suppliers and partners and transforming relationships with their employees.

Exhibit 1.11 **Comprehensive Approach to Network Commerce Business Model**

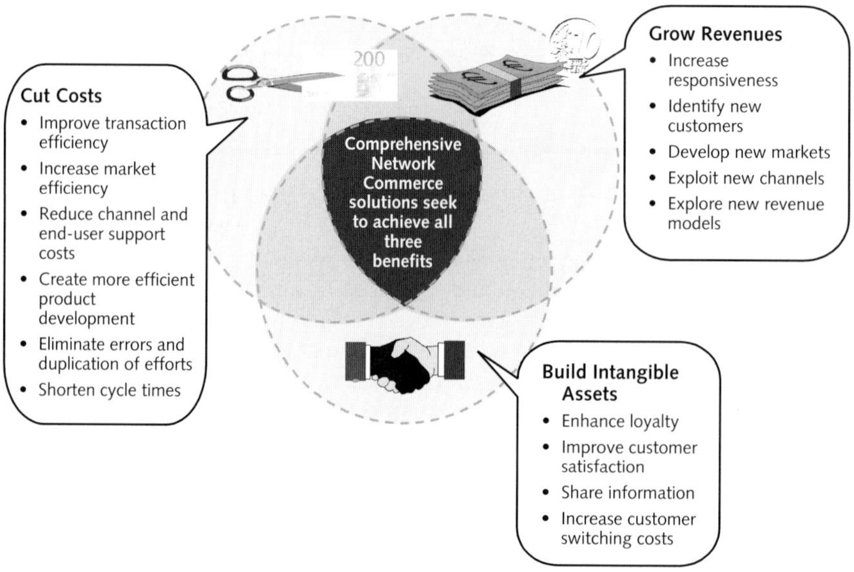

Cut Costs
- Improve transaction efficiency
- Increase market efficiency
- Reduce channel and end-user support costs
- Create more efficient product development
- Eliminate errors and duplication of efforts
- Shorten cycle times

Grow Revenues
- Increase responsiveness
- Identify new customers
- Develop new markets
- Exploit new channels
- Explore new revenue models

Comprehensive Network Commerce solutions seek to achieve all three benefits

Build Intangible Assets
- Enhance loyalty
- Improve customer satisfaction
- Share information
- Increase customer switching costs

Source: Gemini Strategic Research Group.

At the most basic level, network businesses may pursue one or a combination of three revenue models: subscription-driven, advertising-driven, and transaction-driven. With a few exceptions (online services such as Line 1 in the UK, or newspapers such as the *Wall Street Journal*), subscriptions are not well-accepted by consumers used to getting free information on the Web. Advertising is the most effective revenue source as of today, but most of this revenue is concentrated in the top sites: about 80 percent of advertising revenues generated in 1997 world-wide went to approximately two dozen sites (e.g. Yahoo!, Lycos, AOL, CNN). Therefore, the most promising models will be based on transactional revenues. There are many different ways of generating revenues from transactions, ranging from the direct sale of products and services to commissions and other less direct transactional models. For example, ETN (European Travel Network) in the Netherlands sells sales leads to travel agencies for about 3 euro each. Other sources of transactional revenue include the sale of additional services (such as Web design), the marketing of client databases (although this raises significant privacy concerns), or even simply generating incremental telecom traffic, as in the case for Scandinavia Online and Telia in Sweden.

While it is difficult to generalise, successful revenue models have typically met two key requirements: they have delivered substantially more service and at lower prices than can be obtained in the physical world. For example, the *Wall Street Journal* has successfully implemented a subscription model while most other newspapers have failed; its Web-based service offers far more than just newspaper text. It also offers access to all of its international editions, extensive background information on businesses and industries, and many other valuable features, all for less than the cost of a newspaper subscription. Another excellent example is Cendant Corporation's netMarket, which, charging $69 annually for access, handled over $1.2 billion in consumer sales over the Internet during 1997. It was able to do so by delivering a selection of more than 1 million items at guaranteed lowest prices. Many German banks have also found — because they have very limited operating hours — that they can deliver superior service to customers less expensively online.

Community building is critical. Over time, all surviving competitors in an industry are likely to capture the cost-cutting efficiencies and the reach of network commerce technologies. Fickle customers will be able to switch between vendors almost effortlessly. In this hypercompetitive environment, other sources of competitive advantage will become critical. Building brand loyalty becomes even more important than it was in the old economy. Communities and the content that they grow up around become a critical competitive advantage in this economy.

To foster development of new business models, players are creating entrepreneurial opportunities both inside businesses (through internal projects) and outside through investments. In 1995, General Electric developed TPNMart, an internal procurement service based on a network Web site that connected GE with its suppliers. The unit was later spun off as TPN Register and now serves a variety of buyers and sellers. Today, General Electric continues to look actively for ways to improve its processes and business models for a network economy. Finally, most major newspapers and magazines in the US and many around the world, have set up Web presences and are actively experimenting with various business models, despite the low likelihood of near-term profits.

RECOMMENDATIONS

Businesses

- Ensure that network commerce is treated as a key business issue and not as an information technology issue (i.e. network commerce is on the agenda of the CEO).
- Ensure that the business model integrates both the sales channel and relationships with suppliers and partners.
- Actively experiment, capture experiences in a consistent manner, and share experiences across the firm so that all parts of the business can learn from the experimentation; promote entrepreneurial opportunities within the firm.
- Focus on developing or allying with strong brands.

Content Firms

- Even if a firm is not an "electronic publisher," examine how the network can transform the rest of the business (e.g. supplier relationships, customer service, relationships with employees and contractors).
- Participate in the development of and promote micropayment and audience-measurement systems.

Governments

- Facilitate the right business and market infrastructure for network commerce (e.g. telecom competition, labour flexibility, efficient capital markets, streamlined regulatory processes).

1.3 Broader Implications of Network Commerce

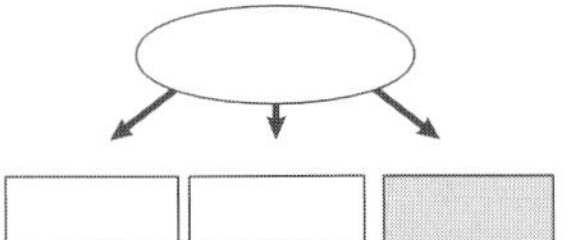

Societies and politics are evolving, but not as rapidly as industries and markets are changing. The evolution of a network economy has several far-reaching implications. More than just a new market or new way of selling things, this new economy will ultimately drive real change in societies and politics.

1.3.1 Requires Adjustments in the Workforce

The network economy will change the nature of work and has already begun to create new jobs in Europe. Over the next five years, the network economy is likely to both create and eliminate many jobs within the European Union, while altering the day-to-day activities of millions of other employees. Individuals will require new skills and flexibility to compete effectively in this economy. People will become increasingly responsible for creating their own value. Already workforces in the US and some European countries are showing signs of strain because of a shortage of information technology (IT) workers (e.g. programmers, computer engineers, systems analysts). These demands are being exacerbated by the demand for IT workers to fix systems with the "Year-2000 bug" and to upgrade systems in anticipation of the European Monetary Union. Microsoft Corporation maintains eighty full-time recruiters and earmarks over $500 million for training, yet recently had over 2,500 unfilled positions. In the spring of 1998, Lucent Technologies had openings for 14,000 computer specialists world-wide. The Information Technology Association of America estimates that 345,000 IT jobs are currently unfilled in the US. Germany currently has 50,000 unfilled IT jobs, and a recent study by IBM found that the UK alone will have to find another 250,000 IT specialists in the next five years. Giga Information Group estimates that 10 percent of Europe's IT jobs are unfilled.

The network economy will also destroy some jobs, especially in middle management and other "intermediary" functions that do not provide clear value. For example, many recently privatised European telecommunications firms need to cut their workforces significantly to remain competitive with aggressive new carriers emerging in the wake of deregulation. The good news is that many of these employees will have skills needed to fill other, currently unfilled positions. The net impact of this wave of job creation and loss will ultimately depend on the ability of European governments, businesses, and the citizens themselves to build the skills necessary to fill new roles.

Network commerce will affect the nature of work qualitatively as well. Already many firms have physically relocated employees to offices closer to their homes and used network technologies to closely link remote locations. "Telecommuting" has been developing, allowing employees to enjoy more autonomy, but also further blurring the lines between work and home. The speed of competition is also placing new pressures on workers, requiring them to manage their own careers and skills, placing special emphasis on independence, flexibility, and motivation. Ultimately, employees will "rent" their competency to businesses. In the multimedia industry for example, free-lancers are widely used and collaboration is based on the renting of specific skills for a given project.

RECOMMENDATIONS

Businesses

- Actively retrain and help to move current employees to higher-value jobs.
- Develop programs to improve employee skills (e.g. in-house training programs, subsidies for continuing education, sabbaticals for employees to upgrade skills).
- Partner with public sector institutions to provide training.

Content Firms

- Ensure that all employees are technology literate and that they develop skills to complement their traditional content skills.
- Develop skills relevant to multiple distribution channels (e.g. Web, television, CD-ROM).

Governments

- Evaluate and, where appropriate, remove limits on employment flexibility (e.g. contracting regulations, "red tape" around hiring and dismissal of employees).
- Develop programs to help redundant workers cope with change.
- Help to create social acceptance of change (e.g. create interest and enthusiasm in the new economy, explain the social and economic costs of not changing).
- Develop life-long learning programs.

1.3.2 Demands More from Education

Education — both formal public education and company training programs — will facilitate the societal transition to the network economy. It will play a major role in ensuring that adequate numbers of skilled workers are available and enabling people to make choices and capture opportunities presented by a new economy. Education will increasingly focus on creating "knowledge workers" (those who add value through interpretation, analysis, and presentation of information) and instill a sense of individual responsibility for the development of skills over a lifetime. The public education system will also need to promote flexibility and entrepreneurial capabilities and attitudes, and businesses will have to devote more emphasis and resources to adequately train their employees on an ongoing basis. Ultimately, the network may become the medium for obtaining life-long education, giving students anywhere the ability to access some of the best educators and materials. Today, students connected to the network may have access to more educational resources than have ever been available before.

The initial stages of the network economy will depend on skilled programmers and computer engineers to build the infrastructure. Ireland, for example, has turned out a wealth of talented IT professionals from its universities, helping to fuel its rapidly growing economy. India (55,000 computer graduates per year) and China (1 million Java programmers), too, have emphasised the skills required to build network infrastructure. In the long term, general education will also have to adapt to teaching for a network world. In 1997, Great Britain adopted a plan (National Grid for Learning) to connect all 32,000 schools in the nation to the Internet by 2002. Canada has undertaken a similar initiative and expects to have completed it by the end of 1999.

RECOMMENDATIONS

Businesses

- Create incentives for employees to pursue continued formal education (e.g. in-house training programs, subsidies for continuing education, sabbaticals for employees to upgrade skills).
- Invest in training programs and actively partner with educational institutions.

Content Firms

- Develop educational products and services to help improve skills.

Governments

- Promote changes in curricula to reflect new skills needed by graduating students, in partnership with businesses; focus on "employability."
- Provide funding to connect schools to network.
- Facilitate interaction between businesses and educational institutions to improve the relevance and quality of education.

1.3.3 Alters Levers of Regional Competitiveness

The network economy promises to alter the levers of competition among regions. Many of the issues discussed in this document stand to affect the ability of regions to attract and build new businesses and continue to compete successfully with established ones. Without flexible and skilled employees, and without adequate infrastructure and capital, regions will be unable to do so. The network economy increases businesses' ability to relocate operations to more favourable environments. It also prompts talented knowledge workers to seek the best conditions in which to realise their potential. Efficient capital, efficient markets, and an efficient workforce become even more critical in the hypercompetitive network commerce environment.

RECOMMENDATIONS

Businesses

- Provide salaries and incentives that are globally competitive in order to attract and retain skilled workers.
- Work with and push governments to create the appropriate business and market infrastructures for network commerce (e.g. competitive telecommunications markets, efficient capital markets, limited regulation).

Content Firms

- Evaluate content quality and value against that of global competitors.
- Make strategic partnerships on a pan-European and global basis.

Governments

- Place network economy issues high on the public agenda (e.g. government leaders should address these issues and ensure that they receive the proper attention).
- Ensure creation of a world-class, inexpensive, ubiquitous network infrastructure.
- Support a world-class education system that prepares students for the network economy.
- Reevaluate the impact of competition laws on firms' ability to compete in the global marketplace (e.g. restrictions on media cross-ownership, media concentration limits).

1.3.4 Changes Culture

The network economy is likely to cause further cultural change on a large scale, creating new "communities" of people across national boundaries. The growth of vast communities sharing common languages is likely to develop an increasing number of cultural and economic ties. For example, the Internet already boasts 25 percent more English-speaking users than the population of the United Kingdom. Within the next two years, Spanish-speaking and Portuguese-speaking Internet users will surpass the populations of Spain and Portugal. Most of these Internet users are located in the Americas.

People will gain exposure to new ideas as the network promotes cultural and linguistic diversity while at the same time creating "global" culture. Such a global culture will have both positive and negative effects, allowing for the preservation of cultural identity while also diluting it; globally advancing positive values while granting negative values and expressions of hatred access to the same broad platform. Naturally, the proliferation of expression on the Internet has led some governments to try to regulate it, but these attempts have generally failed.

RECOMMENDATIONS

Businesses

- Target communities of interest as well as communities of geography.
- Watch for global competitors from countries with similar cultures.

Content Firms

- Seek opportunities to market to global populations with common language.

Governments

- Promote national culture by placing cultural assets on the network; recognise that the global network is a cultural as well as business marketplace.
- Partner with businesses to exploit cultural assets in the global marketplace (e.g. digitise public-domain information and make it available to businesses).

1.3.5 Redefines Roles of Government

The network economy is already altering relationships between government institutions and their citizenry. Interactive networks allow governments to communicate with citizens more often — and in better ways — than ever before. Governments now begin constructive dialogues with concerned citizens in new and innovative ways (e.g. French government officials have noted the unprecedented dialogue between citizens and government officials fostered by its open Internet policy development process). Citizens can mobilise more rapidly and effectively to create and shape political change (e.g. Indonesian student protesters used the Internet to aid them in their efforts to mobilise world opinion in their favour). The network inevitably transfers power to its end users — citizens and businesses. In an excellent demonstration of the potential of the Internet as a vehicle for political organization, the UK Citizens Online Democracy (UKCOD) was established in 1996 by citizens to provide political information and democratic discussion about many issues.

Some governments are recognising that the network does change basic principles and requires new approaches to governance in that it empowers their citizens by giving them new tools to protect themselves. In response, a growing number of governments are taking a "hands-off" (self-regulatory) approach to Internet regulation. Governments have begun to enter into bilateral agreements limiting their involvement in the Internet.

In this environment, governments may find that it is valuable to divide the regulatory issues into three zones:

- A "red zone" for issues which will definitely require legislation (e.g. fraud, money-making scams, data theft);
- A "yellow zone" for issues where business self-regulation facilitated by governments is more relevant (e.g. standards, codes of conduct); and,
- A "green zone" for issues which government should not try to regulate (e.g. cryptography, speech).

In addition, the market has not evolved sufficiently in some areas to determine the best regulatory policies. It is appropriate for governments to enact transitory measures or a moratorium on regulatory activity in these areas until the market has evolved sufficiently. Taxation of network transactions and changes to intellectual property laws should be put on hold until the market has evolved sufficiently to understand best how to respond. Premature actions in these areas could be detrimental to the development of network commerce.

RECOMMENDATIONS

Businesses

- Recognise that relationships between governments and businesses are shifting, providing opportunities for businesses to more actively participate in governance if they choose to do so (and also requiring business to act more responsibly).
- Work with and push governments to address key business issues, but also seek opportunities to partner with governments to resolve these issues.
- Self-regulate whenever practical.

Content Firms

- Work with and push governments to address content-critical issues.
- Develop methods of effectively self-regulating content access (e.g. rating and filtering systems).

Governments

- Facilitate interaction between governments and constituents (e.g. create online forums for constituents, provide citizens with e-mail addresses to which they can address issues and get prompt responses).
- Evaluate the proper balance between role of government and the role of network-empowered individuals.
- Use networks to more effectively communicate with citizens. Move government activities to networks.

1.3.6 Requires Global Approaches to Legal and Regulatory Policies

Network commerce challenges fundamental legal principles. Despite its international nature, network commerce is subject to national regulations, which are far from harmonised in terms of intellectual property, competition, commercial practices, regulation of advertising, privacy matters, consumer protection, or taxation. Many of these legal issues can be resolved by contract, although this is time-consuming and expensive and some difficulties remain concerning sales to consumers (consumer laws vary from one jurisdiction to another, often overriding contractual provisions). In addition, many current trademark regulations are costly, lengthy, and do not encourage network commerce.

Economic governance in the modern system of nation states assumes that transactions take place in some location. All income streams, production, sales, loans, and so forth are also considered to take place in a geographic location. Systems of regulation and taxation are based on the premise that it is possible to determine whose law or regulation applies and in which national market or jurisdiction the transaction takes place. If a computer programmer sitting at a terminal in Bangalore is upgrading code in real-time over the Internet on computer servers located in Frankfurt, London, and New York, where is the "transaction" taking place? In the network economy, both borders and the distinction between domestic and foreign are losing meaning.

The question of nationality of a firm, product, or technology may not even be relevant in the integrated global network economy. The Internet embodies the problem in that it exists simultaneously in many places and in no place. Individual servers and physical network components can be identified precisely in geographic space, but they do not constitute "the Internet" — they are only pieces of it. It is, as one commentator has aptly described, the "nightmare scenario of every government censor" with "no physical existence and [recognising] no barriers."

The European Union has taken steps toward developing its own set of policies, building upon Commissioner Martin Bangemann's "Europe and the Global Information Society" report, published in 1994, widely considered to be one of two most influential documents on the Information revolution (along with US Vice President Al Gore's "The Global Information Infrastructure" report in 1995). In September 1997, Commissioner Bangemann called for an International Charter to develop guiding principles and codes of conduct for global business on the Internet. To this end, he initiated in June 1998 a Global Business Dialogue, which is a business-led effort to address such barriers to global network commerce as inconsistent or inadequate regulation, taxation, tariffs, encryption data protection, and so forth.

RECOMMENDATIONS

Businesses

- Form global self-regulatory organisations to develop business rules and guidelines. Address critical issues first, so that governments do not have to intervene.
- Participate in global standards development efforts.

Content Firms

- Work with and press governments to address content-critical issues on a global basis (e.g. intellectual property protection, censorship, universal access). Help governments to recognise that content regulations have global implications due to the easy flow of content across national boundaries.

Governments

- Facilitate participation of businesses in global self-regulation efforts.
- Participate in global organisations in order to smooth differences between national laws and regulations.

1.4 Summary

The network revolution is real and rapidly changing the world. The ability of European firms and citizens to compete in the global network economy will be crucial to the future economic, social, and political health of the European Union. But much of Europe is lagging behind North America and other major developed countries in network penetration, usage, awareness, adoption by business, and infrastructure spending. If European businesses and governments do not step up now to build the network economy in Europe, the consequences may be disastrous.

This study has highlighted the need for Europeans to foster market infrastructure that promotes network commerce: this means creating and encouraging inexpensive access to the network and related services. It means also that Europeans need to continue to develop and enhance a business infrastructure that encourages innovative and entrepreneurial firms to experiment with new business models and technologies. Finally, European leadership must encourage an overall change in the way business, society, and government approach the network economy.

The political and economic outlook for Europe migrating to the network is improving (e.g. increasing venture capital formation, growing network usage, intensifying telecommunications competition). European businesses and citizens are better positioned to integrate the network economy and some of its practices into the larger European economy, as liberalisation and privatisation add to a competitive economy. Europe's diverse cultural heritage can be a significant advantage in the global marketplace, if its people, businesses, and governments can effectively migrate that diversity to the network.

In the chapters that follow, we examine the evolution of this new economy, focusing on the role of content and the network's impact on content industries. Based on our analysis, we offer several key findings and recommend a number of actions that we believe will be of value to European content firms. Chapters 2 through 10 offer a detailed discussion of the critical issues we have summarised here and provide a blueprint for approaching the new economy and turning it to Europe's lasting advantage.

Notes

1. The Internet is the only widely deployed network that meets this definition today. Other networks with these properties may be deployed in the future. Most existing digital television services do not offer this level of functionality; they are not "networks" as defined in this document.

2. "Convergence" is a widely used term with many meanings. The European Commission Green Paper on Convergence issued 3 December, 1997, defines convergence as "the ability of different network platforms to carry essentially similar kinds of services, or the coming together of consumer devices such as the telephone, television, and personal computer." *Towards an Information Society Approach*, Green Paper on the convergence of the telecommunications, media and information technology sectors, and the implications for regulation, COM(97)623, Brussels, 03.12.1997. Our analysis suggests that Internet Protocol is the critical standard around which these disparate networks and devices are converging.

3. "Gates, Buffett a bit bearish," CNET NEWS.COM, 2 July 1998.

4. According to many industry participants, a year in Internet time is equal to about three months as reckoned by the rest of the world.

Setting the Context

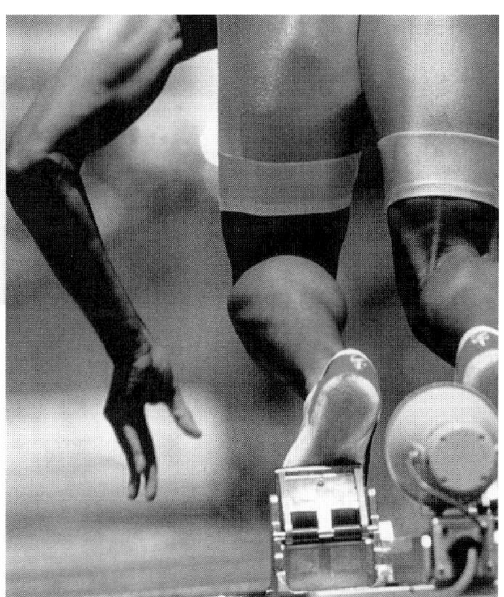

Much about the future is unknowable, but certain key trends that are likely to continue over the next five to ten years can be identified. In this chapter, we discuss several of these global "metatrends" that cut across all areas of analysis and provide context for many of the issues addressed in this study.

We believe a number of digital age "metatrends" (technological, economic, or cultural changes that cut across national boundaries, cultures, and languages) are fueling development of network media industries and the global network economy (Exhibit 2.1). Our assumption is that these metatrends are likely to continue as significant drivers of change affecting all aspects of the global economy — particularly for content businesses — for at least the next five to ten years, and thus can serve as the basis for projections of industry, market, regulatory, and technological developments over that period. Other trends may be identified in a broader context, but the seven identified metatrends are the most significant trends cutting across the issues examined in this study.

Exhibit 2.1 **Seven Digital Age Metatrends**

Moore's Law	• Processing power (speed) of standard microprocessor doubles approximately every eighteen months.
Abundant Bandwidth	• Construction of new networks and utilisation of new technologies, such as cable modems, digital subscriber line (DSL), and wave division multiplexing (WDM), suggest that network capacity will continue to increase exponentially.
Digitisation of Everything	• Analogue content of all types is being converted to easily-manipulated digital formats.
Open Systems and Interconnectivity	• Developers of hardware and software are increasingly building products based on open standards, ensuring greater interoperability and competition.
The Internet and the Packet-Switched World	• The Internet is the most prominent example of the emergence of packet-switched communications as an alternative to circuit-switched networks.
Increasing Competition	• Privatisation, deregulation, and liberalisation are opening telecommunications and media markets to increased competition, driving down prices.
Polarisation	• Trade, communications, and culture continue to cross borders, contributing to a more integrated global economy. At the same time, cultural fragmentation is occurring in many regions — often as a result of the loosening of national and regional controls caused by globalisation.

Source: Gemini Strategic Research Group.

2.1 Moore's Law

In 1964, Gordon Moore, one of the founders of Intel Corporation, predicted that for a given price, the processing power (or speed) of microprocessors would double about every two years. His forecast has proven remarkably accurate; indeed processing power has been doubling approximately every eighteen months since the time of his prediction (Exhibit 2.2).

Exhibit 2.2 **Moore's Law in Action, 1970 – 2005E**

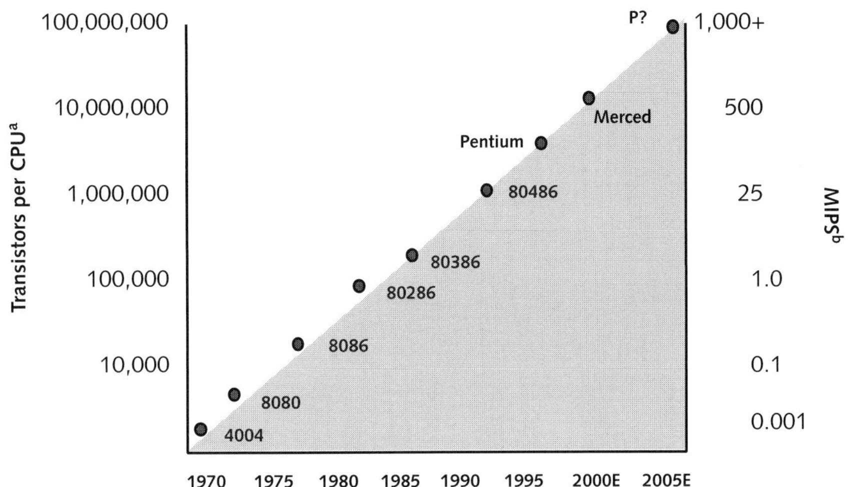

Source: Intel Corporation; *BYTE*; Gemini Strategic Research Group.

a. Central processing unit.

b. Millions of instructions per second.

By the year 2000, semiconductor manufacturers will introduce chips capable of processing data at speeds of 700 to 1,000 Mhz, compared to the 200- to 300-Mhz chips available today. This next generation of chips will process instructions using 64-bit architectures instead of the 32-bit architectures in use today. Every indication is that this trend will continue. Chips will continue to be smaller, faster, and more efficient. Moreover, in 1998 researchers at Los Alamos National Laboratory, MIT, and the University of California at Berkeley announced the development of a rudimentary quantum computer that operates at normal temperatures and solves actual calculations, taking this once-theoretical concept one step toward eventual deployment.[1] While it may take two or three decades to build practical quantum computers capable of performing traditional computing tasks, these devices may provide the next leap in processing performance.

Moore's Law's impact on the business environment has been profound. As computers become smaller, faster, and less expensive, businesses of all sizes increasingly rely on them to process a limitless variety of information from accounting and financial record-keeping to architectural designs and content creation. Consumers, as well, are adopting them into their homes. Computing capabilities have permeated all aspects of our lives, from wireless telephones to automobiles.

The digital media industry — in particular, the Internet — would not exist without the availability of ever-increasing processing power. Transmission devices such as modems, data compression devices, and packet-switching[2] routers rely on microprocessors for high-speed "real-time" transmission. Creating, processing and storing digital information quickly and efficiently depends on the microprocessor power. Computers and set-top boxes are becoming available to the mass market at a low cost. Such developments are allowing industries to produce and deliver digital media while providing the mass market with tools to consume it.

Looking to the future, Moore's Law indicates that those information-processing technologies that cannot be functionally implemented today are likely to be implemented in the not-too-distant future.

2.2 Abundant Bandwidth

"Abundant bandwidth" describes the communications networks' growing capacity to quickly transmit large amounts of information. This growth in transmission capacity is due to an expanding communications infrastructure which in turn reflects new technological developments. In the digital media industry, the communications network is also becoming a primary distribution network. In light of this, having sufficient bandwidth will be essential in determining the continuing commercial viability of digital media. As capacity grows, increased demand will be met, costs will go down, and more products such as on-demand video and audio broadcasting will be available on network platforms such the Internet or digital television.

2.2.1 Physical Infrastructure

Since the invention of the telegraph, companies have been adding to the number of conduits available for communication. Infrastructure expansion continues in the form of main line construction, increasing connections to the home, and the creation of new wireless and satellite transmission networks (Exhibit 2.3).

Expanding infrastructure capacity reflects the emergence of alternative transmission lines such as fibre-optic and coaxial cable. While fibre-optic cable is slowly replacing copper wire main lines, existing television coaxial cable is becoming an alternative transmission conduit for "last mile" connections to the home. Eventually, fibre-optic cable "to the home" will become the preferred conduit, but the time and costs involved in reaching every home remain significant. Satellite and wireless networks such as Teledesic and Alcatel's SkyBridge will expand the wireline communications infrastructure, particularly affecting last mile capacity since additional users of wireless technologies can be added quickly, at low marginal cost to the operator.

2.2.2 Transmission Technologies

As has been stated, new transmission technologies are increasing the infrastructure's capacity. Wave Division Multiplexing (WDM), for instance, expands the capacity of existing fibre-optic cable by simultaneously transmitting multiple wavelengths of light through one fibre-optic cable (Exhibit 2.4, Exhibit 2.5).

Exhibit 2.3 **Increasing Cable and Satellite Capacity on Transoceanic Routes, 1986 – 1995**

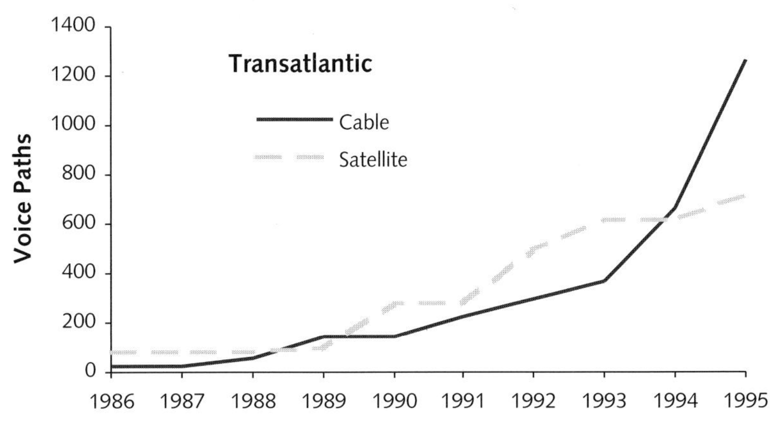

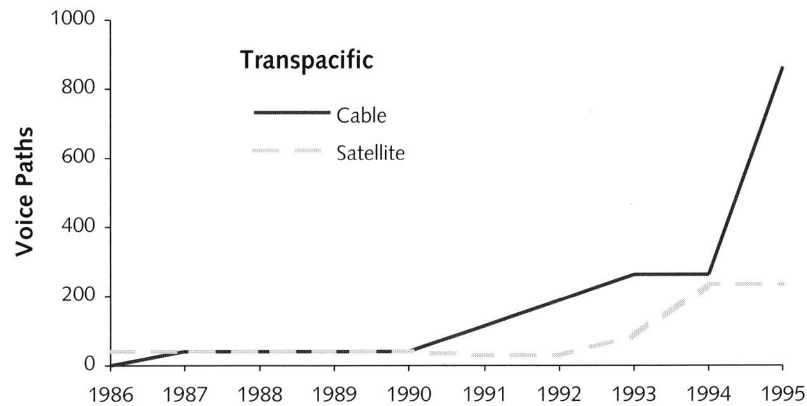

Source: CTR Group; Telegeography via OECD: Information Infrastructures.

Exhibit 2.4 **Cost of Transatlantic Cable Systems, 1956 – 1998**

Year	Cable System	Cost (euro) per voice path	Capacity (voice paths)
1956	TAT-1	491,000	89
1965	TAT-4	322,000	138
1970	TAT-5	43,000	1,440
1983	TAT-7	20,000	8,400
1988	TAT-8	7,900	37,800
1993	TAT-10	2,400	113,400
1996	TAT-12/13	900	604,000
1998	AC-1	<110	2,457,600

Source: The World Bank Group; Telegeography.

Technologies are also improving copper cable transmission capacity, affecting the last-mile portion of the network. Integrated Services Digital Network (ISDN) technologies now allow for transmissions of up to 2 Mbps over copper line, while Asymmetrical Digital Subscriber Line (ADSL) technology can provide transmission rates of up to 7 Mbps over the same network.

Exhibit 2.5 **Capacity of One Fibre-Optic Cable, 1983 – 1997**

Year	Bandwidth (millions/ bits/second)	Simultaneous Phone Conversations	Text Pages/ Second	Books/ Second
1983	90	1,406	4,500	22.5
1985	140	2,188	7,000	35.0
1986	560	8,750	28,000	140.0
1992	2,500	39,063	125,000	625.0
1995	10,000	156,250	500,000	2,500.0
1996	40,000	625,000	2,000,000	10,000.0
1997	80,000	1,250,000	4,000,000	20,000.0

Note: Gemini Strategic Research Group Estimates in Exhibit 2.5 are based on several assumptions: That non-compressed voice conversation requires 64,000 bits per second; the average text page has 2,500 characters representing 20,000 bits; the average book length is 200 pages.

To summarise, more bandwidth increases network ability to deliver high-quality text, audio, and video anywhere in the world at significantly lower cost. These lower costs and a greater availability of delivery channels will perpetuate an increasingly competitive environment for content companies.

2.3 Digitisation of Everything

Conversion of analogue information into digital information dramatically improves the ability to manipulate and transmit that information. Currently, all forms of content are being transformed into digital information permitting more effective editing, storage, and distribution of that material (Exhibit 2.6, Exhibit 2.7). In addition, all forms of digital content such as text and video can be combined to create and distribute innovative new products using the same platform.

Exhibit 2.6 **Examples of Digitisation**

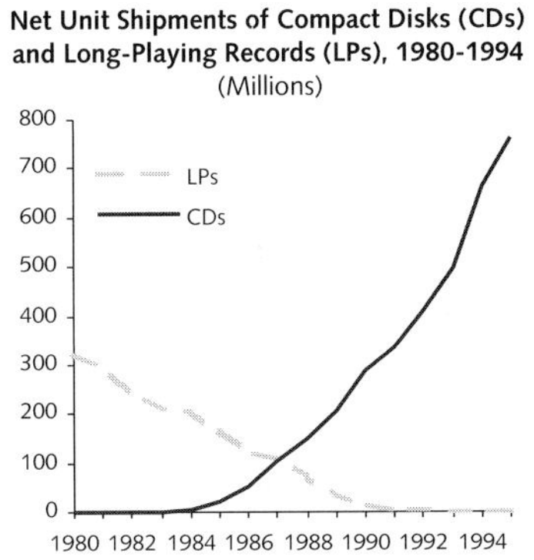

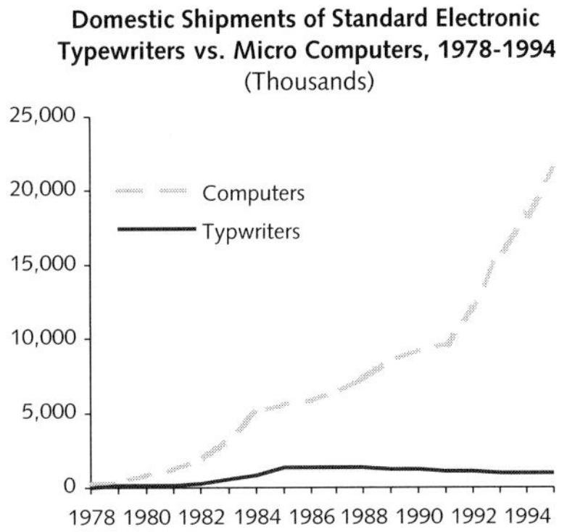

Source: *1996 Information Technology Industry Databook*; Veronis, Suhler, & Associates.

Digitisation will free content industry players from the constraints, including many labor-intensive processes, associated with analogue content (e.g. reproduction, distribution, storage). The importance of traditional content formats and distribution networks in the media industry will diminish relative to the importance of content creation and market-making capabilities. However, digitisation has produced a stumbling block. The very flexibility of digital content creates problems in controlling distribution of information and raises issues around taxation, copyright laws, and illegal dissemination of information.

Digitisation of content maximizes communications network functionality. The Internet operates on an Internet Protocol (IP) network using packet-switching technologies to greatly enhance efficiency. Information must be digitised in an IP network. Similarly, wireless technologies such as Code Division Multiple Access (CDMA), which provides greater transmission capacity through compression of information and packet transmission, require information to be digital in form.

Exhibit 2.7 **Market Share of Digital versus Analogue Phone Services**

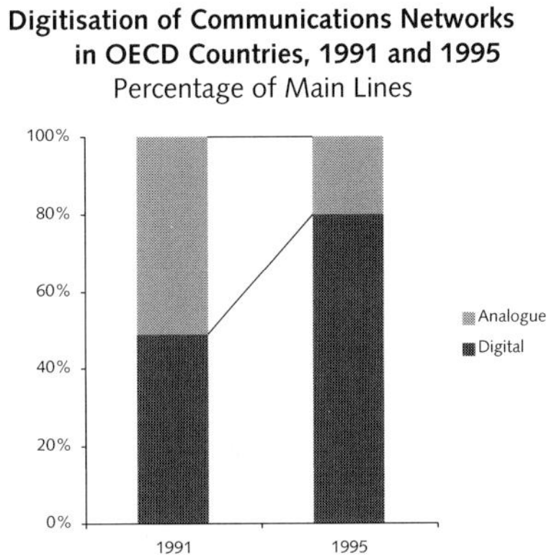

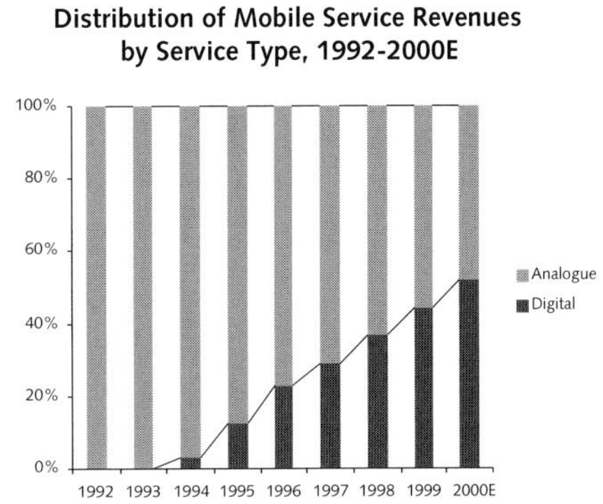

Source: Frost & Sullivan; OECD; Gemini Strategic Research Group.

2.4 Open Systems and Interconnectivity

Proprietary hardware and software standards are giving way to "open" standards (Exhibit 2.8). Open standards make all hardware and software systems compatible, allowing for easy interconnectivity. Moreover, development of new and innovative hardware and software applications is not constrained by the proprietary control of the standards needed to make those applications compatible with all systems.

Exhibit 2.8 **Open Networking Standard Examples**

Acronym	Name	Description
TCP/IP	Transmission Control Protocol/Internet Protocol	Suite of transport and application protocols for linking dissimilar computers over many different networks.
HTML	Hypertext Markup Language	System of text tags that format a document's display for viewing with a World Wide Web browser.
HTTP	Hypertext Transfer Protocol	Network protocol used to request and transfer HTML documents on the World Wide Web.
ANSI X.12	American National Standards Institute X.12	Standards specifying the content and form of messages for electronic data interchange (EDI).
MPEG-2	Motion Picture Experts Group	Compressed digital video format used by most direct broadcast satellite (DBS) service providers. Allows for compression of standard broadcast video channel into a 4 to 6 Mbps datastream.
IEEE 802.3	Institute of Electrical and Electronic Engineers 802.3	Physical layer standard for Ethernet networks.

Source: Gemini Strategic Research Group.

Before open standards are adopted there is a risk associated with choosing to use any particular technology, since the choice of aligning with one technology over another could prove instrumental in the eventual success of a product or service. Open standards eliminate this risk and promote the use of technology. Success of the home video industry can be partially attributed to the open standards (VHS) that eventually allowed all video cassette recorders to be compatible with all home video cassettes (Exhibit 2.9).

Exhibit 2.9 **Open versus Proprietary Standards**

Standard / Product	**Proprietary** (unsuccessful)	**Open** (successful)
VCR	Betamax	VHS
Computer	Apple	IBM (PC)

Standard / Industry	Standard 1	Standard 2
Music/Video	DVD	DVx
Cellular	CDMA	TDMA
Financial	OFX	GOLD
Programming Language	Java	ActiveX

Source: Gemini Strategic Research Group.

The Internet is one of the best examples of the success of open standards. The standards upon which the Internet was built (e.g. TCP, IP, HTTP, FTP, SMTP) enabled the creation of a highly-integrated network infrastructure using less expensive, standardised components chosen from a competitive hardware and software market. The Internet is now a platform in which competing hardware, software, and content products can be used or consumed interchangeably, in an environment that allows the introduction of new products that increase the Internet's functionality.

2.5 The Internet and the Packet-Switched World

Packet-switched networks, particularly the Internet, are playing a growing role in the global communications network. Packet-switched transmission of information uses the total capacity of a communications network efficiently by allowing devices to share the total available bandwidth. During packet-switched transmissions, information is broken down into small packets encoded with information that routes them to the proper destination. Each packet takes whatever path is available to arrive at a common destination, where the information is reassembled and delivered. Public Switched Telephone Network (PSTN) transmissions, unlike packet-switched transmissions, are circuit-switched, meaning that a dedicated connection is made between the sender and the recipient. Information is transmitted back and forth between the sender and the recipient for the duration of the connection; no other information can travel over the path used in that connection (Exhibit 2.10, Exhibit 2.11).

Packet-switched traffic's dramatic growth on telecommunications networks is forcing carriers to confront the implications of this profound change to their business environment. Packet traffic volume is now growing so rapidly on global networks it is likely to surpass circuit-switched traffic volume within five years. Packet traffic through major US Internet network access points has grown at 7 percent per month throughout most of the decade, compared to a growth rate of 5 percent or less per year on most circuit-switched networks.[3]

Exhibit 2.10 **Circuit-Switching versus Packet-Switching**

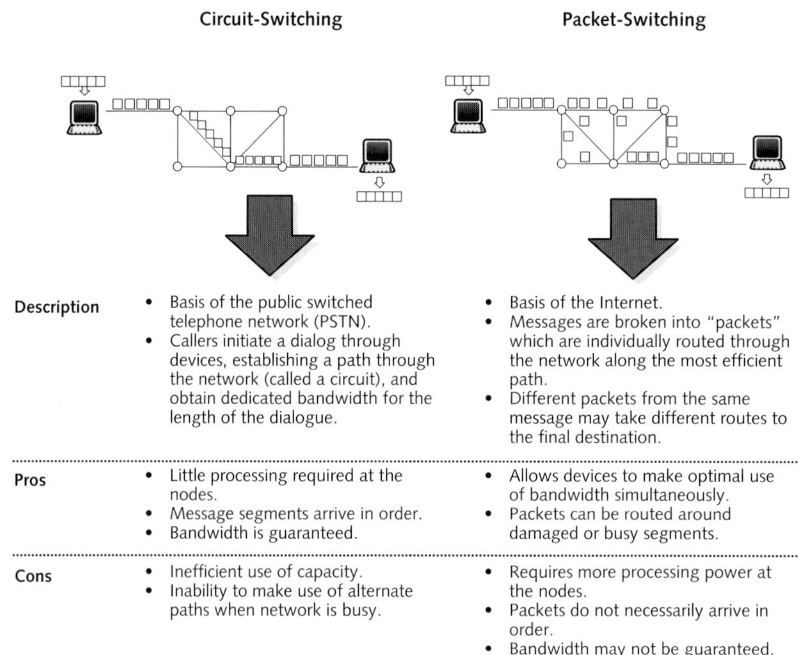

	Circuit-Switching	Packet-Switching
Description	• Basis of the public switched telephone network (PSTN). • Callers initiate a dialog through devices, establishing a path through the network (called a circuit), and obtain dedicated bandwidth for the length of the dialogue.	• Basis of the Internet. • Messages are broken into "packets" which are individually routed through the network along the most efficient path. • Different packets from the same message may take different routes to the final destination.
Pros	• Little processing required at the nodes. • Message segments arrive in order. • Bandwidth is guaranteed.	• Allows devices to make optimal use of bandwidth simultaneously. • Packets can be routed around damaged or busy segments.
Cons	• Inefficient use of capacity. • Inability to make use of alternate paths when network is busy.	• Requires more processing power at the nodes. • Packets do not necessarily arrive in order. • Bandwidth may not be guaranteed.

Source: *Networking with Microsoft TCP/IP*; Gemini Strategic Research Group.

Exhibit 2.11 **Connection between the PSTN Network and the Internet**

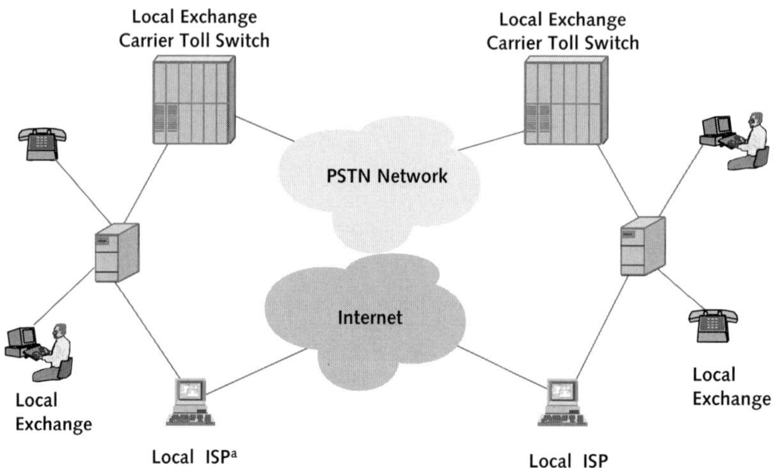

Source: Mutooni & Tennenhouse (1997); Gemini Strategic Research Group.

a. Internet service provider.

The US Regional Bell Operating Company (RBOC) Bell Atlantic reported in the spring of 1998 that 55 percent of its network traffic was data traffic[4] and WorldCom President John Sidgmore has frequently predicted that by 2003 only 1 percent of communications bandwidth will carry voice traffic.[5]

Packet-switched networks will doubtless enhance the digital media industry's ability to combine various forms of media in innovative ways. Further, the low cost of packet-switched transmission will make economically feasible the distribution of robust content products that are more user-friendly than those currently available.

2.6 Increasing Competition

Privatisation, deregulation, and liberalisation of markets and industries has changed the competitive environment in which local and global businesses operate (Exhibit 2.12). Countries around the world have been shifting ownership of commercial entities from the public sector to the private sector, reducing barriers to competition, and opening trade and investment to foreign competitors.

Exhibit 2.12 **Components of Increasing Competition**

Privatisation	• Shift of ownership from the public sector to the private sector.
Deregulation	• The removal of restrictions or barriers to competition within an industry.
Liberalisation	• The opening of a market's trade or investment barriers to foreign competitors.

In the telecommunications industry, removing restrictions has allowed new competitors to offer both long distance and local telephone service, increasing the service supply while lowering service price. The digital media industry relies heavily on the communications network, particularly since local operating companies provide consumers with the access connection to Internet Service Providers (ISPs). Consequently, the cost of local access to the Internet affects the total price of Internet service. For example, telecommunications liberalisation in Europe is likely to drive down prices, increase levels of service, and consequently lead to higher demand for network media and commerce (Exhibit 2.13).

Exhibit 2.13 **Selected International Competitors in Europe**

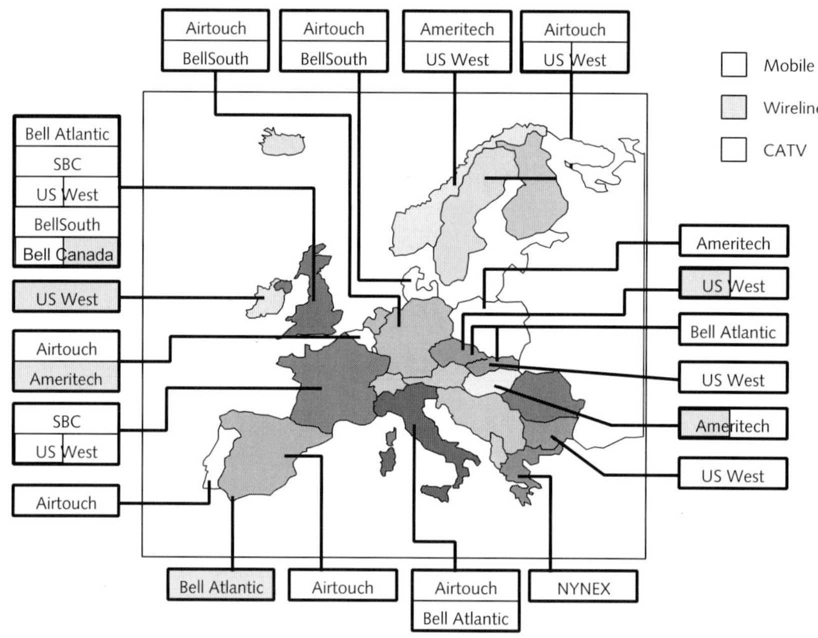

Source: *Telecommunications*, July 1997.

2.7 Polarisation

"Polarisation," as we use the term, refers to the existence of two opposing global trends occurring in parallel. On one side, a global community is emerging, served by multinational companies offering products to a mass market. On the other side, the world is fragmenting into small cultural segments that demand customised products and services and are fighting to maintain their individuality.[6]

Competition for global markets is intense; companies are increasingly operating and investing on a global basis and creating global brands (partially as a result of liberalisation). Consumers are demanding, however, and companies are delivering, a growing number of individually customised products and services.

The Internet reflects this polarised global society. The Internet can bring the world together through communication and interaction, but at the same time strengthens divisions by enabling the creation of an infinite number of unique "virtual communities" formed around mutual interests. The digital media industry's evolution will be closely linked to the polarised nature of the Internet and society.

The relative success of large media companies and specialised niche companies is another example of the trend toward polarisation. Some large media firms will enjoy increasing opportunities to serve a global market with many common needs. There will also be many opportunities for flexible firms to address the demands of small, fragmented markets.

2.8 Summary

This chapter provides an overview of seven digital age metatrends that are likely to influence the evolution of network commerce and content industries over the next five to ten years. They include:

Moore's Law. Named after one of the founders of Intel Corporation, this "law" holds that the processing power of the standard microprocessor doubles approximately every eighteen months, meaning that the amount of computing power one can purchase for a given amount of money today will double in eighteen months.

Abundant Bandwidth. New networks and network technologies will massively increase the amount of bandwidth available for communications.

Digitisation of Everything. Analogue content of all types is being converted to digital formats, making it easier to store, edit, manipulate, and transmit.

Open Systems and Interconnectivity. Hardware and software are increasingly built around open standards, ensuring universal compatibility among network components and encouraging the growth of innovative network products and services for the network.

The Internet and the Packet-Switched World. Packet-switched traffic, especially Internet Protocol (IP) traffic over the Internet, is becoming the dominant form of telecommunications traffic, increasing flexibility and decreasing transport costs.

Increasing Competition. The forces of deregulation, liberalisation, and privatisation are transforming telecommunications markets around the globe, increasing competition and subsequently driving down telecommunications prices.

Polarisation. The world is becoming more integrated and more fragmented at the same time. Trade, communications, and culture continue to cross borders, driving the creation of a heterogeneous, yet integrated global economy and culture. However, cultural and political fragmentation is also occurring as individuals fight for their identity.

These seven metatrends provide context for forecasting future developments and building winning network commerce strategies. Throughout this study we will address the implications of these metatrends on a number of business issues.

Notes

1. While, in the traditional world, a particle or element is either zero or one and can be present in only one place, in quantum physics, elementary particles can be both zero and one, or neither, and can be present in every possible place at the same time. As a result, a quantum-physics–based computer could provide all possible answers to a question, all at the same time. See Ron Wilson, "Research verifies quantum process — Experiment reveals that data can be encoded in molecular quantum states," *Electronic Engineering Times*, 18 May 1998.

2. See Section 2.5: The Internet and the Packet-Switched World.

3. Gemini Strategic Research Group analysis of data from NSFNet, Gilder Technology Group, the ITU, and Telegeography.

4. *InternetWeek*, 2 March 1988.

5. E.g. *Computergram International*, 5 December 1997.

6. The many dimensions of this complex metatrend are richly described by political scientist Benjamin Barber in his book, *Jihad vs. McWorld*, Ballantine Books, 1996.

Introducing the Interactive Content Value Web

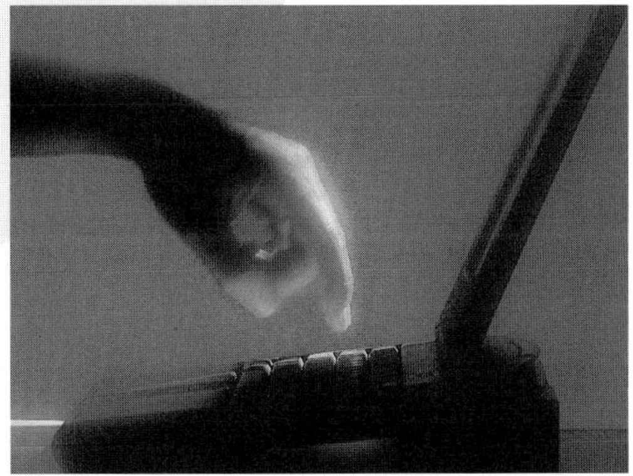

Traditional frameworks for thinking about media and communications industry structure are proving inadequate for describing the complex relationships between firms in the network economy. In this chapter, we introduce the interactive content value web, which places the end user at the centre of a complex web of players and helps capture the dynamics of market evolution.

While metatrends provide the context for the ongoing media industry evolution, the interactive content value web offers a framework for analysing it. The framework helps define the various industry segments and players, map their relationships, and provide a visual representation of the interrelated "ecosystem" that is the network media industry. The various forces (economic, technological, financial, and regulatory) that are driving these changes will be discussed in detail throughout this study.

3.1 From Value Chains to Value Web

Traditionally, separate media industries delivered distinctly different types of content products, each of which had a distinct value chain.[1] For example, the traditional publishing industry value chain consisted of four segments — content development, packaging, distribution, and retailing — describing the different functions performed by publishing companies from product conception to completion. Similar traditional value chains can be created for the film, music, and television industries. Most of these value chains represent the sale of physical products, such as books, recorded music, or television programs; however, because of digitisation, packet-switching, and open standards (Exhibit 3.1), newly-evolved distribution networks can effectively deliver all types of content (Exhibit 3.2), suggesting the need for a common descriptive framework.

Exhibit 3.1 **Effects of Metatrends on Traditional Media Industry**

Metatrend	Traditional Media Industry	Sample Effects
Moore's Law	Content created and used in analogue format.	Low-cost, high-capacity processors; the demand for "instant" digital content.
Abundant Bandwidth	Content distributed in physical form (e.g. books, CDs, newspapers).	Digital content quickly and inexpensively transmitted over communications networks.
Digitisation of Everything	Different media content types (e.g. audio, visual, text) are not compatible in analogue form.	All types of content can be "bundled" for consumption by end user and distributed over multiple networks.
Open Systems Interconnectivity	Content developed and managed by many incompatible devices.	Content development, hosting, connectivity, and end-user interfaces are not constrained by proprietary technologies.
The Internet and the Packet-Switched World	Content transported via a cumbersome network of shipping services.	Transmission of large amounts of digital content becomes more efficient using existing networks, reaching audiences more quickly.
Increasing Competition	High cost of connectivity keeps demand for digital content low.	Access to content through communications networks becomes less expensive.
Polarisation	Distribution infrastructure constrained by distance and regulations.	Content developers world-wide can more easily access end-user markets.

In the emerging network content industry all content will be in digital form. Various types of content (e.g. text, video, audio) will be stored and transported digitally, and ultimately delivered to the consumer through an interface that converts digital information into analogue content — all over a large network such as the Internet. The digital media value chain attempts to capture those components of the network content industry that result from the convergence of separate content industries on digital platforms. The result is an entirely new value chain that describes the components of a content industry that supplies text, video, and audio over a common network environment.

Exhibit 3.2 **Transformation of the Media Value Chain**

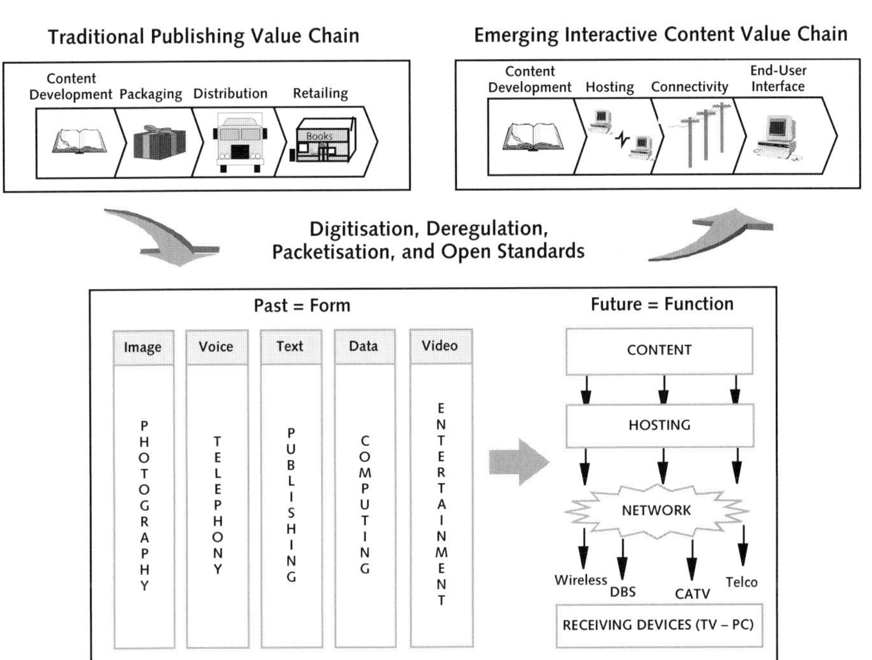

Source: Professor Jag Sheth, Emory University; Gemini Strategic Research Group.

According to the EC Green Paper on Convergence, issued 3 December 1997,[2] "convergence" is "the ability of different network platforms to carry essentially similar kinds of services, or the coming together of consumer devices such as the telephone, television, and personal computer." We agree with the Green Paper that the first of these forms of convergence is going to have the greatest immediate impact. As we have stressed previously, the key drivers of this type of convergence are digitisation, Moore's Law, open standards, and abundant bandwidth, which enable content to be more easily and readily created, manipulated, copied, and distributed. The most important consequence of this type of convergence is that the competitive landscape becomes much more crowded as many forms of media compete equally over a variety of platforms for consumer attention.

The network over which the emerging digital media industry delivers products incorporates many of the features of other media types. For example, similarly to broadcast television, the network can reach a mass market at a low marginal cost per consumer; and, like magazines or books, an almost unlimited amount of products are simultaneously available to consumers. But unlike any other media, it can support interactivity, or two-way communication, between those delivering content and consumers. The ability to instantaneously interact over a common platform sets the digital media industry apart from traditional media industries.

The Internet is the most important interactive network platform to emerge thus far because it embodies the concept of transporting data over any type of network using Internet Protocol (IP). IP transport can carry almost any type of multimedia content over any wireline, terrestrial wireless, or satellite network. Further, IP transport offers a wide range of interactive media types to anyone with access to an IP network. Reflecting the impact of Moore's Law on price/performance, inexpensive network access devices are now available in the marketplace, enabling a growing portion of the population to gain access. Improvement in network access is also occurring as cable television operators upgrade their networks to support cable modem access. A few public switched telephone network (PSTN) operators have introduced digital subscriber line (DSL) services as well. This process is occurring very slowly however, and will take several years to reach most consumers. Competition from new carriers, including satellite operators and new terrestrial wireless technologies, will ultimately provide the bandwidth necessary to offer significantly more robust interactive services. As this occurs, television network operators are also launching digital television services, which they believe will offer more and better traditional video content and succeed as an alternative to the Internet in terms of interactive content and services.

As transaction costs decrease due to network efficiencies, relationships become more fluid and tied to value creation instead of cost savings. The result is that industry components can be assembled, often by end users, to provide desired products and services. For instance, a consumer who wishes to view content can choose from a variety of aggregators (e.g. CNN, BBC), decide which network to use (e.g. Internet, ITV), choose who will provide the access (e.g. cable operator, PSTN, satellite operator), and select an interface (e.g. TV, computer, handheld). Today's range of possibilities is greater than ever before and requires a more thorough description of the value-added relationships that will exist between firms. In the case of a business, many of its non-core functions can be now be easily and effectively performed by component firms that are interconnected through the network, creating a much more dynamic production process.

3.2 The Interactive Content Value Web

Traditional value chains are an inadequate model to capture and describe the dynamics of the emerging network media industry in which many once-distinct industries are converging. Consider how value actually flows through the network. For example, an individual interested in British comedy troupe Monty Python might create a Web site on the subject as part of a "neighbourhood" section of one of the online community sites such as GeoCities, Tripod, Angelfire, or Hotmail. These communities might be hosted on servers operated by a commercial hosting service such as USWeb. The content creator might use local telephone lines to access a local Internet service provider, such as Demon Internet in the United Kingdom. Visitors to the site might consist of hundreds of thousands of Monty Python fans from around the world, connected to the Internet using their own local telephone carriers and any of maybe 10,000 Internet service providers. These visitors may have discovered the site through "portal" services such as Yahoo! or AOL. GeoCities creates "value" by aggregating users and — in providing them services — deriving revenue through the sale of targeted advertising on the site. The advertising is typically placed by a firm like Doubleclick, which places ads for advertisers. Telephone carriers and Internet service providers generate value through the sale of network connectivity. Commercial hosting services derive value from the sale of hosting services to firms like the community organiser. Portals also generate revenues through the aggregation of users, only on a larger scale than the community organiser in our example. The value to content creators in this instance is purely psychological.

The value web represents an environment much like the biological ecosystem and, like a model of a biological ecosystem, describes the totality of relations between a wide range of distinct organisms (companies) and their environment, without isolating any one relationship that might exist.

Exhibit 3.3 **Interactive Content Value Web**

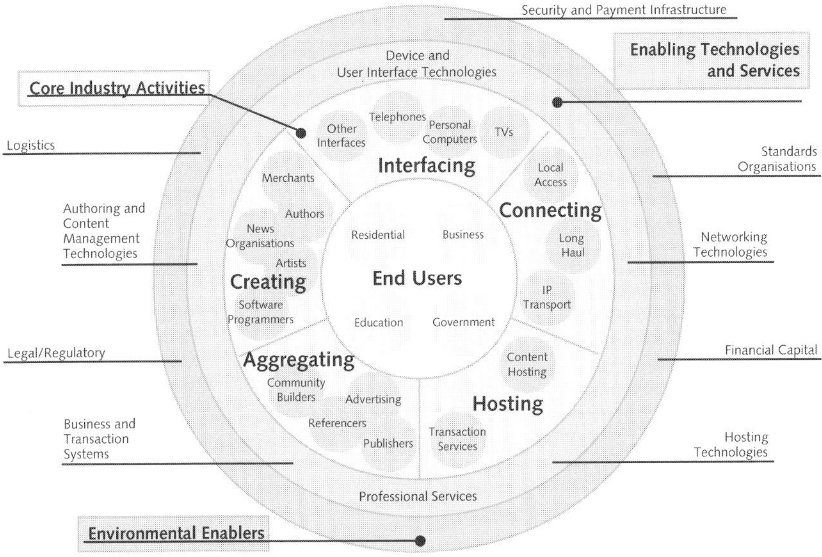

Source: Gemini Strategic Research Group.

The interactive content value web is composed of concentric layers of products and services as seen from the end users' perspective. Segments which physically touch the end-user circle represent areas in which the user has the highest awareness; the other layers are enablers and influencers of those primary segments. In place of the traditional industry value chain, the interactive content value web takes into account the impact of technology and financial and regulatory issues on activities performed within the industry and relationships between end users and industry players. Because end users participate interactively throughout the creation, delivery, and consumption of the content, they belong at the centre of the value web rather than at one end of the value chain.

3.2.1 End Users

End users are individuals, businesses, governments, and other organisations (e.g. educational institutions) that purchase and use network products and services. Because of changes in the content industry, many of which are enabled by technology, end users are much more involved in many aspects of the industry (Exhibit 3.4)

Exhibit 3.4 **End-User Interaction with Content Value Web Segments**

Creating	• End users have become content creators, or contributors of content offered in interactive environments (e.g. GeoCities).
Aggregating	• Purchase, use, or participate in content products provided by aggregators.
Hosting	• End user interacts with transaction service providers when purchasing products.
Connecting	• End user chooses local access (e.g. telephone, cable, satellite) and pays connectivity company for services.
Interfacing	• End user chooses and purchases type, quality, and functionality of gateway.

3.2.2 Core Industry Activities

The network media industry consists of five distinctive activities:

Creating
The act of producing one or more media formats, including text, voice, music, video, and software. In the interactive "ecosystem," we believe that end users create as much content as commercial organisations.

Commercial players actively involved in the creation of content include news editorial departments, motion picture studios, recording artists, software developers, game designers, advertising agencies, and more.

Aggregating
The packaging and marketing of content, including the following participants:

Publishers. Display content in an end-user accessible format. Examples of publishers in the interactive content industry include CNN, Pathfinder, the Weather Channel, *The Wall Street Journal*, *Financial Times*, and many more.

Referencers. Provide directories, indices, search engines, and editorial content leading end users to other content. Examples include Yahoo, InfoSeek, Lycos, HotBot, and AltaVista.

Community Builders. Foster the creation of "network communities" around specific topics of end-user interest, such as hobbies, geographical locations, professional interests, self-help materials, etc. Examples include GeoCities, PlanetAll, Whole Earth Network, Planet Soup, and much of the America Online offering.

Advertisers. Facilitate placement and management of advertising within the interactive environment. Examples include companies like DoubleClick.

Hosting
Physically host content and perform transaction processing, including the operation of Web servers, provision and monitoring of redundant network connectivity, and conducting of payment and other transactions. Examples include dedicated hosting services like USWeb and most ISPs.

Connecting
The distribution networks that connect end users to content. In the interactive ecosystem, this includes local access providers (e.g. local telephony, cable television, wireless networks), long-haul networks (e.g. long distance telephony, satellites, terrestrial microwave), and IP transport (e.g. Internet service providers). Traditional analogues include familiar physical distribution channels (e.g. bookstores, video rental stores, newsstands) as well as broadcast systems (e.g. television and radio transmission systems, cable television). Examples of companies operating in this segment include most Internet service providers as well as specialised services like Eunet, Club Internet, or Demon Internet.

Interfacing
The interfaces that serve as "gateways" to content. In the interactive ecosystem, gateways include personal computers with communications software, network-equipped televisions, enhanced telephones, and other technologies. In the traditional content industries, gateways include items like books, newspapers, movie theatres, televisions, and audio equipment.

Examples of specific products in the gateway segment include computers running Netscape Communicator or Microsoft Internet Explorer, televisions connected with Sony and Philips' WebTV devices, Internet-enabled telephones, and digital set-top boxes.

3.2.3 Enabling Technologies and Services

These are the hardware and software technologies and related services that enable/facilitate the value web segments. Enablers include:

Devices and User Interfaces
Hardware devices, software applications, and other technology components that make up user gateways. Enablers also include software plug-ins, processors, memory, and peripherals.

Networking Technologies
Equipment and software used within communications networks, including switches, routers, head-end equipment, transceivers, network management software, and other components.

Hosting Technologies
Equipment and software used in hosting content and providing transaction services. Includes the World Wide Web, e-mail, FTP, discussion groups, video and chat servers, as well as database and transaction processing systems.

Authoring and Content Management Technologies
Equipment and software used in the development and management of content, including computer equipment, authoring software, user-tracking software, and input devices.

Business and Transaction Systems
Equipment, software, and processes used to link "virtual" storefronts to existing business systems. They include connections to legacy systems (middleware), Electronic Data Interchange (EDI), and Electronic Financial Transactions (EFT), among others.

Professional Services
These are the services that develop, integrate, and maintain the technologies that enable network commerce activities.

3.2.4 Environmental Enablers

Organisations or services that affect the development of one or more internal value web segments, including:

Security and Payment Infrastructure
Systems, standards, and organisations that allow for the secure and timely completion of payments.

Standards Organisations
Organisations that develop, influence, or approve standards used within the value web.

Financial Capital
Public and private equity and debt markets that provide financial capital to organisations operating within the value web. Includes venture capitalists, investment banks, commercial banks, fund managers, and private investors.

Legal/Regulatory Entities
Other government or regulatory organisations that influence one or more segments within the value web.

Logistics
Organisations providing logistics or distribution support to companies operating within one or more value web segments. These include courier systems such as Federal Express and DHL.

3.3 Value Web Analysis

Businesses and other entities can use the value web to develop a comprehensive picture of their role in the network economy. Those involved in either the content creation or aggregation segments of the value web can map out the existing and potential links to other players in the value web, and describe the nature of each relationship. Managers can perform this analysis for other successful industry players and consider the significance of those relationships as well. If they find segments with which they have no apparent relationship, they should consider why this is so, and whether such a relationship might be worth creating. One of the key lessons of the value web is that all players in all segments are to some degree related to one another.

3.4 Summary

Chapter 3 begins with a discussion of the limitations of traditional value chain analysis for describing the evolving network content industry. In particular, traditional value chain analysis fails to capture the central role of end users in the creation and use of interactive media. Such value chain analysis may also fail to capture many relationships that could be critical to the development of strategy in the network economy. Our interactive content value web consists of four concentric layers, including End Users, Core Industry Activities, Enabling Technologies and Services, and Environmental Enablers.

Using the value web can help create a comprehensive picture of a company's position in the network commerce ecosystem and better map and compare strategies with those of their competitors.

Notes

1. For a detailed discussion of traditional value chain analysis, see Michael E. Porter, *Competitive Strategy: Techniques for Analysing Industries and Competitors* (New York: The Free Press, 1980).

2. European Commission Green Paper, Towards an information society approach, 3 December 1997, COM(97)623, Brussels.

4 Mapping the Industry Landscape

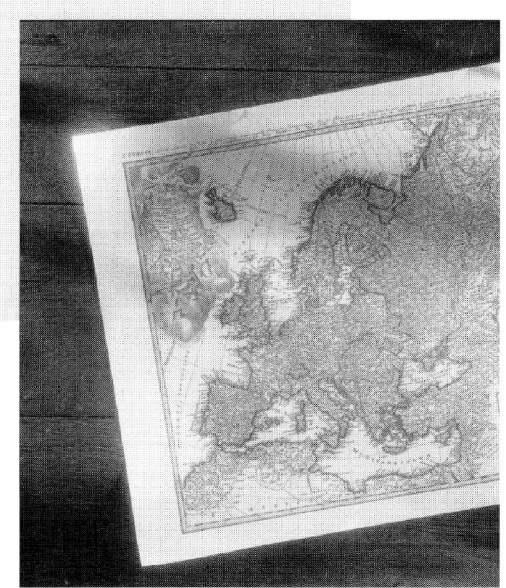

The content and telecommunications industries continue to go through tremendous world-wide change. In mapping the dimensions of this change, we explore the changing roles of traditional content players and take note of the many new entrants intensifying the competition as they bring innovative forms of content and telecommunications services to market.

As we have argued, several metatrends underlie a number of complex and dynamic environmental changes within the content and communications industries. In mapping these changes, we can discover what different industry segments have in common and gain a better understanding of the economics of content and by extension, of network commerce.

The relationship between content supply and demand is changing industry-wide, altering the structure and performance of traditional content industry firms. The organisation, partnerships, and integration strategies of some global content and telecommunications players are adjusting to meet the demands of the network economy. Many traditional firms now recognise that they must focus on attracting and maintaining consumer attention in an environment that has become clamorous with competitors.

This chapter aims to provide a high-level overview of certain major European and US content and communications industry segments[1] and is intended as a preamble to the more detailed discussion of specific network commerce business models and strategies that follows in Chapter 5.

4.1 Supply, Demand, and Complexity

Put simply, three observations may be made about the media industry today:

- The supply of content is increasing dramatically.
- Aggregate demand is inherently limited by time and population.
- The industry is becoming increasingly complex.

4.1.1 Supply

As Exhibit 4.1 illustrates, we have seen a drastic increase in the number of content options available to the consumer.

Exhibit 4.1 **Growth of US Media Consumption Choices, Mid-1950s – 2000E**

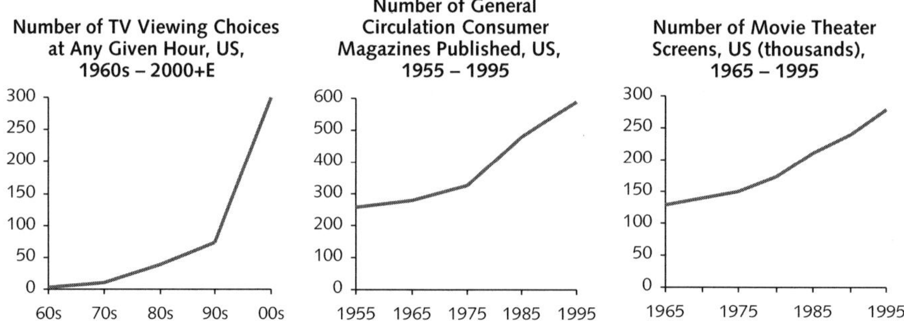

Source: Audit Bureau of Circulation and Magazine Publishers of America; News Corp.'s News Digital Systems Unit via *Business Week*.

Today, cameras, TVs, computers, wireless and satellite broadcast, world-wide communications networks, VCRs, and other technologies allow us to create, store, and deliver more content than anyone could consume in a lifetime. The growth of the Internet clearly demonstrates the staggering deluge of content available today. Vast quantities of information are available to anyone with a connection, at any time of the day or night.

As the capacity for content delivery continues to expand, content creators are rapidly trying to fill magazines, books, television channels, compact discs, and Web sites with bewildering varieties of information or entertainment that might attract consumers. Moreover, the creation, reproduction, storage, and distribution of content is becoming less expensive, reducing barriers to entry for many content products. Consumers have more content to choose from than time to consume it.

4.1.2 Demand

One's ability to watch television, attend a movie, listen to the radio, or read the newspaper is limited to twenty-four hours per day. Despite the fact that content choices are multiplying rapidly, demand — in the form of consumer attention — can only expand as quickly as the population. More and more content products are competing for each consumer's daily attention. On average, US citizens spend more than nine hours per day consuming media, an amount that has barely grown over the past decade.[2]

Despite limitations on consumption, media revenues continue to grow steadily. In some cases, new content products drive sales revenue growth; in other cases, the availability of new content delivery methods increases the industry's capacity to draw advertising revenue. However, because attention is limited, the growth of available content products is far exceeding demand. As a result, industry profit margins are being squeezed (Exhibit 4.2).

Exhibit 4.2 **Revenues versus Operating Cash Flows for Selected Public Media Communications Companies, 1992 – 1996**

Annual Revenues for Media Communications Companies,[a] 1992 – 1996
(Euro billions)

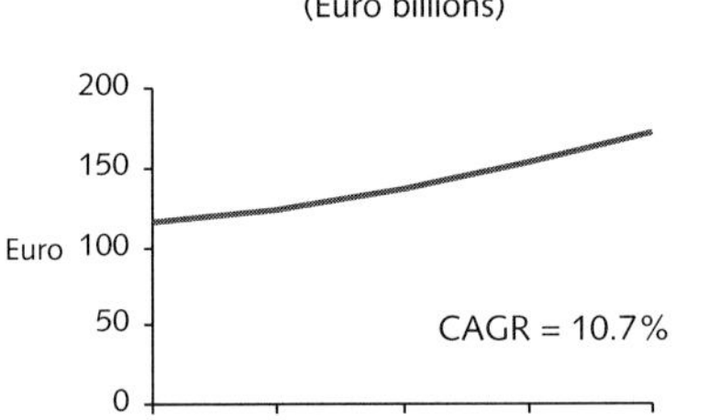

Operating Cash Flow Return on Assets for Communications Companies, 1992 – 1996
(Percentage)

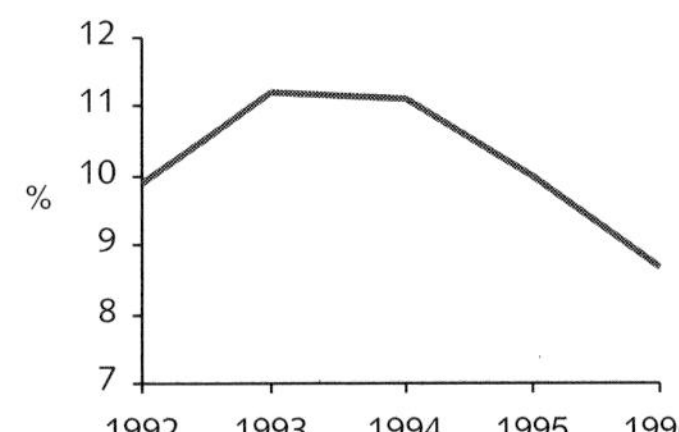

Source: Veronis Suhler & Associates, *Communications Industry Report 1997*.
Note: Graph reflects publicly reporting US media communications companies with annual sales of more than euro 880,000 (443 such companies in 1996). Note also that operating cash flow ROA for communications companies is divided by an average of the current and prior year's assets.

4.1.3 Complexity

An "ecosystem" of component firms is emerging and competing with traditional companies in an open network environment. Under these conditions, polarisation is occurring within the content industries. At one end, companies are actively enlarging to achieve economies of scale, as can be seen in the consolidation of many companies in the media industry during the past ten years. At the other end, companies are honing their core competencies, targeting niche markets, and achieving higher profit margins. The network is enabling component niche firms to work together with the cost efficiency of larger integrated firms.

While more money is being pumped into media, particularly in the form of advertising revenues, the money is spread over a much larger range of content types and players. To illustrate, compare the differences in the breakdown of advertising expenditures by medium across Europe (Exhibit 4.3). While newspapers still capture much of advertising revenue in most European countries, the relative mix of media varies from country to country.

Exhibit 4.3 **Advertising Expenditure Breakdown by Medium, 1996, Percentage of Total Advertising Expenditures by Medium**

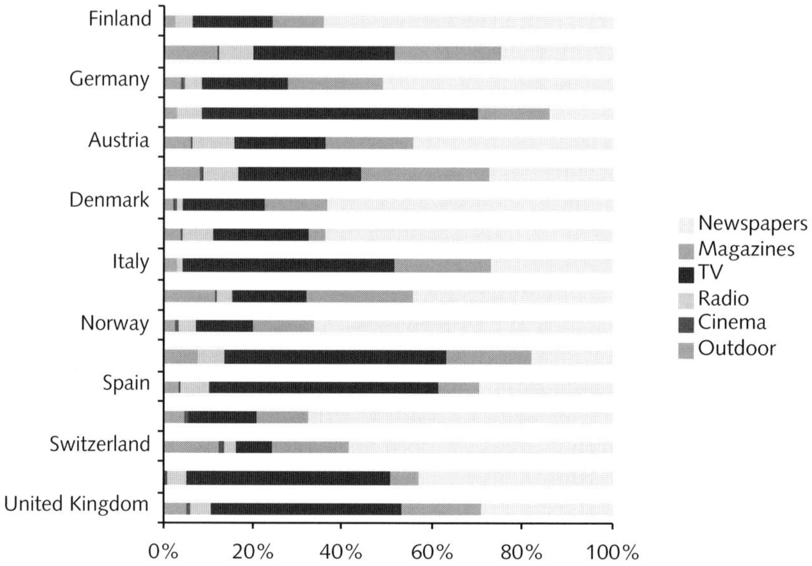

Source: *Campaign*, November 14, 1997.

Firms have adopted an array of business models to meet changing demands. The variations suggest significant differences in the number of choices and organisation existing in various media sectors in each country.

4.2 Creating and Aggregating

Creating and aggregating content remain the most fundamental activities in the media industry. Such activities require talent, skill, and, more recently, technology. In this section, we will describe these industry segments and document the status of some of the major players. We have categorised players into subsegments, based on content form.

4.2.1 Overview

Traditionally we define content by its form:

> Text, voice, graphics, audio, video, or any multimedia combination thereof, represented in analogue or digital format on a variety of media (e.g. paper, microfilm, magnetic or optical storage).

A full understanding of any content product requires that we analyse a product's function:

> Informing, educating, communicating, entertaining.

In the past, media companies were often organised around the form of content product: newspaper, book, or magazine publishers; television producers; television broadcasters; film producers; etc., who might diversify by delivering content products with different functions in the same form. Because of the consolidation of companies and the convergence of media, a shift is apparent toward organisation around product function rather than product form. Today's companies deliver products of the same function using many forms.

Pure entertainment content, such as that created around the character "Batman," usually is based on a concept, which can be marketed to the same end user in many forms (e.g. comic book, television series, film, toys, amusement park rides). The creators own both the content and the concept. In contrast, pure information content, such as sports scores, can usually be marketed and consumed once only. Information content is not in and of itself owned by any individual or group. Most content products fall somewhere in between entertainment and information, often depending on the way they are marketed. The models for deriving revenues from content (Exhibit 4.4) are in part based on the function of the content.

This discussion is organised around major content industry groups. Broadly, these are the print publishing industries, including newspapers, magazines, and books; video industries, including film, video, and television production; and the audio industries, including recording and radio broadcast. We will also briefly examine the sports and video-gaming industries as they relate to content.

Exhibit 4.4 **Content Revenue Sources**

Direct Revenues	Indirect Revenues
• **Content Creators** – Sale or licensing of content product. – Sale or licensing of image, concept, or name of content product or creator. • **Content Aggregators** – Advertising along with content product. – Subscription for access to content. – Re-sale of content product.	• **Content Creators** – Building of reputation or name. • **Content Aggregators** – Promotion by proximity of other content, products, or services (horizontal promotion). – Promotion of other revenue-producing entities (vertical promotion).

4.2.2 Print Media

Print media industry players create and aggregate text-based content products in analogue or digital media. We will break out this content sub-segment into news, magazines, and books, corresponding to the main forms in which this content is presented today.

News and Information

News content creators are predominantly involved in data collection, the compilation of available information into one product such as news, statistics, or research.

The news content creation sub-segment comprises people who provide content for newspapers or other publications, as well as companies and organisations devoted to the collection of data, such as Reuters, private associations, or government agencies.

Rivalry among news content creators is intense, with a large number of fairly undifferentiated players. Entry into this sub-segment is relatively easy, and becoming less expensive as computer and other document production technologies lower costs.

News content creators derive revenues either from employment contracts with aggregators or by licensing content to several aggregators. Content aggregators control distribution networks and marketing capabilities, reducing creators' bargaining power.

News content creation companies have formed to increase content creators' bargaining power by providing a great number of news content products from a single source. As companies grow and begin to create more news content, creating and aggregating naturally merge into one activity.

Newspapers
Newspapers are usually published daily, presenting a large amount of content of which only a small portion is relevant to any particular consumer. Newspapers, like the relevance of content within them, are, in general, temporary, intended for disposal and replacement by tomorrow's edition.

Newspapers earn the majority of their revenues through advertising. Although there is a high demand, newspapers are similar to commodity products in that consumers are not willing to pay much for the content. Because of newspapers' wide audience reach, most media advertising spending goes to newspaper publishers (Exhibit 4.5).

Exhibit 4.5 **Media Share of German Advertising Expenditure, 1985 – 1995**

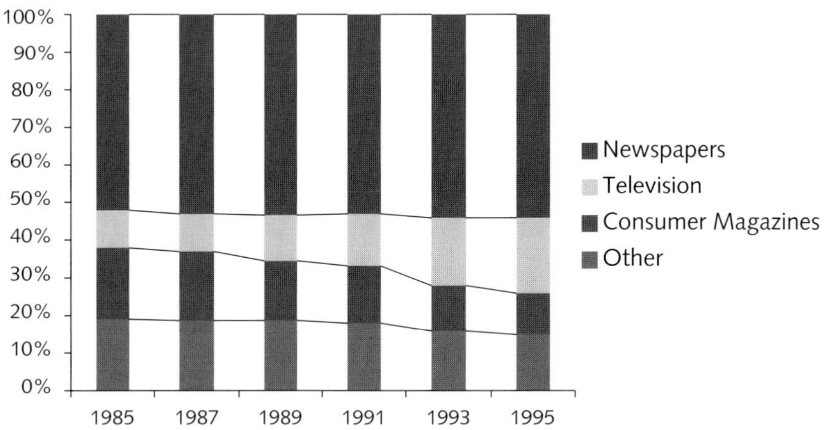

Source: FT Management Report, European Consumer Magazine Publishing, *Facing the Electronic Challenge*.

Newspapers have also traditionally attracted more advertising revenues than the other major advertising-supported print medium, magazines (Exhibit 4.6).

The newspaper sub-segment is fairly fragmented, with no big players controlling international market share. Local brand names, however, can hold a large portion of the market share in a city or region. The newspaper market in Europe varies significantly from country to country, (Exhibit 4.7), and no newspapers can genuinely claim to be "pan-European."

Exhibit 4.6 **US Newspaper and Magazine Advertising Spending, 1990 – 2000E, Euro in Millions**

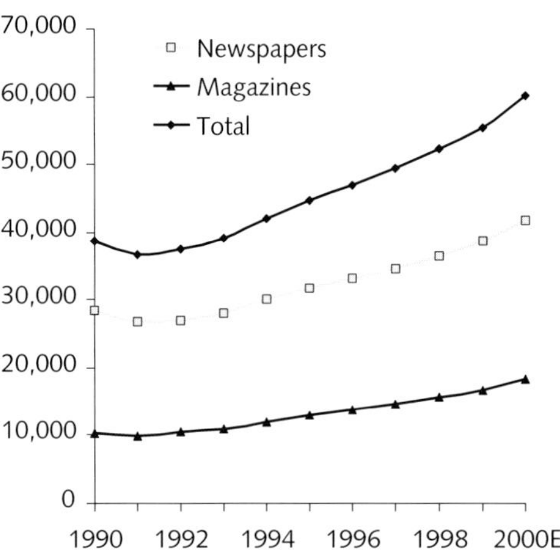

Source: Veronis Suhler & Associates, *Communications Industry Report 1997*.

Exhibit 4.7 **European Newspaper Distribution, 1995**

Country	Total Daily Circulation	% of Population
Austria	2,529,000	31%
Belgium	1,672,000	17%
Denmark	3,034,000	58%
Finland	1,612,000	32%
France	2,367,000	5%
Germany	8,951,000	11%
Greece	25,467,000	248%
Ireland	1,980,000	56%
Italy	495,000	1%
Netherlands	6,281,000	42%
Portugal	5,697,000[a]	61%
Spain	4,285,000	12%
Sweden	4,041,000	46%
UK	18,342,000	32%

Source: World Press Trends (FIEJ) European Campaign Planner.
a. 1993 figure.

Newspaper sales appear to be healthier than the average TV or radio audience figures. All forms of traditional media are suffering from diminished interest as consumers turn to a wider range of leisure alternatives. However, new media appear to be capturing more audience share from broadcast media than from print (Exhibit 4.8).

Exhibit 4.8 **Impact of Internet Usage on Consumer Media Usage**

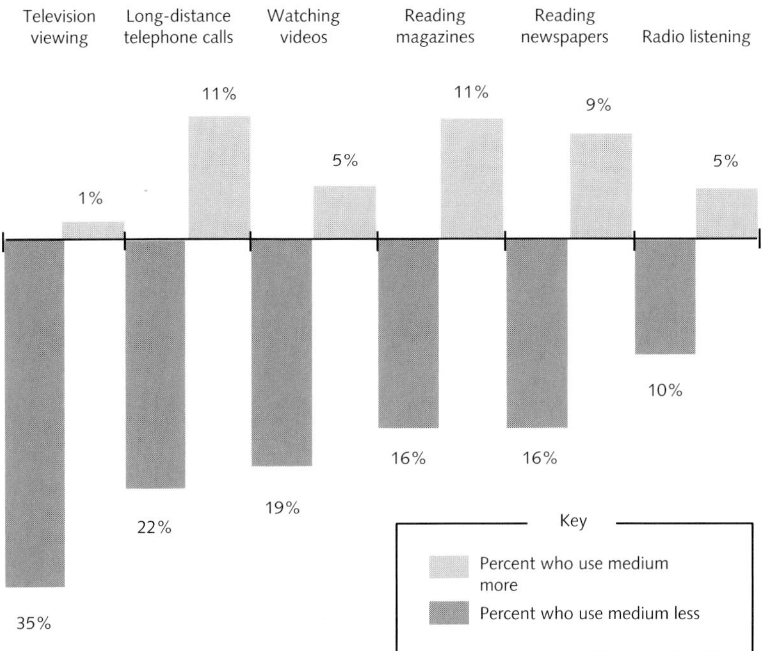

Source: Find/SVP, American Internet User Survey.
Note: Percentage of respondents citing an increase or decrease in usage of other media due to using the Internet.

The main concern within the European newspaper industry in recent years has been falling circulation; but since 1992, newspaper sales in Western Europe have in fact declined by less than 1 percent per year.[3] In France and Germany, the decline has been even less than that. The majority of newspaper titles in the UK are showing circulation increases, and in Spain and Portugal, sales are rising dramatically. In Ireland, indigenous papers are growing despite an influx of less expensive UK newspapers; in the Netherlands, the market is also expanding.

Although substitute physical products are a minimal threat to the newspaper industry, the threat of competition from a new channel, like the Internet, is high. Data collection costs are relatively low compared to the costs of printing and distributing hard-copy news. Use of the Internet eliminates these costs, thereby attracting a greater number of potential entrants. Additionally, switching costs for consumers to try different news content products is very low, a positive characteristic for potential entrants.

Newspapers often have strong brand names locally, thus raising one barrier to entry. Even so, early entry into the market via the Internet may bring substantial rewards to Internet-based newspaper content aggregators who can deliver customised news content products.

Globalisation is a developing issue. An increasing number of newspapers are becoming available in multiple countries. More newspapers are producing international editions, and the market for international advertising in these papers is growing rapidly. International advertising will be an important area of growth and opportunity during the next few years, and given the widespread use of English around the world, the UK will enjoy a particular advantage.

Newspapers are also emphasising tailored content. Continental readers want their newspaper to get things done. They want relevance and material value. In response, publishers seek to directly affect the advertising environment while providing well-defined special-interest subjects in tailored supplements and sections to target markets.

Many newspapers are moving to provide a variety of news content and services on the Internet. Sites such as *The Wall Street Journal's* www.wsj.com and *The Financial Times'* www.ft.com have aggressively entered this arena, providing constantly updated news along with other community information.

Business Information. In the US, business information revenues have been growing steadily since 1992, with operating profit for the same companies rising slightly from 15.7 percent in 1992 to 16.4 percent in 1996. The business information sub-segment is relatively concentrated compared to other publishing sub-segments, perhaps reflecting the benefits of brand and scale.

Having reliable information is very important to news content consumers. Brand name, therefore, can be an important asset to news content creators. While the Internet might encourage entry to this sub-segment due to reduced printing and distribution costs, a strong brand name and established market presence will continue to be relevant issues for incumbents and potential entrants alike.

Companies in this sub-segment are integrating horizontally in an effort to more efficiently market and distribute content products. One of the largest business information firms, Reed Elsevier, for instance, has expanded its business information holdings by purchasing subscriber-based research service Lexis-Nexis, and more recently, the legal publishing holdings of Times Mirror Company.

Magazines

Content creators for magazines are primarily involved in data analysis, the examination of or commentary on any events, data, or other content, including editorial and educational materials, critiques, etc. Historically, magazine content products have been delivered on high-cost paper with low-cost bindings, to be read over the period of a week to a month and then discarded.

Because magazine content tends to be created through data analysis, greater product differentiation exists than in news content. This provides a competitive advantage for some players, as well as a barrier to entry in a sub-segment for which entry is relatively easy.

Most companies involved in magazine content creation are content aggregators as well as content creators. Additionally, much vertical integration exists between aggregators and creators.

Publishers of consumer magazines deliver mostly data analysis content to consumers on a weekly or monthly basis. Magazines tend to be more specialised than newspapers, providing analysis and commentary on a particular topic such as travel, cooking, or sports.

As with media in general, the number of content products available in the magazine sub-segment is growing rapidly. Because total circulation is not growing nearly as quickly as the number of content products available, the average circulation of each product has gone down (Exhibit 4.9).

Exhibit 4.9 **Indices of Audited Titles and Circulation in Germany, 1985 – 1995, Index: 1985=100**

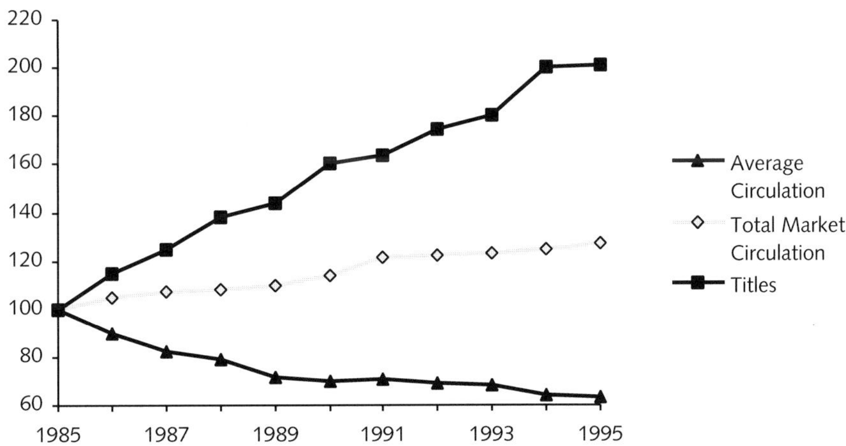

Source: *FT Management Report: European Consumer Magazine Publishing, Facing the Electronic Challenge.*

Magazine publishers have enjoyed only modest revenue growth (Exhibit 4.10), reflecting the maturity of the sub-segment. Now, some large companies are horizontally integrating by controlling many magazine products, publishing content in many different areas of interest in an effort to gain economies of scale by leveraging marketing and distribution channels. Still, operating margins remain modest, with those in the US rising from 9.8 percent in 1992 to 10.7 percent in 1996.

Exhibit 4.10 **Top Consumer Magazine Publishers in US by Revenue, 1992 – 1996, Euro in Billions**

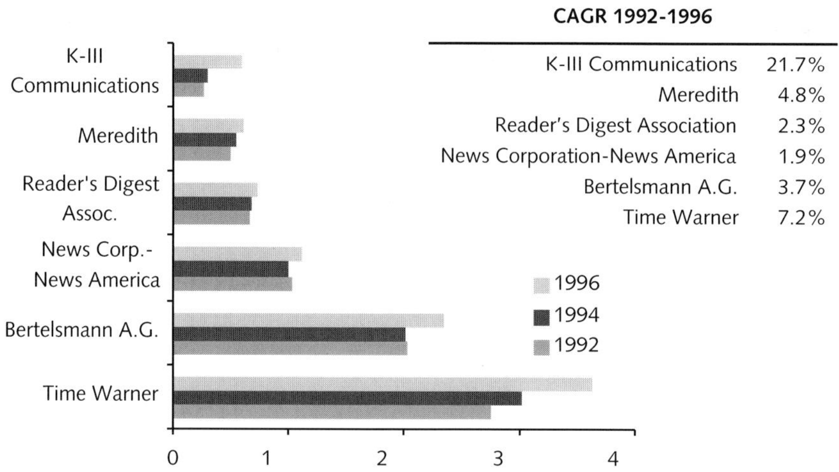

Source: Veronis Suhler & Associates, *Communications Industry Report 1997.*

Industry consolidation has led to a few players controlling most of the top publications, but because magazines target specific interest areas, entry is still possible in niche markets that are not yet saturated (Exhibit 4.11).

Exhibit 4.11 **Publishers' Share of Top 100 Magazines in Europe by Circulation, 1996**

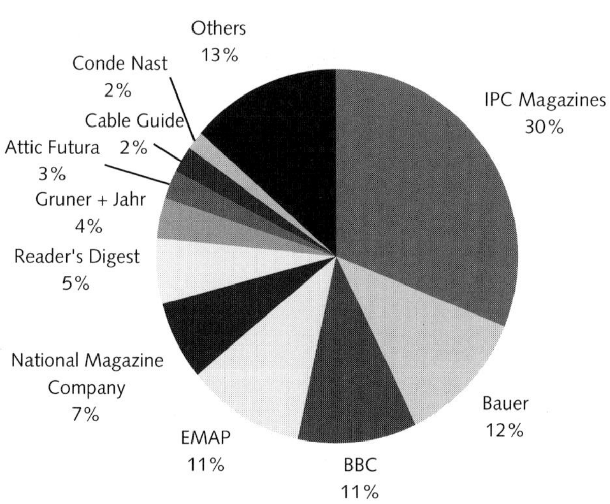

Source: *FT Management Report, European Consumer Magazine Publishing, Facing the Electronic Challenge.*

Historically, consumer magazine revenues are derived equally from circulation and advertising sales. Recently, however, they have depended more on advertising for their revenues, reflecting increased consumer power. Because the market is becoming more segmented, and because consumers have not increased their spending on magazines substantially (Exhibit 4.12), advertisers have been forced to disperse their expenditures across an ever-growing number of publications to reach their target audience.

Exhibit 4.12 **Spending on Consumer Magazines, 1990 – 2000E, Euro in Millions**

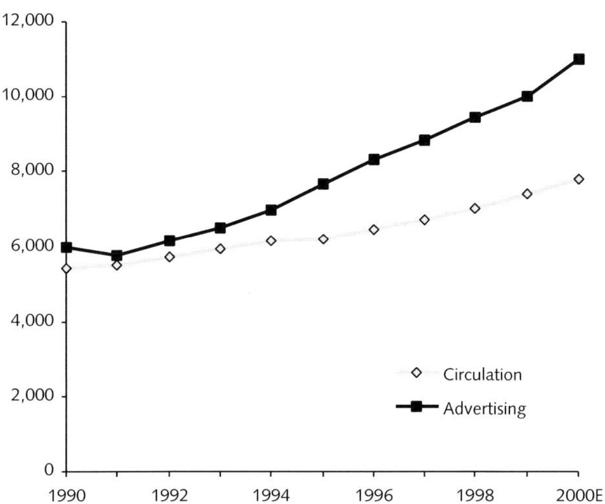

Source: Veronis Suhler & Associates, *Communications Industry Report 1997.*

Due to its multilingual and multicultural heritage, the European magazine industry is fragmented, producing magazines that are local, national, or multilingual. Most international titles are produced separately in the countries where they are distributed in an effort to reflect the national culture. Media markets in Germany and the UK are highly developed. In 1995, for example, in the UK, 2,164 different consumer magazines were in circulation, widely available in chain store outlets such as W.H.Smith. In much of continental Europe, the dominance of the newspaper kiosk, which has limited display space, may be partially accountable for constrained title growth.[4]

In France, about 800 titles are currently published. France has the second-largest consumer magazine market in Europe and boasts the largest circulation title in Europe, *Tele 7 Jours,* published by Hachette Filipacchi. Germany is the largest European magazine market, averaging 124.8 million copies sold per issue. There are about 2,000 titles published in Germany, with 8 titles regularly achieving circulation exceeding 2 million copies. The Italian consumer magazine market is dominated by three large Italian companies, Fininvest, RCS, and Rusconi. The Italian market is characterised by discounted advertising rates and declining circulation. The Spanish consumer magazine market is underdeveloped, with low readership levels. Even television listings magazines have suffered in the face of competition from television: television schedules change too often for listings guides to keep up with them. In the UK, the level of magazine subscriptions remains small, at about 5 percent. Following the lead of their American counterparts, European magazines have started to make inroads in supermarkets.[5]

Subscription levels vary from country to country in Europe. In the UK, subscriptions make up only about 5 percent of all magazine sales, while 43 percent of Germany's titles are sold by subscription. In Italy, subscriptions represent 17 percent and in France 33 percent. European subscription rates pale in comparison to those in the US, where more than 80 percent of copies are sold by subscription. The level of subscription also varies widely by type or title, with some titles achieving the majority of their sales through subscriptions. In Italy, almost half of the circulation of general-interest and business magazines are paid via subscriptions, while less than 1 percent of television listing magazines are sold through subscriptions. Ninety percent of family magazines in France sell by subscription.

Competition among business magazines is a bit different than competition among consumer magazines. The reliability of the information is very important in business magazines, presenting higher barriers to entry. Any magazines that gain recognition and trust in a particular industry can gain a large share of readership in their niche market.

Exhibit 4.13 **Top Business Magazine Publishers in US by Revenue, 1992 – 1996, Euro in Billions**

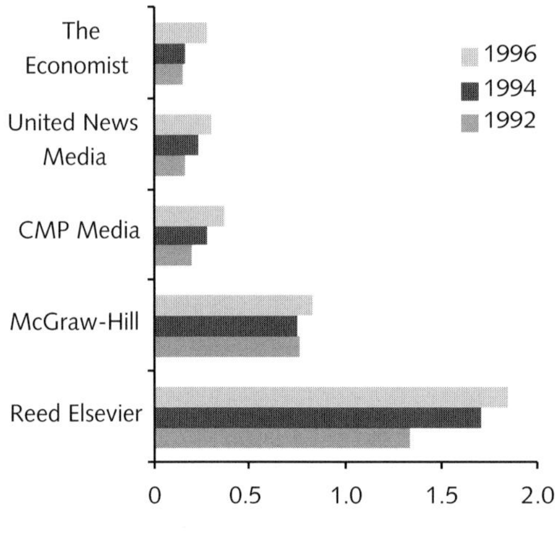

The Economist
United News Media
CMP Media
McGraw-Hill
Reed Elsevier
1996
1994
1992
0
0.5
1.0
1.5
2.0

Source: Veronis Suhler & Associates, *Communications Industry Report 1997*.

On the new media front, many magazine publishers have established Web sites around specific magazines or related content. A variety of strategies are being used by magazines that are experimenting with this new media.

Books

Consumer book industry revenues barely rose from 1992 to 1996, and operating margins fell appreciably from 14.8 percent in 1992 to 10.1 percent in 1996. Book publishers' ties with book content creators tend not to be as close as for magazine and newspaper publishers; competition is fierce for content developed by top creators. Barriers to entry include access to distribution networks and lack of bargaining power with content creators (Exhibit 4.14).

Exhibit 4.14 **Breakdown of Costs for a Best-Selling Book Retailing for $25, Spring 1998**

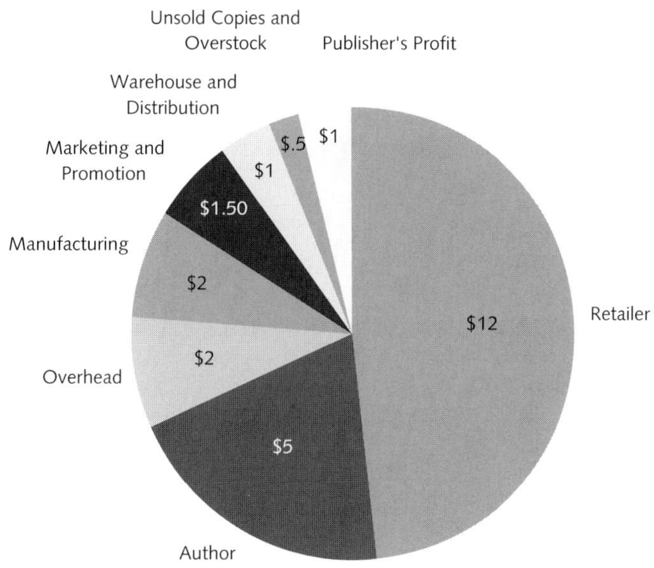

Source: *Time*, April 6, 1998.

As book publishing industry margins become thinner, one company has aggressively expanded through acquisitions to gain economies of scale. Bertelesmann A.G. has added its own publishing holdings by acquiring Bantam Doubleday, Dell Publishing Group, and more recently, in early 1998, Random House, the US's biggest book publisher. Following these acquisitions nearly 40 percent of Bertelsmann's $16 billion in revenues will come from books.[6]

Professional/educational book publishers, like business magazines in the magazine sub-segment, produced higher revenue growth than aggregators for consumer-focused publications. Their operating margins have also outperformed consumer books; however, consolidation in this segment is also evident in Pearson's acquisition of Simon & Schuster's educational publishing units, a move that may make Pearson a world leader in educational publishing.

Book publishers are increasingly using the Internet to sell their work and to develop "communities" around specific books. Many books now have their own Web sites, inviting feedback and discussion among readers.

Exhibit 4.15 **Selected Book Publishing Companies by Revenues, 1992 – 1996, Euro in Millions**

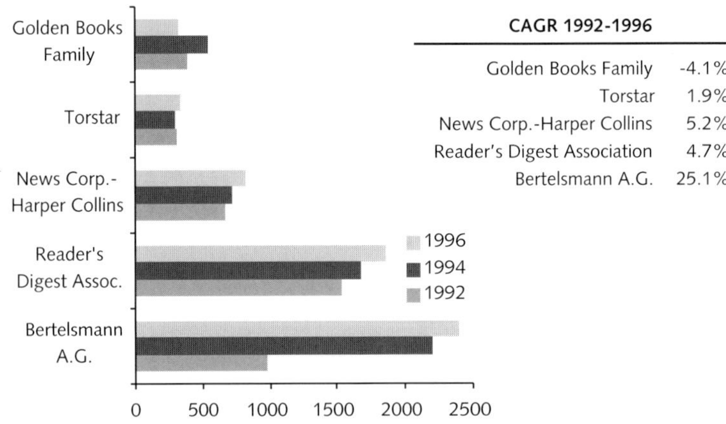

Source: Veronis Suhler & Associates, *Communications Industry Report 1997.*
Note: Companies publicly traded in the US.

4.2.3 Video

Video encompasses content ranging from taped footage of daily events to full-length feature films costing millions of euro. For purposes of this discussion, video divides into two major components: film production and television production. In both cases we have predominantly studied the more mature US industry which has operated with fewer regulatory restrictions in a much larger market.

Film Production
Film content creators are predominantly involved in the conception — the manifestation of an idea in a digital or analogue format, such as audio, text, video, or any combination thereof — of movies or films to be presented in theatres. These include large production companies such as Universal Studios and 20th Century Fox, as well as smaller, independent film companies.

Competition among industry players has always been intense in this sub-segment. Operating margins for major US studios remain moderate and steady, rising from 10.1 percent to 10.9 percent from 1992 to 1996. Although revenues have grown appreciably during the same period (Exhibit 4.16), a small percentage of films generate a large percentage of the revenues (Exhibit 4.17). Film production companies rely on a few highly successful movies to support the enormous production and promotional costs of most films produced (Exhibit 4.18).

Exhibit 4.16 **Revenues for Top European Film and Television Production and Distribution Firms, 1993 – 1996, Euro in Millions**

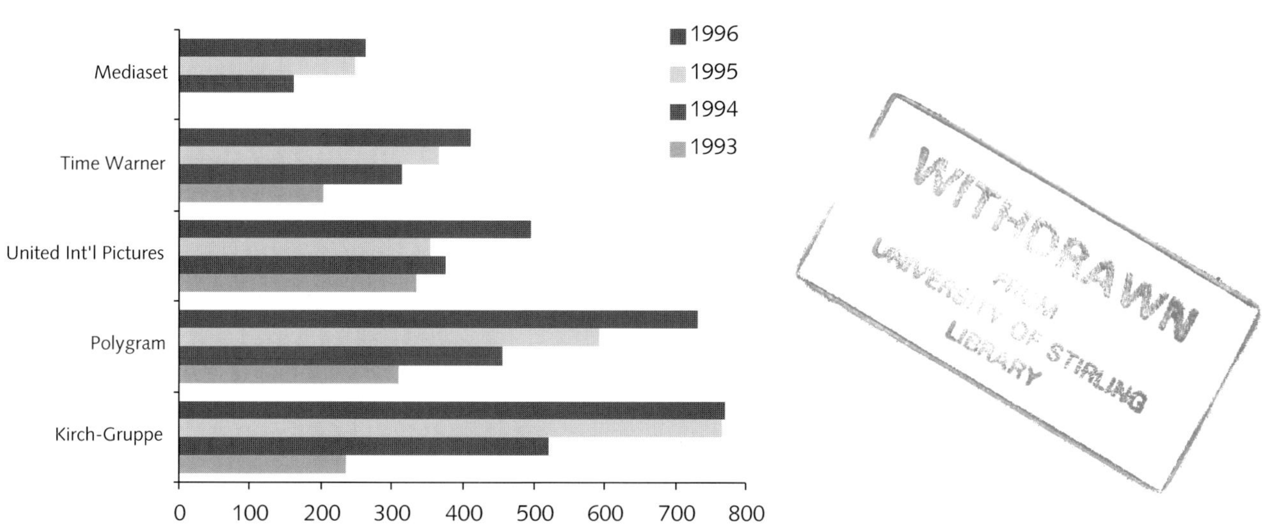

Source: European Audiovisual Observatory, Statistical Yearbook 1998.

Exhibit 4.17 **Number of Films Produced versus Percentage of Box Office Sales**

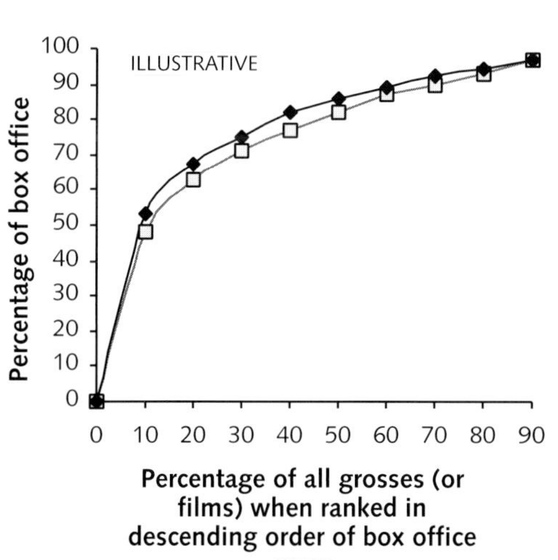

Source: Vogel, *Entertainment Industry Economics: A Guide for Financial Analysis.*
Note: Box-office results of individual films are ranked in order of, for the top curve, total gross, and for the bottom curve, weekly gross.

Exhibit 4.18 **Revenue from Disney's "Lion King" as a Percentage of Disney's Creative Content Division Revenues**

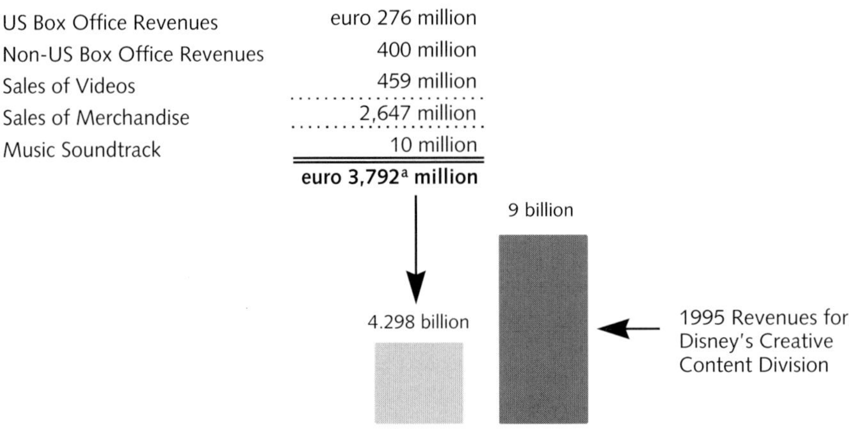

Source: Company Reports; *Business Week.*
a. Revenues earned over a period of several years.

A correlation apparently exists between the amount of money invested in a film and its commercial success (e.g. "Titanic"), and while films with high production costs often produce more revenues, a film with a large budget does not always guarantee success at the box office. This combination high-cost production and the "hit or miss" nature of films makes market entry by potential competitors relatively difficult (Exhibit 4.19).

Exhibit 4.19 **US versus EU Investment in the Film Industry in Europe**

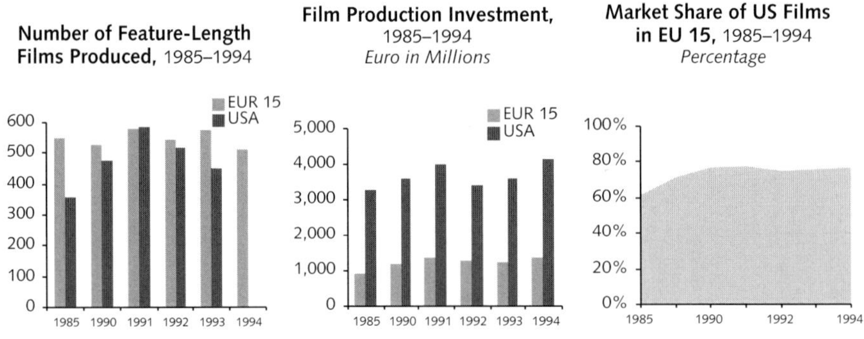

Source: *Panorama of EU Industry*, 1997.

For feature films presented in theatres, substitute products are not a threat to film producers. Films viewed in a theatre constitute a different experience in comparison to video viewing, (even more so in comparison to video via the Internet). Live productions (plays, operas, etc.) provide a theatre experience, but are much more expensive to the consumer. Further, while box office sales provide most of the revenues, videocassette sales and rentals, and licensing to television, cable, and pay-per-view networks also provide revenues for film producers.

US film producers are dominant in markets around the world (Exhibit 4.20). In the past ten years, US films have controlled 60 to 70 percent of the feature film market, taking the top box office revenues consistently world-wide. Although this success could be attributed to the high-budget films that originate in Hollywood, other countries may potentially capture global market shares from the US in the future.

Although films cannot yet effectively be delivered over the Internet, movie studios are creating promotional movie-specific Web sites.

Television

Television content creators produce programs and movies for broadcast or cable television. Players include producers of situation comedies, dramas, talk shows, movies, documentaries, sports, and news programming.

Television production companies have historically achieved higher operating margins than film producers; however, operating margins for US television producers

Exhibit 4.20 **Top Three Grossing Films by Country, 1991 (Bold face = non-US film)**

Country	1	2	3
Argentina	Terminator 2	Dances/Wolves	Godfather III
Austria	Dances/Wolves	Home Alone	Robin Hood
Brazil	Terminator 2	Dances/Wolves	Robin Hood
Chile	Terminator 2	Dances/Wolves	Wild Orchid
Denmark	Dances/Wolves	**The Crumbs**	Robin Hood
Egypt	Dances/Wolves	Ghost	Lethal Weapon 2
Finland	**Mr. Numbskull**	Naked Gun $2^1/_2$	Terminator 2
France	Dances/Wolves	Terminator 2	Robin Hood
Germany	Home Alone	Dances/Wolves	Robin Hood
Greece	Hook	Silence/Lambs	Robin Hood
Hungary	Look Who's Talk 2	Terminator 2	Kindergarten Cop
Iceland	Dances/Wolves	Home Alone	Naked Gun $2^1/_2$
Italy	**Johnny Stecchino**	Robin Hood	**Women In Skirts**
Japan	Terminator 2	Home Alone	Pretty Woman
Malaysia	Terminator 2	**The Banquet**	**Armor of God II**
Mexico	Terminator 2	Robin Hood	**Pelo Suelto**
Netherlands	Dances/Wolves	Robin Hood	Kindergarten Cop
Poland	Dances/Wolves	Robin Hood	Pretty Woman
Spain	Dances/Wolves	Terminator 2	Robin Hood
Sweden	Pretty Woman	Little Mermaid	**The Gas Station**
Switzerland	Dances/Wolves	Home Alone	Robin Hood
U.K.	Robin Hood	Terminator 2	Silence/Lambs

Source: Variety International Film Guide, 1993.

fell almost 22 percent from 1992 to 1996. Demand for programming has grown; however, as programs become less differentiated, increased television content production is driving margins down.

Unlike feature film revenues, television production revenues are mainly derived from the sale or licensing of content to television, cable, or satellite networks. Another difference between film production and television content is the preference, in the case of television programming, for locally produced content (Exhibit 4.21), lowering the chances of the international dominance of the subsegment by a few companies.

Exhibit 4.21 **Top Five Television Programs[b] in Each Country by Origin**

Country	Local	Foreign
Netherlands	5	0
Norway	4	1
Portugal	1	4[a]
Spain	5	0
Sweden	4	1
UK	5	0

Source: *Forbes,* April 15, 1996 via *Market Share Reporter 1997.*

a. Brazil

b. Daily or weekly shows, not special events and movies.

Television networks deliver video content via terrestrial broadcast, cable networks, or satellite broadcast. Until the 1970s, broadcast networks had complete control of the television market. Since that time, cable and satellite networks have not only increased the market for television, but taken much of the market share away from broadcast networks. Increased transmission capacities of cable and satellite broadcast systems are bringing us toward a day when several hundred television viewing choices will be available at the same time. Competition for viewer attention is fierce and will continue to increase as new players enter the market, Internet video streaming technologies improve, and bandwidth capacity grows. Most television aggregators derive the majority of their revenues from advertising; only a few derive revenues from subscription or pay-per-view offerings (Exhibit 4.22).

Broadcast television aggregators offer video content options ranging from news reporting to full-length movies via terrestrial broadcast. Broadcast aggregators often specialise in a particular area of interest, varying programming based on the time of day.

Exhibit 4.22 **Revenue and Profit Growth of Major UK Television Channels, 1993 – 1996, Euro in Millions**

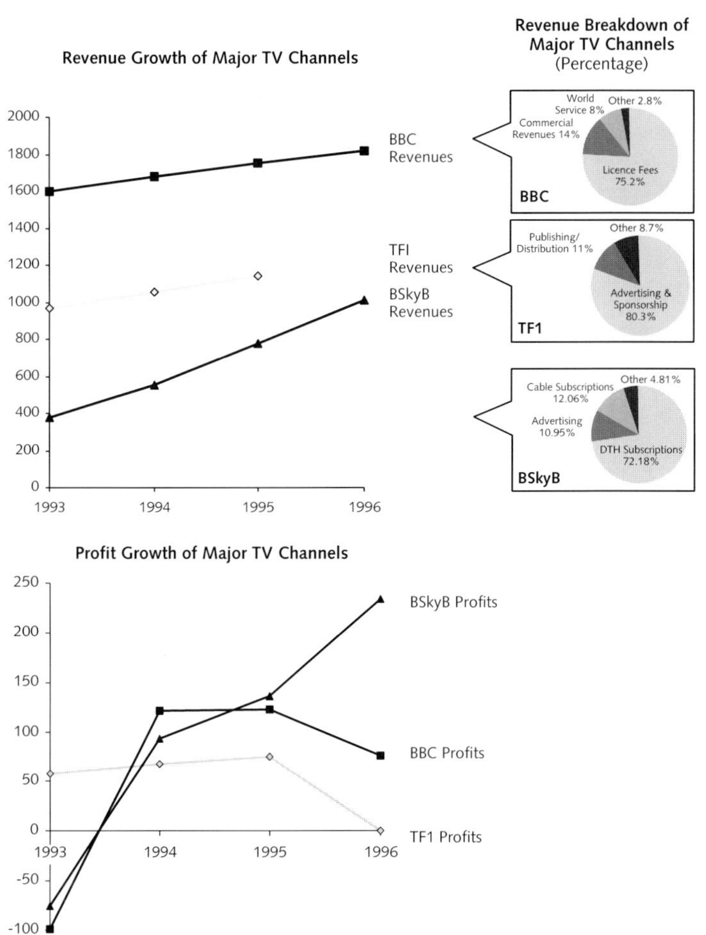

Source: Company Reports.

The US has six national broadcast networks; they control most of the evening and weekend programming, broadcasting via smaller, locally operated stations. Europe does not have large pan-European broadcast networks; instead, local networks and stations dominate the market. A few exceptions are Canal Plus and BSkyB that deliver content in more than one country.

Broadcast television content products compete with one another and with substitute products like cable and satellite programming. As a result, viewers are lost to other choices. Despite this, advertising revenues, making up almost all of broadcast networks' earnings, continue to increase even as viewer share is growing smaller (Exhibit 4.23).

Exhibit 4.23 **Revenues of US Television Stations**

Percentage of Viewers Watching, November 1993 – November 1997

NBC
ABC
CBS
FOX

Advertising Revenues, Euro in Billions, 1993 – 1996

NBC
ABC
CBS
FOX

Advertising Revenues, Euro in Millions, 1990 – 2000E

Television
Radio
Total

Source: Veronis Suhler & Associates, *Communications Industry Report, 1997.*

US broadcasters' operating profits have increased since 1992 and are higher than other aggregating sub-segments. Although competition for audience share is high, broadcast television has consistently drawn more advertising revenues than cable or other television aggregators. Established broadcast networks have a perceived advantage over cable networks in the eyes of advertisers, allowing them to charge rates up to twice as high as those commanded by cable networks.[7] Because demand for television advertising space is higher than for similar space in substitute products, operating margins remain high despite the surplus content.

In the US, the broadcasting sub-segment is highly concentrated (Exhibit 4.24). The top four networks control 49 percent of advertising revenues while three smaller groups claim 7 percent, leaving small stations to battle for the remaining 44 percent. Local stations compete against other terrestrial broadcast stations with a limited spectrum constraining the number of competitors in a given area. Market size for local stations is minimal compared to that of broadcast networks. Broadcast networks reach viewers through a network of local stations; thus gross network revenues are naturally higher than those earned by individual stations.

Content is the biggest expenditure for television stations, accounting for roughly 50 percent of total costs (Exhibit 4.25).

US television broadcasters are turning to new media to enhance product interactivity and reach new markets. Some programming is available globally on the Internet using various streaming technologies. Other television networks have produced text-based Web sites to compete directly with newspapers that have gone online.

Cable and Satellite Networks

Cable networks present video content via cable or satellite broadcast systems. Unlike broadcast networks, cable networks tend to aggregate programming

Exhibit 4.24 **Top US Television Broadcasters' Percentage Share of Total Advertising Revenue, 1996**

Walt Disney-CapCities/ABC 17%
General Electric (NBC) 14%
CBS 11%
News Corp. (FOX) 7%
Grupo Televisa 3%
Tribune Company 2%
Gannett 2%
Other 44%

Source: Veronis Suhler & Associates, *Communications Industry Report, 1997.*

Exhibit 4.25 **Percentage Distribution of Expenses of US Television Stations, 1996**

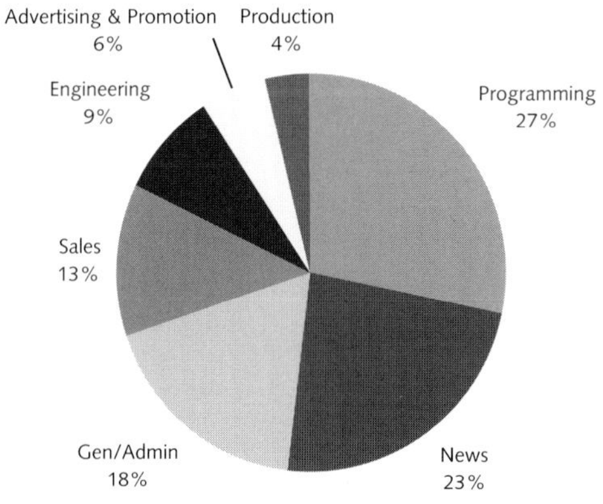

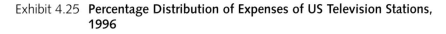

Source: 1997 NAB/BCFM Television Financial Report.

Exhibit 4.26 **Percentage Distribution of Gross Advertising Revenues, 1996**

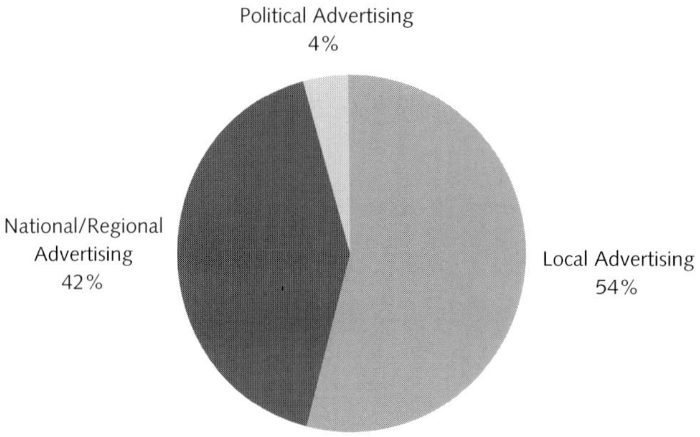

Political Advertising
4%

National/Regional Advertising
42%

Local Advertising
54%

Source: 1997 NAB/BCFM Television Financial Report.

that focuses on a particular area of interest such as music, sports, or news. While competition for viewer attention is intense, many networks attempt to reach niche markets and gain higher market share within those particular areas.

Most cable networks are owned by or in partnership with a few large companies (Exhibit 4.27). Given their bargaining power with connectivity networks, these large companies have a distinct advantage over potential entrants.

Exhibit 4.27 **Cable Network Assets of Major Media Companies, 1996, Percentage of Equity Owned**

- BET (15%)
- Cartoon Network (100%)
- Cinemax (100%)
- CNN (100%)
- Comedy Central (50%)
- Court TV (33.3%)
- E! (50%)
- HBO (100%)
- Headline News (100%)
- TBS SuperStation (100%)
- Turner Classic Movies (100%)
- TNT (100%)

TCI

- BET (22%)
- The Box (5%)
- Court TV (33.3%)
- Discovery Channel (49%)
- Encore (90%)
- Faith & Values (49%)
- Family Channel (20%)
- Home Shopping Network (80.4%)
- International Channel (45%)
- Learning Channel (49%)
- QVC, Q2 (43%)
- Starz! (48%)

- Comedy Central (50%)
- Flix (100%)
- Movie Channel (100%)
- MTV, VH-1 (100%)
- Nickelodeon (100%)
- Sci-Fi Channel (50%)
- Showtime (100%)
- USA Network (50%)

The Walt Disney Company

- A&E (37.5%)
- Disney Channel (100%)
- ESPN/ESPN2 (80%)
- History Channel (37.5%)
- Lifetime Television (50%)

Source: Cable World; Paul Kagan Associates.
Note: TCI also owns large stakes in numerous regional and national sports networks (e.g. Prime Sports, SportsChannel), as well as 23 percent of Turner Broadcasting.

From 1992 to 1996, revenues for companies controlling cable networks grew much faster than those of broadcast networks, perhaps reflecting the consolidation of many networks under a few companies. However, operating income has exceeded that of other aggregating sub-segments. As cable and satellite networks become established, advertising revenues will more closely reflect viewership levels. Currently, cable networks attract 42 percent of the US viewing market, but only about 25 percent of television advertising revenues. If advertising expenditures adjust to correct this phenomenon, cable network revenue growth will eventually far exceed that of broadcast networks.

In Europe, media alliances and mergers and pan-European ownership have been increasing, worrying many European governments. Commercial television's success over the past few years has exposed many government-subsidised television operating inefficiencies. As a result, European governments have been increasingly unwilling to subsidise public broadcasters, and some broadcasters have been forced to make drastic cuts. Britain's BBC, Germany's ARD, and Italy's RAI were the three largest public broadcasters in Europe in 1995. While they are likely to maintain these rankings, they may also watch their shares diminish in comparison to those of commercial broadcasters.

According to Kagan World Media, in 1995 there were eleven television networks in Western Europe with more than $1 billion in revenues. Kagan projects that by 2004 there will be about eighteen networks earning such revenues. In 1994, the top five television networks accounted for 35 percent of western European television revenues, the top ten, 56 percent, and the top twenty, 79 percent. This distribution or revenues is expected to remain fairly unchanged through 2004.

Pay television services continue to grow in popularity across Europe. In 1995, there were an estimated 8.5 million pay-TV subscribers; Kagan World Media forecasts this number to reach 18.3 million by 2004. In the European pay-TV market, Canal Plus France, the oldest pay-TV service in Europe, led the ranking of the top five channels in 1995 with revenues of $1.4 billion, but by 1996, BSkyB took the lead with an estimated $1.6 billion of the total. The growth of pay TV is largely attributable to the emergence of "bouquet" services and mini pay-TV packages. Pay-TV operators such as Canal Plus and BSkyB have been developing "bouquets" of niche television channels, often with cable network partners, to attract new audiences.[8]

4.2.4 Audio

In this sub-segment we will focus on audio content creators and aggregators. Creators in this field include musicians, composers and arrangers, and recording technicians. Aggregators include recording studios and broadcast stations.

Competition in the music business is intense. There are a large number of creators, only a small percentage of which gain any significant market share over time. Market shares of specific content products (songs or albums) are transient, rising and falling with the popularity of the content. Considerable advantage can be gained in this arena by developing a well-known brand name or by gaining "celebrity status" as a content creator.

Music content creators derive profits from licensing agreements or sale of content to aggregators, such as music companies, or from box office sales of live performances (Exhibit 4.28). For creators, live performances can provide revenues, but just as importantly can establish or reinforce brand name and promote packaged products.

Exhibit 4.28 **Top US Concert Tours, 1995, Euro in Millions**

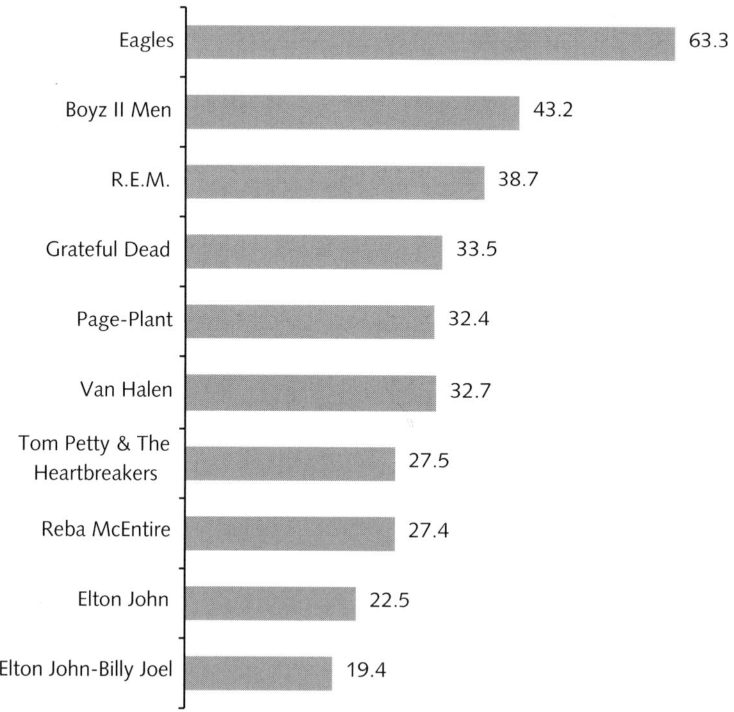

Source: *Detroit Free Press*, December 19, 1995 via *Market Share Reporter, 1997*.

Music creators are constantly threatened by new entrants since there are virtually no barriers to becoming one. On the other hand, music companies are constantly searching for new content products, providing the opportunity for new players or products to gain market share. Once a brand name or reputation is established by a content creator, power shifts from the buyer of that content to the creator. The Internet will eliminate the need for extensive content distribution networks. However, it will not be able to replace the aggregators' market-making capabilities.

Packaged Audio

This sub-segment records, packages, and sells music primarily in the form of tapes and compact discs. Revenues for this sub-segment are generated through direct sales of these products or the licensing of such products to other aggregators.

Five companies dominate the packaged audio sub-segment of the music industry (Exhibit 4.29). Extensive marketing and distribution capabilities give these companies a considerable advantage over potential entrants as well as strong bargaining power with content creators. Intense competition among all music aggregators for "hit" content products transfers this power to the content creator.

Exhibit 4.29 **Media Giants and Their Music Holdings**

- BMG
  - RCA
  - Arista
  - Windham Hill
  - Ariola

- MCA
- Geffen
- Polygram
  - Motown
  - Metronome
  - Decea
  - Deutsche Gramm
  - A&M
  - Island

- CBS Records
- Columbia Records

- Atlantic Records
- Warner Records
- Elektra

- Virgin
- Capitol

Source: Company Reports.

The value of global music sales is expected to grow 26 percent to $50.7 billion by 2003, with Eastern Europe, Asia, and Latin America representing the strongest growth markets.[9]

The retail value of sales by the year 2003 in Eastern Europe is forecast to rise 139 percent, followed by a 112 percent rise in Latin America and a 101 percent increase in Asia. Brazil will remain the star performer in Latin America, with sales growing 132 percent to $3.2 billion, equivalent to a compound annual growth of 13 percent.[10]

Sales in Japan, the world's second-largest market, are, by contrast, seen as remaining stagnant in 1997 and 1998. By the year 2003, the value of the Japanese music market is expected to fall marginally below the 1996 level to just under $6.8 billion.

Despite the abundance of content available, consumers continue to spend increasing amounts on packaged music. Revenues for recorded music companies in the US generally increased from euro 6,425 million in 1992 to euro

7,387 million in 1996, with operating margins rising steadily from 10.5 percent to 12.3 percent over the same period.

Music producers from Germany (BMGE), the US (Warner and Seagram), the UK (EMI) and Japan (Sony) have dominated the global market to date, acquiring many smaller companies in an effort to diversify both geographically and in terms of product (Exhibit 4.30).

Exhibit 4.30 **Top Recorded Music Companies by Revenues in Terms of Product, 1992 – 1996, Euro in Millions**

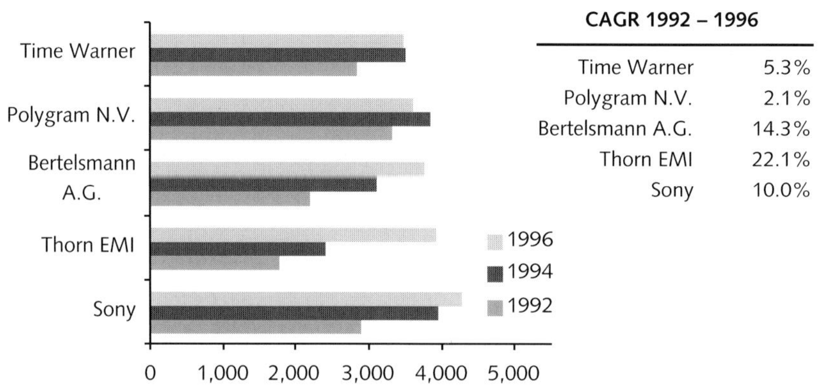

Source: Veronis Suhler & Associates, *Communications Industry Report 1997.*
Note: Companies publicly reporting in US.

The big five music companies battle for market share throughout Europe. Because music is a "hit-driven" industry, market shares vary regionally as popularity of content varies. Local music content has a strong presence throughout Europe. In the UK, the top ten albums of 1996 were created by British acts. In France, local artists accounted for 54 percent of sales, while in Spain only 36 percent of sales were from local artists.[11] To exploit this demand, the big six companies own the rights to many local artists or own small local labels within many countries.

Record companies are employing new media and selling their product directly online. While concerns around intellectual property and piracy have limited this practice, recording firms recognise the Internet as a valuable medium for driving sales.

Radio Broadcasting

This sub-segment is composed of audio content aggregators and broadcasters. In France, Spain, Italy, and the UK, Europe's most mature private radio markets, a handful of players dominate. In these countries, national networks have emerged or have purchased a number of local networks; however, a significant number of specialised independent players, such as NRJ in France and Capital in the UK, still participate. Independents derive nearly all of their revenues from home markets.

This sub-segment is highly consolidated in the US, with six companies increasing their market share from 31 percent to 56 percent between 1992 and 1996 (Exhibit 4.31). Market entry is becoming more difficult as incumbents leverage ties with content creators and packaged audio companies to boost marketing and attract listeners.

Exhibit 4.31 **Top US Radio Broadcasters' Percentage Share of Total Advertising Revenues, 1992 and 1996**

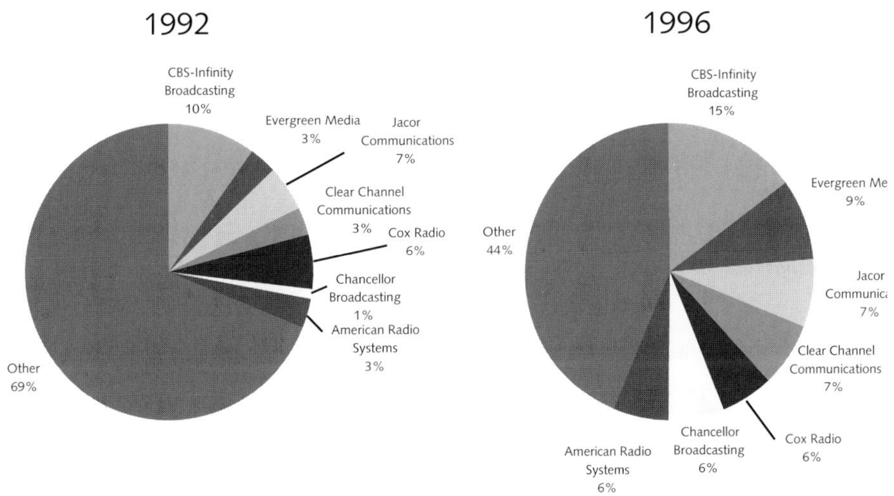

Source: Veronis, Suhler & Associates, *Communications Industry Report 1997.*

While consolidation in US radio broadcasting has occurred during the 1990s, broadcasters have not faced the emergence of many new substitute products as have television broadcasters (e.g. cable and satellite services). Thus, radio broadcasters have increased operating income.

As might be expected, the European radio landscape is more fragmented than that of the US. In 1996, total radio revenues in Europe were estimated at roughly $8 billion, with revenues divided between licensing fees and advertising revenues.

Until the 1970s, European radio was dominated by state-owned national networks, but over the last two decades, European radio broadcasting has undergone considerable deregulation, competition has increased, and now over 6,000 radio stations are in operation across Europe. In about half of Europe, the private sector's audience share has risen to over 50 percent. In France, Greece, Spain, and other countries, new private broadcasters have formed national networks and compete on equal terms with the public broadcasters. Meanwhile, in some countries (e.g. Denmark, Sweden, and Finland), private stations have only local licenses and limited ability to form national networks. Based on licensing policies, European governments also regulate the number of private stations in each country. The number of local private stations ranges from 2 in Austria (where 8 are planned) to over 2,500 in Italy. These local private stations account for about 90 percent of all European radio broadcasters, but can claim less than half the total audience. Their share is greatest in Germany and the UK, where full-scale networking is not permitted, and is lowest in such countries as Belgium and Norway.[12]

With 25 percent and 21 percent of market share respectively, Germany and France account for almost half of European radio advertising revenues. Spain and the UK bring in 10 percent each, while some countries with poorly developed commercial radio sectors generate virtually no radio advertising revenues.

Using streaming technologies, hundreds of radio broadcasters are now reaching global audiences by broadcasting over the Web. New, solely Web-based, radio broadcasts have also emerged. As computers and other network access devices become better able to receive and play music, traditional broadcasters' dominance will be severely threatened.

4.2.5 Sports

Creators of sports content include athletes, coaches, and sport event organisers (e.g. professional soccer leagues, the Association of Tennis Professionals, the International Olympic Committee).

Participants
This sub-segment is extremely concentrated. Of the large number of participants, only a few succeed financially. Participant turnover in sports is very high, creating an environment in which new entrants and existing participants compete constantly for market share.

Because they are differentiated from others, exceptional athletes gain power over organisers and aggregators, adding great value to sports content products.

Event Organisers
Event organisers are an extremely concentrated sub-segment. High entry costs and intense competition for top athletes and coaches create a natural monopoly for most professional sports leagues. Revenues are derived by licensing content products to aggregators and advertising revenues from corporate sponsors.

In recent years, relationships between major sporting leagues and television broadcasters have grown stronger. Believing it can provide key anchor content to build global viewership, News Corp. has forged a number of important long-term relationships with various sports leagues around the world. Most recently, a News Corp. subsidiary went one step further, purchasing a US Major league baseball team, the Los Angeles Dodgers, for $320 million. News Corp., a stakeholder in twenty regional television sports networks in the US, also owns 20 percent stakes in the New York Knicks, a National Basketball Association team, and the New York Rangers, a National Hockey League team. Disney, which owns 80 percent of the ESPN television sports networks, also owns a professional team in the US.

Ted Turner, founder of Turner Broadcasting System and CNN, pioneered combining team ownership with television network ownership. Turner used rights to broadcast the Atlanta Braves Major League Baseball games on his small independent television station to help build regional appeal for his network. He bought the team in 1975 and soon began broadcasting to cable television network operators across the US via satellite. The Braves broadcasts, and later the NBA's Atlanta Hawks games — Turner purchased the Hawks in 1977 — provided anchor content on Turner's TBS Superstation, enabling his small independent television station to gain entry into almost every cable household in the US.[13]

Using popular sporting events to build viewership is occurring in markets around the world. Those broadcasters able to offer lucrative contracts to sports leagues or international events obtain a competitive advantage in the now-crowded broadcasting markets.

4.2.6 Video Games and Entertainment Software

More children now recognise Nintendo's key character, Mario the Plumber, than recognise Disney's Mickey Mouse. By the middle of 1997, Sony expected to start earning more from its video game subsidiary than from film-making.[14] The video game industry has become an important sub-segment of the digital media industry.

Game playing now ranks with movies, sports, and music as a popular leisure pursuit of people under thirty: In the US, 40 percent of households have a Nintendo system. Competing with Sega and Sony, Nintendo's systems have grown in capacity and ingenuity — the company has recently released a 64-bit machine.

Video game creators develop digital interactive games to be played on a variety of electronic devices. Although Sony has made huge inroads with its popular PlayStation console and software, the video game segment is so far dominated by Sega and Nintendo (Exhibit 4.32); game developers pay licensing fees to create games for Sony and Nintendo systems. Sony first introduced its PlayStation in 1995. Since then, it has proven equally adept at developing game software. Three of the six best-selling PlayStation titles are made by Sony Computer Entertainment.

Although revenues for 1996 were down, the video game business underwent an unprecedented boom in 1997. In recent years, Sega has fallen behind Sony and Nintendo.

Exhibit 4.32 **Top Video Game Console Software Companies by Revenue, 1992–1996, Euro in Millions**

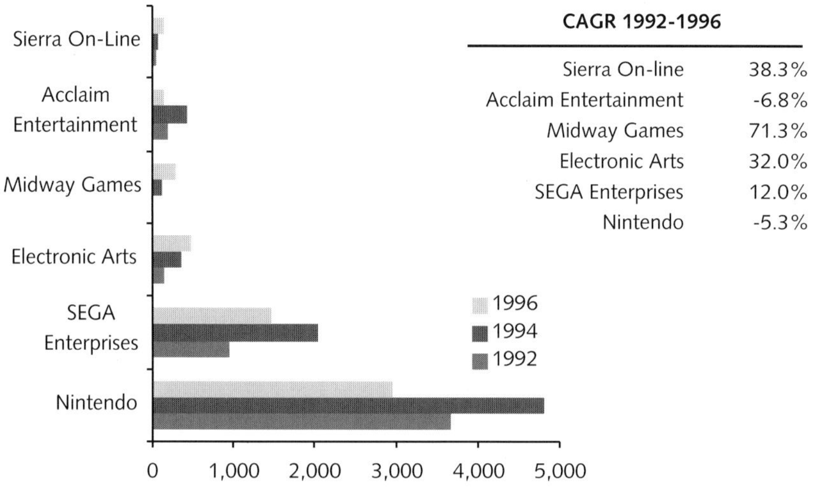
Sierra On-Line
Acclaim Entertainment
Midway Games
Electronic Arts
SEGA Enterprises
Nintendo
0
1,000
2,000
3,000
4,000
5,000
1996
1994
1992
CAGR 1992-1996
Sierra On-line 38.3%
Acclaim Entertainment -6.8%
Midway Games 71.3%
Electronic Arts 32.0%
SEGA Enterprises 12.0%
Nintendo -5.3%

Source: Veronis Suhler & Associates, *Communications Industry Report, 1997.*

Sony's strength in the United States, Japan, and Europe has recently made it a leader; it now produces 2 million PlayStation units per month, more than any single consumer product in the company's history.

Until recently, PCs were not equipped with enough memory and were too slow to run the graphics-intensive video games customarily played on game consoles. In 1998, however, an estimated 100 million PCs will be sold world-wide — all with the processing power to run advanced games.[15]

As with other media, an apparent glut of video games has hit the market — mostly due to Sony. The Sony PlayStation offers 300 games to Nintendo 64's 36.[16] Sony has shipped 135 million games since 1995, with Japan buying 70 million, the US 35 million, and Europe 30 million.

Video Game software has become a "hit-driven" industry like the film industry. Production costs are also becoming very high. "Final Fantasy VII," which cost $35 million to develop for the Sony PlayStation, is the most expensive game made to date and has already grossed more than $200 million in retail sales. Given rising costs of production, distribution, and advertising, smaller software developers are facing a squeeze in the video game market.

4.3 Connecting

"Connecting" is the analogue or digital transmission of content over a network. Most players in this segment provide the infrastructure hardware and software as well as the connection necessary for aggregators and end users to exchange information. The technological aspect of the connecting segment will be covered in Chapter 7, but issues pertaining to the structure of the industry are briefly discussed here.

4.3.1 Telecommunications

Analogous to many of the industry segments discussed above, the telecommunications industry is undergoing a major transformation. Once heavily regulated, this sector is being deregulated in much of the world (Exhibit 4.33).

Exhibit 4.33 **Realignment of the Telecommunications Industry**

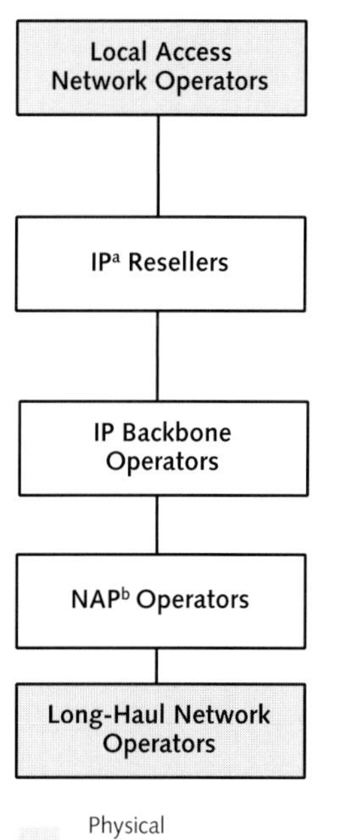

- Physical network that end users use to reach POP, LEC switch, or headend:
  - May be POTS[a] telephone line, ISDN line, leased line, wireless, or cable TV coaxial, (e.g. Deutsche Telekom, Norkabel, Iridium, France Telecom).
- Carriers that resell IP transport to end users by leasing connection to Internet bandwidth operators are either building and operating or leasing POPs:
  - A majority of US Internet service providers operate as IP resellers (e.g. EarthLink, MindSpring, and HarvardNet).
- Carriers that operate the backbones that carry IP traffic over leased lines between high-speed routers and ATM switches located in multiple locations:
- Lease access to resellers (e.g. UUNET, Ebone, and Ukerna).
- Major connection points between multiple Internet backbones:
  - Usually operated by carriers or consortia of carriers (e.g. MAE-East, DGIX, and deCIX).
- Operators of physical networks on which IP backbone operates:
  - Typically carry both voice and data traffic (e.g. WorldCom, Hermes Railtel, Qwest, and Telenor).

Source: Gemini Strategic Research Group.

a. Internet protocol.

b. Network access point.

This transformation will ultimately have profound consequences for a wide range of players.

The biggest telecommunications companies are Nippon Telephone and Telegraph (NTT) of Japan, followed by American Telephone and Telegraph (AT&T) of the United States, Deutsche Telekom of Germany, France Telecom, and British Telecom of the UK.

Germany has the largest telecommunications market in Europe. The industrial group Mannesmann, A.G., also the leading operator of mobile-telephone services in Germany, has linked with Germany's railway system to create a telecommunications network called Arcor. Overall, about thirty companies are offering services in specific sectors. During 1998, three energy companies will launch telecommunications services to compete with Deutsche Telekom and Arcor. These firms are Veba and RWE, which have launched a jointly-owned business called o.tel.o, and VIAG, which is backed by British Telecom and Telenor. France Telecom has one direct competitor, Cegetel, a subsidiary of Compagnie Generale des Eaux (recently renamed Vivandi), which opened its network in February 1998. Bouygues, the construction and television conglomerate, also entered the market.

Italy has been slow to adapt to the new environment; licences to operate fixed telephone lines have not yet been awarded and no group has named a date for the launch of services. Three big operators making preparations to enter the market include Olivetti and Mannesmann, with a project called Infostrada; the Banca Nazionale del Lavorno with British Telecom and Mediaset, to be joined soon by Eni, with Albacom and Enel; and Deutsche Telekom and France Telecom with Wind.[17]

Europe's telecom market is valued at euro 114 billion. Despite efforts by long-established telecoms to maintain full control of their territories, eager and aggressive start-ups are developing detailed strategies to compete for this lucrative market. British Telecom, Deutsche Telekom, France Telecom, and other industry giants have devised a sophisticated alliance defence strategy of their own.[18]

This competition is likely to produce varied results. In Great Britain, where competition has been a reality for several years, the latest figures for the uptake of cable services (most of which provide telephone services and Internet access in addition to video entertainment) show that penetration is actually less than half of the 45 percent of the population predicted to be cabled up by the start of 1998. Nevertheless, telephone services have proved popular, with some 34 percent of cable customers having purchased these services along with the video services, exceeding the number of subscribers by three times.[19]

In November 1997, the EC threatened seven European countries with legal action unless they moved to meet the required rules and timetables associated with the telecommunications deregulation process. In response Deutsche Telekom announced price cuts for long distance calls. The new tariff offers the biggest rate cuts in areas where competition is expected to be most pronounced. In the local market, however, Deutsche Telekom is likely to remain the dominant force for years to come.

Across the EU, the process has been set in motion, bringing tremendous change for telecommunications competition over the next few years.[20] Many new operators will be investing in more advanced, cost-efficient, and flexible technology than that owned by incumbents. Higher-level synchronous digital hierarchy (SDH) systems, Internet protocol (IP) over asynchronous transfer mode (ATM), and others are a few of these technologies. In comparison, incumbents will have no option but to retain copper and 800 MHz technologies in some parts of their networks. The comparatively higher cost of these technologies will be reflected in their financial performance.

Most alternative networks are expected to be well-capitalised. New operators will be able to offer broader product ranges, have lower unit costs, and be well-positioned to offer bundled services. As price caps are removed, the new industry structure will change. "In five years' time, the telecommunications industry will look like any another free-market industry," says communications analyst Martin Warwick. "Markets will become highly segmented, marketing costs will increase, approaching those of popular branded products in the retail sector, and the industry in general will have low predictability."[21]

Market segmentation trends are already becoming apparent. Large incumbents are forming consortia with a sole aim of serving business customers. Experience has shown this area as being richest in potential revenues, and this is where size and global presence count. Increasingly, residential markets will be served by cable operators or similar companies that provide a mix of telephony and entertainment/interactive services.

In the business services area, the emphasis on network reliability and end-to-end manageability will lead to the increased importance of owning infrastructure. Leasing and interconnection arrangements will be the choice of the typical reseller or small operator serving domestic or regional markets. This is borne out in the case of WorldCom, which, in the early days of its alliance with the long distance operator LDDS, served as a reseller earning $1 billion without owning significant infrastructure.

New global carriers like WorldCom will mount a tremendous challenge to European incumbent carriers. WorldCom is estimated to have spent $50 billion acquiring other telecoms and building new fibre-based infrastructure. "We are in the process of building the first global broadband network," declares John Sidgmore, WorldCom's CEO.[22] In fact, monumental changes are forecast for global backbone operators. The commissioning of submarine cables and terrestrial fibre backbones over the next two years will effectively quadruple the bandwidth on some international routes. The addition of physical lines combined with the use of SDH and other cost-efficient technologies are likely to lead to the commoditisation of voice. "We expect basic voice service tariffs to fall by about 80 percent over the next five years," asserts Martyn Warwick. The billions of minutes of voice traffic that will be carried on these networks will mean that per-minute costs of plain old telephony will effectively approach zero. Commoditisation will emphasise the added value that service providers will be forced to offer in addition to basic packages.[23]

4.3.2 Terrestrial Broadcast

Terrestrial broadcast consists of high-bandwidth data transmission over television or radio frequencies. Separate transmission equipment is necessary for each frequency and terrestrial broadcast only serves local areas. All consumers receive terrestrial broadcasting free of charge; they require only a television or radio in order to receive the signals. As other networks that can offer a much greater variety of programming, such as cable, satellite, and the Internet, become less expensive and more popular, terrestrial broadcasting networks may be forced to adapt.

4.3.3 Cable Systems

In the US, cable systems began transmitting television programming to end users over twenty years ago. Since then cable systems have been growing as these companies invest in their infrastructure. Cable systems provide high-bandwidth transmissions of digital information through coaxial cables; all allow transmission of information in both downstream (host to end user) and upstream (end user to host) directions.

Cable systems require large initial investments by operators, creating a large barrier to entry for potential players, and creating monopolistic economies for cable transmission within local areas. However, the advent of satellite networks has dramatically increased competition, reducing profitability for cable operators (Exhibit 4.34).

Exhibit 4.34 **Percentage Operating Income Margins of US Cable Systems Operators, 1992 – 1996**

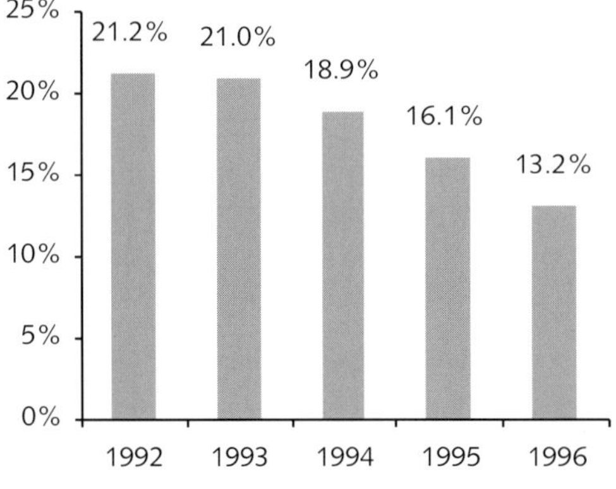

Source: Veronis, Suhler & Associates, *Communications Industry Report 1997.*
Note: 1992 vs. 1996 Margin Change (Points) = -8.0.

4.4 Interfacing

In Chapter 7 we will discuss fully the types of electronic devices consumers use to access content. From a technology perspective, one of the most important trends in this sector is the convergence of many access devices that were once distinctly different. Increasingly, these devices contain more common components and approximate each other in functionality. Consumer electronics giants have responded to this trend by diversifying their product lines in an attempt to capture the wide range of potential revenues. These firms have forged important alliances with content firms to supply devices like digital set-top boxes for television and cable modems.

4.5 Achieving Economies of Scale in an Attention Economy

In a network economy, attention has become the most scarce resource. Many companies compete for consumer attention while consumers are more careful where they allocate it, creating an "attention economy." Firms are evolving to compete successfully in this attention economy.

New technologies and more efficient markets are creating a web of specialised firms that can easily, cheaply, and seamlessly interact with each other to provide products and services to consumers. Because technologies are decreasing the transaction costs among and within companies, it is no longer clearly a cost advantage to control many components of a product value chain. However, with the abundance of products and services, strategic power resides in the ability to draw the attention of consumers. A firm can achieve economies of scale by capturing the attention of a large market and then selling and promoting a variety of products and services to that market. Many content firms are organising themselves to achieve these advantages.

4.5.1 Moving Away from Product-Focused Integration Strategies

Large investments in upstream or downstream activities can reduce a firm's flexibility, rendering it less able to adjust to changing markets. Because the use of networks has the potential to squeeze out many of the traditional inefficiencies in markets, the emerging global network economy is often described as "frictionless." Theoretically, such a frictionless economy should facilitate the externalisation of many more functions than could ever be externalised without the network, and speed the development of dis-integrated industries. The network allows cheap, efficient global markets to develop for almost any type of raw materials, components, or services that a firm might require for its product or service.

As we examined the various segments that make up the content industry, one of the most salient distinctions among segments was the relative degree of vertical integration. For example, newspapers, in addition to maintaining staffs of reporters and editors, also tend to own printing plants and extensive fleets of vehicles to transport newspapers to news agents and subscribers. On the other hand, many smaller book publishers consist only of editorial and marketing staffs, with everything from the actual content creation (by individual authors) to printing and distribution accomplished by third parties. Levels of integration are changing significantly as firms attempt to develop strategies in response to the changing environment. Fluid networks are emerging to produce and deliver many of the media products traditionally created by vertically integrated media concerns. Companies are focusing less on integrating functions of the production and delivery of specific products.

4.5.2 Moving toward Attention-Focused Integration Strategies

In the content industry integration strategies are shifting focus to delivering various products to a single market. Once a firm has the attention of a market, it can leverage that attention to promote other products and services.

Today, these firms often possess extremely flexible and well-managed webs of component suppliers, and function as sophisticated, efficient organisers and marketers of resources. Horizontal integration is taking place to leverage synergies in marketing of content products, as well as to expand the competencies of firms in an effort to become flexible in a changing marketplace.

We will analyse companies that are not necessarily organised around products, but rather around markets to gain a different perspective on the industry and an understanding of the drivers of integration within the industry. We will look primarily at large media companies that operate in several segments of the industry — at companies that are organised around content function. Earlier in this chapter we considered content as having two major functions: On one end of the spectrum they are providing entertainment, and on the other end of the spectrum, information.

Entertainment

Through their many subsidiaries, large media conglomerates such as Viacom, Bertelsmann, News Corp., Time-Warner, and Walt Disney create, aggregate, and distribute entertainment content throughout the world. These media empires realise the full value of the content products they own and control extensive market-making capabilities for content creators and content aggregators. A key factor in their market-making power comes from having the attention of a captive audience or "community" of consumers.

We saw earlier the example of Walt Disney's "Lion King," a film that not only grossed 676 million euro at the box office, but also drew revenues from the sale of Lion King merchandise, video cassettes, and a soundtrack. This example gives us an idea of the importance of "hit" content products for media companies, and also how entertainment concepts can be exploited through various revenue streams. However, the promotional and market-making capabilities of "Lion King" can also indirectly drive other revenues streams controlled by Walt Disney. Disney has captured the attention of the market of families with young children through the popularity of "Lion King" and then sells and promotes other products to this particular market. By Integrating assets that produce these other products into its company, Disney has realised significant promotional and financial benefits (Exhibit 4.35).

Exhibit 4.35 **Revenue from Disney's "Lion King" as a Percentage of Disney's Creative Content Division Revenues**

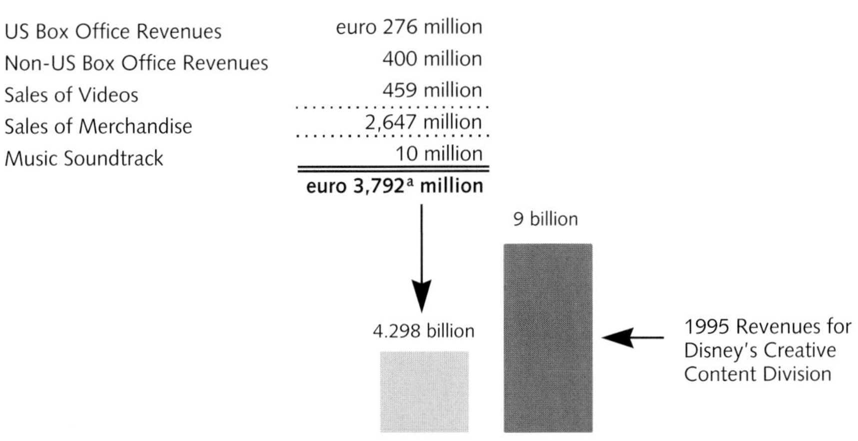

Source: Company Report, *Business Week.*
a. Revenues earned over a period of several years.

Walt Disney uses the popularity of content products such as "Lion King" to promote other assets such as its ABC broadcasting network, the Disney Channel cable network, Disney World, Disney Land, and EuroDisney amusement parks. These assets then promote other Walt Disney content products. The ability to make markets for products is the ultimate competitive advantage that media empires possess, and a reason why it is so difficult for new players to enter into any of the creating or aggregating sub-segments.

Media companies build their market-making ability by controlling many assets including content products, content creators, and content aggregators across different content forms. These companies can then promote new content products through various aggregators or by linking them somehow to other popular products. The large scale of media giants allows them to create and promote many content products, increasing the chances that one of those products will become a "hit."

News Corp.'s Fox Network followed a strategy similar to Walt Disney's when its television show "The X-Files" became a hit. Capitalising on the popularity of the show, News Corp. not only drew revenues from advertising and syndication directly associated with the show, but has released a movie based on the show (which grossed $30 million in it first weekend in the United States), sells merchandise associated with the show, and drives demand for FX, its cable network

(Exhibit 4.36). Fox and FX will also promote other television shows by programming them before or after "The X-Files," increasing awareness of those shows.

Exhibit 4.36 **Capitalising on the Success of "The X-Files"**

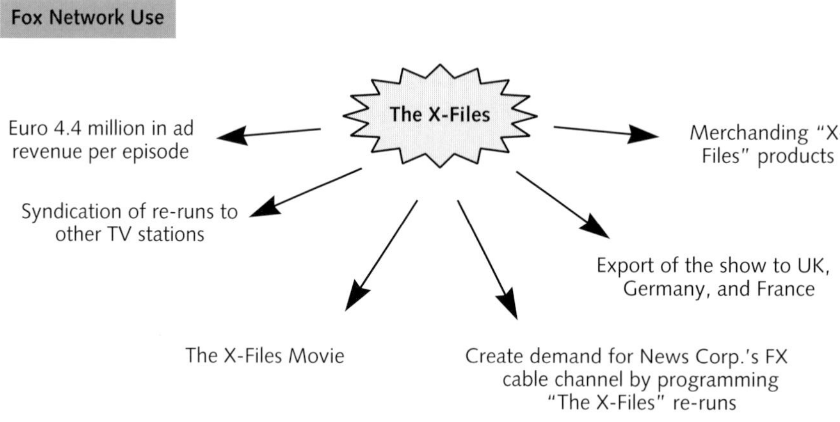

Source: *Fortune*, January 12, 1998; Gemini Strategic Research Group.

Looking at the US television market we can see that most major companies such as Viacom, Disney, News Corp., Time-Warner, and Sony have secured control of television-related assets to create, promote, and support content products (Exhibit 4.37). Assets in the television market complement assets in publishing, film, music, retailing, and other content products. These media giants dominate the entertainment business, creating high barriers to entry.

Exhibit 4.37 **Media Communications Company Relationships**

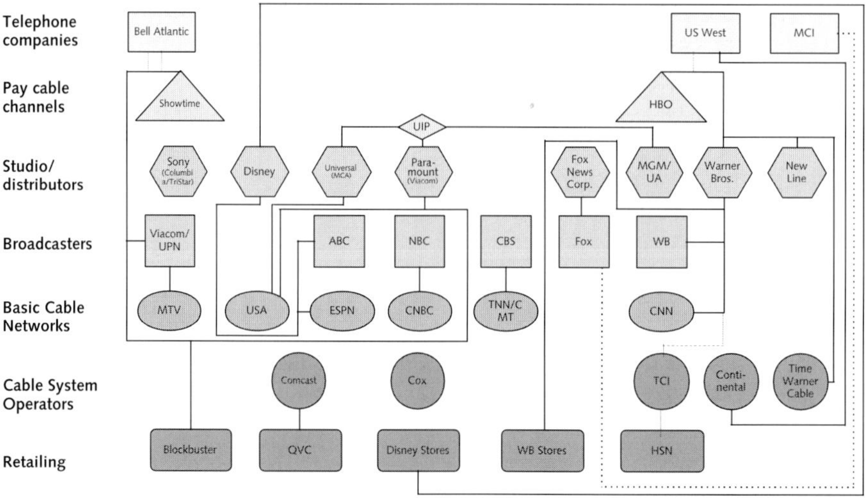

Source: Vogel, *Entertainment Industry Economics: A Guide for Financial Analysis.*

Although most media companies own assets throughout the digital media industry, these assets' revenue streams and ability to create operating income naturally vary widely. Even though some segments within a company perform poorly compared to others, they might be key components of the overall strategy of the firm. Thus, although CBS's TV network performs poorly compared to the company's radio stations (Exhibit 4.38), much of CBS's power as a media company is derived from its TV network.

Exhibit 4.38 **News Corporation's (Fox) 1996 Revenues and Operating Income and CBS's 1997 Revenues and EBITDA, Euro**

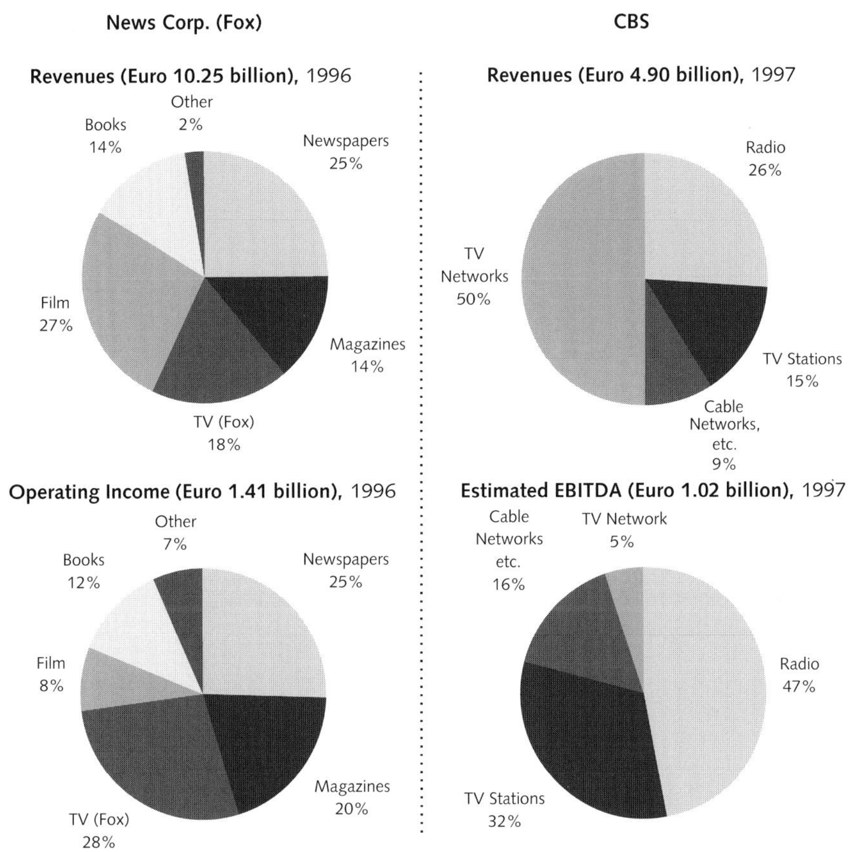

Source: Morgan Stanley Equity Research, 1997.

Publishing assets can also drive indirect revenues. Books are often adapted to become movies or television shows, while magazine brands or concepts are used in television or radio shows, merchandising, or exhibitions relating to areas of interest (Exhibit 4.39)

Exhibit 4.39 **Brand Extension Benefits for a Magazine Brand**

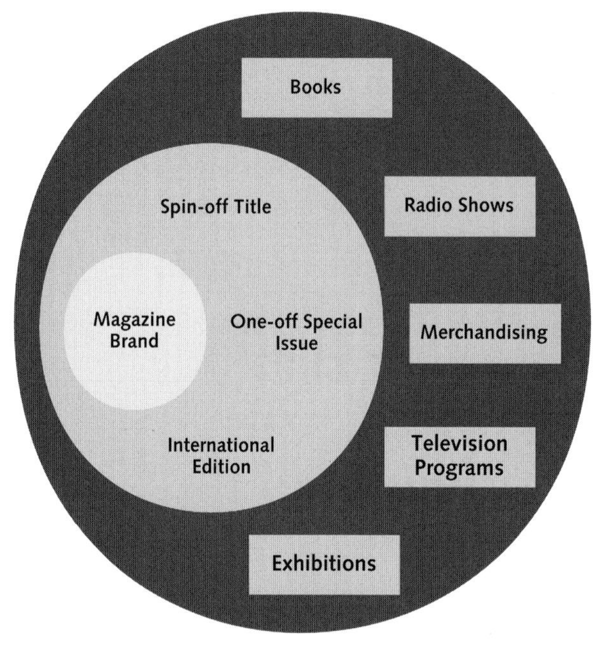

Source: Datamonitor.

Internet content creation and aggregation can become both an extension of the market-making network that media giants control and an additional revenue stream from which these companies can profit. Even though the Internet promises to reduce reproduction and distribution costs for many products, competitors in any sub-segment will be at a disadvantage because of the control that media companies have outside the Internet.

Niche players have been better able to provide their customers with highly relevant and sometimes individually customised products. However, the Internet will allow creation of customised content products based on electronic user profiles. Large media companies can thus reach a mass market, yet provide "customised" products.

Information

Companies like Reed-Elsevier, Dunn & Bradstreet, and Reuters create, aggregate, and distribute information content for many different markets. They have become dominant in the information media segment by assembling and controlling large content-creating networks and gaining economies of scale in the aggregation and distribution of content. Their competitive advantage rests largely on brand name, reputation, and the assets they control.

Unlike entertainment-based companies that deliver content on a "hit or miss" basis, information companies must strive to provide accurate information at all times to maintain their reputations. Within the niche markets that these companies serve, their brand names become the seal of quality of the information they provide. This allows them to gain market share and reinforces the credibility of their related content products. Again, these companies are focusing on capturing a market and then leveraging their position to sell other products to that market or to similar markets.

4.6 Summary

An overabundance of content and content delivery methods has been causing many changes in the digital media industry. Many firms have been vertically dis-integrating to focus on their core competencies and horizontally integrating to leverage economies of scale in the attention economy. Many content firms have organised their assets roughly based on the function of their content products (information versus entertainment) to more effectively realise the economies of scale gained from controlling the attention of a market, particularly in the marketing and promotion of products.

RECOMMENDATIONS

The traditional content and telecommunications industries are undergoing profound change. Increasing levels of competition and the globalisation of competition in these industries are forcing all players to re-evaluate their strategies and seek new sources of advantage. Businesses in general and content businesses in particular must move now to adjust to these changes.

Businesses

- Focus on the customer relationship as a key source of competitive advantage. While it may sound like a cliché, the customer relationship is more important now than ever. Product-oriented firms may find that customer-oriented firms squeeze them out of markets that they have held for years.
- Become more flexible by outsourcing many non-core functions. Vertical de-integration has been taking place for many years, but now it is accelerating as digital interactive networks based on open standards make it easier for firms to acquire non-core products and services in the open market. Those firms that understand this and take advantage of this flexibility are likely to be the most successful in the marketplace.

Content Firms

- Promote and link network products with traditional content products. There is a tremendous amount of "noise" and confusion in the network marketplace. Those firms that can successfully exploit traditional content channels to drive traffic to their network services have an advantage over firms that do not have access to these traditional channels. Many of the current Internet retail and media success stories have relied heavily on advertising in traditional media to build market awareness and drive traffic.
- Differentiate content as much as possible to compete with traditional and nontraditional firms (e.g. manufacturers, governments, professional services) that are also developing and distributing content. The incredible proliferation of media described in this chapter means that content must be unique in order to compete successfully in the marketplace. Only content that is timely, personalised, original, or sensational is going to attract the attention of consumers bombarded by an ever-increasing choice of content. Doing this will require a concerted focus on developing products and partnerships to attract and retain customer attention. Again, controlling a market's attention is the key competitive advantage in the network economy.
- Constantly re-evaluate how you derive revenues from content products. Be prepared to use all network delivery channels as well as traditional formats. Simply put, print publishers should explore network and broadcast channels; network publishers should explore print channels; content firms should separate the content from the delivery medium and explore new opportunities for delivering that content to potential consumers. Preparing to do this means investing in digitising content and storing it in easily manipulated formats. It also means continuously observing technology and market developments in order to spot emerging opportunities.

Governments

- Adjust market definitions and statistical categories to reflect changes in markets and industry structure, since many categories based on outmoded definitions may distort market statistics. Governments base many decisions about regulation on examination of the activities in given markets.

Businesses make decisions about investment based on market data, a significant portion of which is developed by government statistical agencies. As market boundaries blur and whole industries are transformed, government agencies must take care that antiquated statistical categories do not lead to faulty data collection and bad policy decisions.

Notes

1. In the absence of consistent pan-European data on aggregate industry performance in some segments, we have relied on US market data for our analysis, comparing the structure and performance of industry segments across different European markets and the US market wherever possible.

2. Veronis, Suhler & Associates.

3. Jim Chisholm, "Global publishers predict rosy future for newspapers; Top European Newspapers," *Campaign,* November 14, 1997.

4. Dr. Helen Bunting, "European Consumer Magazine Publishing: Facing the Electronic Challenge," Financial Times Telecommunications & Media Publishing, London, 1997.

5. Ibid.

6. I. Jean Dugan, "Boldly Going Where Others Are Bailing Out," *Business Week,* April 6, 1998.

7. Robert La Franco, "Entertainment and Information," *Forbes,* January 12, 1998.

8. Kagan World Media, *European Television Markets,* 1996.

9. "UK: Global Music Market Expected To Grow 26 Per Cent By 2003," *AAP Newsfeed,* January 14, 1998.

10. Ibid.

11. *Music Business International,* December 1997.

12. Dave Laing & Bob Tyler, "The European Radio Industry," Financial Times Telecommunications & Media Publishing, London, 1996.

13. Richard Sandomir, "Warily, Baseball Prepares to Make Murdoch Owner of the Dodgers," *The New York Times,* March 8, 1998.

14. Tom Shakespeare, "The games people play. Super Mario is now bigger than Mickey Mouse," *The Irish Times,* August 18, 1997.

15. Philip Manchester, "PC as a Games Platform," *Financial Times,* December 3, 1997.

16. Joseph Gelmis, "New Technology Takes Games into the Mainstream," *Newsday*, December 31, 1997.

17. *Agence France Presse,* December 30, 1997.

18. Martyn Warwick, "The wake up call; Europe's telecommunications industry," *Communications International*, January 1998.

19. Bhawani Shankar, "The brave new world," *Telecommunications*, January 1998.

20. Martyn Warwick, "The wake up call; Europe's telecommunications industry," *Communications International*, January 1998.

21. Ibid.

22. Ibid.

23. Ibid.

24. Bhawani Shankar, "The brave new world," *Telecommunications*, January 1998.

Building Network Commerce Business Models

Ultimately, every successful business model is unique, but all share certain elements. In this chapter, we examine several network commerce business models, exploring successful and unsuccessful strategies for building businesses in this new environment.

Building on our discussions of industry landscape and the broad environmental context, we turn to the evolution of business models for content-driven network commerce. While we do not propose to offer a set of business models for firms seeking to enter the network commerce arena, we are beginning to understand the key characteristics of many network commerce business models. Network commerce offers the ability to address major business objectives, particularly sustainable revenue growth and cost reduction. In this section, we describe three basic revenue sources for companies doing business over a network media platform, focusing on the role content plays in driving these revenues. We briefly describe how firms can use network commerce to reduce operating costs and build intangible assets. Throughout this chapter we detail several categories of products and services that are now being delivered via network commerce, examining some successful and unsuccessful players in each of these areas.

5.1 Overview

Interactive media, such as the Internet and interactive television, now compete with television, radio, film, and printed matter in the delivery of content products. The Internet and other interactive media bring something different to the marketplace, including their interactive features, which simultaneously enable broad content distribution and two-way communication between end users and content aggregators, as well as an almost limitless capacity to present and support content. In the past, media companies "controlled" most content delivered over communications channels (e.g. television or newspapers). Today, the Internet and the growth of network commerce allow virtually anyone to sell or promote products while presenting content to gain consumer attention. For media companies, network commerce represents an opportunity and a threat. Because content companies have traditionally controlled most content products, they are well-positioned to leverage those products on the Internet. However, companies not traditionally involved in the business will also present content in an effort to generate demand for other products, adding to the complexity and the competitiveness of the content industry environment. According to the director of production for a scientific publishing firm in France, "In the specific healthcare area, pharmaceutical laboratories are prevented by law to propose free services to doctors. This protects publishers. But in other areas, you can imagine competition coming from anywhere. For example, lawyers can use their specific knowledge and case law to propose (by themselves, therefore bypassing publishers) very effective information to corporate lawyers or to specific targets. Banks can become genuine competitors for the financial print media."[1]

5.1.1 Defining Network Commerce

Network or electronic commerce has been defined in many different ways.[2] According to the European Commission's DGXV:

> Network commerce refers to any activity which involves enterprises interacting and doing business with customers, with each other, or with administrations by electronic means.[3]

Although network commerce encompasses a broad range of activities, we will focus on commerce that takes place on open networks, such as the Internet.

5.1.2 Role of Network Commerce

Firms consistently try to ensure their survival, producing goods and services, allocating resources to sales and marketing, brand-building, and honing their strategies. Network commerce presents firms with a new opportunity — a new way to reach consumers. Network commerce can help firms to grow revenues, cut costs, and build intangible assets. (Exhibit 5.1).

By offering opportunities to seamlessly and cost-effectively connect all components of the digital media industry, from product creators to consumers, network commerce facilitates component-based commerce, allowing firms to devote more resources to serving their markets by outsourcing many non-core functions.

Exhibit 5.1 **Objectives of Network Commerce**

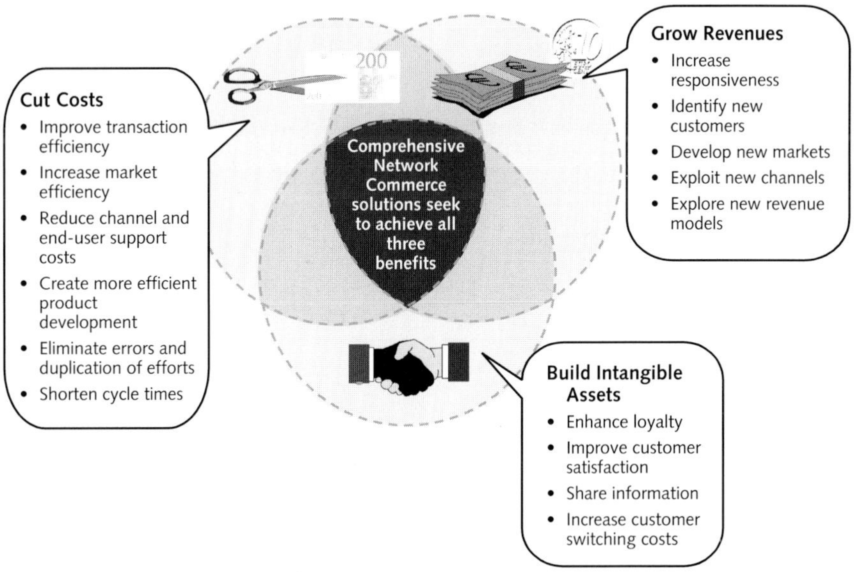

Cut Costs
- Improve transaction efficiency
- Increase market efficiency
- Reduce channel and end-user support costs
- Create more efficient product development
- Eliminate errors and duplication of efforts
- Shorten cycle times

Grow Revenues
- Increase responsiveness
- Identify new customers
- Develop new markets
- Exploit new channels
- Explore new revenue models

Comprehensive Network Commerce solutions seek to achieve all three benefits

Build Intangible Assets
- Enhance loyalty
- Improve customer satisfaction
- Share information
- Increase customer switching costs

Source: Gemini Strategic Research Group.

According to a broad-based survey by US Internet market research firm ActivMedia, over 80 percent of firms maintaining a Web site say one major reason for doing so is to market and sell products and services (Exhibit 5.2).

Exhibit 5.2 **Reported Purposes for Maintaining Web Presence**

Direct Online Sale of Products and Services	49%
Pre-sale Support and Purchasing Information	66%
Post-sale Customer Support/ Technical	28%
Maintain Private Cust./ Vend. Relationships	18%
INFORMATION/ DISTRIBUTION (NET)	82%
Publish Information/ On-line Entertainment	63%
Collect Information/ On-line Entertainment	25%
Provide Free Links to Third Parties	35%
Provide Paid Ad Space/ Links to Third Parties	12%
Distribute or Download Products Online	19%
Internal Communication with Staff & Associates	13%
MARKETING COMMUNICATIONS	81%
Public Relations/ General Image Enhancement	78%
Investor Relations/ Market Value	15%
Membership/ Association/ Newsletter	11%

0% 10% 20% 30% 40% 50% 60% 70% 80% 90%

Source: ActivMedia.

Network commerce can enhance many different business activities, but because of the variety of businesses engaged in network commerce via the Internet, these activities obviously vary greatly from one company to another.

GeoSystems

Expanding the Customer Base

GeoSystems Global Corporation is a leading supplier of maps and mapping-related products, services, and technology to companies in the publishing, travel, yellow pages, and real estate markets, as well as directly to consumers. Products and services range from supplying highly customised maps for textbooks, travel guides, reference books, and multimedia products, to providing mapping technology and related components for hotel reservation systems, driving directions, information kiosks, cellular telephone directory assistance systems, and Web sites. MapQuest is GeoSystems' Internet-based interactive mapping service available to consumers and businesses. MapQuest translates GeoSystems' content and expertise to the network, offering a variety of interactive maps — from very detailed neighbourhood maps to more general regional and national maps. The Web site has also been posting other content, such as detailed point-to-point driving directions; restaurant, activity, school, and business listings; links to home and apartment rental and sales services such as Rent.net; and information for people planning to relocate. MapQuest has registered 1.5 million users on its site and boasts roughly 35 million page views per month.[4] Some revenue comes from leased advertising space, including banner ads and incorporation into the various resource lists available on the Web site. MapQuest gives consumers a multifaceted offering relating to GeoSystems' mapping and travel services. It provides advertisers with a variety of advertising options that are closely tied to the content being delivered.

MapQuest also derives revenues from licensing fees paid by other Web sites that use its mapping services. For example, a restaurant that wishes to display a map showing its location with directions on how to get there can easily incorporate MapQuest's interactive content and technology on its site.

The Internet has expanded GeoSystems' customer base from a few large clients, such as the American Automobile Association (AAA), to thousands of firms of all sizes by allowing it to create customised mapping solutions quickly and at a low cost.

www.mapquest.com

5.1.3 Importance of Content

Depending on the firm and the type of product being sold, content serves various functions in a network environment. For some companies, content is the primary offering. For other companies, the content provided may be a digital representation of their primary product, a complementary content product, or an unrelated content product used only to attract attention. Many firms have not yet learned how to derive revenues from content presented over a network. Frequently, too, content overload occurs on the Internet. Still, as illustrated in Exhibit 5.3, content plays an important role in the network commerce buying process.

Exhibit 5.3 **Role of Content In Network Commerce Buying Process**

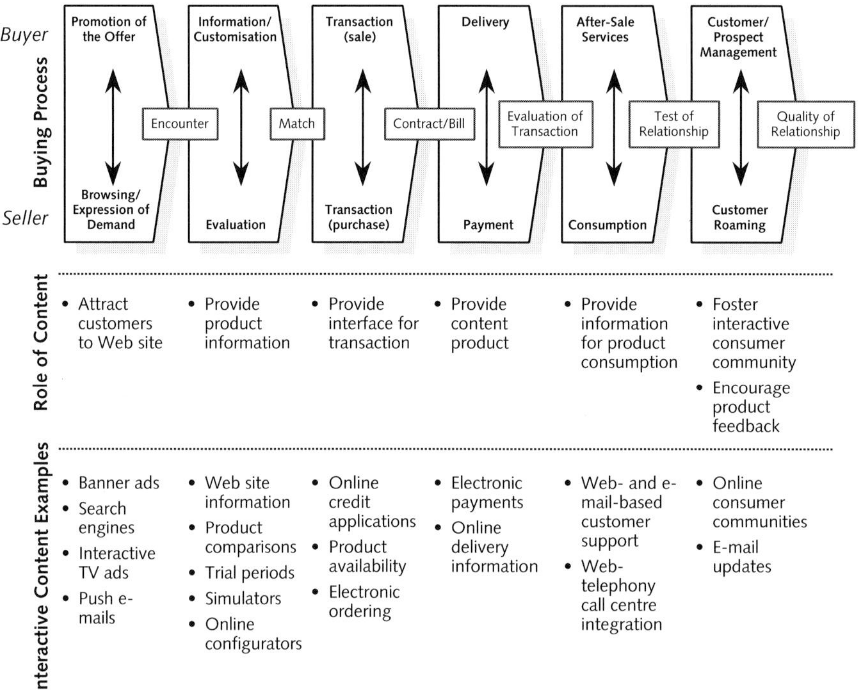

Source: Gemini Strategic Research Group.

The head of the electronic banking division of a major German Bank remarked that "We have a network and calculation systems, which we manage and monitor, spanning over 100 countries. We have customers, whom we know intimately. But to sell content, we need editorial, design, and marketing skills. Therefore, we will still need content providers. All players should concentrate on their core competencies and make the relevant partnerships."[5] One example of content's significant role in the buying process, NetGrocer, a seller of non-perishable food over the Internet, provides viewers with descriptive pictures of its products, health and nutritional information, transaction instructions, and customer service information.

Helicon

Positioning Content for Re-Use

Helicon is a British company that publishes the Hutchintson Encyclopaedia — one of the best selling encyclopaedias in the UK — both on paper and electronically. Created in 1992, Helicon has a staff of twenty-five and employs seventy-five free-lancers. Revenues for 1998 are expected to reach 6 million euro, an increase of 13 percent over 1997. The company started off through an MBO from Random House. It acquired the Hutchinson reference fund, the databases, and the trademarks. Random House and Microsoft (24 percent) are shareholders of Helicon.

Helicon derives half of its revenues and 40 percent of earnings before interest and taxes (EBIT) from the production of the encyclopaedia on paper. The offline and online electronic products provide the other half (40 percent offline, 10 percent online) and 60 percent of EBIT. Helicon produces around twenty paper volumes and three CD-ROMs per year. The CD-ROMs are distributed through three different channels of equal importance in volume: retail outlets, bundling (with PCs, etc.) and other channels such as mail order, book clubs, etc.

But Helicon is not profitable yet. It is still in the investment and experimentation phase and considers achieving significant market share as a long-term objective. Its main competitor, Microsoft Encarta, is in the same situation.

The Database Is the Model

The SGML, platform-neutral content database is at the heart of the business model. It allows for the same content to be re-used on various platforms with minimal modifications. Therefore, revenues can be generated from various channels at the same time while the cost of updating the content is greatly reduced. Helicon has invested 11.8 million euro since 1992 to develop this "industrial" infrastructure for storing and structuring the content.

Helicon's mid-term strategy is to position itself as a wholesaler of marginal-cost content, for all media (paper and electronic), selling to professional clients wishing to distribute that content to final customers. In fact, Helicon adds value by collecting, structuring, and updating information in all formats (text, images, video, graphics, sound), thus providing "raw content" which can be transformed by clients. For example, it provides content to such aggregators as CompuServe. That activity generates very high margins (around 80 percent) and has the biggest growth potential. To meet this objective, Helicon's databases still need to reach a critical volume of content, estimated at two to three times its present size. This could be achieved through acquisitions.

As far as online content is concerned, delivery is restricted to the Internet. This market should develop as more schools connect to the network. Other online platforms, such as interactive television of mobile phones, are not yet seen as market opportunities. In fact, clients for the online content today are libraries (80 percent) and consumers (20 percent).

Helicon believes that European companies can deal with competition from the US, provided that partnerships are established for "localising" and translating products Europe-wide. Start-ups alone do not have the resources to develop products for several EU markets at the same time. Help to identify quickly and efficiently the right partners in Europe will be required.

www.helicon.co.uk

5.2 Grow Revenues

Network commerce generates revenues through advertising, subscriptions, and by selling products and services. Most companies use combinations and variations on these three models (Exhibit 5.4), but according to the CEO of the online division of a major Swedish publisher, "There is not one revenue model, it is early to say. You have to try them, you should understand all of them. You will need to mix them anyway. Banner advertising is hopeless. If it works, fine, otherwise, too bad. But you cannot build a business on it. People are willing to pay subscriptions, even in the Business-to-Consumer market. We have products which are very focused, others which are for a wide audience. Those products have different revenue models."[6]

Exhibit 5.4 **Three Basic Network Revenue Models**

Model	Description	Examples
Advertising	Revenues generated through advertisers' fees paid to the operator of the network service.	Yahoo!
Subscription	Revenue generated through fees paid by customers in exchange for access to online information, entertainment, or services.	PKBaseline
Selling Products/ Services	Revenues generated from the on-line sale of products or services.	Amazon.com

Source: Gemini Strategic Research Group.

5.2.1 Advertising

Selling advertising "space" is one of the most important ways to generate revenues in the traditional media world. It has also emerged as one of the most significant revenue sources in the network commerce world. The Internet has provided new opportunities for aggregators, permitting the creation of new products (e.g. search engines or chat rooms), access to new markets, and the power to directly link consumers to vendors through advertising.

Attracting Viewers

Many of today's Internet-based content products are reincarnations of traditional content products, but they have taken on new roles and importance in a network environment. Traditional media products such as directories and news services have been most successful at attracting viewers thus far (Exhibit 5.5), and have played a central role in defining how aggregators can derive advertising revenues on the Internet.

Exhibit 5.5 **Top-Trafficked Web Sites, 29 December 1997 – 25 January 1998, Unique US Visitors Ages 12-Up**

Rank	Site	No. of "Hits" (Visits)
1	yahoo.com	26,726,000
2	netscape.com	20,723,000
3	microsoft.com	15,674,000
4	excite.com	12,502,000
5	infoseek.com	11,696,000
6	aol.com	11,243,000
7	geocities.com	10,498,000
8	lycos.com	6,787,000
9	altavista.digital.com	6,764,000
10	msn.com	6,315,000
11	hotmail.com	6,016,000
12	four11.com	4,499,000
13	webcrawler.com	4,477,000
14	zdnet.com	4,066,000
15	whowhere.com	3,280,000
16	real.com	2,965,000
17	cnn.com	2,924,000
18	att.net	2,888,000
19	weather.com	2,880,000
20	tripod.com	2,745,000
21	hotbot.com	2,703,000
22	switchboard.com	2,696,000
23	gte.net	2,550,000
24	compuserve.com	2,536,000
25	usatoday.com	2,518,000

Source: RelevantKnowledge.

By providing a much-needed service for navigation in a seemingly chaotic environment, search engines and Web directories have been the most successful in attracting Internet users (Exhibit 5.5). Companies such as Yahoo! and Excite routinely sell advertising space alongside the content that they provide, in the same way traditional media companies draw advertising revenues from their content. However, much of the free information these companies provide has become a commodity since barriers to entry are low. Strategies for attracting viewers are now developing in the network environment.

Portals. During much of 1997, directory and search engine sites such as Yahoo! and Lycos feared they would become commodities. In response, they began touting themselves as "networks" that, as in the TV world, would act as "channels," funnelling programs, information, and news to subscribers. Now they are moving one step further, attempting to become one-stop, full-service sites. From this has emerged the concept of the "portal." The portal is the "doorway" through which customers access the Internet. Portal operators understand that by aggregating users, they create a huge potential market for advertising and product sales. The portal concept (e.g. America Online) is rapidly blurring the lines between traditional "online services" and search engines or directories (e.g. Yahoo!, Lycos). All are competing in the same space and offering the same services; all are seeking to become the dominant portal for millions of Internet users around the world.

America Online (AOL) is currently the leading portal to the Internet, with 11 million subscribers accounting for 39 percent of all Web traffic.[7] AOL's services include content offerings, shopping, chat rooms, and e-mail, and have drawn millions of users to the proprietary site. To compete with other portals, AOL now offers its subscribers free features such as instant messaging — a real-time e-mail exchange much like chat — and NetMail, which lets subscribers check e-mail from the Web without accessing the AOL service. In the first quarter of 1998, company revenue from advertising and the electronic sale of goods and services rose to $118 million, up from $69 million one year earlier. Despite this success, AOL is facing stiff competition from the others. CNET Inc., for example, is attempting to enter this space by licensing Snap!, a collection of Web content created by others, to firms such as Toshiba, GTE, and Compaq Computer. "Our bet," says Halsey M. Minor, chief executive at CNET, "is that everybody combined will be able to generate more customers than AOL."[8]

AOL has enjoyed some success in Europe, having reached 1 million customers within two years of its launch there, with services in Germany, France, Great Britain, Austria, Switzerland, and Sweden. Additionally, AOL's acquisition of CompuServe's customers in 1997 brought it CompuServe's European division. Heinz Wermelinger, chief executive of AOL Bertelsmann Europa, Bertelsmann and AOL's joint-venture that operates AOL Europe, boasted in 1998 that "We have exceeded our own expectations and achieved a breakthrough as a pan-European mass medium."[9]

Microsoft approaches the portal business from several angles. Microsoft's ten Web sites are already among the biggest draws on the Internet, visited by one-third of all US Web surfers. Microsoft is reportedly creating a super site that will showcase all its Web properties, from travel to car-buying to news, and include such services as free e-mail and a search engine for Web exploration. The new site is called "Microsoft Start," reflecting Microsoft's strategy of making it the portal to the Internet.[10]

A US consulting firm, the Yankee Group, attributes MSN's appeal to its promotion of customisation. Half of MSN users customise their start pages, choosing what news categories they want to read about, etc. Yahoo! also has a personalised Web page service called My Yahoo!, which lets end users customise the content they receive and promotes Yahoo! as the preferred portal.[11]

To supplement its offerings, Yahoo! acquired a $5 million minority stake in GeoCities, one of the largest communities online. As part of the deal, Yahoo! users can 'build' their own home pages based on communities of interest. Yahoo!'s competitor, Lycos, is following a similar strategy with its $58 million acquisition of Tripod, another virtual community. Both Yahoo! and Lycos have made deals with large Internet service providers (MCI and AT&T respectively) to provide online services that more closely resemble AOL's. For example, by bundling a browser with Internet access, Lycos could ensure that its subscribers use Lycos as their portal.

Lycos has been generating revenues through its shopping channel by licensing out its technology and partnering with content providers such as GTE's Interactive Yellow Pages. Lycos has been aggressively advertising via television, radio, and in movie theatres.[12] Following in the footsteps of AOL, Yahoo!, and Excite, which have all entered into a string of marketing partnerships with companies, Lycos has secured a three-year deal with Electronic Newsstand, a site that brings Lycos a guaranteed revenue stream of $10.5 million plus commissions on the sale of magazine subscriptions.[13]

Netscape has also joined the race to become a Web portal by leveraging its brand name to build on its already popular site. Under an agreement with Internet mail provider USA.net, Netscape now offers free, easily accessible e-mail service. It has redesigned its home page and added other new features, including a Netscape-brand search engine that was created as part of a two-year, $70 million deal with Excite.

As competition for portal dominance increases, barriers to entry for new portals are growing as well. Yahoo! licensed a search service two years ago; since that time it has developed features in-house and purchased some additional ones in the past year, at a total cost of $205.5 million. Recreating that same service from the ground up today would cost between $500 million and $1 billion. "The separation between the haves and the have-nots will begin in earnest in 1998," according to analyst Mary G. Meeker of Morgan Stanley, Dean Witter, Discover & Co.[14]

Even those traditional content companies like Time Warner or Disney that have been slower to pursue portal strategies are moving, and could pose a substantive threat to current leaders.

A differentiator among Web portals appears to be the type of consumers they attract. Interestingly, members in different communities have very different characteristics as potential customers. The Yankee Group's

InteractiveConsumer97 survey found that, relative to customers of other access communities, MSN users said they are much more likely to offer personal information about their interests and lifestyles in return for incentives. To benefit from tailored advertising, discounted fees, frequent flyer miles, or points redeemable for goods and services, MSN users were 30 percent to 56 percent more likely to offer information about themselves and their families.[15]

The Yankee Group also found that, relative to other communities and Internet access providers, AOL and MSN are far better positioned to profile their customers' buying habits, and that this knowledge will ultimately translate into new revenues. Further, the survey indicates that MSN may very well be intending to exploit this potential before AOL does. Such information is important to many industries — ISPs looking to move into commerce services, retailers looking to move into direct marketing, media buyers seeking to leverage the online channel, and various commercial service providers concerned about Microsoft's ability to supplant them.[16]

Commercial sites are trying to strike deals with the most popular portals in an effort to reach millions of daily viewers. Online bookseller Amazon.com paid $50 million to AOL, Excite, and Yahoo! in exchange for prime advertising space. AOL has announced a string of multi-year deals that will generate large amounts of revenue, including $100 million from TelSave, $50 million from CUC International (NetMarket), $30 million from software maker and personal finance service provider Intuit, and $40 million from Barnes & Noble.[17]

Virtual Communities. Most Web sites are pursuing an implicit virtual community strategy; several sites are openly attempting to create communities of interest on the Web.

In the book *Net.Gain*,[18] John Hagel and Arthur Armstrong argue that, in its simplest form, a virtual community should be viewed as a group that shares interest, even passion, for a particular activity (such as travel) or product class (such as racing cars). They describe four needs that create such communities — information, transaction, fantasy, and relationship. Members "chat" with one another and with community organisers to share concerns, opinions, or questions about their common interests. Collectively, they have bargaining power with vendors because they possess group information about commercial interests and the transaction history of group members. For example, members share their product experiences with other members and generate valuable content for the community members in general in the process. Increased interaction among members means more member-generated content, an increase in the community's ability to attract new members, more loyalty to the community, and possibly more transactions conducted.

Some of the largest online communities include AOL, GeoCities, Tripod, and TheGlobe, each possessing a high degree of end-user involvement. They provide free Web hosting as well as software tools to facilitate Web site creation, putting an emphasis on user-created content.

GeoCities

Creating Virtual Communities

GeoCities generates revenues primarily through advertising sales. Launched in 1994 by David Bohnett to provide free hosting services to people wishing to post content on the Internet, GeoCities provides individuals with 6 MB of server space and some simple tools required to build a Web page (an additional 6MB of server space can be purchased for $4.95 per month). The Web sites are categorised into areas of interest such as Sports & Recreation, Business & Money, and Health, and into forty sub-categories called "Neighborhoods." As of March 1998, GeoCities had signed-up 1.7 million members with unique Web sites and was receiving 789 million "hits" and 115 million visits each month,[19] making GeoCities one of the top-five visited Web sites on the Internet. The number of viewers GeoCities attracted led to roughly $5 million to $6 million in revenues in 1997, 80 percent of which were derived from advertising. The remaining 20 percent came from other activities, including selling premium services. Large advertisers such as CDNow, Fist USA, and Auto by Tel receive premium banner space throughout GeoCities, while other advertisers can target specific markets by advertising in specific neighbourhoods. Sales transaction fees ranging from 2 percent to 10 percent brought in additional revenues on the GeoCities site. GeoCities controls costs by having its user base of "homesteaders" create the content presented on the site in exchange for a small amount of server space.

In March 1998, GeoCities launched "GeoShops," an inexpensive service ($24.95 per month) that enables small firms to establish network commerce sites on the Web. GeoCities partnered with Netopia, Inc. to develop a software application called "Netopia Virtual Office" that allows small and home office firms to create Web sites with network commerce capabilities. GeoCities also provides transaction processing capabilities to GeoShop members. The GeoShops are categorised by areas of interest and are grouped with non-commercial sites.

GeoCities aggregated enough original content to become one of the most frequently visited sites on the World Wide Web, and is working to become an influential network media company. In April 1998, GeoCities hired president and publisher of *US News and World Report*, Thomas Evans, as Chief Executive Officer, bringing traditional media industry expertise to the world of network commerce. While GeoCities will continue to leverage its viewership to gain advertising revenues, Evans has stated that in the future, "more and more goods will be sold (on GeoCities),"[20] opening up the possibility for more transaction revenues as well as revenues transaction-enabled services.

www.geocities.com

Major search engines and other portals are trying to enter this arena as well. Yahoo! began the trend in January 1998 by acquiring a $5 million minority stake in GeoCities. Lycos Inc. followed by acquiring Tripod Inc. — a Web community targeting twenty-year-olds which has about 1 million members — in

February 1998 for $58 million in stock. Today, AOL is considering a similar service. "This space is very unforgiving because your competition is one click away," says Jeff Mallett, Vice-President of Business Operations at Yahoo![21]

Because sites such as Yahoo! and Excite publish content to build consumer communities, they may become less concerned about the separation of editorial and advertising content. As a result, these online publishers may find their brands becoming less distinguishable from one another. This problem is even greater for traditional media with the emergence of Web sites such as the *Wall Street Journal*, *Business Week,* and the *San Jose Mercury News*, all of which will presumably reflect the editorial integrity of their parent publications while aggressively pursuing advertising and transaction-based revenues.

E-Zines and Online Newspapers. Many new and traditional content aggregators have appeared on the Internet and are presenting advertising-supported content to end users. The majority of these sites derive revenues solely from advertising, but, future revenue sources for many of these sites will likely combine subscription and advertising-based earnings.

Some of the new magazines, or "e-zines," that only publish content on the Internet include *Slate* (owned by Microsoft), *Salon*, and *Suck*. All combine original editorial content with news and information targeting narrower markets than portals or virtual communities. One e-zine, *Feed*, incorporates its readers' comments into the margins of the articles it presents, bringing a sense of online community to its publication. E-zines face competition from other Web sites as well as traditional magazines. Their future success will depend on their ability to leverage interactivity, consumer willingness to read online (or at least print it from their computers), promotion of the site either formally or through word of mouth, and of, course, presentation of interesting and popular content.

Traditional publishers like *Money* magazine, *The New York Times*, and *USA Today* also offer editorial material and news stories on the Web — again, relying on advertising sales for revenues. Unlike most Web publishers who are moving more and more toward a subscription-based service, the Merc Centre is moving toward an advertising-based service. In April 1995, subscribers were asked to pay $4.95 a month for complete access to the Web site. Now, the *San Jose Mercury News* online newspaper is free to users. The Merc Centre pioneered online newspaper offerings, debuting on AOL in 1993 and on the Web in 1994. Although readership for Web products is probably not as high as for physical publications, the risk of placing content on the Web is minimal while the potential rewards could be very high.

Dagens Nyheter

Experimenting with Revenue Models

The newspaper *Dagens Nyheter* is part of the Bonnier Group, one of Scandinavia's leading media companies. *Dagens Nyheter* publishes one paper edition and now also produces an online edition. The electronic edition was launched in 1996 and is read by about 50,000 visitors every day.

The online edition was started in response to a decrease in the number of subscribers, which decreased for three reasons according to Fredrik Åkerman, IT manager at Dagens Nyheter and part of the management group:

1. The Internet has a competitive advantage by providing real-time news, like TV and videotext. In contrast, "the morning papers give the background, a more thorough editorial content and analysis."[22]
2. VAT on newspapers increased in Sweden.
3. Free newspapers, such as the Metro distributed in Stockholm, are thriving.

Dagens Nyheter wishes to connect the electronic brand with that of the paper edition. Brand name and reputation for trustworthiness are major levers in its effort to drive revenues for its online paper. Users could use both products to satisfy their information needs:

- Real-time news on www.dn.se,
- Background and analysis in the paper edition,
- Article archives with searching capabilities on www.dn.se.

Dagens Nyheter is going through a learning process, which does not appear to be an easy one. It does not charge readers for access to www.dn.se and does not earn as much money as expected from advertising. Additionally, it has lost ground to sites such as www.passagen.se and www.torget.se, that are becoming more like portals and attracting many visitors.

Dagens Nyheter has invested about 3 million euro in hardware and software for www.dn.se. Revenues from the online edition are expected to cover the running costs for the editorial staff within two years. Revenue sources for the online edition today include only advertising, but in the future it expects to derive increasing revenues from interactive advertising as well as from subscriptions to the online edition. Meanwhile, revenues from traditional advertising and subscriptions will decrease.

www.dn.se

Broadcasters. Traditional television and radio broadcasters have already begun transmitting live programming over the Internet. Thousands of radio stations now reach a global audience through their Web sites. Www.broadcast.com provides many stations with the technology necessary to broadcast over the Internet and aggregates those stations much like a cable operator aggregates

ITV

New Broadcasting Channels

ITV is the only Video-On-Demand (VOD) service in the world running commercially in 1998. One month after the launch, 40,000 subscribers to this private network in Hong Kong were able to choose a film, at any given time of the day, from a regularly updated catalogue of sixty titles. They can also listen to music-on-demand, place online bets on horse races, or shop in virtual malls (Netvigator). ITV is also bound to offer home banking and network gaming applications. ITV will be accessible to 1.6 million households (85 percent of the population) by the turn of the century.

The required investments are huge. HK Telecom invested 113 million euro in the last three years to build the network and plans to invest another 1.21 billion euro over ten years. It has to bear most of the production cost of the set-top boxes (530 euro per unit), the cost of digitisation, and huge royalties to ensure exclusivity for the movies from studios such Golden Harvest, China Star, or Walt Disney.

Meanwhile, Hong Kong is a very competitive marketplace for TV services: four analogue channels, five others by satellite, plus a cable channel (Wharf Cable) offering pay-per-view to 400,000 subscribers. Hong Kong authorities also announced that they will award shortly a second interactive TV license. As a consequence, ITV had to slash prices.

In front of high costs and price cuts, revenues do not quite make up for the difference. They are mostly derived from subscriptions and pay-per-view charges. Set-up fees, commissions on transactions, and advertising are only minor sources of revenues. Given that video-on-demand does not provide but a very scattered audience, advertising is not attractive to advertisers.

Because of low revenues, other revenues sources are necessary. Providing Internet access at broadband speed is a possible option. With 500,000 Internet users, Hong Kong provides a large potential market. Provided that technical problems related to connecting the PC to the set-top box, Internet access, sold for a relatively low price (28 euro per month, plus 0.7 euro per out-of-office hour), should provide additional revenue.

In this new model ITV runs a new risk: Its proprietary services (shopping, banking, etc.) all have competitors on the Internet; therefore, providing Internet access could endanger those services by losing the advantage of a captive audience. In fact, if ITV has no choice but to follow this strategy, it may mean that the proprietary models are doomed. Once broadband access to the Internet is made available at low prices, only operators of IP-based services may be able to thrive.

www.itvhk.com

television stations. Similarly, many television stations such as MTV Europe (www.m2europe.com) and Fox News (www.foxnews.com) continually broadcast over the Internet the same programming that is being broadcast over cable networks. Today these services are only additions to existing broadcasting services, but as the network as well as the interfaces (computers, WebTV, etc.) improve, the Internet will pose a serious threat to traditional broadcasters and their networks and Internet broadcast services will be able to draw revenue on their own.

Connecting Consumers and Advertisers

The network environment brings new possibilities and dilemmas to advertisers. New technology allows advertisers to instantaneously connect directly to consumers. However, the complex environment and oversupply of content makes it difficult to develop uniform pricing schemes or to monitor viewership. For small and medium-sized Web sites, advertising networks have arisen, enabling them to attract advertisers.

Advertising Technology. Web-based advertising has evolved very quickly, moving through a number of stages in its brief history. (Exhibit 5.6).

Exhibit 5.6 **Evolution of Web-Based Advertising Models**

Late 1994

Simple banner advertisement: The first and simplest advertising revenue model; sites priced banner ads on a monthly basis, and sites with higher traffic were generally able to charge more for banner ads than those with lower traffic.

Mid-1995

Guaranteed ad model: In this scenario, sites continue to price advertisements on a monthly basis but guarantee advertising traffic levels.

Mid-1995

CPM (cost-per-thousand) revenue model used by traditional media: Ads are sold by the number of impressions delivered.

- CPM is inversely related to traffic: sites with high traffic are mass marketing vehicles and charge lower CPMs, while low-traffic sites which are targeted vehicles can charge higher CPM rates.

Mid-1996

Click-through revenue model: Advertisers only pay for the actual number of users who click on their ad banner.

- Yahoo's contract with Procter & Gamble calls for ads to be charged on a basis of click-throughs.
- Average click-through rates are between 0.4 percent and 2.8 percent, which compares favorably with the average response rates for other media including direct mail.
- More targeted Web sites and advertisements have led to reported click-throughs ranging from 8 percent to 30 percent.

Source: I/PRO Research; Gemini Strategic Research Group.

The standard banner ad has been criticised since its inception, but with banner spending reaching at least $600 million in 1997, banners will likely continue to be widely used.

Web advertising technology has grown more sophisticated. While consumer-oriented sites have made the most use of pop-ups and interstitial ads to date, some analysts believe such ads have clear business-to-business applications for Web site managers seeking to generate consumer loyalty to their sites and draw more revenue from those consumers.[23]

Interstitial ads increase the amount of information Web visitors see, popping up briefly on the screen while content pages load. Interstitials remain the most popular at free game sites such as Berkeley Systems's bezerk.com, where they are treated as a user's "payment" for playing, much like broadcast television and radio. "The problem is they take a long time to load," says Sean Cafferky, President of the Professional Presence Network (http://www.ppn.org), a Texas-based organisation for Web developers. A full screen of graphics might take a 28.8 kbps modem forty-five seconds to download, he says. Mr. Cafferky expects interstitials to become more popular as telephone and cable companies roll out faster access services. When consumers can access the Internet at 1 Mbps, delays in loading graphics will disappear.[24]

One of the main business issues concerning Web advertising at this time is metering. Fixing the number and demographic characteristics of unique users visiting a site and being exposed to a particular advertisement is still difficult and will limit advertisers' ability to maximise revenues. Yet, even in its current infant state, the accuracy and sophistication of Web usage metering far exceeds that of methods used to project television and radio audiences, or magazine and newspaper readership. Web sites are already capable of generating huge quantities of user information that extend beyond the expectations of other types of media firms. According to the head of a French online advertising space purchasing agency, "Newspapers and magazines have a very important potential on digital networks, on the condition that they provide real usage value on their sites and that they are able to provide to advertisers sophisticated tools to measure and qualify their audience. The capacity to provide audience data of high quality and with maximum availability is a key differentiating factor."[25]

A problem for advertisers is the lack of a logical and widely accepted Web advertising pricing model. Click-through models raise questions about the value of environmental ads and challenge the fundamental premises of most other types of advertising. Again, as Web advertising proliferates and the Web advertising marketplace develops, logical pricing models will become available for different types of Web sites.

The "caching" effect presents an additional challenge to Web advertising. Web browsers and proxy servers cache frequently used Web data to prevent repeated downloading, making Web usage difficult to measure. A possible solution

Télévision Par Satellite

Interactive Advertising Possibilities

TPS (Télévision Par Satellite), one of the two major digital satellite TV offerings in France, is a joint venture between TF1, France Télévision, France Télécom, Lyonnaise des Eaux and M6. It is integrating a whole range of interactive services into its offering. Whether it be malls, home banking services, or interactive advertising, the same logic applies: "We sell the space," says Alain Staron, Director of New Services at TPS, "We sell space on the satellite along with access to our subscribers."[26]

Close to direct marketing

Since October 1997, TPS has led five interactive advertising campaigns for cars (Renault Kangoo, Renault Clio, Citroën), toys (Lego) and detergent (Skip). "Our subscribers hate advertising," says Staron. Therefore, the programmes are not interrupted. But click buttons appear on the screen, saying for example: "Press OK to know more about product X." According to Alain Staron, 85 percent of those who saw such buttons clicked on them. Since the commercials are not declared into a channel, viewers then quit the TV programme they are watching.

"The first message talks to people's hearts (emotional) and once they've clicked we must talk to their brain (rational)," explains Staron. The latter message can then be of three types:

1. Decentralised sales-lead generation (for the distribution network): "Do you want to be called by the nearest dealer?" This was used for the car campaigns.
2. Centralised sales-lead generation (mail order): "You can order the catalogue, or even buy in our interactive mall." Lego, who has a mall on TPS, used this kind of message.
3. Loyalty, brand switching, building a database: "Tell us more about yourself and we will send you coupons and/or samples." Skip used this message.

The five campaigns totalled 75,000 clicks. The transformation rate for the Kangoo campaign reached 3.6 percent. It did not have the objective to generate sales directly but it created traffic in the dealers' network. "For the sale of physical goods, we just facilitate the contact," says Staron. In fact, interactive advertising comes very close to direct marketing.

Selling opportunity rather than success

TPS does not commit to the results which merchants or advertisers can obtain. "We sell the opportunity rather than success," says Staron, "We are a mediator."

In the future, TPS will try to integrate the Internet into TV programming. Viewers will be able to link up to an Internet site. "But it will stay in the TV paradigm," says Staron. As a consequence, for example, "those Internet sites will probably need to be re-designed," he says.

www.tps.fr

to this problem may be the use of "cookies," which track browsing histories and end-user activity despite caching.

Finally, firms are developing ad-blocking technologies, such as PrivNet's Internet Fast Forward freeware, that will enable an advertising-free Web environment. The ad-blocking software is currently complicated to use, but if widely adopted, it will force advertisements to become more like content, perhaps raising their overall value and quality.

Advertising Networks. Advertising networks play an important role in generating revenues, even for small sites. Niche publishers, like *Salon Magazine* and *The Onion*, have sustained themselves through advertising as part of these larger networks. The combined ad inventory, offered media buyers by networks like DoubleClick and Petry, allows small sites to compete with high-traffic sites like Microsoft Sidewalk and Yahoo!

Today, a sophisticated network is emerging to meet the needs of Web-based advertisers. Further, content aggregators offer a variety of advertising options that more effectively link consumers with advertisers.

Web-based advertising is one of the earliest and most established examples of component-based commerce. Many sophisticated advertising services automatically upload banner ads from remote servers, enabling publishers to generate advertising revenues without building additional systems.

The cost per thousand impressions (CPM) of network-based advertising can vary significantly based on two factors: The broad range of advertising capabilities available through use of the Internet, and online advertising's early state of development. (Exhibit 5.7) As Web-based advertising evolves, the CPM will probably stabilise and look more like that of some traditional media.

Exhibit 5.7 **Comparison of Average CPM for Different Types of Media, United States**

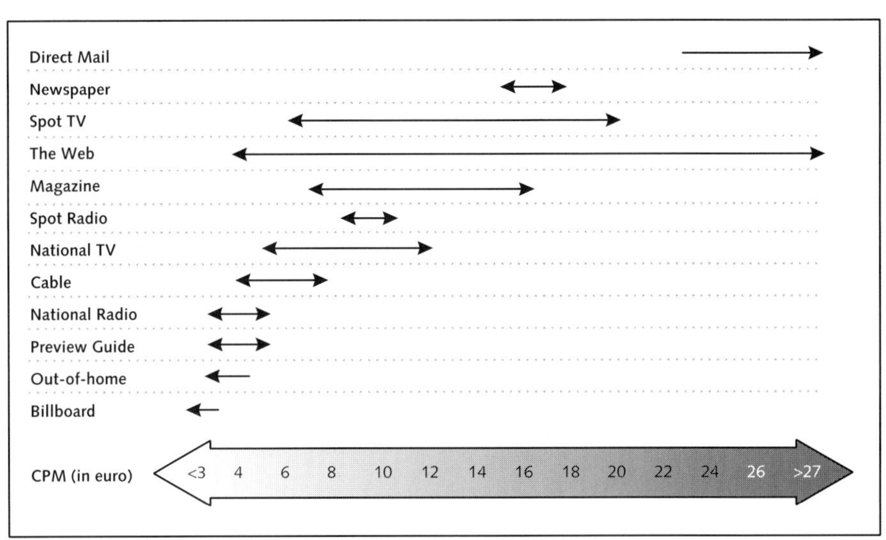

Source: I/PRO Research.

Currently, Web-based advertising is still in its infancy; aggregators and advertisers are uncertain about how to measure its value. Bundles of ad space from various smaller sites have stepped in to bring advertisers and aggregators together.

5.2.2 Subscriptions

Subscriptions provide an important source of revenues for many traditional forms of media. A number of content providers have been optimistic about the revenue potential of subscriptions, but have been disappointed in many cases. Today, subscriptions do not represent an attractive consumer revenue model for most types of content, but as we look to the future, content aggregators capable of providing high-value content services may eventually achieve success by charging subscription fees.

Many plans to offer online subscription services have been derailed as Web users seem unwilling to pay subscription fees to access information. Much of Internet culture is infused with a belief that information should be free. According to the Georgia Tech GVU surveys, about 65 percent of Internet users say that they will not pay fees to access information on the Web.[27] Consumers feel they are paying a sufficient amount of money to access the Web in the first place; they think they should not have to pay additionally for information. This belief is reinforced by the huge amounts of information available on the Web for free. If a subscription service is successful, other similarly structured services are likely to come quickly into being. With so many advertising-based news services, virtual communities, directories, and others providing information to consumers for free, content aggregators wishing to charge for content must be able to provide unique value for the consumer.

Business Information

According to some analysts, the business of selling news, research, and information to corporations is undergoing a huge transformation.[28] Recent events in the $34 billion information-publishing industry suggest that many key assumptions about the Web's impact on electronic publishing are wrong.

First, *NewsNet*, the subscription-based online information provider, announced in September 1997 that it was shutting down because of competition from free Web news services. Within weeks, other small- and mid-sized subscription services began closing as well. Amulet Inc. shut down its InfoWizard pay-per-view research service in October 1997, citing competition from free ad-supported services. The DataTimes Corp., EyeQ service from UMI Co. (a Bell & Howell company), and Infoseek's corporate information division also shut down around this time. In late November, Dow Jones & Co. announced layoffs and other cutbacks at its troubled financial information division, Dow Jones Markets, in what may be a prelude to the sale of the unit.

Meanwhile, other large information services announced mergers in an effort to strengthen their positions. Individual Inc., which offers the NewsPage, First, and HeadsUp personalised news services, engineered an $84 million merger with Desktop Data that extended its reach into the corporate information market. M.A.I.D., a $35 million information firm, purchased Dialog from Knight-Ridder for $420 million in an effort to deepen its content by adding Dialog's 6 billion pages of searchable text. Reed Elsevier Inc., owner of the premier news and legal-information provider, LEXIS-NEXIS, tried to merge with Wolters Kluwer, a leading professional and scientific publisher, but the merger was later called off due to regulatory concerns.[29]

The advent of free, advertising-supported news and information services such as CNET's News.Com and Excite's NewsTracker, has apparently upset the business models, pricing and cost structures, and marketing and sales practices of the major traditional providers.

By the mid-1980s, new technologies and a rapidly growing appetite for news and information had already spurred a host of new players to enter the once-monolithic market. In particular, the financial information market grew tremendously, led by new electronic publishers such as those created by Reuters, Telerate (now Dow Jones Markets), Bloomberg, McGraw-Hill (Standard & Poor's), and Thomson Financial Services. New entrants such as Individual Inc. and SilverPlatter began delivering information by fax and CD-ROM at lower prices, expanding use among mid-size businesses, professionals, and end users.

Masson

Expanding the Product Base

e2med is an online information service targeting physicians in France that leverages Masson's portfolio of publishing activities in the medical sector. Masson, a subsidiary of French media and publishing conglomerate Havas, is the leading medical publisher in France with about 40 scientific journals, a daily newspaper, a 3,000-book back-list, and 150 new titles every year.

e2med offers physicians and specialists access to database of articles with an AltaVista-powered search engine, forums, news, classified ads, and selected links. Articles from about thirty medical journals are accessible in HTML or PDF[30] format. Abstracts are free for non subscribers, even some of the hundreds of books in the catalogue are made available in full text. In addition, the recent buy-out of Le Quotidien du Médecin, the major French medical daily, brings complementary content.

Less than six months after the launch in January 1998, statistics show that around 250 identified viewers[31] surf the site every day, most of them from work. Users seem to be interested primarily in news (conference schedules, etc.) and classifieds, followed by articles.

"It is the first time that I have a chance to know my customers," says Stéphane Boudon, Production Director at Masson. "I can determine who they are, what they do and when they do it. I can also see how they search for information."[32]

Business has picked up very quickly. e2med has as a mid-term objective to reach a penetration rate of 15 percent of its present client base, or about 11,700 paying subscribers. In 2000, e2med hopes to have 7,000 paying clients. This success is probably the sign that e2med is the right service and that network commerce meets an underlying need in the medical community. e2med could further develop if subscriptions become eligible for vocational training points (authorisation is pending). In France, physicians have to accumulate a number of points which correspond to an annual amount of required vocational training courses. e2med would then offer a free service allowing physicians to manage and track their points.

Today, 100 percent of the revenues are provided by subscriptions. In the mid-term, they should amount to 80 percent with advertising providing the rest. Various forms of subscriptions are proposed: electronic bundled with paper, electronic only for those who are already subscribers to a paper edition, or paper only.

The changes brought by e2med internally have far ranging implications. It is not only a way to leverage existing content and to develop network commerce, it is an opportunity to drive internal change towards new, digital editorial production processes.

www.e2med.com

With the Internet's arrival, the information business exploded. The Internet not only gave rise to dozens of new niche-market groups but also dramatically expanded the depth and breadth of the information market. Hundreds of Web-based news and data services were launched to serve millions of new customers.

During the 1990s in the US, investment in information tools and content became the highest value-added component of large-scale economic activity. One good example of this is the "consumerisation" of the stock market, in

Lexis-Nexis

Adjusting to the Network Environment

LEXIS-NEXIS is the world's leading news and legal-information provider. It has 1.3 million subscribers and more than a billion documents from 18,300 sources in its 5.7-terabyte database. This archive adds sixteen new documents per second, compared with one document every four seconds being added to the Web. Moreover, its search and retrieval engine is regarded as a premier achievement in information science.[33]

Despite these advantages, LEXIS-NEXIS faces some critical long-term challenges. The biggest of these was to make its searchable archives accessible via the Web. LEXIS-NEXIS began running its new Web service in early 1998, an effort that required huge resources, including a reported 300-person development team.[34]

Current challenges include the need to design both higher and lower value-added complements to the company's core service. To profitably meet the needs of specific, under-served market segments. LEXIS-NEXIS has already begun moving in that direction with a new service that connects university local-area networks to LEXIS-NEXIS via the Web. The company is reportedly considering pricing of $2 to $4 per student per year, as compared with the minimum $5O per month plus usage fees charged for its core service.

LEXIS-NEXIS also faces a challenge in that its archive providers self-publish their original content online using cheaper service providers. Annual reports that once cost upwards of $25 each for example, are now available free on the US Securities and Exchange Commission's EDGAR site. To counter that threat, LEXIS-NEXIS must make its service indispensable to high-margin large-business customers so that they will continue to pay for the service, even if the information is partially (but freely) available elsewhere.

Finally, LEXIS-NEXIS could re-intermediate content to an entirely new level. Knowledge-management tools such as data mining and visualisation could be applied to vast storehouses of data, enabling LEXIS-NEXIS to deliver high-calibre strategic decision-making intelligence to corporate customers.

www.lexis-nexis.com/forbusiness

which an unprecedented 40 percent of US citizens are now active investors. The rapid growth of the small office/home office sector and the burgeoning influence of small businesses in the US economy are additional examples.

For the top-tier services such as LEXIS-NEXIS, Dow Jones News Retrieval, and Dialog, their depth and breadth of content, and highly sophisticated search and retrieval technologies would appear to have established their long-standing relationships with major corporate customers. Yet, as the recent cutbacks at Dow Jones Markets demonstrate, the top-tier suppliers face serious long-term threats, which will require heavy investment and careful attention to product design and market segmentation.

The critical mandate for business information publishers in the network economy is to transform information products into integrated services aimed at delivering enterprise-wide business solutions. This means that for firms like LEXIS-NEXIS, the corporate intranet market is as important as that of the Internet.

Consumer Content

Many firms have experimented with subscription services on the Internet, but very few have succeeded. Some sites, however, are successfully charging subscriptions, many only for premium services.

Exhibit 5.8 **Variations of Subscription Revenue Models**

Fixed Monthly Fee, Unlimited Access	The standard model for most subscription services, this model was adopted by firms like Encyclopedia Britannica.
Per-Hour or Per-Minute Fee	The traditional business information service and BBS model, it has proven difficult to implement over the Internet because of metering expenses and other technical issues.
Combination of Fixed Monthly Fee and per-Minute or per-Hour Fee	The traditional online service model in which the online service maintains considerable quantities of proprietary content. It is easier to implement over proprietary networks such as AOL and T-Online.
Free or Advertiser-Supported Combined with Fixed Fee	More popular with many content firms, this model allows the service provider to experiment with the mix of advertising- and subscription-based fees in order to maximise revenues. A leading example of this model is ESPN SportsZone.
Combination of Fixed Fee and Transaction Fee	This model was first employed by business information firms such as PKBaseline that offer time-sensitive or highly-valuable information saleable on a piecemeal basis, as well as access to other valuable data. This model has also been adopted by some marketplace organisers who charge fees for membership in the marketplace and derive commissions from the product sales.
Free with Plans to Institute Subscription Fee after Audience Established	Pursued by many newspapers and magazines, like the *Chicago Tribune* and online magazines like Microsoft's *Slate*, this model is likely to fail (as it did for the *Tribune* which chose to pursue an advertising model instead).

Publications such as *The Economist*, the *Wall Street Journal*, and *Business Week* provide added value by publishing original editorial content, and can attract customers through brand names that have been built in the traditional publishing world.

ESPN, the top television sports network in the United States, operates a Web site offering complete sports news and events coverage free of charge. It also offers additional services, such as "fantasy" sports leagues, for a subscription fee of $39.95 a year. Similarly, Disney's Daily Blast Web site offers content and games for $39.95 a year, while its sister site, Disney Online, offers content for free. Other sites that provide premium services by paid subscription include Money.com, *Salon Magazine,* and newspapers like *USA Today* and the *New York Times* that offer access to their archives for a fee.

One example of a subscription-based revenue model on the Web today is the shopping site netMarket created by Cendant Corporation (formerly CUC International). Subscribers to this site pay $69 per year to access of thousands of consumer products at prices below retail. NetMarket is able to offer products at low prices because it relies on subscriptions as its primary revenue stream.

Subscription services will continue to develop as more original and value-added content and service offerings appear on the Internet, and as consumers shift their spending from traditional content and service options, such as newspapers and print magazines, to Internet-based sources.

5.2.3 Transactions

Network-based transactions have the potential to affect a broad range of industries ranging from books to automobiles. In addition to providing a transaction platform, the network enhances many aspects of the buying process. Firms are combining content and the network environment to attract and retain customers, and to drive sales. Additionally, the network environment provides many cost-cutting benefits.

According to the head of a French online advertising space purchasing agency, "The role of content is changing. As content is used more and more to sell all types of products, content production and the ability to use it to attract viewers is a major challenge on the Internet, which goes well beyond the sale of content as a stand-alone product. The challenge is to build the most appealing site to attract viewers, to make them loyal and to generate stable traffic, in order to "lock in" a target and to market advertising and services to that target. As a consequence, production of content on the network is not the monopoly of traditional content firms anymore. New players coming from other sectors provide more and more free information, for example, with the sole purpose of creating traffic (e.g. Yahoo!)."[35]

The Buying Process

Most commercial Web sites exist either to directly or indirectly sell products and services. These range from simple "brochureware" sites containing basic product information, to sophisticated transaction systems that provide customised pages and automatic order processing. Network commerce can provide many solutions to customers' and sellers' needs during the buying process (Exhibit 5.9).

Exhibit 5.9 **The Network Commerce Buying Process**

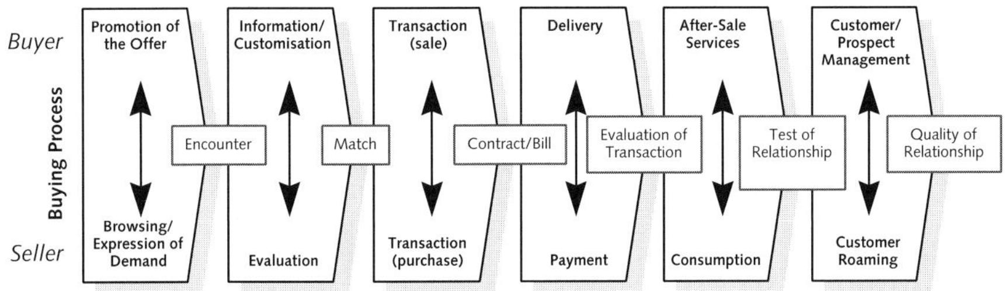

Encounter. Network commerce offers firms a medium to showcase products and services while providing consumers with a convenient platform on which to access these items. As the Internet becomes increasingly popular, consumers will come to rely on it as a channel for products and services. Strategies used during this first stage of the buying process are focused on attracting consumer attention to a particular site.

Ravensburger Interactive

Adapting Content for the Network

Ravensburger Interactive, a subsidiary of the board-games manufacturer, is representative of the potential for content firms to shift gears and to sell content to retailers, enabling them to sell other products online.

Ravensburger Interactive has a catalogue of fifty children's software titles. It also entered the games market at the end of 1997. Moving into the online world, it now uses the Web to sell those products. "That is a first step. The second step is online gaming," says Thomas Kirchenkamp, Managing Director.[36] An online, multiplayer board-game based on the "Scotland Yard" game (spot a spy in London rebuilt in 3D) bound to be released in September 1998, in co-production with Cryo (makers of the 2ème Monde 3D interface). The online service, as well as the first elements of the game, will be free of charge, so as to build a customer base. Then, Ravensburger Interactive will charge for the next game levels. Players will be able to communicate between them in real-time. Advertising panels will be posted in the 3D environment. "We expect huge growth for online gaming," said Kirchenkamp.

But while selling its products on the Web and developing online gaming are natural extensions of traditional games, Ravensburger Interactive is moving even one step further: Providing content to merchants for generating sales of whichever product they may sell online. Based on its experience and reputation on producing board-game puzzles, Ravensburger Interactive has designed "moving puzzles." Video pictures are broken into pieces and must be rebuilt as the picture moves. "Moving puzzles are a good prospect. They are simple, popular, and there is no problem of language. They can be used to sell other products: Content in this case is a mediator," Kirchenkamp explained.

For those moving puzzles, Ravensburger Interactive developed a video engine. Any video content can be put into it. Those puzzles allow for the presentation of products in an entertaining, relaxing fashion. In this case, Ravensburger Interactive licenses its own content. If they cannot sell the idea to retailers, they will use it for their own branding purposes on their Web site. "It is a huge opportunity. The advantages (of having developed it) outweigh the disadvantages," Kirchenkamp said. The promises of this new product were already confirmed by a 'Milia d'Or'[37] award in February 1998.

With the moving puzzles, Ravensburger Interactive is also able to target new segments. While its games usually target families with young children, the content sold to retailers is targeted at adults. "It is all a matter of content, whatever the medium. Our goal is to have a huge database of content, plus a strong brand. Having the content is a huge comparative advantage," Kirchenkamp concluded.

www.ravensburger.de

Match. The most basic examples of matching can be seen in simple Web sites that present information in the form of electronic brochures. These sites post static product information available to consumers at any time via any computer.

The network environment has enabled companies to follow much more elaborate strategies. Some companies provide complementary content and services while partnering with sellers of related products to support the sale of their core products. Many travel agencies have Web sites that offer free news and information about travel destinations, tips and travel advisories, and other services such as currency exchange calculators. Quicken.com, a site promoting Intuit's Quicken personal finance software package, offers investment information and advice, related news, and links to financial institutions (Exhibit 5.10).

Exhibit 5.10 **Quicken.com's Internet Site**

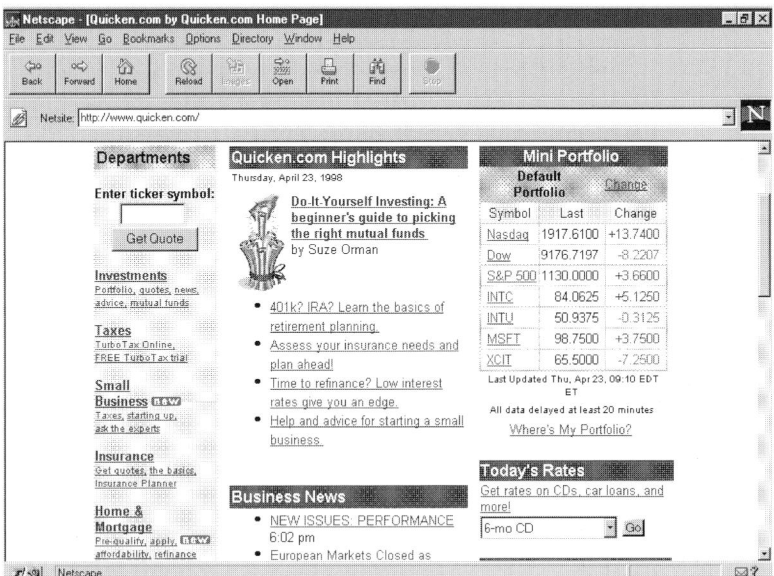

Source: Company Web site.

This matching process can also include consumer information gathering, including contact information, demographics, preferences, and other relevant details. This information is used to update the consumer of changes in products or services, or to tailor the Web site according to consumer preferences.

Contract. The ability to request a product over an electronic network provides considerable convenience to the consumer. Network commerce allows users to find, research, and order a product with the click of a button, making the Web site a point of purchase or sales channel for the product or service. At this point, the purchasing decision has been made by the consumer; the subsequent request is executed immediately.

Transaction Logistics. Transaction logistics describe the actual exchange of a payment for a product, and are an extension of the contracting segment. As in the contracting of a purchase, facilitating payment for and delivery of products can be an advantage to a firm.

Test Relationship. Content plays a role in "testing the relationship." In this segment, network commerce provides support for users in the consumption of products, providing tips and advice on use, troubleshooting help, complementary information, and reassurance of the quality of the products and the firm.

Maintain Relationship. The final segment of the buying process concerns the establishment of a long-term relationship between the consumer and the seller. The experiences that a consumer had when purchasing and consuming the product are largely responsible for shaping this relationship. In some ways, the consumer's perception of the buying process is as significant as the products themselves are. However, the connection a consumer feels with the company — many consumers feel strong ties to Coca-Cola and remain loyal to the brand, even paying higher prices — as well as the connection a consumer feels with fellow consumers of the same product, remains a factor. Maintaining a rela-

E*Trade

Serving Many Customer Needs

E*Trade has moved its entire transaction process to the network, making securities trading easier and cheaper than ever. E*Trade provides trading services at $14.95 to $19.95 per transaction, and offers information about markets, companies, and accounts. Its revenues are growing rapidly as more consumers use the Web and gain confidence in conducting transactions online.

E*Trade facilitates the entire securities buying process. Its services are easily accessible via the Web, eliminating the need for proprietary software or dial-in networks. Information and a demonstration of services are available on the Web site, along with information about investing, companies and stocks, and recent news provided to help users research and track potential investments. Trades are initiated through the site and the user is notified when the actual trade has taken place. Personal portfolios and other account information can easily be tracked on the Web site as well, with a variety of customer service capabilities available to answer investor questions.

For the first six months of fiscal 1998, E*Trade reported revenues of $104 million, up 83 percent from $57.2 million for the same period in 1997. Income for the first half of 1998 was $11 million, up 108 percent from $5.3 million in the first half of 1997. E*Trade has over 400,000 customer accounts, after adding 80,000 in the second quarter of 1998 alone, 10 to 13 percent of the estimated 3 to 4 million total online accounts.[38] E*Trade has established a name brand as one of the first providers of Internet-based trading services. Its brand name is reinforced through free information, provided for customers and the public at large, in order to draw attention to its Web site.

E*Trade is trying to extend its reach by allying with complementary financial service providers. BancOne has incorporated E*Trade's brokerage services as part of a comprehensive suite of services provided to its online customers. Similarly, E*Trade has allied with E-Loan, Inc. in order to provide information on mortgages, shop for the best rates, and apply for a loan over the Internet. Additionally, E*Trade is partnering with brokerage companies throughout the world, licensing its brand and technology in exchange for royalty payments. Through these services and alliances, E*Trade hopes to create a strong name brand and establish a clientele.

www.etrade.com

tionship resembles, and even becomes, the creation of a virtual community that revolves around a product, or interests related to the product.

According to the CEO of a major interactive publishing firm in France, "There is a traditional physical value chain and an 'information value chain.' The question is: where will value be created in the latter and who is going to capture it? What really is at stake is the business-to-consumer market because that is where one-to-one marketing will be used. The challenge is to develop customer relationships and to capture this relationship's value. The customer (with whom you have established a relationship) has a quantifiable value. This value is not the same whether, for example, it is a France Loisirs or a Canal+ customer.[39] At the same time, multi-channel distribution strategies will develop. End users will assemble the content components they need. One must bear in mind that one-to-one marketing is very nice but it requires specific competencies."[40]

A long-term relationship can be most important to consumers and sellers when the product is time sensitive or must be replaced frequently. Having completed the buying cycle once, a consumer is likely to buy again if satisfied with the product and the company. The link between firms that provide time-sensitive products and services and their clients is often closest. For example, if a ski equipment seller provides updated skiing conditions and weather forecasts on its Web site, then clients and potential clients are likely to return to the Web site.

In addition to being an important part of the buying process, maintaining a customer-seller relationship is also is an integral part of building brand names and corporate image.

Successful Industries

The sale of goods over the network has been highly successful thus far. Although margins have typically been low in the network retailing world, many firms see network retailing as a hugely lucrative market that will develop in time. In the US, Amazon.com has created panic at rival booksellers Borders and Barnes & Noble, just as Dell Computer has among personal computer re-sellers. More recently, the automotive industry distribution system is beginning to show signs of strain as customers turn to the Web to get accurate pricing information.

Books. Book sales on the Web are expected to rise to $400 million in 1998. This represents about 3 percent of the $13 billion US book market.[41] Amazon.com currently leads the industry, followed by US retail giant Barnes & Noble. Borders Group, another US retail giant, launched its long-delayed online bookstore in early 1998, and Bertelsmann A.G. is constructing an international online book mall that will offer books in English, French, Spanish, German, and Dutch.

Amazon.com has begun to sell music and is expanding into Europe as it considers distribution sites in Britain and Germany. Meanwhile, Barnes & Noble is significantly increasing its advertising and has reached a deal with an antiquarian bookseller to offer rare and used books.

Amazon.com

Changing the Book Retailing World

Amazon.com has become one of the most publicised network commerce firms by selling books over the Internet. However, Amazon.com lost $27.6 million on sales of $147.8 million in 1997. As many competitors, such as Barnes & Noble, enter the online book sales arena, Amazon.com will continue to struggle to turn a profit; however, Amazon.com has established a strong brand name that may be its greatest competitive advantage going forward.

Created in July 1995, Amazon.com, has over 2.2 million customer accounts, making it the Web's busiest retail site.[42] The bookseller offers over 2.5 million book titles and has begun to sell music CDs as well. Avoiding costs related to maintaining physical retail outlets, Amazon.com has been able to offer discounts of 20 to 40 percent off retail prices. Additionally, the Web site offers an abundance of general and customer-tailored ancillary services. In the first quarter of 1998, sales rose to $87.4 million, more than half the revenues for all of 1997. Yet, the company still recorded a loss.

Because it will be relatively easy for new and established competitors to offer the similar prices and selections online, providing distinct, or value-added services and building a brand that will attract many customers are keys to Amazon.com's future success. The retail Web site has been adding and refining ancillary services on its site, making it a model for other firms seeking to promote their Web sites. Amazon.com provides book reviews via a variety of sources, contains best-seller lists, as well as book suggestions listed by category, including "customised" lists based on individual customer preferences. It also offers original interviews and articles, and provides news and events listings.

Amazon.com is aggressively seeking to draw traffic to its site and attempting to increase sales volume. In the first quarter of 1998, the company had $28.2 million in operating expenses, $20 million of which were spent on sales and marketing to promote its products and Web sites. Amazon will have to compete with companies like Barnes&Noble.com, who paid AOL $40 million at the end of 1997 to be the exclusive bookseller on the subscription-based site. Amazon.com is also seeking to attract traffic and sales by creating an "associate" program in which any site, (e.g. Merriam-Webster online) can earn 5 percent of any sale referred to Amazon.com, or 15 percent of sales for books featured on the site.

www.amazon.com

To compete, Bertelsmann has formed regional teams around the world to begin building Web sites in various languages for its bookstore. Bertelsmann's goal is to be able to sell any book in print and use its distribution network to keep costs low. It also wants to provide marketing and service to its huge book club membership numbering 35 million people.

"I can see (Amazon) being an enormous boost to the business because it's not just about selling more big, best-selling authors," says Michael Lynton, chief executive of the Penguin Group, a subsidiary of Pearson P.L.C.[43] Network-based customers tend to prefer older back-list titles and less well-known authors to the best-selling authors. Readers are buying in such broad patterns that, during November 1997 alone, Amazon customers bought at least one copy of 84 percent of Simon & Schuster's 10,000-book backlist and at least one copy of Penguin's 15,000-book backlist. Readers are also buying works by obscure small presses that may not appear on the shelves in most bookstores. Many of these smaller publishing houses are finding that a significant and growing percentage of their traffic is coming through online sales. The Foundation Press reports, for example, that 15 percent of its sales are through online bookstores.[44]

Music. Like books, packaged music is also being sold over the Internet. Two of the biggest competitors in this market are CDNow and N2K's Music Boulevard. Other major players in this arena include Tower Records, mail-order retailers Columbia House and BMG, and even the online book seller Amazon.com, all of which offer thousands of titles at discounted prices. CDNow has over 250,000 titles available, which can be delivered in three to five days. Online retailers like Music Boulevard offer a variety of additional services, including music clips, articles and reviews of albums and artists, recommendations based on user preferences, and even broadcasts of albums, concerts, and radio stations. Music Boulevard has begun selling ninety-nine cent "singles," or individual songs, that are delivered to the customer via the Internet. This delivery method is not entirely attractive to most consumers as downloading one song with a 28.8 kbps modem may take an hour or longer. Other sites such as CDuctive offer the ability to create custom compilation CDs from a choice of songs available on that site.

In 1997, CDNow lost $10.8 million on sales of $17.4 million, while N2K (Music Boulevard) lost $28.7 million on sales of only $11.3 million. In the fourth quarter of 1996, N2K had sales of $679,000; while one year later, in the fourth quarter of 1997, sales reached $4 million. Today Internet music retailers are struggling to make a profit. However, if sales continue to grow at the current pace, large sites that can generate sales volume will be able to profit.

Automobiles. Consumers have traditionally been deterred by dealer network because of ambiguous pricing schemes and high pressure sales techniques. Internet sales channels shift the power to consumers by providing them with much more information as well as a variety of choices. Car shopping services such as Auto-By-Tel and Microsoft's CarPoint allow the consumer to conduct much of the buying process at home by providing detailed information about a variety of cars (including the dealer's cost), enabling to pick an exact model and get a price quote, and even arranging financing for the purchase.

In 1997 16 percent of new car buyers used the Internet for shopping, up from 10 percent in 1996,[45] and 10 percent of consumers said that they would be willing to buy a car online without a test drive.[46] Today many consumers are using car purchasing sites to prepare themselves with the necessary information needed to buy a car at a dealership. Sites such as AutoWeb or GM's www.gmbuypower.com provide quotes and refer customers to specific dealerships that will sell the car at the specified amount. Some car dealers are finding that 50 percent of referred customers are completing the purchase as opposed to 18 percent to 20 percent of consumers who are not referred by a Web site.

In 1998 Auto-By-Tel claimed to be responsible for about $500 million in monthly car sales although 1997 revenues were only about $6 million. Revenues are derived from a variety of sources including a payment from car dealers for every referral, monthly fees for exclusive referrals, and bonuses for car sales or financing arrangements. As more car dealers move into the Internet sales space, the consumer will be able to order custom made cars and expect prompt delivery and still pay relatively low prices since many of the distribution inefficiencies will be removed.

Computers. The computer industry is a perfect example of how the Internet can become a direct sales channel between the manufacturer and the consumer, providing speed flexibility and low prices. In the past five years, Dell Computer Corporation has rocketed to become the third-largest computer manufacturer (behind Compaq and IBM) by reaching directly to the consumer, initially through the telephone and now through the Internet, to provide made-to-order computers at low prices.

In July 1998, the CEO of Dell, Michael Dell, announced that the firm was generating $6 million of sales per day over the Internet and that $1 million of that was from Europe. Cisco Systems, which sells networking equipment, sells $9 million per day over the Internet, about 50 percent of the company's total revenue. These companies, along with many others like them, are redefining the role of retailing in the network economy by closely integrating sales, marketing and manufacturing processes through a common network platform.

Retailers. One of the more interesting models to emerge is the broad-based discount retailing operation of netMarket. Cendant Corp. (formerly CUC International) has created this subscription-based shopping service. With little promotion, the site pulled in 140,000 memberships in December 1997. NetMarket is pursuing a business model as the ultimate network retail intermediary, and, if its projections are correct, has the potential to be significantly more profitable than any other retailer. For year three, Cendant is currently projecting 4 million members that will generate a cash profit of $200 million and net profits of $160 million. NetMarket is a member-only shopping site, where each subscriber pays an annual fee of $69 to become a member. Cendant makes a profit of $14 per new subscriber in the first year and $50 in the second year in addition to margins earned through the sale of goods and services.[47]

By charging a membership fee, Cendant can offer items at cost and can leverage this low-pricing ability to capture market share. Because Cendant's software engine and databases allow it to track local prices for goods and services, the company's prices may be lower than those of any local retailer (which

The Gap

Expanding Customer Relationships

The Gap is a retailer of its own line of casual clothing with several thousand shops throughout the US and Europe. The company is incorporating an aggressive image-building campaign into its effort to enter online retailing. A recent advertising campaign features famous performance artists promoting Gap clothing lines. Gap.com offers these advertisements along with an online catalogue from which end users can select purchases.

For the most part, the Gap's image-building campaign features US rock musicians. While traditional endorsements use celebrity names and images to attract attention and build an image, the Gap goes one step further by using original material created specifically for the Gap. The video spots are viewable on the Gap Web site as a means of attracting customers and reinforcing brand and image simultaneously. This strategy uses the Internet to maximise the reach of the Gap's television advertising campaign. Such "extensions" might be ideally suited for the Internet, since a good deal of exposure is achieved at a low cost. According to the company, the Gap's Web site has had success as a retail services channel, particularly during the Christmas buying season.

www.gap.com

could still be higher than a national price point offered by a competing service that doesn't track local prices). Cendant claims that its experience in direct marketing and its infrastructure for managing pricing are so far ahead of the competition that no one else can match its capabilities.[48]

Travel Services. The travel industry has been among the first to suffer seriously as a result of the Internet. Travel services have enjoyed great success on the Web, displacing travel agents. Forrester Research Inc. forecasts that ticket sales volume will quadruple to nearly $5 billion by 2000. As a result, smaller travel agents are de-emphasising airline ticket sales. Commission caps were behind the initial impact on travel agents' income, but online competition — which emboldened the airlines to slash commissions that they paid to agents — accelerated the displacement. For one independent agent, between 1995 and the end of 1997, airline ticket commissions dropped from 62 percent of revenues to less than 30 percent. In response, many agents are offering new services and becoming more customer-focused. Other agencies are focusing on speciality offerings such as adventure trips, travel for people in specific age or social groups, and eco-tourism. Yahoo! has entered this market segment with its accommodation services.

The explosive growth of online reservation services combined with reductions in agency commissions by US airlines is rapidly thinning competition in the trav-

La Compagnie des Voyages

Seeking to Add Greater Value

La Compagnie des Voyages (LCDV), a French travel agency, receives an average of 350 orders per month and makes 20 percent of its revenues on the Internet (revenues reached 5.3 million euro in 1997). "Business is picking up very strongly," says CEO Stéphane Van Son.[49] The company started to sell online in September 1996 and has already recovered its investment.

The value proposition is very simple and based on choice, price, and service. The Web site lets users compare prices, timetables, and availability of seats in real-time, and to book and pay online. International flights (departing from France) for seventy airlines, 900 destinations, and 250,000 negotiated prices are ranked by price. La Compagnie des Voyages is also part of a world-wide network of travel agents through the ITA (International Travel Association) to integrate up to 5 million price offerings.

LCDV, in effect, disintermediates as much as possible to avoid commissions. Prices are guaranteed at the time of booking. Automation in the booking processes also reduces costs and hence prices. The company claims that a light organisation allows them to be more reactive. LCDV also claims to be a in a neutral position towards the airlines and to be able to aggregate all the offers and to allow a fair comparison. The CEO encourages users to send him email messages personally in order to improve the service.

The Web site has several services such as promotional offers posted by airline companies and special offers available only by e-mail through a "virtual counter." The site will soon be upgraded with a mailing list for loyal customers, and probably a forum and a magazine.

The information system is linked to Airquest, an American database used by US travel agencies, through an application developed by a German company, TISS. It also interfaces with the Sabre reservation system. The Web site is hosted in Washington, DC, by Digiweb.

www.lcdv.com

el business. "There are about 32,000 travel agencies in business right now. I would be shocked if a year from now there are 15,000 left," said Peggy Lee, president of Lee Travel Group. "If all Lee Travel did was book airline reservations, I wouldn't be able to sleep nights."[50]

The number of travel agencies in operation dropped 6 percent between January 1997 and October 1997 alone, according to Addison Schonland, director of aviation travel and marketing research at CIC Research Inc. "The soft part of the market is gone."[51]

"The agencies that offer value-added services for travel will still get a lot of business, but the companies that simply take orders are history," said Terrell Jones, president of Sabre Interactive, which runs the Travelocity Web site.[52]

Financial Services. A whole range of financial services is moving rapidly to the network, including banking, brokerage services, and insurance.

Banking. Financial services firms offering products and services over the Internet are adopting so-called "reintermediation" or "neo-intermediation" as a means of building profitable relationships with customers.[53] In effect, disintermediation — withdrawing savings from a bank to invest elsewhere at a higher rate of return — continues to be a major problem for banks, whether non-bank rivals originate in the financial district or over the Internet. Successful network-based firms provide personal, interactive services at little or no cost. This "trust-building" approach allows these firms to learn what each customer values. Armed with detailed customer knowledge, these companies are well-positioned to build loyalty and increase profits for the long term. US mutual funds giant Fidelity Investments, for instance, uses personal financial goals entered by consumers at the fidelity.com Web site to advise those customers on how much they need to save and invest and where. As another example, Infinity Financial Technology (riskview.com) will analyse consumer investment portfolios and make a calculation of the relative risk.

This "trust-building" approach, of course, is really an old practice that many banks have moved away from. Now, rightly or wrongly, customers view banks as aggressive sales organs or as faceless corporations interested only in fees — the downside of overdone cross-selling. New online financial services firms capitalise on this view as they compete with banks to serve the needs of the mass market.

Brokerage. Brokerage concerns have also moved to the network. Piper Jaffray Inc. expects online securities trading to account for 60 percent of the discount brokerage industry and 10 percent of all retail securities brokerage commissions by 2001, up from about $268 million in 1996.[54] Further, according to Piper Jaffray, the online trading industry will generate $2.2 billion in commissions in 2001, over eight times the $268 million in commissions it generated in 1996. This growth may be attributed to the Internet's growth, easing consumer fears about Internet security, and an increased number of online trading offerings. US discount brokerage leader Charles Schwab & Co. has the largest share of the online trading industry currently with 35 percent of all online trades. Rapidly growing E *Trade has moved into third position with 13 percent market share just behind Fidelity Investments.[55]

Competition is driving down commissions. Average online trading commission rates fell almost 50 percent from $30 to $35 in 1996 to $15 to $20 in 1997. However, Piper Jaffray forecasts that rates should stabilise due to recent US Securities and Exchange Commission (SEC) rule changes and the move toward smaller quote increments on the New York Stock Exchange and NASDAQ.[56]

The growth of the online trading industry has come at the expense of traditional full-service firms as well as banks. Merrill Lynch and Paine Webber have risked alienating their existing brokers by a move into online trading.

Insurance. Insurance sales are another area especially well-suited to the network, but channel conflict issues have slowed the move to the network by major insurance firms.

Life insurance agents, who have traditionally made sales in person, face competition on the Web. LifeQuote of America Inc., a life insurance agency in Miami, Florida, invested less than $50,000 to develop its Web site (www.lifequote.com). Soon after the site's launch in 1995, it accounted for 60 percent of the eleven-year-old company's overall business. According to LifeQuote, of the 300 people per month who use the site to request quotes, 17 percent become paying customers, surpassing the conversion ratios for both direct mail (1 percent to 2 percent) and cold calling (5 percent). LifeQuote still acts as an insurance agent, representing more than fifty insurance companies. And for each policy it sells online, it collects 50 percent of the first year's premium as its fee.[57]

Despite clear indications that consumers want quotes, information, and the ability to buy insurance via the Internet, few insurance companies are rushing to meet that demand, according to Mark L. Trencher of Conning & Company, Hartford, Connecticut.[58] Citing a 1997 survey by Booz-Allen & Hamilton of 170 multi-line insurers, Trencher listed consumers' top five wants regarding Internet insurance capability, including quotes, ability to change personal information, ability to make policy changes, more agent information, and ability to purchase policies.[59]

Insurance firms are concerned about angering their current sales channels. While more than 30 percent of participating companies said their customers wanted more services, fewer than 10 percent of insurers said they would provide such services in 1998.

A 1996 survey of insurance companies by the Des Plaines, Illinois-based National Association of Independent Insurers, indicated that about 20 percent of 129 respondents had a Web site, while nearly 40 percent said they were planning one. Insurance companies usually have "static" Web pages, containing information only and offering no ability to transact business. Meanwhile, the insurers' competitors in banks and brokerages are moving toward Internet-based transactions.

While less than 3 percent of insurer Web sites offer transactions, 33 percent of bank Web sites have that capability, according to a 1997 study by Meridien Research, in Needham, Massachusetts. The study looked at Web sites for the top 200 insurers and retail banks globally. Among the top-grossing fifty brokerages (world-wide) participating in the survey, 20 percent reported having Web sites offering transactions.[60]

Information technology spending among insurers has been steadily increasing since 1992, now reaching an estimated 4 percent of the amount of their written premiums. Return on equity for this spending has been inconsistent.

Real Estate. Real estate brokerage agencies are also adapting swiftly to a network business model. Real estate brokers maintain databases of properties for sale and provide potential buyers access to these databases. This classic intermediary function does not add significant value and can be superseded by a Web-based business model.

For example, San Francisco-based Abele Information Systems Inc. runs a ten-employee Web service called Abele Owners' Network (www.owners.com). The site, launched in early 1996, was still small, listing 140,000 homes in forty-five states over the course of its first year. At owners.com, sellers enter basic price and property data and add such extras as pictures for a small fee. The attraction for both buyer and seller is that they can negotiate the price directly, thus avoiding the brokerage fee. Owners.com's potential and fast growth have inspired traditional brokers to create their own sites. "The industry feels threatened by the release of online listing information," says Becky Swann, a former real estate broker in Grapevine, Texas, whose International Real Estate Digest (www.ired.com) rates hundreds of real estate Web sites run by agencies and entrepreneurs. "They got carried away with controlling the information. The ones that think their job is providing access to the MLS, those are the folks who will be out of business."[61]

Large, national real estate brokerage firms are quickly following the start-ups onto the Web. Coldwell Banker Corp., for example, says its Web site lists 150,000 properties and generates 100,000 user sessions per week. A Coldwell Banker executive says that instead of seeing it as a replacement for its traditional sales channels, "We see it as a tool for generating sales leads for our brokers."[62] However, this easy access to listings will force change on the business. Customers, after doing much of their own preliminary research online, may challenge the notion of paying the standard 5 to 7 percent commissions charged by real estate brokers. To stay in business, agents may have to lower their commissions or charge fixed fees for such tasks as preparing documents, negotiating prices, marketing, or holding open houses. As in so many other businesses in this highly competitive network economy, exemplary personal service and customised advice will become essential survival tools for traditional real estate brokerages.

For content creators and aggregators, the emergence of Web-based real estate brokerages creates a number of potential opportunities. Firms that own content related to real estate purchasing, home repair, specific geographical communities, and so forth, may be able to leverage this content or the brands associated with it to create Web-based marketplaces. This represents an opportunity, especially for newspapers that have often earned significant revenues selling classified advertising space to individuals and brokerages selling properties. By creating focal points for property buyers and sellers, newspapers can preside over significant traffic that can be used to sell advertising and related services.

5.3 Cut Costs

Network commerce can reduce costs in three main areas — supply management, internal operations, and marketing and sales. In an ideal network commerce environment, open standards would ensure that almost every aspect of supply management, internal operations, and marketing and sales were efficiently connected. Firms would be able to switch suppliers, add internal capabilities, or use new distribution networks easily, without losing efficiency.

5.3.1 Supply Management

Large companies have reduced information transfer costs for many years using Electronic Data Interchange (EDI) over private networks. These expensive private networks proved economically viable only for large companies conducting billions of euro of transactions annually. Today, however, almost any company can transmit electronic data over the Internet because the cost of the network is shared among all its users.

General Electric Information Service (GEIS) and Thomas Publishing have jointly created Trading Process Network (TPN) Register, an network commerce service designed to link purchasers and suppliers. TPN Register has two Internet-based marketplaces, TPNMart and TPNPost. TPNMart facilitates MRO procurement through online catalogues from various suppliers. TPNPost facilitates the Request for Price Quotations process by electronically distributing product specifications to suppliers who then provide " blind" bids. (Exhibit 5.11). GE Lighting has reduced quote processing time from about twenty-one days to only nine, and it has cut the cost of related faxes, mail, and labour by 30 percent. Although TPN Register was designed originally for General Electric's use, other companies can use the network by paying a membership fee. Firms seeking a network relationship with suppliers can develop their own network with suppliers or use intermediaries such as TPN register to aggregate suppliers for them.

Exhibit 5.11 **TPNPost's Online Bidding Process**

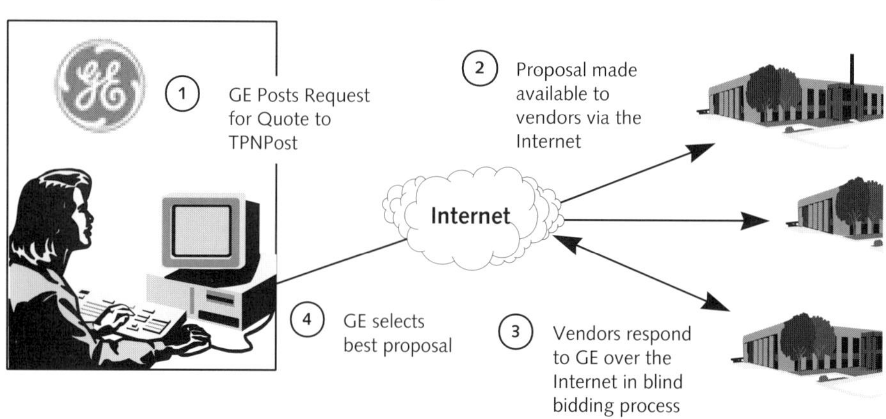

Source: Company Reports.

5.3.2 Internal Operations

In much the same manner that producers cut costs by connecting to suppliers through digital networks, co-ordination of internal activities digitally has proven beneficial.

The cost of communicating via digital networks as opposed to paper exchange need not be documented here. As is well-known, filling out, delivering, and filing paper work is slow, labour-intensive, and costly. In contrast, for most companies, network commerce solutions can facilitate communications and information transfer between and among all departments. For example, as sales are made, a firm's sales department can easily check on inventory status and place internal orders that include all the relevant information regarding each sale. Based on historic sales data over time, the firm's manufacturing arm can more accurately forecast production needs. Using the network, the accounting department can easily keep track of accounts receivable and inventory as both sales and shipping automatically update the status of in-process orders.

Using their networks efficiently has allowed such computer manufacturers as Gateway, Micron, and Dell to produce made-to-order computers for individual buyers, delivering product to their customers in a timely manner. These firms have not just reduced inventories, they have continued offering the latest technology available.

5.3.3 Marketing and Sales

Network commerce can bring similar cost savings to marketing and sales efforts and customer relationships. Making the customer part of the ordering process can have beneficial effects. In the case of Dell, consumers can research and specify the exact computer that they wish to purchase and access the Web site for any customer support they might need following the transaction. Each week about 20,000 people use the Web site to check the status of their orders. If 10 percent of these customers had called Dell for this information (assuming a cost of $3 to $5 per call in terms of customer service), Dell would incur an additional $6,000 to $10,000 in costs per week.[63] Additionally, about 30,000 software files are downloaded from the Dell Web site each week. Dell's cost to process software file orders by phone and mail the software would total roughly $150,000 per week.[64]

In another example, bank transaction-processing costs have gone down more and more as consumers turn to the Internet to conduct their own transactions directly. (Exhibit 5.12).

Exhibit 5.12 **Banking Services Cost per Transaction by Method**

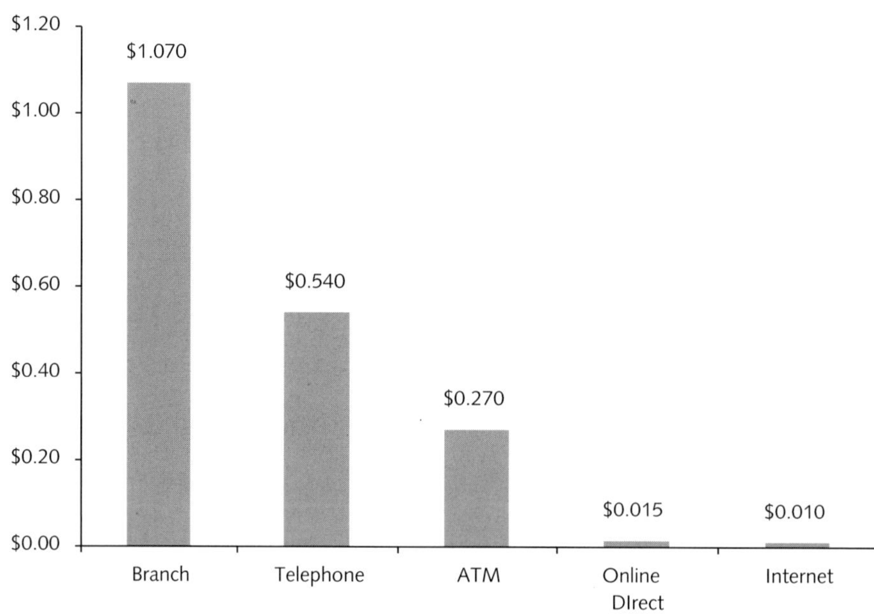

Source: Booz Allen & Hamilton.

The Internet has enabled firms to reach consumers directly and has created a cost incentive for many firms to do so. As the Internet gains popularity, traditional distribution channels will be forced to contend with this new force (Exhibit 5.13).

Exhibit 5.13 **Network Commerce and Channels**

Disintermediation	Some traditional "intermediaries" (middle men) will be displaced by direct dealings between producers and customers, and producers and suppliers.
"Reintermediation"	New intermediaries are emerging to broker/facilitate transactions among producers, suppliers, and customers.
Channel Conflict	Many firms face obstacles with existing distribution channels as they attempt to engage in network commerce and reach customers directly.

Source: Gemini Strategic Research Group.

Exhibit 5.14 **Distribution Channel Models Today and Tomorrow**

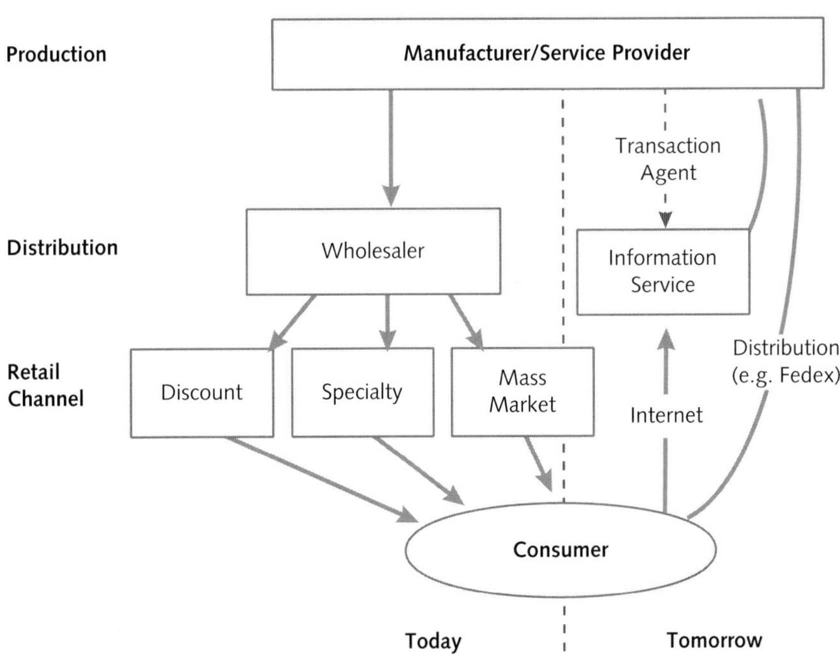

The Web is generating new forms of channel competition. From a historical perspective, some portion of Dell's PC business has always been sold direct first by mail order, then via toll-free numbers, and now on the Web.

The network economy is already creating complications for an industry relying on major dealer/agent networks for product distribution (e.g. automobiles, insurance). In the US and Canada, cars are typically sold through independently owned dealerships affiliated with manufacturers. Some manufacturers are interested in using the Internet to more effectively market their products, but are wary of disturbing their dealer network too radically. It is possible, ultimately, that many smaller dealers will be displaced by Web-enabled intermediaries.

Today's particularly effective channel participants may become even more successful by leveraging the Web. In the automobile industry, for example, some independent dealers are already using the Web to expand their reach. These dealers will become the Web-enabled intermediaries who survive the consolidation that is likely to occur in the distribution network. Those intermediaries who broker products and information without adding value are unlikely to survive in this competitive environment.

As customers come to expect immediate, continuously updated information on the Web, they will also develop higher expectations about actual delivery of goods and services. An individual who orders a book from an online bookseller may not be willing to wait a week or two weeks to receive that product. If the

N2K

Bypassing Traditional Distribution Networks

N2K represents another successful example of network commerce direct marketing. N2K is one of several music companies providing a variety of products and services directly to customers. The core of N2K's online offering is Music Boulevard, an Internet-based retail music store. N2K also has three Web sites devoted to specific music Interests ("Rocktropolis.com," "JazzCentralStation.com," and "Classicalinsites.com." The company has combined retailing, publishing, and music broadcasting into a complete business, driving revenue from transactions from Music Boulevard and advertising from all the sites.

Music Boulevard offers consumers all the benefits of online shopping (access to over 200,000 titles, opportunities to listen to over 350,000 music clips before making a buying decision, and the convenience of shopping from home or office. Because of the importance of local, regional, and musical artists in this market, N2K maintains foreign language versions of its sites that contain localised content and sell music from local artists. In addition, N2K has an exclusive agreement with Ticketmaster, one of the world's largest live-event ticketing firms, to provide online ticket purchasing capabilities for its customers and attract more viewers to its sites.

N2K's online network provides an abundance of articles, reviews, and news categorised by genre. Additionally, N2K offers radio broadcasts over the Web, including live concerts, selected albums, and other musical programming. The sites offer information on specific artists and albums, provide audio clips of many songs, and offer a direct link to Music Boulevard, where consumers can purchase music. By creating separate sites for specific music market niches, N2K can effectively build an online community while creating a strong brand name for N2K. Consumers are directed from each of the various Web sites into Music Boulevard for the retail transactions.

Although for 1997 N2K lost $29.3 million on sales of $11.3 million, the increasing popularity of the Internet is driving high revenue growth. Revenues for the first quarter of 1998 reached $7 million, compared to only $1.1 million for the same quarter in 1997. Revenues grew nearly 100 percent in the six months from October 1997 to March 1998.

www.n2k.com

distribution and transportation infrastructure does not support fast, cheap product distribution, this form of commerce will be hindered. Logistics have changed significantly in the US and are beginning to shift in Japan. Retailers are working with transport firms like Federal Express to ensure low-cost shipping almost anywhere in the US within twelve to twenty-four hours. In the US, Web-based grocers CUC International and NetGrocer use Federal Express to deliver non-perishable groceries from central facilities to customers across the continental US.

5.4 Build Intangible Assets

The final reason for actively pursuing network commerce opportunities resides in a business' need to build intangible assets (image or brand identity, or cachet that plays a role in a firm's long-term success). Intangible assets, such as actors' names, can make a difference to the success of feature films. Unlike revenues or costs, intangible assets are not easy to measure.

Product type, sales method, customer service, marketing, corporate culture, media exposure, and many other issues contribute to a firm's image and product brand names. Firms doing business via networks have the opportunity to build their intangible assets.

Disney Online

Leveraging a Strong Brand

Walt Disney is a traditional media company that has ventured onto the Internet with Disney Online. The Web site aggressively parlays the success of Disney's cartoon products, including all its original cartoon characters, but presents new content designed to take advantage of the network environment.

Disney Online's flagship Web site, Disney.com, is organised into four channels: "Today @ Disney" contains news and information about what's happening throughout Disney, (movies, schedules for DisneyTV, information about books, records, travel, theatre, and more). "Kids" offers activities and games for children aged three to twelve. "Family" provides parenting tips and suggestions for activities based on a child's age. "Shop" encompasses the Disney Store Online, and online "boutiques," like Pooh Grams and the Disney Design Online studio, which enables users to purchase items online. Disney Online has also developed Web sites for Germany, France, Spain, Japan, and other countries that target local audiences.

Disney's Daily Blast (www.disneyblast.com) was launched in April 1997. It delivers original interactive programs every day, including games, stories, activities, and kid-centric sports and news. Disney's Daily Blast is a subscription-based service that charges users $5.95 per month or $39.95 per year. Daily Blast is also available on MSN, the Microsoft Network, at no extra cost to MSN members.

Disney Online derives revenues through banner ads, subscriptions from its Disney Blast service, sales from the Disney Online Store, and from indirect revenues by promoting Disney TV, Disney Amusement Parks, Disney Cruise Lines, and others products. Disney Online attracts viewers by combining popular Disney content related to movies, books, and music; new content such as games and activities that feature Disney characters; and content unrelated to Disney products that may be of interest to Disney's target markets.

Disney Online has used its image and content to drive demand for its Web site. Simultaneously, the company has created new, Internet-tailored content calculated to build a loyal and growing audience predisposed to buying its products.

www.disney.com

Finally, Netscape Communications Corporation, creator of the Netscape Navigator Web browser, is attempting to leverage its reputation as an innovative Internet company and its extremely well-known brand name to become a portal to the Internet. In early 1998, after losing market share to Microsoft's Internet Explorer browser, Netscape began offering its browser for free. Netscape shifted its focus to other revenue streams in the hope that its name will position it to compete successfully with Yahoo!, Excite, and others in attracting viewers and drawing advertising revenues.

5.5 Summary

The network environment is changing the way many firms do business. Network commerce will help achieve several traditional business objectives — increasing revenues, cutting costs, and building intangible assets. Firms using network commerce are building revenues through advertising, subscriptions, and transactions; reducing costs by enhancing connections with vendors, internally, and with clients, and building intangible assets by promoting their brands and creating virtual communities. In this environment, content has taken a central role in many business models.

RECOMMENDATIONS

A successful network business model has several components, and it is far from certain what the specific components of that model should be in a given instance. However, at this early stage in the development of the network economy, it is possible to identify a number of key lessons from the experiences of leading firms on the network.

Businesses

- *Become leaders in establishing a network presence, focusing on learning more than your competitors or potential competitors.* The emergence of the network economy is changing the rules under which many businesses will operate in the future. Those firms that learn the rules now will be much better positioned to compete in the new economy than those firms that wait until later. Most network markets may not yet be mature enough to support profitable businesses, but most are mature enough for firms that invest with an eye toward learning to develop valuable insights about the opportunities of the new economy. The challenge is to invest prudently and to make sure that the lessons learned through experimentation are systematically captured and shared throughout the firm.
- *Actively experiment, capture experiences in a consistent manner, and share experiences across the firm so that all parts of the business can learn from the experimentation.* This means that firms should seek ways to promote entrepreneurial opportunities within the firm.
- *Implement a continuous process of competitor analysis to track who your competitors and potential partners are (e.g. a content firm's strongest competitors may not be other content firms).* In this rapidly evolving environment competitors (not to mention potential partners and customers) may come from completely unexpected industries and markets. Firms cannot afford to sit back and wait for the market landscape to become clear. Active and vigilant monitoring is necessary.
- *Ensure that the business model integrates both the sales channel and relationships with suppliers and partners.* In other words, be comprehensive: where practical, migrate transactions, both internal and external, to the network. Much of the hype about network commerce focuses on the new sales channel and the network commerce revenue model. The firms that have been most successful to date at exploiting network commerce have been those that have built comprehensive network commerce business models, using networks transform or build new-to-the-world organisations that link everyone from the smallest supplier to the customer in a nearly seamless web.
- *Evaluate in-house content and explore ways to leverage it.* Firms that do not think of themselves as being part of the content industry may find that they own significant quantities of valuable content. Examine the data produced within your firm and evaluate its value to your industry, your customers, and perhaps to others with whom you have not had relationships in the past.
- *Decide where to place brand emphasis and develop strong branding strategies to generate trust.* Again, the amount of "noise" in the marketplace makes a strong brand an important competitive advantage for those firms that can develop and effectively exploit that brand.
- *Create active customer communities.* Create facilities for easy and meaningful customer interactions with each other (e.g. discussion groups, chat servers). Over time, this may become the only source of competitive advan-

tage. Customers have more and more choices for purchasing most products and services. The only thing that may differentiate one seller form another may be the web of relationships that a customer builds around a seller's products and brand.

- *Build a more flexible organisation, capable of responding readily to change (e.g. lean management, culture of innovation and experimentation, telecommunications technologies effectively leveraged).* Firms are increasingly finding that as markets evolve, they must also rapidly evolve their strategies. Firms that have built the capability to rapidly change direction, have a huge advantage over firms that cannot change direction or can only change direction very slowly. Here again, outsourcing non-core functions and understanding and effectively utilising new telecommunications technologies can be critical advantages. The firms that are best at this anticipate, prepare for, and embrace fast change. They constantly re-evaluate what value they are creating for their customers.
- *Ensure that network commerce is treated as a key business issue and not as an information technology issue.* Network commerce is the most important business issue that most firms will face in the next eighteen months. It must be on the agenda of the chief executive or managing director.
- *All employees, especially top management, should have Internet access and use it.* If management and employees don't use the Internet, they won't understand it capabilities and limitations. If they don't understand it, the competitor who does is likely to destroy them.
- *Work with and push governments to create the appropriate business and market infrastructures for network commerce (e.g., competitive telecommunications markets, efficient capital markets, limited regulation).* Business leaders cannot sit idly by and wait for government to take the appropriate steps. Businesses should actively pursue appropriate action to speed market and business infrastructure development. Beyond pushing government to act, they should seek ways to partner with government to move forward.

Content Firms

- *Market content creation and aggregation competencies to non-content firms.* Content firms possess two things that every firm trying to sell on the network is going to require: content and content creation skills. Content firms are already adept at selling content, but identifying and learning to market content creation skills to other firms will require a change of focus for many content firms. The sale of these services to non-content firms offers a huge new market for many content firms.
- *Develop acquisition and partnering strategies to address need for rapid change.* It will be difficult to develop all of the necessary capabilities to compete in the new economy internally. Savvy managers will develop a game plan for identifying acquisition and partnering candidates that can help quickly address new market opportunities and threats.
- *Develop skills relevant to multiple distribution channels (e.g. Web, television, CD-ROM, print).* Digitisation means that content can be repositioned relatively rapidly for a number of distribution channels. To exploit the widest range of market opportunities, firms should have an understanding of the technical and market requirements of each of these channels and, either internally or through partnerships, should possess the skills to exploit these channels. content firms that can learn to package their content appropriately for this marketplace.

- *Evaluate content quality and value against that of global competitors.* The network content market is a global marketplace. Potential customers will have access to the best content that the world has to offer. All content firms must measure themselves against the quality of the best global content.
- *Make strategic partnerships on a pan-European and global basis.* The fragmented European marketplace means that it can be even harder to build a critical mass of network customers in Europe than it is in other parts of the world. One way to overcome this handicap is to partner with firms in other countries to share technology development and administration costs and to learn more rapidly about the realities of marketing in the network world.
- *Even if a firm is not an "electronic publisher," examine how the network can transform the rest of the business (e.g. supplier relationships, customer service, relationships with employees and contractors).* The Internet can make as much, if not greater, difference to the operations of a traditional print publisher or broadcaster as it can to an online publisher. Explore how the network can be used to transform production and internal communications processes.
- *Participate in the development of and promote micropayment and audience-measurement systems.* Micropayment systems and advertising provide important potential revenue sources to content firms on the Internet. Content firms should participate in the development of micropayment and audience measurement systems in order to ensure that capabilities develop to capture new revenue streams in these areas.
- *Explore the potential value of content to a variety of firms doing business on the network.* Every firm on the network needs attractive, high-quality content to attract potential customers and sell its products and services. This opens up a huge new market of potential customers to those. In particular, this means that firms should create content products that can be easily customised and licensed for integration into other firms' network content products.

Governments

- *Place network economy issues high on the public agenda (e.g. government leaders should address these issues and ensure that they receive the proper attention).* By placing network economy issues prominently on the public agenda, government leaders can play an important role in ensuring that network commerce issues are on the agenda of every business.
- *Facilitate the right business and market infrastructure for network commerce (telecommunications competition, labour flexibility, efficient capital markets, streamlined regulatory processes).* Again, these basic issues must be addressed in order to ensure that European firms have a level playing field on which to pursue network commerce initiatives in an intensely competitive global marketplace.
- *Use the network for transactions with citizens (tax collection, automobile registration, etc.) as well as with suppliers (bidding and collaboration on contracts, payments, and collections).* Governments can use components of network commerce business models to more effectively and efficiently deliver government services to their citizens.

Notes

1. Gemini Consulting interview.

2. For a valuable discussion of the many definitions of "network" or "electronic" commerce, see "Measuring Electronic Commerce," OECD, Paris, 1997.

3. Communication by the European Commission, "A European Initiative in Electronic Commerce," April 1997, COM(97)157.

4. GeoSystems Global Corporation.

5. Gemini Consulting interview.

6. Ibid.

7. Media Metrix.

8. Heather Green & Linda Himelstein, "Portal Combat Comes to the Net," *Business Week*, 2 March 1998.

9. AOL Press Release, 24 February 1998.

10. Heather Green & Linda Himelstein, "Portal Combat Comes to the Net," *Business Week*, 2 March 1998.

11. Ibid.

12. Ibid.

13. Ibid.

14. Ibid.

15. Yankee Group, 1997.

16. Ibid.

17. "America Online Increases Shelf Space For Barnes & Noble," *Newsbytes*, 17 December 1997.

18. John Hagel & Arthur Armstrong, *Net.Gain*, Harvard Business School Press, 1997.

19. I/PRO March 1998 Report.

20. Kenneth Li, "Cyberspace Calling: US News President Taking Internet Post," *Daily News* (New York), 16 April 1998.

21. Heather Green & Linda Himelstein, "Portal Combat Comes to the Net," *Business Week*, 2 March 1998.

22. Gemini Consulting interview.

23. Dana Blankenhorn, "Marketers Toy with New Ways to Keep Eyes on Site," *Business Marketing*, 1 February 1998.

24. Ibid.

25. Gemini Consulting interview.

26. Ibid.

27. Georgia Tech GVU Survey.

28. David Bodwin & David Kline, "Information publishing enters a post-Web world," *Upside*, February 1998.

29. Ibid.

30. Portable Document Format. Used by Adobe's Acrobat software, this format allows publishers to reproduce documents electronically while maintaining the original document's layout and look.

31. Users who have entered personal details when subscribing.

32. Gemini Consulting interview.

33. David Bodwin & David Kline, "Information publishing enters a post-Web world," *Upside*, February 1998.

34. Ibid.

35. Gemini Consulting interview.

36. Ibid.

37. Award presented at Milia (an international interactive media trade fair held every year in Cannes, France) to honor European multimedia products.

38. Steve Bailey and Steven Syre, "It's a Bull Market for Web Brokers," *Boston Globe*, 5 May 1998.

39. France Loisirs is a company equally owned by Havas and Bertelsmann and is involved in the Books On-Line project, Bertelsmann's global alternative to Amazon.Com. Canal+ is part of the Vivendi group, like Havas.

40. Gemini Consulting interview.

41. Baker & Taylor Books, via *The New York Times*, 9 March 1998.

42. Media Mextrix.

43. Doreen Carvajal, "The Other Battle Over Browsers," *The New York Times*, 9 March 1998.

44. Ibid.

45. Larry Armstrong, "Downloading Their Dream Cars," *Business Week*, 9 March 1998.

46. Ibid.

47. Paul Kagan Associates, "Netmarket — to Be the E-Commerce Leader?", *Interactive Multimedia Investor*, 20 January 1998.

48. Ibid.

49. Gemini Consulting interview.

50. Evan I. Schwartz, "How Middlemen Can Come Out on Top," *Business Week*, 9 February 1998.

51. Ibid.

52. Ibid.

53. Alan Tobey, "Back to the Right Future: The Case for Neo-Intermediation," *The American Banker*, 10 November 1997.

54. Piper Jaffray.

55. Ibid.

56. Ibid.

57. Ara C. Trembly, "Insurers Move Online."

58. Ibid.

59. Ibid.

60. Ibid.

61. Evan I. Schwartz, "How Middlemen Can Come Out on Top," *Business Week*, 9 February 1998.

62. Ibid.

63. US Department of Commerce, *The Emerging Digital Economy*, 1998.

64. Ibid.

Determining End-User Needs and Market Potential

Determining the size of the potential market for interactive content and network commerce is a difficult challenge. In this chapter, we provide an overview of the many forces shaping market demand.

The network economy is underpinned by market needs — both expressed and latent. While observers debate whether "market pull" or "technology push" triggers innovation, the probability is that markets and technology evolve together. Expressed needs create market "pull" — end users demand that their product and service needs be fulfilled more effectively, more conveniently, less expensively, and faster. In contrast, technology "push" occurs where technology fulfils expressed needs in unexpected ways or fulfils latent needs (needs for goods or services that end users would value but have never experienced or would never think to ask for).

6.1 Network Commerce Statistics and the Perils of Forecasting

"Forecasting is always difficult," the Danish physicist Niels Bohr is said to have remarked, "and it is especially difficult when trying to forecast the future."[1] This is certainly true of network commerce. While no one can be certain how large the network commerce market is going to be or how long it will take to develop, many observers are optimistic about both aspects. Our projections suggest that network commerce will significantly impact EU businesses over the next five years (section 6.1.5).

One problem in assessing network economy growth is that the Internet is a classic example of a "market discontinuity" — a "shift in any of the market forces or their interrelationships that cannot be predicted by a continuation of historical trends," and one that "can dramatically affect the performance of a firm or industry."[2] Like any market discontinuity (e.g. the 1929 stock market crash, the oil price shocks of the 1970s, the introduction of mass-produced automobiles), it is not possible to predict precisely the specific impacts of the Internet.

From a practical business perspective, timing of market evolution is critical. Even those who believe that the network economy is going to change everything recognise that this is not going to happen immediately. As with so many other aspects of this phenomenon, a look back at the Industrial Revolution will provide an analogy for the timing of the network revolution. John Chambers, CEO of Cisco Systems, believes that, "The Internet Revolution...will have every bit as much impact on society as the Industrial Revolution.... [I]nstead of happening over 100 years, like the Industrial Revolution, it will happen over seven years."[3]

Among other things, facing the network revolution will require many businesses to develop a deeper understanding of end-user needs and consumption behaviours. This could be a complex task, primarily because network commerce players are becoming so tightly interconnected through the network economy that the boundaries between markets and competitors are beginning to blur.[4]

6.1.1 Understanding Network Commerce Statistics

Measures of network usage and commerce have been difficult to develop — some of the key difficulties being definitional. Defining "users," "subscribers," "individuals with Internet access," and so forth has varied among surveys, making statistical comparisons across surveys and markets difficult. Uncertainty about current market sizes creates even greater difficulty in developing reliable forecasts of growth.

A survey of the literature suggests the range of forecasts and their typical lack of grounding in objective reality. The wide variation in estimates of current activity and forecasts for future activity were well documented In 1997 by the Organisation for Economic Co-operation and Development (OECD) in a paper called "Measuring Electronic Commerce."[5] The OECD paper provided an analysis of the issues involved in attempting to measure electronic commerce volume and collected in an appendix many of the then-available electronic commerce forecasts. This and other analyses stress the need for better measures of network activity.

Measuring current Internet usage is also difficult. In the US, four major Internet usage rating services — Media Metrix, RelevantKnowledge, NetRatings, and Nielson Web — are fighting to become the standard for measuring Web site traffic and usage habits.[6] Each uses different rating techniques, and results vary widely. "I think it's important to remember that no rating service has got it completely 'right' yet in terms of online measurement," says Chris Charron of Forrester Research.[7] Over time, however, measurement of Internet usage is likely to become more accurate than current statistical sampling techniques for measuring traditional media usage.

In addition, measuring network commerce's impact is complicated by the fact that few estimates attempt to quantify both transactions completed over the Web and those enabled by the Web. Data suggests that the Web plays a significant role in sales not directly transacted over the Web (e.g. a recent ActivMedia survey found that 91 percent of Internet users use the Web to compare product prices). Most market volume measures and forecasts of market volume do not include this element (one exception being ActivMedia's forecasts). The Web is also beginning to play a role in the pricing of products, such as computers, books, and automobiles. Particularly in the US, today's consumer culture increasingly revolves around price competition. According to a *Wall Street Journal* writer, the Web has emerged as the ultimate tool for finding the best bargains, forcing businesses to respond to pricing moves by Web-based competitors around the world.[8] Many of the key values of network commerce are also difficult to measure financially — including such intangibles as convenience, variety, and ease of access to information.

6.1.2 Segmentation

Interactive digital network technologies allow businesses and other participants in the interactive content value web to more closely link their activities (Exhibit 6.1).

Exhibit 6.1 **Network Commerce Relationships**

High-Level Segmentation of Business Relationships

Government Agencies
Organisation
Financial Institutions
Partners
Suppliers
Channels
Market
Business Customers
Consumers
Key
Business-to-consumer
Business-to-business

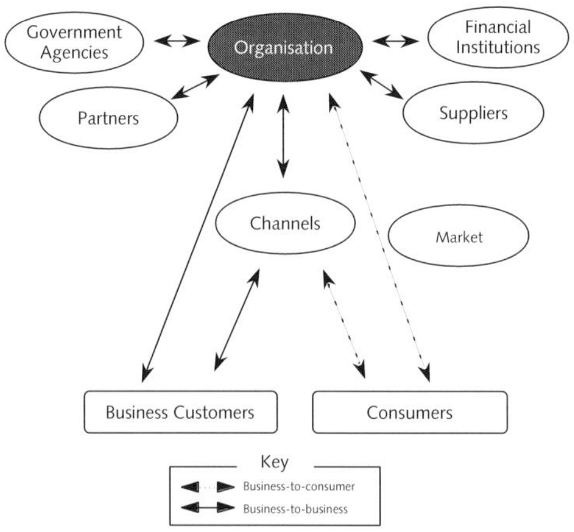

Types of Business Relationships and Examples

Types of Partners	Examples
Customers	Businesses, consumers
Channels	Distributors, wholesalers, sales agents
Suppliers	Core inputs, MRO[a] suppliers, health care, transportation
Partners	Joint ventures, alliances, consortia, trade associations
Government Agencies	EU, Member States, local
Financial Institutions	Banks, capital markets

Source: Gemini Strategic Research Group.
a. Maintenance, repair, and operations.

These relationships can be broadly classified into two categories, business-to-business and business-to-consumer. Business-to-business relationships are typically higher volume, longer term, and more structured than business-to-consumer relationships. In this network environment, the relationship between businesses and governments tends to be similar to business-to-business relationships, while the relationships between governments and citizens are more like those between businesses and consumers. Observers are nearly unanimous in predicting that the financial value of business-to-business commercial activity will continue to exceed that of business-to-consumer transactions for some time to come — primarily because many business-to-business transactions are much larger and more regular than typical business-to-consumer transactions and, therefore, can be more cost-effectively automated.

6.1.3 Market Size

There are many ways to measure the network market (Exhibit 6.2).

Exhibit 6.2 **Various Network Market Size Measures**

Measure	Definition
User	Individual Internet user who may or may not be using a paid subscription; access over last week or month usually counts as usage.
Remote User	A user only having access to employing firm's resources (e.g. a teleworker); not directly connected to the Internet.
Subscriber	An individual or organisation that has paid for its own Internet access subscription. May support multiple users and have more than one subscription.
Host	A computer connected to the Internet; may provide access to the Internet for 1 or 100 users.
Port	Point at which a subscriber line (e.g. PSTN modem line or leased line) accesses the Internet via its service provider.
Seat	Individual corporate user license; may be used by more than one user.
Household	Household with Internet access; may have more than one subscription and may support multiple users.

Source: EITO; Gemini Strategic Research Group.

The most common of these measures is the "user." Although the definition of "user" varies, most market analyses describe a "user" as anyone who has used the Internet in the previous week or month. For example, the surveys conducted by Nielsen Media Research and CommerceNet in the US define "Internet users" as any person who has used any part of the Internet — e-mail, the Web, FTP, telnet, chat rooms or discussion groups — during the past month and still has access to it at the time of the survey interview.[9]

An estimate of the number of users in the world (generally, the number of people who say that they have used the Internet in the last month) compiled from multiple sources, is about 120 million individuals. The vast majority of users (approximately 114 million) were located in the major industrial nations. Of these, about 22 million (6 percent) are located in the fifteen EU member states (Exhibit 6.3).

6.1.4 Online Sales and Economic Impact

Another difficulty measuring the size of the network market is in defining network commerce. However, there are many additional definitions of "network commerce," electronic commerce," e-commerce," "e-business," and so forth, many of which encompass smaller or larger portions of the market. For example, does "network commerce" include electronic data interchange (EDI) transactions or not?

Overall Network Commerce Measures

Overall network commerce market estimates and forecasts vary widely (Exhibit 6.4).

Exhibit 6.3 **Estimated Internet Users and Penetration for OECD Nations, Early 1998**

Country	Internet Users	Internet Users as % of Population
Australia	3,000,000	16.3
Austria	500,000	6.2
Belgium	478,000	4.7
Canada	8,900,000	29.1
Czech Republic	200,000	1.9
Denmark	600,000	11.4
Finland	1,040,000	20.3
France	1,300,000	2.2
Germany	5,800,000	7.1
Greece	100,000	1.0
Hungary	100,000	1.0
Iceland	121,630	45.0
Ireland	150,000	4.2
Italy	700,000	1.2
Japan	12,100,000	9.6
Korea	700,000	1.6
Luxembourg	29,547	7.1
Mexico	370,000	0.4
The Netherlands	1,500,000	9.6
New Zealand	560,000	15.4
Norway	1,400,000	31.9
Poland	700,000	1.8
Portugal	1,080,000	10.9
Spain	1,340,000	3.4
Sweden	1,900,000	21.5
Switzerland	500,000	7.1
Turkey	600,000	0.9
UK	6,000,000	10.2
US	62,000,000	23.2
Total OECD	113,769,177	11.1
EU15	22,517,547	6.0
EEA	24,039,177	6.3

Source: NUA; National Statistics Agencies; Gemini Strategic Research Group Analysis.

Exhibit 6.4 **Comparison of Selected Network Commerce Market Estimates and Forecasts, In Euro**

Source	Today	Year	Future	Year
IDC	7,054,424,888	1997	293,640,435,963	2002
VSAComm	42,326,549	1994	3,086,310,889	2000
Verifone	308,631,089	1995	57,317,202,215	2000
ActivMedia	66,135,233,325	1998	1,058,163,733,202	2002
Killen & Associates	--		683,397,411,026	2000
Yankee Group	749,532,644	1996	126,979,647,984	2000
Jupiter	39,681,140	1995	511,445,804	2000
e-land	396,811,400	1995	8,818,031,110	2000
EU	--		201,051,109,308	2000
US	176,360,62	1995	--	
EITO	320,094,529	1995	176,360,622,200	2000
AEA/AU	176,360,622	1995	47,617,367,944	2000
Hambrecht & Quist	1,031,709,640	1995	20,457,832,175	2000
Forrester	456,744,011	1995	5,801,382,667	1999
Price Waterhouse	--		382,702,550,175	2002
Stephens Inc.	6,437,162,710	1997	3,042,220,732,955	2005
Nicholas Negroponte			881,803,111,001	2000

Source: OECD; Gemini Strategic Research Group.

Actual 1997 network-based sales figures for individual firms suggest that many of these estimates undercount the true volume of network commerce. There are at least four firms that recorded 850 million euro or more in direct purchases (purchases which were actually completed via the Internet without the customer having to use an alternative means of placing an order) over the Internet in 1997: Cisco Systems (3.53 billion euro); Dell Computer (882 million euro); netMarket (1.06 billion euro); and General Electric (882 million euro). Several other firms reported sales worth billions that were facilitated by the Web in some way, although the transactions were not directly executed on the Web. For example, eSchwab, handled transactions of 23.8 billion euro; Auto-by-Tel claims to have initiated at least 1.76 billion euro in automobile sales; and several other firms reported sales of greater than 44 million euro.

Most network commerce forecasts suggest that in the first years of the next century, global network commerce volume will reach into the tens of billions of euro. Some prognosticators suggest that it will exceed 882 billion euro, with the largest estimate suggesting a total of more than 3 trillion euro in online activity by 2005. Measured against a current GDP among the OECD nations that reaches about 22 trillion euro, the 3 trillion euro forecast, if it is reached, will be significant.

Most of the estimates reviewed here measure US network commerce activity, although some are purposefully vague about whether they are measuring the US market or the global market. Some forecasts specifically for Europe do exist. International Data Corporation, for example, estimates that Europeans spent about 882 million euro online in 1997 and that they will spend more that 26 billion euro online in 2001, with Germany being the main engine of growth.[10]

Business-to-Consumer

Not surprisingly, business-to-consumer forecasts vary dramatically in magnitude as well (Exhibit 6.5).

Exhibit 6.5 **Comparison of Selected Business-to-Consumer Network Commerce Market Estimates and Forecasts, In Euro**

Activity	Today	Year	Future	Year	Source	Date of Estimate
General	1,637,634,349	1997	22,926,880,886	2002	eMarketer	1998
Apparel	40,562,943	1995	283,940,602	1999	Forrester	
Apparel & Footwear	81,125,886	1997	453,246,799	2001	Forrester	1998
Gifts/Flower	39,681,140	1995	580,266,447	1999	Forrester	
Books	14,108,850	1996	352,721,244	1998	Amazon.com	1998
Books	190,469,472	1998	1,939,966,844	2002	Jupiter Communications	1998
Food and Beverages	34,390,321	1995	405,629,431	2001	Forrester	1998
Clothing	78,480,477	1996	283,940,602	2000	Forrester	
Other	32,626,715	1995	290,113,224	1999	Forrester	
Miscellaneous Merchandise	306,867,483	1996	--		European Commission	1997
Entertainment	74,953,264	1995	1,102,253,889	1999	Forrester	
Entertainment	262,777,327	1997	2,380,868,400	2001	Forrester	1998
Subscription Services	105,816,373	1996	851,821,805	2000	Jupiter Communications	
Pornography	45,853,762	1995	--		Forrester	
Music	7,936,228	1997	164,015,379	2000	Jupiter Communications	
Images	3,527,212	1997	--		Photodisc	1997
Tickets to Events	70,544,249	1998	--		Ticketmaster Online	1998
Tickets to Events	69,662,446	1997	1,763,606,222	2001	Forrester	1998
News	5,290,819	1996	--		Individual, Inc.	1997
Online Games	111,988,995	1997	893,266,551	2000	Forrester	
Online Gambling	5,290,819	1995	--		Sports International	
Online Gambling	141,088,498	1996	7,583,506,755	2000	Christiansen Cummings & Assoc.	1997
Consumer Finance	59,962,612	1997	--		E*Trade	1997
Financial Services	1,058,163,733	1997	4,409,015,555	2001	Forrester	1998
Consumer Insurance	34,390,321	1997	978,801,453	2001	Forrester	
Books and Music	137,561,285	1997	969,983,422	2001	Forrester	1998
Total Business-to-Consumer	4,409,015,555	1997	82,889,492,434	2002	Price Waterhouse	1998
Total Business-to-Consumer	2,116,327,466	1997	22,045,077,780	2002	Forrester	1998

Source: OECD; Gemini Strategic Research Group.

Most forecasters recognise that certain categories of goods and services, such as computer-related products, books, music, banking services, brokerage services, and travel are being affected more significantly by network commerce than others. Forrester Research has developed one of the more comprehensive sets of forecasts for business-to-consumer network commerce revenues, although its forecasts are only for North America (Exhibit 6.6). These forecasts suggest that the largest growth area for this category of network commerce is in travel, with online revenues for travel services forecast to reach nearly 6.6 billion euro by 2001.

A study by the University of Michigan Business School found that the leading category of goods purchased online was computer software (16 percent), followed closely by books (14 percent), computer hardware (13 percent), and music (11 percent).[11] In a recent Yankelovich Partners poll of Americans using the Internet, between 65 and 75 percent who had not yet purchased anything online said that they would consider using it to make hotel reservations, pay for online subscriptions, buy computer software, buy airline tickets, or buy music and videos.[12]

Exhibit 6.6 **Consumer Online Shopping Revenues by Product or Service, 1997 and 2001E, Euro in Millions**

Category	1997	% of Total	2001E	% of Total	CAGR
PC Hardware	979	35%	4,282	22%	45%
Travel	742	27%	8,441	43%	84%
Entertainment[a]	338	12%	3,037	15%	73%
Books & Music	177	6%	1,229	6%	62%
Gifts, Flowers & Greetings	169	6%	910	5%	52%
Apparel & Footwear	104	4%	583	3%	54%
Food & Beverages	102	4%	525	3%	51%
Jewellery	43	2%	159	1%	39%
Sporting Goods	23	1%	95	<1%	43%
Consumer Electronics	22	1%	162	1%	66%
Other	74	3%	306	2%	43%
TOTAL	2,773	100%	19,729	100%	63%

Source: Forrester Research.

a. Includes adult entertainment.

Business-to-Business

The business-to-business market is generally forecast to be significantly larger than the business-to-consumer market, as in the forecast in Exhibit 6.7.

Exhibit 6.7 **US Internet Commerce, 1997-2002F, Euro in Millions**

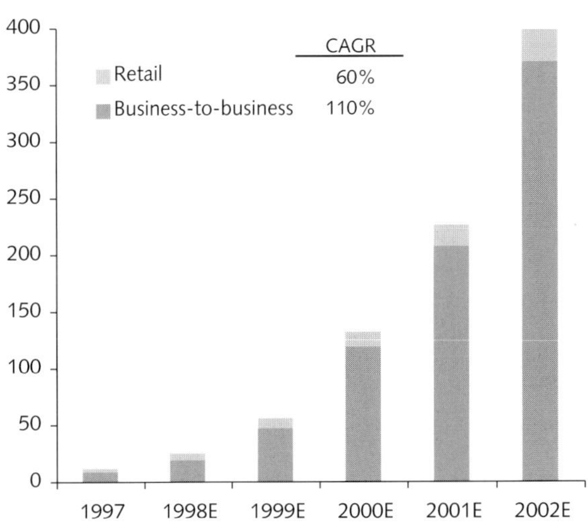

Source: Forrester Research.

However, we again encounter a significant variation in forecasts (Exhibit 6.8).

Exhibit 6.8 **Comparison of Selected Business-to-Business Network Commerce Estimates and Forecasts, In Euro**

Activity	Today	Year	Future	Year	Source	Date of Estimate
General Electric Purchasing	881,803,111	1997	4,409,015,555	2000	General Electric	1998
Cisco Systems Sales	3,527,212,444	1998	--		Cisco Systems	1998
Dell Computer Sales	1,763,606,222	1998	--		Dell Computer	1998
Automobiles	6,172,621,777		--		OECD "Sacher Report"	
Computers	10,581,637	1995	--		NECX Direct	1997
Computers	264,540,933	1997	--		Dell Computer	1997
Computers	284,822,405	1996	1,856,195,549	2000	Forrester Research	
Software	186,942,260	1996	3,084,547,282	1998	Soft*Letter	1997
Software	220,450,778	1996	4,056,294,311	2000	IDC	
PC Hardware and Software	760,996,085	1997	3,350,851,822	2001	Forrester Research	1998
Travel	243,377,659	1996	3,968,114,000	2000	Jupiter	
Travel	576,699,235	1997	6,525,343,021	2001	Forrester Research	1998
Airline Ticket Sales	705,442,489	1998	7,848,047,688	2002	Jupiter Communications	1998
Transportation	--		264,540,933	2001	Forrester Research/Business Week	1998
Wholesaling	--		78,480,476,879	2001	Forrester Research/Business Week	1998
Durable Goods	--		87,298,507,989	2002	Forrester Research/Business Week	1998
Professional Services	--		16,754,259,109	2002	Forrester Research/Business Week	1998
Total Business-to-Business	--		299,813,057,740	2002	Price Waterhouse	1998
Total Business-to-Business	--		617,262,177,701	2000	Nicholas Negroponte (MIT Media Lab)	1998
Total Business-to-Business	--		236,323,233,748	2002	eMarketer	1998
Total Business-to-Business	7,054,424,888	1997	288,349,617,297	2002	Forrester Research	1998

Source: OECD; Gemini Strategic Research Group.

As the forecasts reviewed here suggest, no one yet has a clear picture of the actual size and speed of the development of network commerce. We are still at an early stage in the development of this new economy, in which firms and analysts are struggling to develop the methods required to more accurately measure and forecast network market trends.

6.1.5 Gemini Forecasts

The evolution of network commerce in some countries has now reached a point where we can reach some reasonable assumptions about how network commerce is likely to evolve in those European nations where it is not yet well established. Based on current growth rates and the observed growth rates in nations like Norway, Canada, and the US, we can project potential growth for network usage and network commerce activity across Europe. As a result, we have developed a fairly conservative estimate of network usage in the EU but a more aggressive forecast of network commerce activity (Exhibit 6.9).

Exhibit 6.9 **Gemini Estimates of Network Population and Market Impact, 1995 – 2002E**

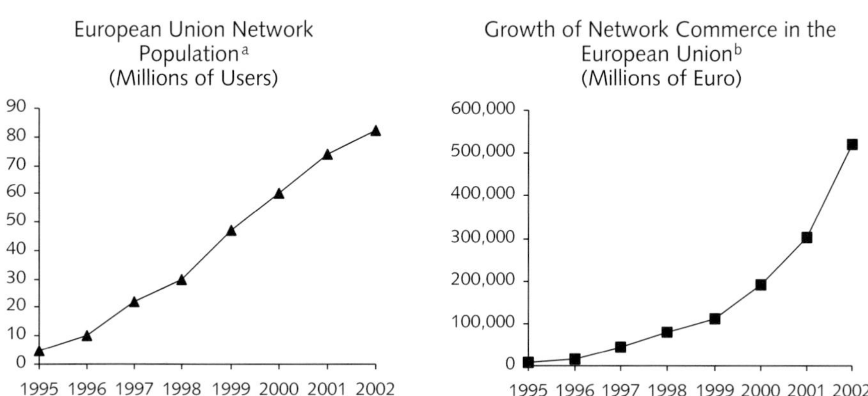

Note: Gemini Strategic Research Group Estimates.

a. Estimated growth of Internet users in EU15 nations based on observed growth rates in individual nations and historic growth rates in advanced markets.

b. Includes direct network-based transactions in all categories of goods and services (business-to-consumer and business-to-business) and transactions consummated offline but directly affected by use of the network (e.g. offline automobile purchase facilitated by Web-based research).

These forecasts reflect our belief that network usage will take off relatively slowly in many EU markets due to a relatively low penetration of PCs, the lack of local content, and the high cost of telecommunications. All of these factors will improve significantly by 2002, but they will not be sufficiently overcome to rapidly make up for the low starting point in some of Europe's more populous nations (e.g. France, Italy). The 82 million interactive network users in 2002 (individuals who use the network at least once per week) will represent about 20 percent of the EU's projected population. This is slightly less than the Internet user penetration in the US in early 1998, but a significant increase from the current 6 percent penetration rate in the EU. The aggressive network commerce growth projection suggesting an impact on EU commerce reaching 552 billion euro — approximately 5 percent of projected EU GDP — reflects both a broad definition of network commerce and a belief that relatively high-value business-to-business network commerce will gain a significant foothold in Europe by 2002.

6.2 Understanding Consumption Behaviour

The reason why network commerce takes off in some markets and not in others is deceptively simple: for network commerce to succeed, the expected utility — the perceived subjective value — of the network option must be significantly greater than the expected utility of the traditional option. An individual user's expectation of the utility of network commerce is affected by a wide range of factors. We will examine factors shaping consumer and business network consumption separately, but we will begin with a critical factor shaping both: telecommunications costs.

6.2.1 Telecommunications Costs

One of the most critical factors shaping the ability of network technologies to address end-user needs is the cost of telecommunications. This issue provides context for both the discussion of consumer and business adoption of network commerce, and neither market can be considered in isolation from this issue. The cost of telecommunications services and equipment is a fundamental determinant of the speed and breadth of the development of the market for network commerce.

Telecommunications access prices and Internet penetration can be correlated (Exhibit 6.10).

Exhibit 6.10 **Comparison of Internet Penetration and Access Costs, Selected OECD Nations[a]**

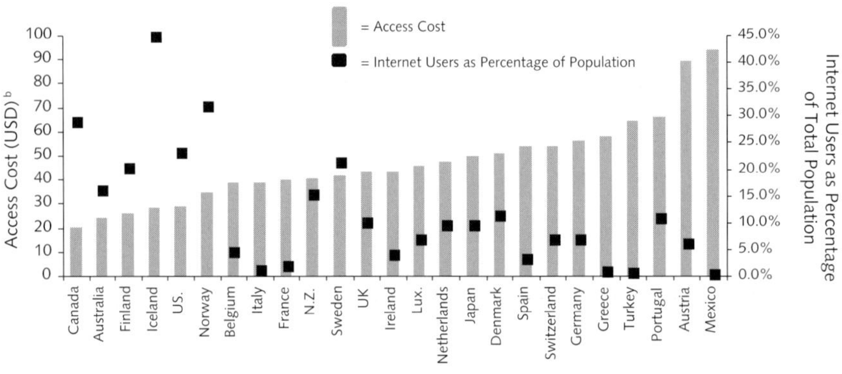

Source: NUA; OECD; Gemini Strategic Research Group Analysis.

a. Internet user and penetration data for first quarter 1998.

b. Internet and PSTN tariffs for off-peak usage from August 1996, based on twenty hours per month of usage.

In most of the major developed nations the correlation is strong. Some of the exceptions can be explained by special circumstances, such as the substantial installed base of Minitel terminals in France. Lower telecommunications costs resulting from telecommunications competition in the EU are likely to have a significant positive impact on the growth of network commerce activity in the EU.

The role of network access costs in the consumer market is apparent in AOL's decision to switch from metered charges to a flat-rate pricing policy. In response, many more subscribers joined the service and increased their time online. AOL's flat rate, combined with flat local telephone rates in the US, allows many users stay online indefinitely without incurring additional costs. Consequently, AOL is able to charge more for advertising; chat and discussion groups have become more populated, and therefore more valuable; and many new products and services have been added to support the growing market. AOL's value rose for subscribers, merchants, and advertisers, alike.

Telecommunications costs pose a significant problem for business-to-business network commerce development as well. For example, the cost of a 300-kilometer two-megabit circuit in the US is around 1,570 euro; in Europe, an equivalent leased line (between Italy and Switzerland, for example) would cost 25,572 euro.[13] Paul Offen, President of the UK-based Society of Information Technology Management, says, "Figures show that in many cases European prices are ten times more than they are in the United States — after discounts have been applied — for commercial users."[14] Phil Sayer, global communications manager for Reuters, worries that these high prices are a significant hindrance to European businesses adopting network commerce. "It's cheaper to host websites [sic] in the US, so that's where all the business is going," he says.[15]

6.2.2 Consumer Market

The consumer market consists of all the individuals and households that purchase goods and services for personal consumption. In 1996, the EU consumer market consisted of 372 million people in an economy with a gross domestic product of 6.8 trillion euro.

European consumers vary greatly in age, income, language, educational level, mobility, and taste. As we seek to understand the evolution of the network economy across Europe, it is useful to study these consumers in segments.[16]

Cultural Factors

Factors such as culture, subculture, and social class shape consumer attitudes toward and adoption of network commerce. When examining culture, we consider an individual's values, perceptions, preferences, and behaviours. These cultural characteristics are developed through socialisation within the familiar and institutional groups, such as schools and religious denominations. North Atlantic democracies share common characteristics that might allow them to be categorised as "modern technologically advanced societies."

While a number of cultural factors influence consumer-market receptiveness to technology and network commerce. Nationality and language appear to be the largest determinants. Content and commerce services available in the language

of a particular market will drive rates of adoption.

Among Internet users in the major developed nations, English speakers predominate (Figure 6.11).

Exhibit 6.11 **Distribution of Global Internet Users by Language, OECD Nations, First Quarter 1998**

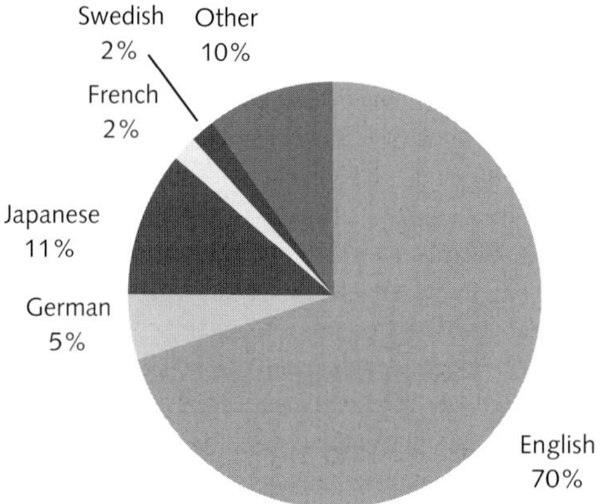

Source: NUA; OECD; Gemini Strategic Research Group.

However, speakers with a first language other than English are the fastest growing group of new Internet users (Exhibit 6.12), a fact that could profoundly affect the Internet's use and development.

Exhibit 6.12 **First Language of Non-English-Speaking Internet Users, 1998**

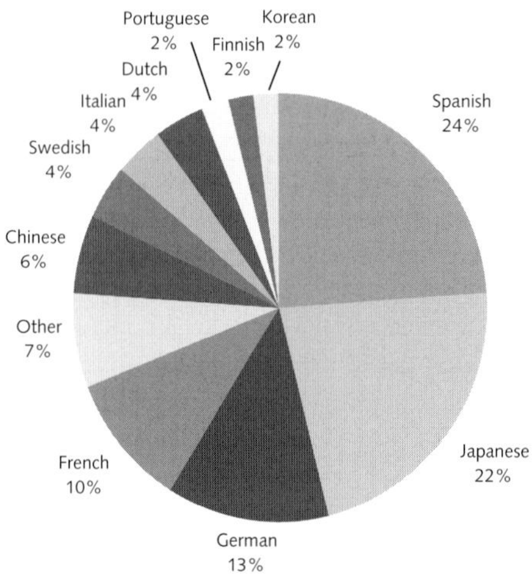

Source: Euro-Marketing Association.

Major Internet portals such as Yahoo! and Excite have already begun offering services in multiple languages. Netscape Communications has partnered with Star Media Network, a Latin American Internet service provider, to develop portals in Spanish and Portuguese.

In the EU, the number of people who report that they have mastered English sufficiently to take part in a conversation far exceeds the number of Europeans who have mastered other languages. However, there are more than 100 million Europeans who can communicate in German and French, suggesting that there will be significant market opportunities for services in these languages (Exhibit 6.13).

Exhibit 6.13 **Estimated Number of Europeans in Each EU Nation Who Have Mastered Major European Languages Sufficiently to Take Part in a Conversation, 1995[a]**

Country	Italian	Spanish	Swedish	German	English	French
Austria	482,820	160,940	--	7,805,590	3,862,560	724,230
Belgium	506,850	304,110	--	912,330	3,345,210	3,852,060
Denmark	52,280	104,560	1,097,880	2,666,280	3,973,280	522,800
Finland	51,080	102,160	1,838,880	868,360	2,605,080	153,240
France	2,907,050	5,814,100	--	4,651,280	20,349,350	55,233,950
Germany	2,449,860	2,449,860	--	78,395,520	36,747,900	9,799,440
Greece	313,770	--	--	627,540	3,451,470	418,360
Ireland	35,800	71,600	--	214,800	3,401,000	572,800
Italy	56,710,170	1,145,660	--	1,718,490	16,612,070	13,175,090
Luxembourg	45,430	8,260	--	318,010	189,980	355,180
The Netherlands	309,140	772,850	154,570	10,201,620	12,211,030	3,555,110
Portugal	198,420	496,050	--	99,210	2,182,620	2,182,620
Spain	392,100	38,033,700	--	392,100	7,449,900	3,528,900
Sweden	176,540	264,810	8,650,460	2,118,480	6,355,400	617,890
UK	1,172,260	1,758,390	--	5,861,300	56,268,480	14,653,250
EU15	65,803,570	51,487,050	11,741,790	116,850,910	179,005,370	109,344,920

Source: Eurobarometer.

a. Includes individuals who reported that they could converse in more than one language.

A recent OECD study found that, world-wide, English-speaking countries make the best use of high technology because they focus on using it rather than developing it. Historically, these nations have integrated their economies more fully with the US economy, consequently creating environments in which technology has been more effectively implemented.[17]

The EU's multicultural and multilingual environment affects the evolution of network economy in Europe positively and negatively. By fragmenting markets and making it difficult for European firms to build scale and momentum, such an environment hurts the development of these new businesses and their ability to compete. However, in many markets such an environment provides protection from global media players giving local players time to develop their own service offerings in advance of entry by the global media firms.

The European market's fragmented nature has and will continue to hurt the evolution of the new media markets. However, we already see the emergence, primarily in the search engine and directory segments, of a business model that may address some of this fragmentation. Fragmentation has also affected

European capital markets, with venture capital and investment largely being fragmented by national boundaries.

Diversity may make it harder for large multinational firms to compete effectively in individual markets, because the cost of developing localised offerings often is not justified by the size of the potential market. Just as local newspapers and radio programs have continued to withstand the onslaught of new media, local content players may be able to compete effectively in these markets. Many of the major global players are building localised offerings such as AOL's Digital City and Microsoft's SideWalk. Current activity suggests that the key to competing effectively will be to customise for these markets.

Yahoo! now operates fourteen localised services, eleven of them in languages other than English. Yahoo! offers sites in Spanish with variations in dialect and vocabulary targeted at twenty Spanish-speaking countries. Yahoo! also operates a Chinese-language Web site and sites dedicated to the United Kingdom and Ireland, France, Germany, Norway, Denmark, Italy, Canada, Australia and New Zealand, Korea, Japan, and the rest of Asia.[18] In the longer run, machine translation services, such as that already offered on the Internet as part of Compaq's AltaVista service, also hold intriguing possibilities as they improve in capability.

The network economy creates new global opportunities for European businesses. While there were about 8.1 million Spanish-speaking Internet users in 1997, the number is expected to rise to more than 37 million by 2000, with most located in Latin America.[19] The number of Internet users in English-speaking countries is over 20 million more than the entire UK population, and the number of Portuguese-speaking Internet users will likely outnumber the Portugal's population by 2000, with the vast majority of those users located in Brazil. Global online communities sharing common languages create opportunities, especially for content businesses, in any of the countries where the language is spoken.

Social Factors

Social factors, such as reference groups, family, and status, also play an important but nebulous role in shaping the adoption of network commerce and its usage by particular individuals. Of these factors, social status probably plays the most significant role in the development of network commerce. In the US, for example, the use of technology, especially computers and the Internet, is becoming a status symbol, with executives growing used to using their computers for e-mail and other activities. In fact, Microsoft estimates that more than 90 percent of white-collar workers in the US now use PCs.[20] In many European nations, these keyboard-based activities have traditionally been considered lower status and assigned to administrative employees. Only about 56 percent of white-collar workers in Europe use PCs.[21] Clothing and objects emblazoned with URLs have also become status symbols in the US.

Personal Factors

A consumer's behaviour is also significantly influenced by his or her personal characteristics, notably age and life cycle stage, gender, occupation, education, economic circumstances, lifestyle, personality, and self-concept. We believe that age, gender, and education are the most significant of these personal factors effecting the adoption of network commerce.

Age. Over the longer term, the demand for network commerce and content will be significantly affected by changes in the relative growth of different age cohorts. The most important broad, age-related demographic shifts in the EU during the next decade are likely to include a projected shrinkage in the number of eighteen– to thirty-four–year-olds, a projected rapid growth in the number of forty-five– to sixty-four–year-olds, and a significant expansion of the population over age sixty-five.[22]

These general demographic trends vary significantly across EU nations. Ireland, with the fastest growing economy in the EU during the mid- to late-1990s, also has the youngest population. Germany, the most populous nation and the nation with the largest economy, has the oldest population. The age of the German population may prove to be a significant constraint to the growth of a broad-based consumer network commerce economy in Germany.

The median age of adult US Internet users has edged upward from around thirty-two in 1996 to about thirty-eight today.[23] From a generational perspective, the core of the "baby boom" generation (aged thirty-five to fifty-four) account for about 54 percent of all users, while the so-called "Generation-X" group (aged eighteen to thirty-four) make up 35 percent of the total and the over–fifty-five group account for the rest.[24] Among these users, those in older generations are more likely to make purchases on the Internet. A study by Georgia Tech's Graphics Visualization and Usability Centre, found that 42 percent of Internet users sixty-five and older have used the Internet to purchase something and 39 percent of those aged fifty to sixty-four have done so. Many of these older users report that they use the Internet most often for managing or tracking their investments.[25]

In general, the European population is older than the population of the US and of the more dynamic Asian and Latin American economies. These demographics may be a significant disadvantage to European nations as much of the growth of consumer network commerce will likely be driven by youth and young adults who have grown up with and are comfortable with the new technology. In the US in particular, there is a significant cohort of young people (approximately 90 million individuals aged two to twenty-two in 1999), an "echo" of the Baby Boom generation, that have grown up with computers and are already comfortable with the technology. A survey of US teenagers (aged twelve to nineteen) by Simmons, a New York market research firm, found that nearly 65 percent had used or subscribed to online services over the previous twelve months.[26] Market researcher eStats predicts that the number of US children online will grow from about 6 million in 1997 to 38 million by 2002.[27]

Gender. The Internet was once a predominantly male world, but this is changing. Today in the US, women represent between 40 and 45 percent of online users. Various studies suggest that by the turn of the century the percentage of men and women on the Internet will be about equal. Some studies suggest that women will outnumber men and that they will make up a significantly larger share of the consumer market. For example, NetSmart-Research, predicts that women will make up 60 percent of the online population by 2005, and that they are already using it as a tool to find things more quickly and complete common tasks more effectively.[28] At the same time, the study suggests that male users are increasingly using the Internet as a toy. Over 70 percent of women deal with the financial side of running a household, and they are increasingly using the Internet to complete these tasks more effectively. This study suggests that relationships and interactivity are crucial to attracting women to spend online.[29]

Today, however, the typical online shopper remains an affluent male, who tends to spend substantially more money online than his female counterpart. For example, the research firm Binary Compass found that the typical online purchaser in mid-1997 was male (79 percent), affluent (66,000 euro average income), and spent an average of 155 euro per purchase, compared to the average female purchaser (only 21 percent of online purchasers), who earned about 53,000 euro and spent only an average of 82 euro per purchase.[30]

Education. The role of educational institutions in the development of networked commerce in the developed world is closely tied to the role age demographics. Several OECD countries[31] have launched initiatives to ensure that every school or even every classroom will have Internet access within the next five or fewer years. In addition, universities and other institutions of higher education have and continue to play a critical role in socialising new generations of users to the use of the Internet. Those nations with large youth populations will inevitably find that they have much larger populations of active Internet users within the next few years.

In the US and Canada, the percentage of students in higher education significantly surpasses the number of students in higher education in the EU (Exhibit 6.14).

In fact, the number of students in higher education in the US is greater than the number in the much larger EU. The availability of free Internet access to millions of US and Canadian students has already created a generation of young, dynamic consumers, socialised to the use of the Internet for communications, entertainment, work, and shopping. The much smaller percentage of the European population exposed to the Internet through higher education could be a disadvantage in the evolution of network commerce across Europe.

Psychological Factors

Consumer buying behaviour is also influenced by such psychological factors as motivation, perception, learning, and beliefs and attitudes. As with social factors, the impact of these psychological factors on the development of network commerce is significant but nebulous. It is hoped that as the network economy evolves and matures, businesses and researchers will invest in research to better understand the role of psychological factors in determining why and how individuals choose to use network technologies.

Exhibit 6.14 **Number of Students by Level of Education, EU and Selected OECD Nations, 1995**

Country	Total Students (1995)	Total Students (1995) as % of Population	Students in Higher Education (1995)	Students in Higher Education (1995) as a % of Population
Austria	1,402,000	17.4%	234,000	2.9%
Belgium	2,115,000	20.9%	353,000	3.5%
Canada	6,666,000	22.5%	1,784,000	6.0%
Denmark	943,000	18.0%	170,000	3.3%
Finland	1,047,000	20.5%	205,000	4.0%
France	12,148,000	20.9%	2,073,000	3.6%
Germany	14,035,000	17.2%	2,156,000	2.6%
Greece	1,850,000	17.7%	296,000	2.8%
Iceland	67,000	25.1%	7,000	2.6%
Ireland	897,000	25.1%	122,000	3.4%
Italy	9,098,000	15.9%	1,792,000	3.1%
Japan	22,408,000	17.9%	3,918,000	3.1%
Luxembourg	54,000	13.1%	2,000	0.5%
The Netherlands	3,201,000	20.7%	503,000	3.3%
Norway	858,000	19.7%	173,000	4.0%
Portugal	2,161,000	21.8%	301,000	3.0%
Spain	8,637,000	22.0%	1,527,000	3.9%
Sweden	1,698,000	19.2%	246,000	2.8%
Switzerland	1,172,000	16.6%	148,000	2.1%
UK	13,700,000	23.4%	1,813,000	3.1%
US	59,225,000	22.5%	14,279,000	5.4%
Total OECD	163,382,000	16.4%	32,102,000	3.2%
EU15	72,986,000	19.6%	11,793,000	3.2%
EEA	73,911,000	19.6%	11,973,000	3.2%

Source: Eurostat; OECD.

6.2.3 Business Market

The business market consists of all the individuals and organisations that acquire goods and services that enter into the production of other products or services that are sold, rented, or supplied to others. There are about 19 million business enterprises located in the nations of the European Economic Area (EU15 plus Norway, Iceland, and Liechtenstein) and Switzerland, employing about 115 million people.[32] This market is usually segmented into such major segments as agriculture, forestry, and fisheries; mining; manufacturing; construction; transportation; communications; public utilities; banking, finance, and insurance; and services. Most of these businesses are small, with 93 percent having fewer than nine employees and 99.8 percent being classified as small or medium-sized enterprises (SMEs) with fewer than 250 employees.[33] Overall sales to businesses are larger than sales to consumers. Each link in the chain of production to distribution must buy many other goods and services as well, and this explains why more business buying occurs than consumer buying and why this represents such a larger, fertile market for network commerce.

Key Differences between Business Markets and Consumer Markets

To appreciate the differences in the business-to-business and business-to-consumer markets and anticipate the relative impact of network commerce, it is worth examining the differences between these markets. There are several key characteristics that differentiate business markets from consumer markets:

Fewer and Larger Buyers. There are far fewer business buyers than there are consumers. In addition, many business markets are dominated by a few large firms, and a few large buyers account for most of the purchasing. In many industries, four or five top manufacturers account for 70 percent or more of total production.

Close Supplier-Customer Relationships. Because of the smaller customer base and the importance of the larger customers over the suppliers, a close relationship tends to exist between customers and sellers in the business market. Suppliers are often expected to customise their products to meet individual customer needs.

Geographically Concentrated Buyers. Many industries are concentrated in a limited number of geographic areas.

Derived Demand. The demand for business goods is ultimately derived from the demand for consumer goods. The business marketplace is intimately linked to the consumer marketplace.

Inelastic Demand. The total demand for many industrial goods and service is not much affected by price changes.

Fluctuating Demand. The demand for business goods and services tends to be more volatile than the demand for consumer goods and services.

Professional Purchasing with Several Buying Influences. Professionally trained purchasing agents typically purchase industrial goods. More people typically influence business buying decisions than consumer buying decisions.

Other Factors

A number of other factors influence business purchasing decisions. Each buying organisation has specific objectives, policies, procedures, organisational structure, and systems, all of which will impact the use of network commerce. A firm's purchasing function typically includes several participants with different statuses, authority, empathy, and persuasiveness. Group dynamics within the buyer are important. Each participant in the buying decision has personal motivations, perceptions, and preferences. When examining the individual factors in the business marketplace, one must essentially take into account the same factors one examines in the consumer marketplace, such as age, income, education, job position, personality, and the risk profile of each of the key participants in the buying process.

6.3 Market Diffusion and Critical Mass

Forecasters have long attempted to isolate the most critical of the characteristics discussed in the previous section to develop statistical techniques for projecting market development. In 1969, Frank M. Bass, known as the father of diffusion models, introduced a framework for evaluating new product sales over time using communication theory. He believed that the two factors most affecting consumer purchase were mass media and interpersonal networks. Bass hypothesised that mass media and interpersonal networks producing a life-cycle diffusion curve over time. Such a curve has an introductory phase characterised by slower sales, a growth phase reflecting the highest rate of end-user acceptance, and a maturity phase where the product reaches its saturation point.[34]

6.3.1 Diffusion Curves

There are now many product and service diffusion models; however, all diffusion models centre on the development of key diffusion characteristics. The first characteristic is the long-run saturation level. This is simply the maximum number of units a firm can sell of a product or the number of homes connected to a network at some distant point in the future. The second characteristic is the inflection point of the diffusion curve. This represents that time where sales will reach the maximum rate. The third characteristic is the delay factor — a more subjective value — which indicates the intensity of the introductory stage of the life-cycle.

Diffusion of new products leads to S-shaped curves. In the case of world adoption of colour TVs and video games, for example, it took three years before innovators (equivalent to a penetration of 2 percent to 3 percent of the population) started to adopt the product. It took another three years for early adopters (penetration of about 10 percent) to appear. After twelve years, the penetration rates began to plateau, signalling that those products were becoming mature. The adoption of VCRs took even longer (Exhibit 6.15).

Exhibit 6.15 **Household Diffusion of Selected Electronic Devices**

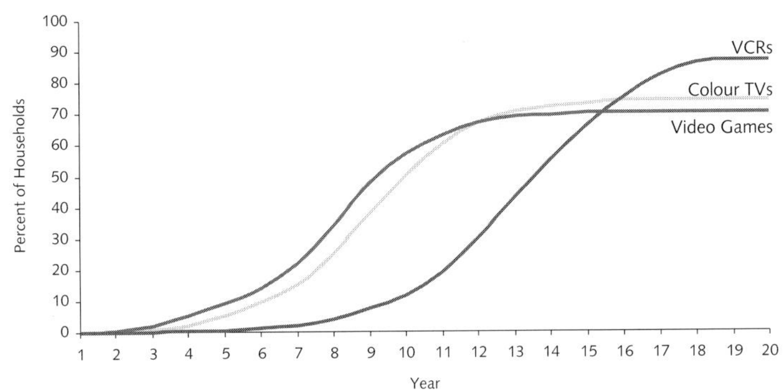

Source: Electronics Industry Association.

Diffusion models, such as the Bass Model, help to forecast this growth, attempting to predict how many customers will adopt and when they will adopt (Exhibit 6.16).

Exhibit 6.16 **Typical Bass Model Curves**

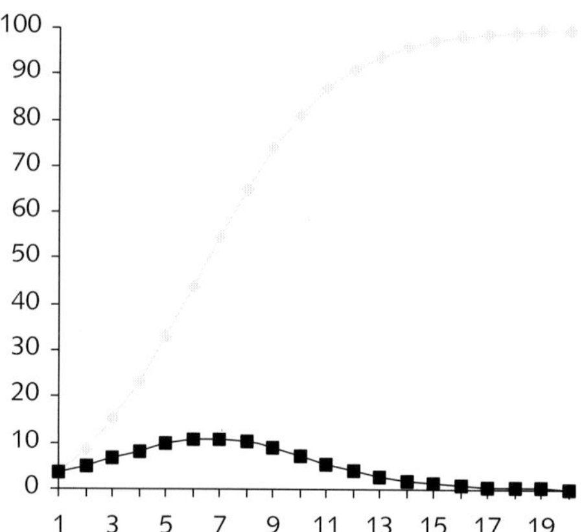

Source: Manoj K. Agarwal, "Forecasting Market Adoption Over Time," School of Management, Binghamton University, Binghamton, NY, November 1997.

The Bass Model is based on the hypothesis that a new product diffuses in a population due to the effect of innovators and imitators. The innovators tend to buy the product by themselves and are represented by an external influence parameter (p). This represents the influences on diffusion process other than the prior adopters. The internal influence parameter, q, represents the effects of word of mouth and interpersonal communications. Different values of p and q will represent various types of diffusion characteristics. Some products have low p values due to price and other characteristics. The q values also range from low to high. The combination provides different types of curves. Some products have a high initial take-up rate, while others may have a long, slow growth period.[35] A twenty-year snapshot of penetration levels for different technologies in US households provides a good illustration of the results of these factors (Exhibit 6.17).

In many markets, the Internet has exhibited a very rapid take-up rate. The key unanswered question in these markets is where the saturation point lies. The experience to date in Canada, Norway, and Iceland suggests that it is reasonable to expect mature markets to reach anywhere from 30 percent to 45 percent penetration. It is unclear however, especially considering the plateau of household PC penetration in markets like the US at around 45 percent, whether this represents the ultimate saturation point or whether penetration will reach 90 percent or greater as with the telephone and television in most developed nations. The answer to this question may ultimately depend on the ability of technology vendors to supply very cheap, easy-to-use access devices.

Exhibit 6.17 **Penetration of Communications Technologies in US Households, 1980 – 2000E**

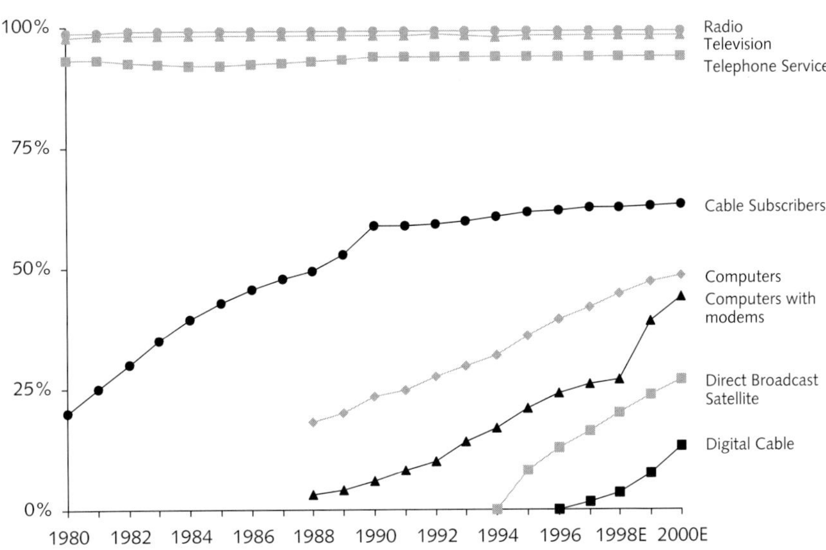

Source: Statistical Abstract of the US, Paul Kagan Associates, 1994 World Satellite Directory; Techno Trends; Veronis Suhler & Associates; Gemini Strategic Research Group.

6.3.2 Metcalfe's Law and Critical Mass

True network commerce only occurs when a significant portion of potential users perceives that a "critical mass" of valuable products and services has become accessible over a given network. The need for this critical mass creates a dilemma: potential users want products before investing in the service, but potential service providers need demand. Once critical mass is reached, adoption takes place through a viral uptake in commercial activity, rising along a steep growth curve. The rapid growth of network commerce has actually occurred in a series of markets "exploding" in succession: the first occurring in the North American and Nordic markets, followed by a number of markets in Europe, and more recently in Japan. These market explosions appear to bear out Metcalfe's Law (named after Robert Metcalfe, inventor of the Ethernet networking protocol and founder of 3Com Corporation), which holds that the utility of a network is equal to the square of its number of users (e.g. one computer connected to the network is useless; three connected computers start to be really useful; a million connected computers are far more valuable than the sum of the parts) (Exhibit 6.18). The differences in the timing of these explosions are attributable to several factors, two issues discussed above — the cost of network access and market fragmentation caused by language differences — being among the most important.

Exhibit 6.18 **Metcalfe's Law and the Succession of Market "Explosions"**

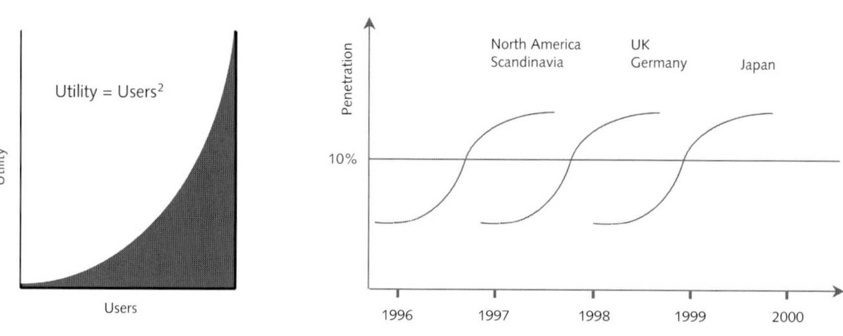

Source: Adapted from Mui & Downes, *Unleashing the Killer App,* 1998, and Jupiter Communications.

The Internet is the ultimate generator of network effects, since it, by definition, enables the interconnection of disparate networks and devices. As such, the Internet has emerged as the most rapidly adapted technology in history. Radio existed for thirty-eight years before it reached a penetration of 50 million listeners; television took thirteen years before it reached 50 million viewers. It was not until sixteen years after the introduction of the Altair PC kit that 50 million people were using personal computers. In contrast to these other successful technologies, the Internet required only four years after it was opened to the general public to reach 50 million users.

6.4 Impact on Traditional Media and Other Consumer Activities

Time is a limited resource. In an economy of plenty it may become the most valuable resource. To some extent, the growth of time devoted to one activity decreases the amount of time available to devote to other activities. Thus, Internet usage have begun to cut into time spent using traditional media such as television and newspapers (Exhibit 6.19).

Recent studies in the US by the Pew Research Centre for the People and the Press and Paragon Research suggest that the use of the Internet is beginning to have impact on newspaper readership.[36] The Pew study found that 36 million Americans now get some new from the Internet during a typical week, up from 11 million in 1996. Paragon Research's survey conducted in May 1998, found that 16 percent of US households regularly access the Internet to read a newspaper site, a figure which holds fairly constant among subscribers, sing-copy purchasers, and individuals who typically don't subscribe to or purchase single copies. Thirteen percent of the households that do not receive home delivery but do access Internet newspapers report that they have dropped their subscriptions because of the ability to access newspapers on the Internet. Another 11 percent of current home delivery subscribers who access the news on the Internet report that they plan to drop their subscriptions. However, 53 percent of those who receive subscriptions and read newspapers online reported that they are not at all likely to cancel delivery of the newspaper, and 56 percent of those who read newspapers on the Web read one other than the one that they purchase in hard copy form. In effect, the Web may actually be allowing individuals to access a wider range of news more conveniently and inexpensively than they could previously have done.

Exhibit 6.19 **Impact of Internet Usage on Consumer Media Usage, 1997, Percent of Respondents Citing an Increase or Decrease in Usage of Other Media Due to Using the Internet**

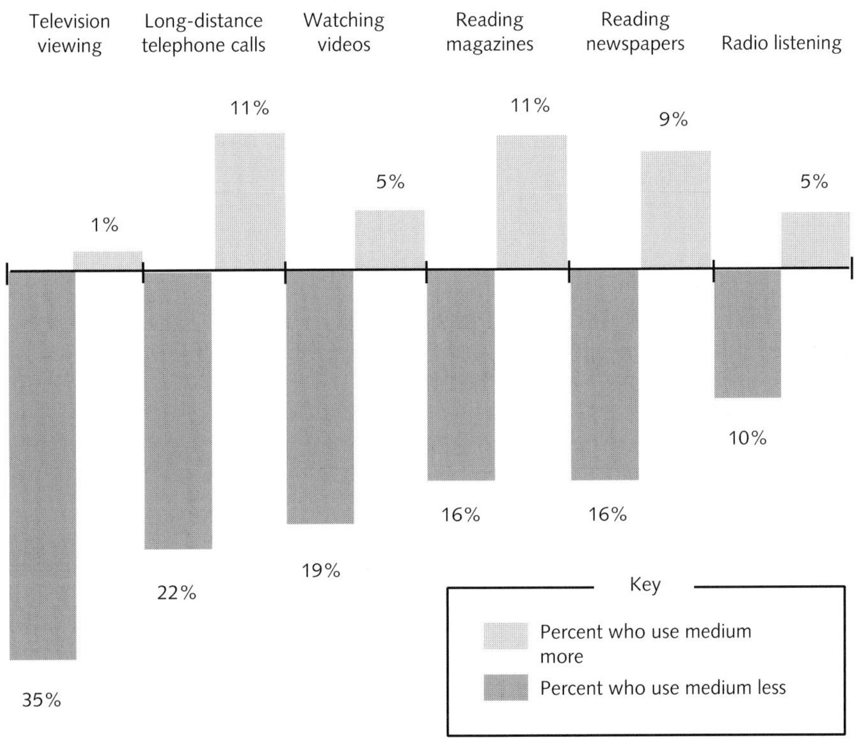

Source: Find/SVP, American Internet User Survey, 1997.

One specific form of traditional media whose readers are migrating to the Internet is the computer media. A recent study by Intelliquest found that 11 percent of computer-related magazine readers now read these magazines less because they can obtain the same information on the Internet.[37]

Other studies have suggested more ambiguous effects. For example, an Arbitron NewMedia study found that the heaviest Internet users have somewhat higher television viewing habits than light Internet users. In addition, these increases in Internet usage were associated with increases in the perceived importance of television. Some studies have also shown that Internet users tend to read more magazines and newspapers than their non-Internet counterparts. Part of the reason for these findings may be that Internet users tend to be more educated and earn a higher income than the general population and that many of them are "media junkies." For this population, the Internet tends to augment, rather than detract from, traditional media usage.[38]

In addition to the variations noted above, the impact of Internet usage on people's time budgets is actually quite complex. While cutting into time spent using some traditional media, the Internet also can also significantly reduce the amount of time that end users must expend completing some tasks. By giving end users ready access to significant amounts of information and a wide range of services aimed at addressing needs, the Internet empowers end users and potentially reduces the time that they must expend completing many purchasing tasks. In addition, network commerce allows people to significantly shift the time in which they do things. For example, a person can order concert tickets or conduct banking transactions over the network seven days per week, twenty-four hours per day.

6.5 Scenario Planning and System Dynamics

Most observers now agree that the potential impact of network commerce on individuals, businesses, nations, and society in general is huge. Five years ago, few predicted the dramatic rise of the Internet. As we have seen, today there are dozens of forecasts of Internet growth and network commerce growth in aggregate and across a wide range of industries and markets, and most of them are based on limited data. Developing intuition about the dimensions of the potential changes and an ability to spot key trends early enough to shape them, respond to them, and take advantage of them, will be a critical challenge. Two useful tools for doing this are scenario planning and system dynamics modelling.

Scenario planning is a powerful business tool, allowing businesses to plan and manage effectively in uncertain environments. Traditional forecasting assumes that it is possible and useful to predict the future. Scenario planning, on the other hand, assumes that the future cannot be predicted and therefore irreducible uncertainty must not be ignored or glossed over. Making predictions where there is fundamental uncertainty can be a dangerous process that takes away from the decision maker the insights needed to come to a responsible conclusion.

Scenario planning concentrates on developing processes that enhance the capability of the organisation to mobilise the resources available towards greater inventiveness and innovation. Decisions are never based on one scenario being more likely than others; planners optimise their plans so that they will achieve desirable outcomes across a wide range of plausible futures. The first objective of scenario planning becomes the generation of projects and decisions that are more robust under a variety of alternative futures. Aided by scenarios, managers learn to recognise patterns of events that point towards specific outcomes and can respond more effectively. Without scenario planning, those same managers would never recognise the significance of certain patterns of events. According to one of the world's leading scenario planners,

Kees van der Heijden, "The ultimate purpose of the scenario planner is to create a more adaptive organisation which recognises change and uncertainty, and uses it to its advantage."[39]

Another useful tool is system dynamics modelling. System dynamics is a theory of the structure and behaviour of complex systems. System dynamics was developed in the late 1950 by Jay W. Forrester at the Alfred P. Sloan School of Management at the Massachusetts Institute of Technology.[40] Forrester recognised that the open-loop approach to the modelling decision making neglected the effect of decisions upon themselves. Forrester proposed a closed-loop approach in which decisions affect the environment and changes in the environment, in turn, providing input to further decisions. System dynamics holds that social systems can productively be studied as information feedback control systems, that is as systems in which a decision affects the environment which in turn affects the decision. An important premise of system dynamics is that the behaviour of a system is primarily determined by the characteristics of the whole and not by the characteristics of the individual parts.

The interactive content value web is a complex system, and only by beginning to account for the dynamism of the relationships and connections between the components in the system can a full picture of the opportunities for network commerce. System dynamics offers a valuable set of tools for describing and modelling the relationships between the players in the value web and even the dynamic relationship between the seven metatrends discussed in Chapter 2.

6.6 Summary

This chapter examines the market for network commerce and the many challenges to accurately measuring network commerce. We begin with an overview of the wide variation in network commerce statistics and forecasts and speculate about the reasons for this variation. We then discuss the factors shaping the evolution of end-user demand for network commerce, focusing on such general factors as telecommunications costs, and on specific factors influencing consumers and business users. Following this, we discuss the concept of diffusion and the significance of reaching a critical mass of users and services. After discussing the impact of network commerce on traditional media, we close with a discussion of two valuable conceptual tools for operating in uncertain markets: scenario planning and system dynamics modelling.

RECOMMENDATIONS

The network commerce market is evolving rapidly, but because it delivers new services to markets and is disruptive of traditional business practices, it is difficult to predict market development. Certain key lessons can be learned about market development, but firms must also develop new approaches to analysing markets and planning to exploit them.

Businesses

- *Implement a scenario-driven strategic planning process that allows the firm to identify key market developments and respond appropriately.* The development of the network economy is volatile and uneven. It is impossible to determine exactly how it will evolve. Given the high degree of uncertainty, firms need to explore alternatives to traditional forecasting and planning techniques developed in stable markets. By using scenario-driven planning processes, firms can better anticipate potential market developments and develop intuition about when and how to respond to these developments.
- *Watch for global competitors from countries with similar cultures.* The network destroys distance as a barrier to market entry. This, of course, creates important opportunities and threats.
- *Investigate end-user needs using new interactive technologies to capture, store, and analyse data to understand those needs and better address them.* The best way to do this is by identifying and focusing on lead users to better understand how the market is likely to evolve. Internet-based server platforms and related technologies provide the best tools ever developed for exploring the habits and needs of consumers on a mass scale and rapidly responding to them.
- *Seek intersections between what customers want, such as ability to communicate, access information, be entertained, or be empowered as consumers, and what is possible to deliver.* Several customer needs are identifiable and met especially well by network technologies. Successful service offerings typically incorporate one or more of the technologies that meets these needs.
- *Recognise that it may take time for a market to develop, but that history suggests these markets grow rapidly once they reach critical mass.* Once network markets reach a critical mass, they rapidly take off, reflecting the effect described by Metcalfe's Law. The firms that create and ride those market explosions often become industry leaders.

Content Firms

- *Recognise that traditional forms of content have evolved to effectively meet certain consumer needs.* Do not abandon them without good reason (e.g. printed books and newspapers will not go away for a very long time, if ever). Despite all of the change in the marketplace, do not assume that everything will change. Human needs evolve slowly. Many traditional forms of content have evolved over very long periods of time to address those needs, and it will take a long time for new types of content to match the comfort and ease of use of those traditional content forms. It is often better to explore how network services and content can enhance traditional forms of media than to try to replace those traditional forms of media with network content.

Governments

- *Ensure competition in the telecommunications services industry.* The availability of inexpensive, easy, and ubiquitous access to the network — in particular the cost of local phone service — is essential to the success of the network economy. Governments must work to ensure creation of a world-class, inexpensive, ubiquitous network infrastructure. Again, this is a critical pre-condition for the development of network markets. All other issues are moot unless this one is addressed effectively.
- *Place public information on the network.* Adding content to the network will help it reach a critical mass of users and services. In this manner, government can play an important role in creating a critical mass of content on the network.
- *Like businesses, governments may also investigate the needs of their citizens using new interactive technologies to capture, store, and analyse data to understand those needs and better address them.* Governments have an unprecedented opportunity to develop closer relationships with their citizens in order to deliver more and better services in a cost-effective manner.

Notes

1. Aphorism attributed to Bohr. Various sources, e.g. Frank Trippett, "Looking for Tomorrow (and Tomorrow)," *Time*, 26 April 1982.

2. Vijay Mahajan and Jerry Wind, "Market Discontinuities and Strategic Planning: A Research Agenda," *Technological Forecasting and Social Change,* August 1989, p. 187.

3. Thomas Friedman, "The Internet Wars," *New York Times*, 11 April 1998.

4. For further discussion of this effect, see Stan Davis and Christopher Meyer, *Blur: The Speed of Change in the Connected Economy,* Addison-Wesley, Reading, Massachusetts: 1998.

5. See *Measuring Electronic Commerce,* OECD, Committee for Information, Computer and Communications Policy, OCDE/GD(97)185, Paris, 1997.

6. Paul Festa, "Net Traffic Ratings Debated," CNET NEWS.COM, 12 June 1998.

7. Jim Hu, "Net Metrics Inching Along," CNET NEWS.COM, 4 August 1998.

8. Bernard Wysocki, Jr., "The Outlook: Internet Is Opening a New Era of Pricing," *Wall Street Journal,* 8 June 1998.

9. Nielsen Media Research, "Number of Internet Users and Shoppers Surges in United States and Canada," 24 August 1998. http://www.nielsen-media.com/news/commnet2.html.

10. International Data Corporation, "The Western European Forecast for Internet Usage and Commerce," 1998.

11. University of Michigan Business School, "eCommerce: What's Selling Online," 1997. http://www.emarketer.com/estats/ec_sell.html, 1998.

12. Yankelovich Partners, Inc. "eCommerce: What's Selling Online," 1998. http://www.emarketer.com/estats/ec_sell.html.

13. Simon Reeve, "High Phone Prices Threaten Europe's E-Commerce Future," *The European,* 20-26 July 1998.

14. Ibid.

15. Ibid.

16. For a good overview of factors shaping market behaviour, see Philip Kotler, *Marketing Management: Analysis, Planning, Implementation, and Control,* Englewood Cliffs, New Jersey: Prentice Hall, 1988.

17. "English-speaking Nations Ahead in High Tech," Reuters, 28 April 1998.

18. "Yahoo! Starts Speaking Spanish," CNET NEWS.COM, 26 June 1998.

19. "Surprise! Surprise! Latin America Internet Use is on the Rise," PR Newswire, 19 November 19 1997.

20. eStat,1998. http://www.emarketer.com/estats/net_geogaphy_exp.html.

21. Ibid.

22. *Eurostat Yearbook '97: A Statistical Eye on Europe 1986-1996,* Luxembourg: Office for Official Publications of the European Communities, 1997.

23. "User Demographics: Net User Age," http://www.emarketer.com/estats/demo_age.html, 1998.

24. Yankelovich Partners/Cyber Dialogue, 1997.

25. GVU, Eighth WWW User Survey, http://www.gvu.gatech.edu, 1998.

26. Simmons, Simmons Teen-Age Research Study (STARS), 1998.

27. "User Demographics: Net User Age," http://www.emarketer.com/estats/demo_age.html, 1998.

28. NetSmart-Research, "What Makes Women Click," 1997.

29. Ibid.

30. Binary Compass Enterprises, Internet Shopping Report, 1997.

31. E.g. US, Canada, UK.

32. European Network for SME Research, *Fifth Annual Report of The European Observatory for SMEs*, 1998.

33. Ibid.

34. Jeffrey Morrison, "How to Use Diffusion Models in New Product Forecasting," *Journal of Business Forecasting Methods & Systems,* Summer 1996.

35. Manoj K. Agarwal, "Forecasting Market Adoption Over Time," School of Management, Binghamton University, Binghamton, NY, November 1997.

36. Steve Outing, "Study: 16 percent of US Households Read Web Newspapers," *E&P Interactive,* 12 June 1998.

37. Net Usage vs. Offline Media, http://www.emarketer.com/estats/usage_net_vs.html, 1998.

38. Ibid.

39. Kees van der Heijden, *Scenarios: The Art of Strategic Conversation,* Chichester: John Wiley & Sons, 1996.

40. See, for example, Jay Forrester, *Industrial Dynamics,* Cambridge, MA: MIT Press, 1961; Jay Forrester, *Urban Dynamics,* Cambridge, MA: MIT Press, 1969; and Jay Forrester, "The Counterintuitive Behavior of Social Systems," *Technology Review,* January 1971.

Understanding Technology Enablers

Technology enables the creation of the network economy, making it critical that firms understand the key technology enablers and their likely evolution. In this chapter, we provide a framework for understanding the components of network commerce technology and address many of the critical decisions that must be made.

Technology enables the global network economy and will continue to shape its evolution. Because the rapidly changing network economy may find some of today's successful vendors out of business tomorrow, in this discussion of technology enablers we have chosen to focus primarily on concepts and principles that we believe will be of lasting use. By identifying and describing these concepts and principles and by drawing essential technological lessons from the experiences of industry participants, we hope to build a firm foundation for thinking strategically about technology.

7.1 Overview

While we will devote attention in this chapter to technology as it relates to the evolution of digital television platforms, we believe that networks and devices based on Internet protocol (IP) will emerge as the principle platforms for the delivery of interactive digital content. On the Internet today, one can see many conceivable types of interactive products and services. In addition, we are also seeing many attempts to combine features of television and the Internet. Regardless of the final delivery medium, the Internet provides the tools necessary to build the products and services that will drive the success of those networks. Firms that ignore the lessons of the network economy as it is emerging on the Internet today are unlikely to succeed in any network medium.

IP-based technologies are profoundly altering the telecommunications market. IP is an excellent example of a "disruptive technology."[1] Disruptive technologies are technologies that bring to market a very different value proposition than has previously been available. At least initially, disruptive technologies do not provide as high a level of performance as existing technologies, but they are also much cheaper, and they improve over time. Once they reach the point that they perform adequately, they tend to rapidly push the legacy or "sustaining" technologies out of the market. The best-managed firms, those that most effectively focus on meeting their best customers' needs, tend to ignore disruptive technologies that many of their most profitable customers find useless or undesirable. As a result, those firms that are most in-tune with their best customers, and identifying those products that promise greater profitability and growth, are rarely able to build a case for investing in disruptive technologies until it is too late. The challenge for many of the managers of established content firms reading this study will to be to determine how to effectively identify and exploit disruptive technologies and embrace them before it is too late.

7.2 Building Network Solutions

The bulk of our discussion will deal with the components of a robust network platform; we will discuss the network interface, connectivity, hosting, and content creation. Before moving on to this detailed discussion, however, we will look at the relationship between technology enablers (such Web servers and fibre-optic networks) and the functions they should support. We will also discuss how a set of Internet technologies based on open standards has emerged providing the key enabling technologies for the network economy.

7.2.1 The Relationship between Technology Enablers and Network Platforms

Network-based service providers build value propositions out of sets of enabling technologies that offer necessary levels of functionality.

Exhibit 7.1 illustrates the relationship between these enablers and the network solutions that they support. Enabling technologies and services provide the fundamental building blocks of hardware, software and expertise. These enablers must provide a variety of key functionalities that help define the network user's experience. Advances in functionality result in applications with increased value. Network-based service providers offer one or more applications over the network.

Exhibit 7.1 **Role of Network Commerce Enablers**

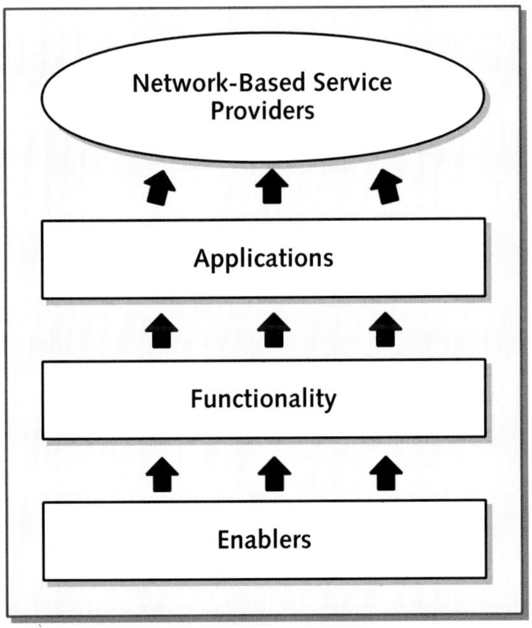

Source: Gemini Strategic Research Group.

7.2.2 Functionality

Any network solution consists of a complex set of tools and services. At its most basic, however, a network commerce platform requires nine basic components:

Access to Customers and Trading Partners

Access is the ability to reach customers and trading partners via a network and with appropriate compatibility. Without access to a meaningful population of potential customers or partners, all other capabilities are useless.

Information Sharing/Querying

An effective network solution must offer users the ability to view, query, and automatically compare products, product availability, company information, and any other information that potential customers or partners might require to make informed decisions.

Community and Communication

This encompasses interaction with customers, partners, and other industry players. At a minimum, this capability entails simple e-mail communication. At the high end, it could involve online communities with chat areas, customised information, and even real-time multimedia communications. Such interaction may enable customers and partners to form separate preferred relationships among themselves.

Transactions

This includes online ordering and selling, payments and receipts, and access to information about order status. Without the use of telephone, fax, or in-person alternatives, this component provides the ability to track product status before, during, and after the purchase.

Security

Security includes identification and authentication, credit verification, encryption, and data privacy. This is the assurance that all stages of the commerce activity, especially financial transactions, are legitimate, secure, and reasonably private. Both software (e.g. encryption) and infrastructure (e.g. separate network) solutions support this capability. Security also includes the ability to ascertain, within reason, a party's ability to pay or deliver.

Reliability

Network users require assurance that software, hardware, and network services will be "up and running" and that information will be properly mirrored and backed-up.

Interconnectivity

Interconnectivity is the ability to link to legacy systems, the ability to link with partners and customers, and the set of standards that make all these systems compatible. This capability is crucial for reaping the full benefits of the network economy. Often interconnectivity is ensured by the adoption of open standards or standards developed by a trading partner or industry.

Professional and Technical Support

This component is the human element — the development and support services that enable all aspects of the creation and maintenance of network solutions and include both in-house and third-party resources. Services include implementation, data management and tracking, training, education, systems integration, business consulting, hosting, and others. Human capital often proves to be the most important and most expensive component of network solutions.

Flexibility

Managers must be able to revise, quickly and easily, both the content and processes of a network solution, including making changes to software components, graphics, descriptions, pricing and inventory. One of the most salient features of Internet platforms is the flexibility of these platforms relative to traditional network platforms.

7.2.3 Open Standards and the Advantages of Internet Technologies

In its simplest forms, network commerce has been with us since the invention of the telegraph in the 1837. In the 1960s, large businesses began attempting to automate some high-volume, repetitive commercial activities by developing a network technology known as electronic data interchange (EDI). EDI allows trading partners to use dedicated networks to transmit orders and other commercial documents directly from one computer to another without human intervention. EDI has proven highly successful at reducing costs and processing errors for some high-volume transactions between large trading partners. However, EDI is too expensive and too limited in its functionality to replace most manual processes. Stronger, more flexible Internet technologies have created a whole range of new network capabilities available to businesses of all sizes and to individuals (Exhibit 7.2).

Exhibit 7.2 **Comparison of Internet-Based and Traditional Network Commerce**

Factor	EDI	Internet Electronic Commerce
Implementation Dynamics	• Built upon existing trading relationships	• Consumer of services initiates request to buy in one-to-one relationship.
Business Case	• Develop only after market or willingness to use channel exists.	• Proven market may not exist.
Financial Transactions	• Financial transactions typically take place over existing networks.	• Internet gateways to financial networks, new financial instruments.
Effect on Business Processes	• Transactions have impact on internal business processes.	• Transaction mirrors physical transaction or simplifies business process.
Frequency and Value of Transactions	• Typically high-value transactions, may be very high volume.	• Mass market, lower frequency, lower value.
Choice of Products	• Comparison shopping does not occur.	• Comparison shopping is a common component.
Level of Trust	• High	• Low to medium
Duration of Relationship	• Long	• Short to medium
Cost	• Higher	• Lower
Reliability	• Higher	• Lower (but improving)
Flexibility	• Lower	• Much higher
Effect of Distribution Channels	• No conflict with distribution channel due to primary focus on uniqueness of transactions.	• Channel conflict may occur.

Source: Gemini Strategic Research Group.

As illustrated in Exhibit 7.3, this new range of capabilities and the tremendous savings over the cost of traditional EDI have enabled network commerce to dramatically expand its reach in the marketplace.

Exhibit 7.3. **How the Internet Expands the Reach of Network Commerce**

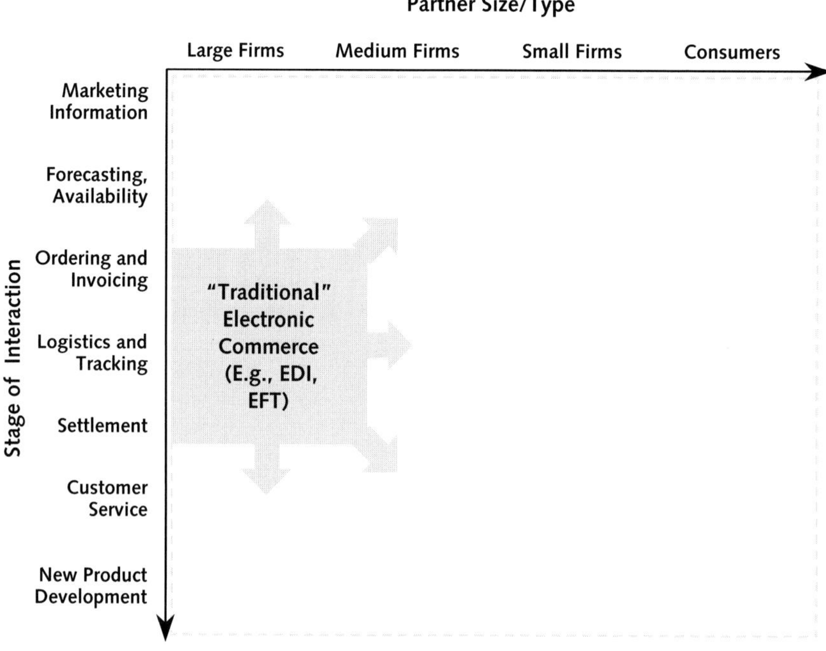

Source: Gemini Strategic Research Group.

The ability of IP technologies to extend the functionality and reach of electronic commerce is just one example of the power of open technology platforms. Earlier we discussed the growth of the Internet and packet networks and open standards as key metatrends. As outlined in Exhibit 7.4, the history of networks in the last seven years shows a shift from proprietary models combining content and network connectivity to open models separating content from transport. Both content firms and network service providers that have failed to heed this principle have watched their business models collapse under the onslaught of competitors that have learned to separate content from conduit.

Exhibit 7.4 **From Proprietary Models to Open Models, 1990 – 1995 and 1997**

	Television		Online Services	
	1990-1995	1997	1990-1995	1997
Business Model	Proprietary	Open Internet	Proprietary	Open Internet
Leading Providers	Time Warner, RBOCs, and many other PTOs.	Progressive Networks, Web-TV, and others.	America Online, CompuServe, Prodigy, Europe On-line, NiftyServe	NetCom, AT&T, EUnet, and more than 4,000 others.
Leading Service Goal	High-quality video on demand; interactive shopping etc. in closed online malls and games.	Low-quality audio/video that can evolve with higher compression rates and higher speed local access networks.	Provide access to proprietary databases of news, information, and other services.	Provide Internet access.
Number of "Information Channels"	Video on demand and 500+ channels.	Unlimited but variable quality.	Closed world of proprietary databases.	Unlimited but variable quality.
Interface	Electronic Program Guides.	Internet browsers with streaming media "plug-ins."	Company proprietary interface.	Netscape and Microsoft browsers.
User Equipment	TV, set-top box, remote control.	PC with PSTN, wireless or cable modem, Web TV, or Internet-ready TV.	PC and modem.	PC and modem.
Infrastructure Costs	Expensive supply-driven infrastructure provision.	Low-cost demand led infrastructure upgrades.	Major cost item customer service, marketing, and content provision.	Relatively low-cost entry to Internet service business. Potential cost increases depending on future of peering and interconnection.
Pricing	Pricing in trials only.	Mostly free content (advertiser-supported) or pay-per-download of content models.	Certain number of hours included followed by measured charges. Premium pricing for some content.	Flat rate per month.
Strategy Shift	Close or dramatically scaled back trials. Shift focus to cable modems, selling existing access products (ISDN, second lines) and high-speed xDSL technologies. Flat rate or volume charges for cable modems.	Work to develop Internet protocols, compression and streaming media technologies. Open Web-TV devices to be non-proprietary and incorporate more multimedia applications.	Open proprietary networks to Internet since 1995. Reinvent themselves as IAPs offering additional premium information services. Reorient pricing toward IAP model.	Incorporate "Push" interfaces such as Pointcast. Differentiate access pricing for value-added service.

Source: OECD; NewsCom.

7.3 The Building Blocks of Network Commerce

Network commerce technology and service enablers can be divided into four basic building blocks. First, network and hosting services are required. These are provided by firms that operate networks and hosting facilities, including public switched telephone network (PSTN) operators, Internet service providers (ISPs), and value-added network (VAN) operators. Second, businesses require a set of hardware components, including personal computers, workstations, routers, remote access servers, cabling, switches, and other physical components of the communications network. The third component is software, required to develop and operate the applications that make up the platform. These may include EDI software, HTTP servers, catalogue servers, authoring tools, business applications, mail servers and clients, security software, databases, middleware, browsers, and usage tracking software. Finally, professional services encompass the people who are required to develop, implement and operate the systems.

These include systems integrators, value-added resellers, Web site designers, trainers, and analysts who create and operate these platforms (Exhibit 7.5).

Exhibit 7.5. **Components of an End-to-End Network Solution**

Components	Description of Services or Products	Examples of Vendors	
Service Bureaus	• Firms to which specific business functions are outsourced.	• Industry.Net • TPN Register	• IBM World Commerce • WOMEX
Real-Time Communications	• Wide array of e-mail, news, audio, video, streaming and push technologies supporting real-time multimedia and community.	• Vocaltec • Netscape	• Progressive Networks • PointCast
EDI	• EDI software, networks, gateways, and related services.	• Harbinger • GEIS	• Premenos • Envoy
Authoring	• Software applications and development environments for creating Web sites and on-line environments.	• NetObjects • Microsoft	• Adobe • Bluestone
Catalogues/ Directories/Agents	• Products designed specifically for publishing online catalogues and directories and automated search and filtering software.	• SAQQARA • iCat	• Cadis • Firefly Networks
Metering/Measuring	• Network service usage measuring and analysis software and related services.	• NetGenesis • Interse	• I/PRO • Netcount
Web Commerce Servers	• Internet servers designed to support commercial transactions.	• Microsoft • Actra	• Open Market • Broadvision
Middleware	• Firms providing software to connect legacy systems to servers.	• Bea • PSDI	• OneWave • Elekom
ERP[a] Applications/ Databases	• Client/server business applications, database software providers.	• Oracle • SAP	• Baan • PeopleSoft
Payments	• Payment instruments and other payment software and providers of payment services.	• Cybercash • First Data Corp.	• First Virtual Holdings • Digital
Security	• Security hardware and software and related service providers.	• Certicom • RSA Data Security	• IBM • TradeWave
Network/Hosting	• Communications networks and content hosting services.	• France Telecom • WorldCom	• Deutsch Telekom • Viag Interkom
Computer Hardware	• Computers and peripherals required to operate the software needed to implement EC solution.	• HP • Sun	• IBM • SGI
Network Hardware	• Hardware required to build and operate communications networks.	• Cisco • Cascade	• Bay Networks • 3Com

Source: Gemini Strategic Research Group.
a. Enterprise resource planning.

Constructing a network platform requires the integration of a number of different products from a range of vendors (Exhibit 7.6). Many vendors, especially those that provide servers and enterprise resource planning (ERP), have developed extensive partnership networks in order to bring complete solutions to market. As the industry evolves, consolidation will occur, and some product categories, such as stand-alone catalogue software, will be incorporated into other types of products.

Exhibit 7.6. **Example of an End-to-End Network Commerce Platform**

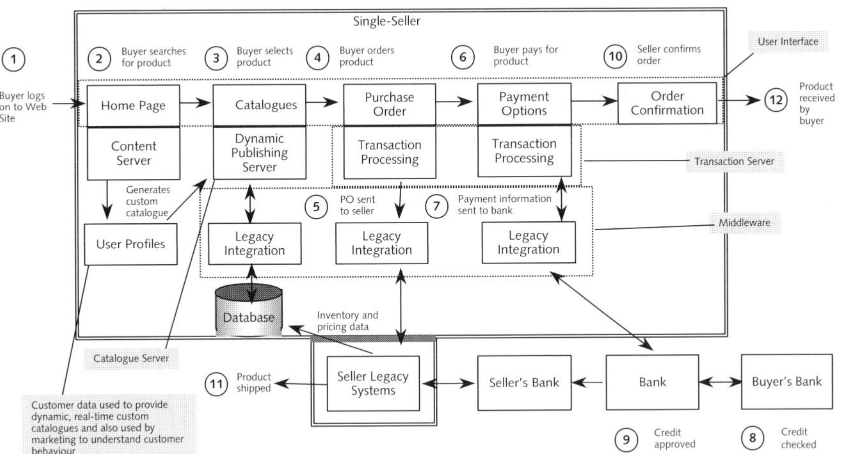

Source: emmerce; Gemini Strategic Research Group.

In the following sections, we will examine these product and services categories in greater detail, from end-user devices to network services, hosting, and content creation and management.

7.3.1 End-User Devices and Client Software

We have already discussed the importance of Moore's Law in driving the evolution of end-user devices.[2] Increases in computing performance have made possible the extensive commerce capabilities that firms are beginning to exploit. Driven by ever-increasing functionality and performance, the computer and consumer electronic industries are gradually merging into one.

Client Software and Operating Systems

The software industry is undergoing important changes driven by the emerging network economy. New standards are emerging, including new programming languages like Java that are unbundling applications into smaller "applets" better suited for networked computing. Platform neutrality is another important goal. Interpreters are being developed for each platform to enable applets and applications to run on any operating system. The network is facilitating access to applets, deemphasising the need to store entire programs locally. The long-term implications of these changes for software makers include the potential loss of influence for conventional players, a loss of significance for platforms, and the entry of many new, smaller players. Conventional players may lose influence as large programs and application suites residing on the desktop give way to applications supported by applets from the network. Platforms could lose significance, as operating systems become less important due to Java interpreters overcoming cross-platform incompatibilities. Finally, many new, smaller players may enter the market due to the ability of open standards to facilitate the entry of applet-specific players (Exhibit 7.7).

Exhibit 7.7 **Rise of Platform-Independent Computing**

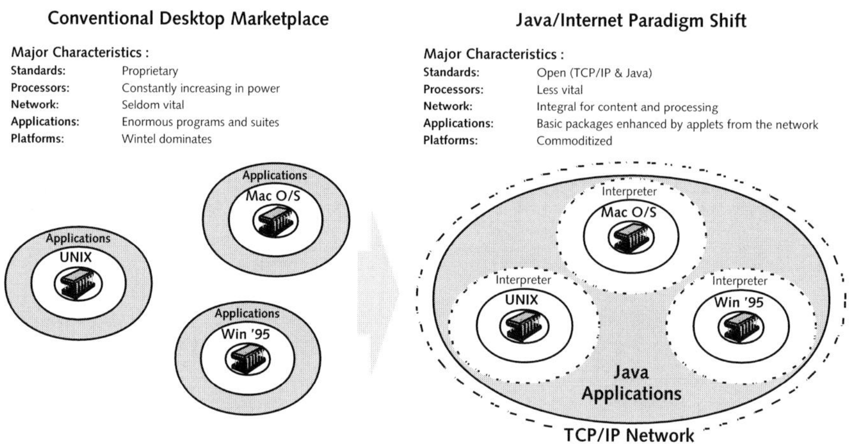

Source: Gemini Strategic Research Group.

Browsers

The browser is the user software interface of choice for accessing the Internet and other forms of digital media. Microsoft and Netscape have seized upon the browser as a unified means of accessing both local and networked resources. Even CD/DVD-ROM publishers now often package browsers with their content instead of developing proprietary interfaces (Exhibit 7.8).

Exhibit 7.8 **Changing Market Shares of Leading Browsers, August 1996 and July 1998**

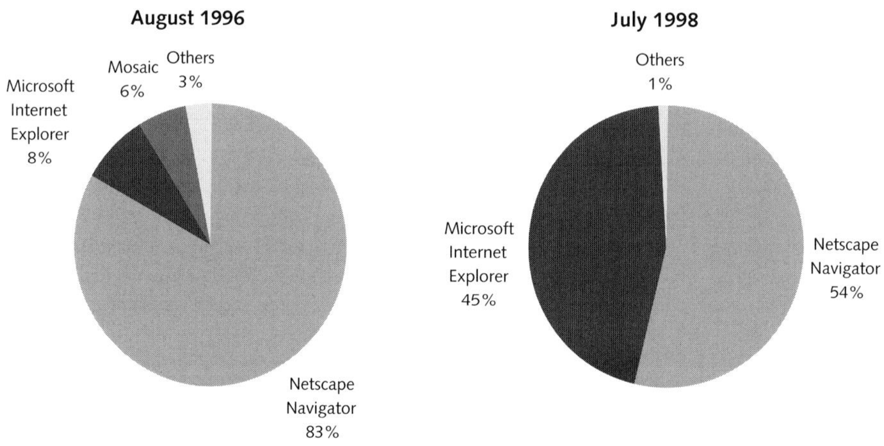

Source: Zona Research Browser Census, 1998.

Devices

The network economy's ongoing effect on hardware is difficult to measure. The most important hardware components will likely be those that mediate between device and network, with devices such as modems increasingly being measured by network access speed. Processor brands are also likely to become less important as open standards emerge and applets and new applications are increasingly able to work with a wide range of processors. Processing speed will remain extremely important despite the emergence of smaller, easier-to-execute applets. Storage needs will also continue to grow as high-speed network access increases the ability to download vast quantities of data.

Today, a wide range of devices are available for accessing digital media. These devices range from stand-alone, non-networked devices like the Digital Versatile Disk (DVD) player to so-called "fat" clients, such as the personal computer (Exhibit 7.9). We believe that fat clients, in the form of personal computers and personal computers integrated with television tuners, will be the most important devices for accessing digital media and transacting networked commerce; however, a wide range of other networked and non-networked devices will play significant roles in this marketplace as it evolves. In particular, as functionality improves, hand-held and wearable wireless devices have the potential to become extremely important access devices. We believe, however, that the minimum time-frame for these portable devices to reach the necessary level of functionality is three years.

Exhibit 7.9 **Digital Content Access Devices**

	Device Type	Examples	Approx. Price
"FAT" Client — Networked	PCTV	Destination *(Gateway 2000)*	2,650 – 4,400 euro
	Consumer PCs	Compaq and others	700 – 2,650 euro
	Network Computer	Oracle and others	440 euro
	Game Players	Sega	175 – 265 euro
	Set-Top Boxes	WebTV and others	265 – 350 euro
	Enhanced Televisions	Mitsubishi and others	880 – 2,650 euro
	Screen Phones	Navitel and others	265 – 440 euro
"THIN" Client	Portable Devices	Casio and others	350 – 530 euro
Non-Networked	Stand-alone Digital Video Players	DVD Player	130 – 265 euro

Source: Gemini Strategic Research Group.

Telephones. Telephones are the most ubiquitous interactive network access devices. Telephone penetration is very high in the developed world where almost everyone knows how to use a telephone to communicate. Many attempts have been made to extend the functionality of the telephone as an interface to information content, the most profitable telephone-based content services being pay-per-call information and phone sex services. For example, firms have created interfaces that allow customers access to product and order information about automated touch-tone dialing. In the last decade, equipment manufacturers and service providers, and banks in particular, have experimented with enhanced telephones and screenphones to offer greater functionality to their customers. Most of these experiments have failed due to low functionality and pricing schemes that set high usage costs. Minitel, a screenphone service offered by France Telecom, was one of a small number of successful ventures of this kind. By giving away Minitel terminals to telephone customers, France Telecom was able to create a huge installed base on which to build an innovative set of services. It has remained an important interactive content access platform in France, but because it did not evolve to provide the functionality and interconnectivity of Internet-enabled PCs, it was eclipsed. With the advent of Internet telephony, many manufacturers have returned to the screenphone concept as a low-cost network access device. About a dozen manufacturers offer screenphones with various levels of functionality, ranging from the ability to send and receive e-mail messages to the ability to browse the World Wide Web (Exhibit 7.10).

Exhibit 7.10 **Screenphone Example**

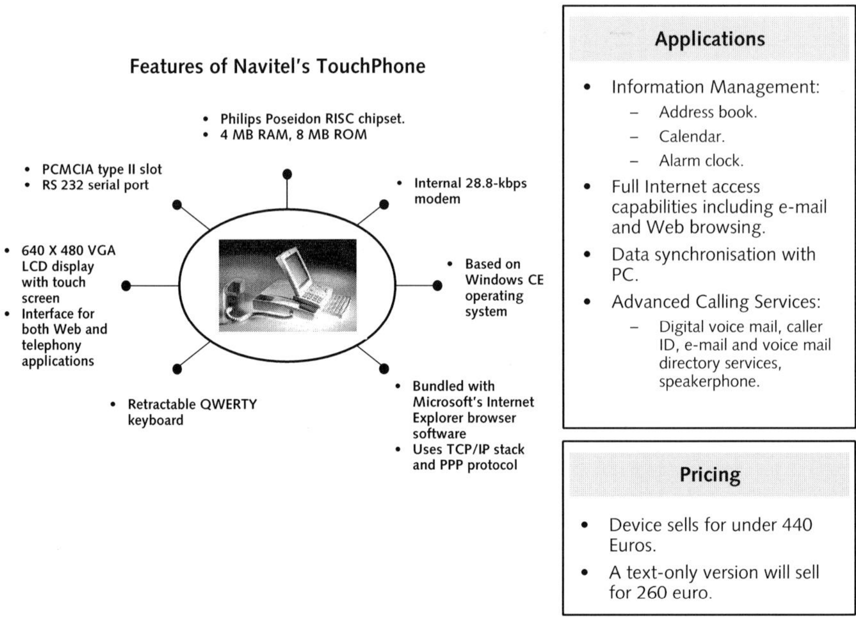

Source: Navitel.

We believe that most telephones manufactured in the near future will include IP-based messaging capabilities. Combined with low network connection costs (less than 2 euro/month above standard telephone tariffs), such devices will likely play an important role in making simple Internet e-mail nearly as ubiquitous as the telephone.

Television. The television has the widest penetration of all network access devices; however, it is not truly interactive (beyond the ability to change channels). Traditional TV manufacturers are beginning to develop devices that extend existing TV capabilities to tap into the interactive services market (Exhibit 7.11). These manufacturers generally fall into two camps: those developing set-top-boxes that attach to existing TVs and those integrating Internet access directly into the TV. The rise of digital broadcasting will help to promote increasing similarities between television and PCs, including greater processing power, more common components, and connection to networks capable of supporting both video and interactive data.

Exhibit 7.11 **Example of Web-Enabled Television Set**

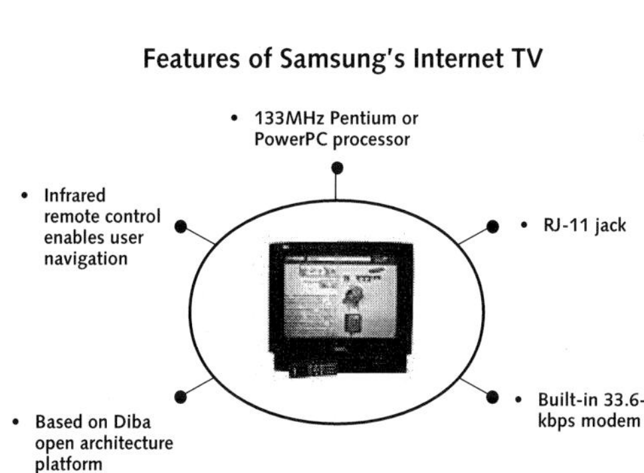
Features of Samsung's Internet TV
• 133MHz Pentium or PowerPC processor
• Infrared remote control enables user navigation
• RJ-11 jack
• Based on Diba open architecture platform
• Built-in 33.6-kbps modem

Description & Applications

- Samsung's Internet TV is based on Diba's open architecture platform (IDEA).
- The company began selling the TV in Korea in 1996 and entered the US market in 1997.
- Provides full Internet access and email capabilities:
  - Users can program favourite sites for on-demand access.
- Enables standard broadcast reception.

Pricing

- Device is priced between 530 and 620 euro.

Source: Samsung.

Within a five- to ten-year time-frame we believe that almost all digital television sets will be manufactured with Internet access capabilities. These television sets will play an important role in extending Internet access to segments of the population that would not otherwise purchase a computer or other device solely for accessing interactive networks.

In Europe, the European Commission's Action Plan for advanced television has funded the development of widescreen programming in an attempt to gradually move Europeans toward widescreen, high-definition television. According to the European Association of Consumer Electronics Manufacturers (EACEM), the cumulative installed base of television sets with the widescreen 16:9 aspect ratio in Europe at the end of 1996 was over 1.1 million. Sales of widescreen sets are doubling every year, and 1.3 million units were forecast to be sold in

1997 alone, bringing the total installed base to 2.4 million at the beginning of 1998.[3]

In connection with the conversion to digital television in the US, the Consumer Electronics Manufacturers Association (CEMA) has released a set of standardised definitions for various digital television types to be used in connection with the marketing of these new products. These standards, which are likely to be used in countries where the Advanced Television Systems Committee's DTV standard is adopted, include Digital Television (DTV), High-Definition Television (HDTV), and Standard Definition Television (SDTV).[4]

For competitive reasons — and because in many cases, they simply don't know — TV hardware executives are loath to say what their first digital TV receivers will look like, what they will contain, and how much they will cost. Both Mitsubishi and Hitachi say their first digital TV receivers will be large — 60-inches and above — rear-projection TVs with 16:9 aspect ratios (as opposed to the current 4:3 National Television Standards Committee (NTSC) standard in the US and elsewhere). The new sets will sell for anywhere from 7,000 to 9,700 euro. While both companies insist that pricing is based on the cost of manufacturing first-generation digital TV receivers, other TV equipment executives argue vehemently that the real cost — even for the first models — should be much lower than that. A study by the Grand Alliance (the consortium of manufacturers who created the current US DTV standard) on receiver costs conducted in 1996 when memory chip prices were higher than today, puts the cost of a high-end digital TV chassis, capable of processing and displaying a full 1080-I (1080-line interlaced) or 720-P (720-line progressive-scan) HDTV signal at 320 euro. Add a widescreen HDTV-capable projection display (cost, about 700 euro), a cabinet, and then multiply by about a factor of three and you get a cost-based retail price of under 4,400 euro. Even assuming the Grand Alliance study underestimated the cost of HDTV-capable MPEG-2 decoder chips and other silicon, some TV makers privately insist that even 60-inch 16:9 digital TV receivers should have retail prices between 4,400 and 5,300 euro.[5] These prices are likely to drop rapidly, however, as demand increases and manufacturers move up the learning curve, with the CEMA estimating that HDTV prices will drop to about 3,500 euro within five years.[6]

Set-Top Box. Analogue cable television set-top boxes have been in use for many years. The most sophisticated of these boxes are addressable systems allowing cable network operators to control customers' access to premium channels and pay-per-view programming. With the advent of digital broadcasting, set-top boxes are becoming a necessity for owners of analogue television sets wishing to access digitally transmitted programming. Most digital set-top box specifications include the ability to add Internet access capabilities. Modular network interface units allow these devices to be upgraded to accommodate different types of access networks. Several manufacturers have already entered the marketplace with dedicated Internet access set-top boxes. The most prominent of these is the WebTV device manufactured by Sony and Philips under license from Microsoft, which is now readying a third-generation WebTV specification built around its Windows CE operating system. Firms from the computer industry, like Microsoft, view these devices as an important step in the eventual integration of the television and the computer. Despite a high-profile national television advertising campaign by Philips in the US, initial uptake of the WebTV device has been slow. The second-generation WebTV device introduced in late 1997 appears to be faring better in the marketplace, and we believe that the ability to combine the WebTV device with cable modem access may allow it and similar devices to become a significant means of network access.

Internet TV using a set-top box made its European debut in October 1997. Launched in the UK through major retailers, NetChannel offers Internet, e-mail and home shopping services without the need for a PC. The set-top box supplied by NetProducts Ltd. costs about 260 euro. It also requires a phone line, smart card, and a "plug-and-play" connection to the family TV set. The monthly charge is about 13 EUCs for unlimited Internet access, five e-mail addresses, localised and personalised services and advertisements, and a bundle of "home channels." Netchannel plans to roll-out similar services in Germany, France, and the Benelux. Netchannel is already wooing UK cable operators and digital broadcast TV operators. According to a Netchannel mission statement, "We intend to become the de facto standard for easy-to-use consumer Internet TV access for all delivery mechanisms, including cable, satellite and terrestrial."

Set-top boxes will also play a role in the transition to digital television. Any analogue TV purchased today will be able to play back digital TV broadcasts when outfitted with the proper converter box, although not at true high-definition resolution. At least a few manufacturers plan to have digital TV converter boxes ready by fall of 1998, with more models following from other manufacturers in 1999.

No one is saying how much these boxes will cost, but they are likely to exceed the original target price of between 90 and 180 euro. Prices will vary depending on whether the converter is capable of sending a full HDTV signal to the TV or whether it will "down-convert" to "standard definition." Most of the boxes will have component-video outputs for a direct connection to the TV display. Sony, Toshiba, Sharp, and a few other manufacturers are starting to ship analogue TV sets with component inputs. Still, if a TV can display only 500 lines of resolution, running a 1080-line signal to it is just wasting processing power. With one or two exceptions, a converter box attached to an existing analogue TV or projector is going to fall far short of HDTV performance.[7]

Personal Computer. The PC landscape is changing quickly as truly low-cost personal computers enter the marketplace. While PC manufacturers have traditionally added features and held market prices fairly constant, during 1997 they began pushing prices downward in hopes of growing their market (Exhibit 7.12). In the US, a highly functional PC can be purchased for as little as 440 euro, placing PCs within the price range of a whole new group of consumers. In addition, some manufacturers have begun to produce hybrid PC/television devices in an effort to compete with traditional television manufacturers. The entry or re-entry of a number of Japanese consumer electronics giants, such as Sony and Toshiba, into the desktop PC business has also led to significant improvements in hardware design and ease-of-use.

Exhibit 7.12 **Price/Performance of Key Personal Computer Components**

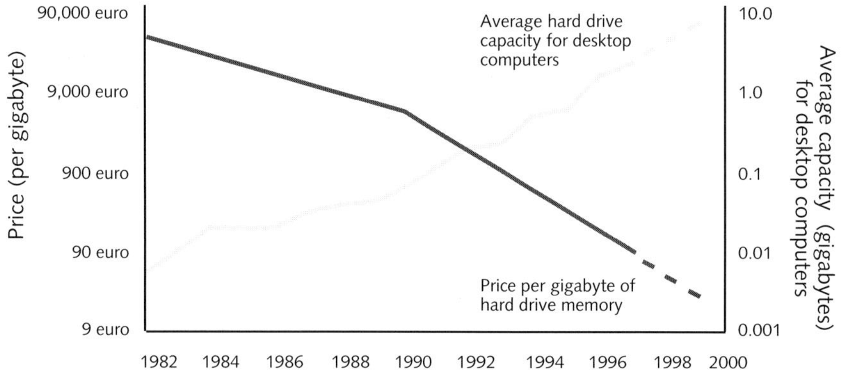

Source: *Forbes*, 14 March 1997.

With continuing improvements in performance and the continuing efforts of hardware and software manufacturers to improve ease of use, personal computers will continue to be the most significant network access technologies in most markets. Questions remain, however, about the limits to household PC penetration. In the US and a few other countries with high household PC penetration, household penetration seems to have levelled at around the fortieth percentile. Whether this is an economic barrier or a cultural barrier is not yet clear.

Network Computer. The term "network computer" must be carefully defined, for many devices are so-labelled (Exhibit 7.13). While originally envisioned as low-cost (less than 440 euro) stripped-down PCs for the consumer market, network computers have been repositioned as low-maintenance, centrally controlled corporate computing devices. Several studies have suggested that potential savings in information technology maintenance costs by large corporations adopting network computers might be the reason.

Exhibit 7.13 **Three Types of Network Computers**

Type	Features	Examples
Client-Oriented Network Computer	• Diskless • Runs thin-client operating system • Code executes locally but resides on server • Some types may not inherently support Windows applications	• Sun Microsystems JavaStation • Wyse Technology Winterm 4000 • NC standard architecture developed by IBM, Netscape, Oracle, and Sun
Server-Oriented Network Computer	• Diskless smart terminal • Applications execute on server	• Citrix Systems WinFrame
NetPC	• Diskless or disk used only for cache • No data stored locally • Identity is server-based	• Microsoft-Intel specifications

Source: *Network World.*

While network computers are likely to be a corporate computing phenomenon, if, indeed, they find any wide-scale acceptance in the marketplace, they may affect the demand for network content and commerce services in interesting ways. Since market research shows that many people access the Internet both from home and work, and that access from the workplace is a common driver of demand for access from the home,[8] the adoption of network computers in workplaces with only limited or controlled access to the Internet may affect the growth of demand for Internet access and Internet-based services. In addition, the centralised administrative features of the network computer may shift purchasing of corporate information in a digital form from individual employees to a centralised authority.

Personal Digital Assistants. A wide range of hand-held computing and communications devices have reached the market (Exhibit 7.14), but beyond the immensely successful mobile telephones, few of these devices have won market acceptance.

Exhibit 7.14 **Example of Personal Digital Assistant**

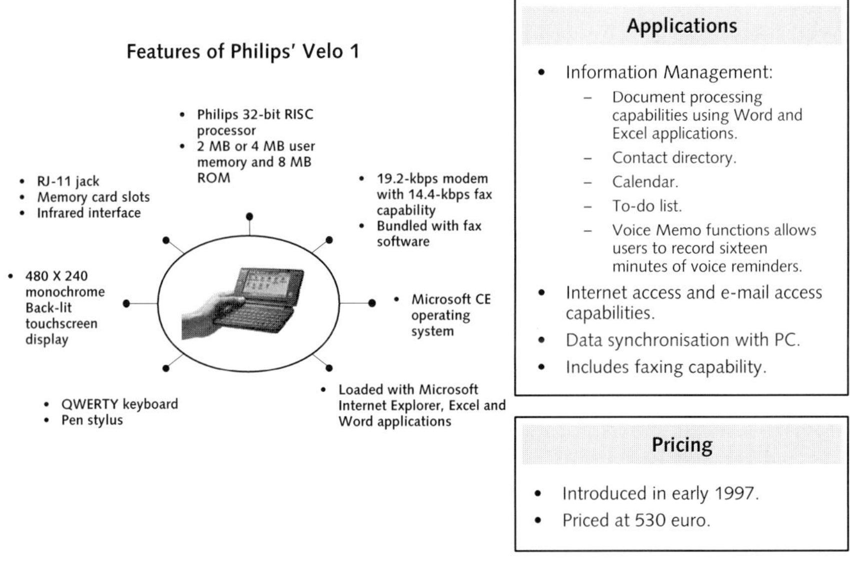

Source: Philips.

3Com's PalmPilot, a hand-held personal organiser, has been especially successful. 3Com recently released a new model with optional wireless network-access capabilities for sending and receiving e-mail. The PalmPilot and similar products are becoming increasingly powerful, functional devices with considerable potential to provide remote access. These devices are too small to offer truly functional keyboards, and the handwriting-recognition capabilities of such pen-based systems are still limited. The displays on these devices are also too small to display Web pages adequately. Eventually, processing power will be sufficient to support voice-recognition capabilities.

Digital Reading Devices. These new devices are closely related to other hand-held computing devices, except that they have been developed specifically to display text electronically in a form similar to that found in a printed book. These devices offer the promise of allowing readers to download the text of books from the Internet and store the text of dozens of books for later use. They combine the ubiquitous distribution system provided by the Internet with the "form-factor" of traditional books. Several manufacturers are introducing these devices in 1998 (Exhibit 7.15), and if they achieve significant market penetration, they have the potential to significantly alter the economics of the publishing industry.

Exhibit 7.15 **Selected Digital Reading Devices**

Name	Weight	Price	Release
Softbook	1.3 Kilograms	265 euro and up	Fall 1998
RocketBook	0.6 Kilograms	N/A	Fall 1998
Everybook	1.7 Kilograms	1,200 euro	Fall 1998

Source: *Wired*, July 1998.

One of the key components of these devices is the screen, which must provide a crisp, bright display, as readable as ink on paper. Recently, a start-up firm in Cambridge, Massachusetts, E Ink Corporation, announced the development of an "electronic ink" that will eventually allow the display of high-resolution images on almost any surface. When the electronic ink, which uses tiny capsules containing a chip of ink that is white on one side and coloured on the other, is exposed to electrical current, it changes colour, allowing the display of words, graphics, or anything else that can be displayed on a computer screen on almost any surface, including normal paper. It is significantly less expensive than other types of displays, draws minimal power to refresh, requires no power to maintain and offers a contrast equivalent to printed media. Within a five- to seven-year time-frame, electronic ink technology will enable newspaper subscribers to download a personalised version of the day's news and display it on the same "paper" each day.[9]

CD/DVD Players. Digital Versatile Disk (DVD) may yet emerge as an important digital medium (Exhibit 7.16). To date, battles over standards and concerns about copy protection have prohibited DVD's wide-scale adoption. DVD-ROM, the computer component version of DVD, will likely take off during 1998. The emergence of mid-priced personal computers with DVD-ROM drives is likely to elevate consumer awareness of DVD significantly and stimulate demand for DVD-delivered content. The market research firm In-Stat projects DVD-ROM drive shipments of 11 million in 1998, a significant increase from fewer than 1 million in 1997. About half these shipments are expected to be in the United States.[10] The uptake of digital televisions will be one potential driver of stand-alone DVD market growth. Assuming that a significant installed base of HDTV-enabled television sets is available, consumers will likely demand packaged or rental video products equal or superior to broadcast quality.

Exhibit 7.16 **Capacity Comparison of Optical Storage Media, in Gigabytes**

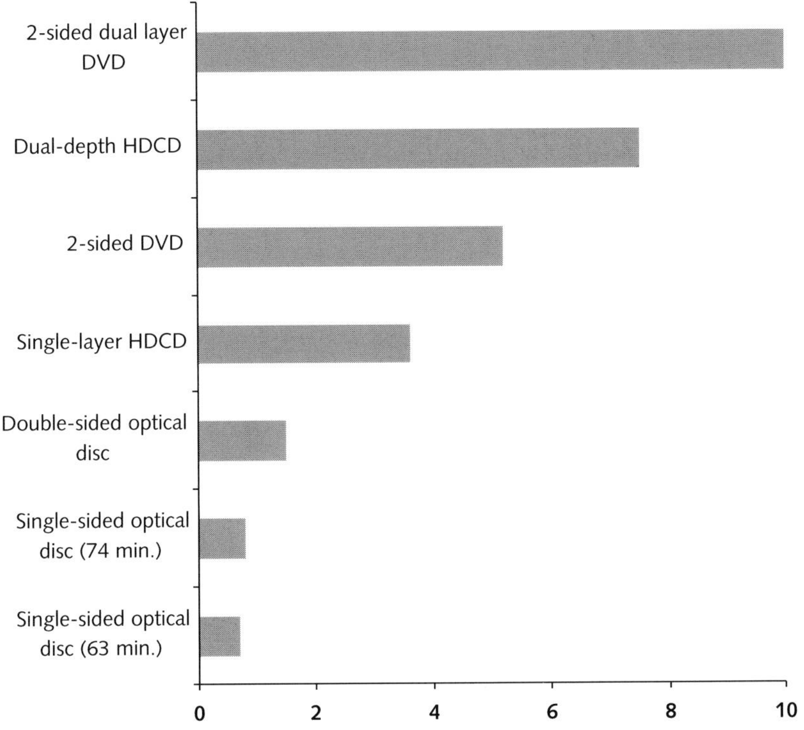

Source: *CD-ROM Professional.*

DVD was launched in Europe in the spring of 1998. Issues such as regional coding, encryption, copy protection, and multichannel sound have hindered DVD's European advance. Panasonic and Thomson have already launched DVD hardware and discs in Europe, and Samsung will release a European DVD player and discs in the fall.

The impact of DVD on networked commerce is difficult to project. Most CD-ROM publishers have moved toward a hybrid publishing model where materials on CD-ROM are supplemented by materials that can be accessed from related Web sites. By creating these hybrid titles, publishers are able to combine the relatively multimedia-rich content on the CD-ROM with the ability to update information continuously and provide greater degrees of interactivity enabled by the Internet. With its much greater capacity, the DVD-ROM offers more local multimedia content combined with the interactivity and currency of Internet-based information. Owners of video and film content may develop new experiences for consumers by combining high-definition, full-length digital films and other programming with access to online communities of interest. The development of such hybrid programming might be significantly helped by the development of hybrid DVD-Internet access set-top boxes.

Game Consoles. Because of the high penetration of game consoles and the historically rapid consumer adoption of new generations of game console technology, we believe that the game console may be another important network access device, assuming that it is bundled with cheap network access service. Some game console manufacturers have developed network add-ons, and we believe that all game consoles will come bundled with network access capabilities within the next three to five years. Online gaming is already a significant and growing market on the Internet with a substantial number of consumers willing to pay a premium for access. The combination of low-cost gaming consoles and inexpensive network access may provide an important conduit for network commerce.

7.3.2 Software Applications

A number of types of software applications are required to support any network platform. In this section we will examine several of the application groups, first reviewing their functionality and common properties, and then briefly examining some examples of products on the market today.

Intelligent Agents/Expert Systems

"Intelligent agents" are software programs that can act autonomously and with a high degree of flexibility (Exhibit 7.17). These applications can be programmed to perform actions and make decisions without direct human control. They may operate proactively, initiating a communication or transaction, or reactively, responding to external events and conditions. Because the Internet provides a vast environment in which agents can explore and interact, the Internet's growth has stimulated great interest in agents and agent-based applications. In addition, the proliferation of material on the Internet has created a tremendous need for help to filter and organise information (Exhibit 7.18). As they become more sophisticated, intelligent agent technologies will play an important role in shaping and delivering content and services and may eliminate much of the integration now necessary to implement network commerce.

Agents can change the way companies market to their customers in an online environment by allowing customisation of content to an individual user's specific needs (one-to-one marketing). Information on user preferences can be determined through inference and observed behaviour, not just through direct user response. User data can be used as part of community-building efforts. However, these technologies may raise issues regarding individual privacy. Many agents require a substantial amount of personal information, and whether they supply such information directly or indirectly, some consumers may not feel comfortable doing so. Service providers must emphasise the additional benefits enabled by intelligent agents and the steps they are taking to protect user privacy. In addition, use of agent technologies limits the benefits of "serendipitous discovery" inherent in Internet browsing. Users often find interesting or useful content without purposefully looking for it. As a result, these technologies will not be appropriate for all situations.

Exhibit 7.17 **Examples of Intelligent Agents**

Vendor/Product	Application	Client vs. Server-Based	Core Algorithms	Learning Capability	Explicit vs. Implicit
Firefly Network • Community Navigator • Catalogue Navigator	• Find people with similar interests • Link users to preferred content	Server	Statistical clustering collaborative filtering	Performance improves with greater user data	Implicitly infers connections based upon previous user input
WiseWire • WiseWire.com	• Personalised news service	Server	Neural network collaborative filtering	Performance improves with greater user rating data	Offers both keyword-guided search and inference-based selection
Autonomy • The Web Researcher • Press Agent • Guardian Agent	• Finds relevant information on the Web • Compiles personal electronic newspaper • Screens Web text and images for objectionable material	Client	Neural network "concept clustering"	Performance can improve with additional sample data	Implicitly makes decisions based on contextual text analysis
Aptex • SelectCast	• Deliver targeted advertising	Server	Neural network	Performance can improve with greater observed user data	Observes user behaviour (clicks, requests, page views) to infer preferences
Net Perceptions • GroupLens	• One-to-one marketing • Community building	Server	Collaborative filtering	Performance improves with greater user data	Enables both explicit queries on user preferences and implicit observation of user behaviour

Source: Gemini Strategic Research Group.

Exhibit 7.18 **Selected Agent Technology Features**

Filtering/Cataloguing

Searches for information fitting a user's preferences, and may then organise it into a structured format (e.g. Verity's Agent Server).

Collaborative Filtering

Analyses data compiled from a large group of users to select items of interest to individual people (e.g. Firefly Network).

Cataloguing

Automatically maintains information database in response to the creation or removal of data in a specific domain (e.g. Web spiders).

Sentinel

Watches for specific events or content and then alerts user or takes other programmed actions (e.g. Autonomy's Guardian Agent).

Source: Gemini Strategic Research Group.

The popularity of intelligent agent software among search engine and Internet directory services indicates its potential for high-volume online applications. Infoseek is using Aptex's SelectCast to target advertising to individual user profiles and its Convectis text analysis system to automatically categorise new Web pages for its Internet directory. Yahoo! has licensed Firefly Network's collaborative filtering software to offer personalised Web site recommendations through its My Yahoo! service. Excite has developed a filtering agent for its NewsTracker personalised news service that receives feedback from users to improve its performance over time. There are more than 1.4 million registered users of Firefly-based services. These initial implementations of agent-based applications on the Internet have generated a great deal of end-user enthusiasm, signalling the potential for strong market growth. However, the range of agent technologies on the market today varies tremendously in degree of functionality and intelligence. Despite their promise, agent technologies are still in a primitive stage.

Communications/Community/Collaboration

New communications technologies allow users to interact in a rich multimedia environment, combining audio, video, text, and graphics (Exhibit 7.19). They allow buyers and sellers to form relationships and create communities on the network. The growing use of these technologies in Internet and online communities indicates increasing acceptance and market potential. Technology vendors continue to integrate a broader range of functions into their products, including messaging and collaborative browsing.

Exhibit 7.19 **Forms of Network Communications**

	Store-and-Forward	Real-Time
Video	• Video messaging	• Video conferencing
Audio	• Voice mail	• Internet telephony
Text & Graphics	• Internet fax • E-mail	• Whiteboard • Chat

Source: Gemini Strategic Research Group.

Communications technologies found on the Internet can be categorised by content type and by mode of communication. Better video and voice communications are being made possible by increasing availability of bandwidth and by improvements in compression technology. The Internet can be a platform for both asynchronous and synchronous communications. In store-and-forward mode, messages are sent to a server to be retrieved by the recipient at a later time. In real-time mode, parties to the conversation (two or more) are online at the same time.

Scores of technology vendors are making significant investments in communications and community applications, including dozens of start-up firms, such as VocalTec, ichat, Volano, NetiPhone, and The Palace (Exhibit 7.20). Smaller software and service companies such as Quarterdeck, White Pine, Camelot, and Galacticomm, and established hardware and software companies such as Lucent, Intel, and Microsoft are also producing communications and community products.

Exhibit 7.20 **Selected Internet Communication/Community Vendors and Products**

Vendor	Product	Media/Functions	Layer
VocalTec	Internet Phone	Voice, video, voice mail, text chat, whiteboard, file transfer	Client
	Telephony Gateway	Interface between PSTN and the Internet	Server App.
Third Planet	DigiPhone	Voice, voice mail, conference calling, video in development	Client
Netscape	Conference *(integrated into Communicator)*	Voice, voice mail, text chat, whiteboard, file transfer, collaborative browsing	Client
Microsoft	Net Meeting *(integrated into Internet Explorer)*	Voice, text chat, whiteboard, file transfer	Client
White Pine Software	Enhanced CU-SeeMe	Voice, video, text chat, whiteboard	Client
	White Pine Reflector	Hosting of CU-SeeMe sessions	Server App.
Voxware	TeleVox	Voice, voice mail, text chat, file transfer	Client
	VoxChat plug-in	Multiple-user text and voice chat	Client
Volano	VoxChat Server	Hosting of multiple-user text and voice chat rooms	Server App.
	Volano Chat	Real-time text chat via Java applets	Server App.

Source: Company Reports; Gemini Strategic Research Group.

The development of quality, real-time voice/video communications could make the Internet an ever-present part of our daily lives. Successful deployment in corporate environments may drive greater penetration across industries and in consumer markets, as more users adopt such technologies, gradually making the Internet the preferred platform for interpersonal communications. In fact, as we have discussed elsewhere,[11] user-generated content may become more important than that provided by Web site operators and content companies. The ability to form relationships with like-minded individuals may be the most compelling value proposition for Internet users. For example, AOL, which cultivated community and communications, has been far more successful than Prodigy, which did not.

Push Technologies

"Push" technologies change the way users obtain information over the Internet. Until recently, users had to click a series of hypertext links to pull relevant information from the Internet. Push software works in the background to package Internet text, graphics, and audio and automatically deliver the information onto the client machine. Because push technologies mimic the ease-of-use of television and appeal to "passive" needs of consumers, many content firms eagerly rushed to adopt push technology during the first half of 1997, making it one of the hottest Web technologies at that time. Much of the excitement over push technology appears to have faded, however, and it may play a more limited role than originally envisioned (Exhibit 7.21).

Exhibit 7.21 **Overview of Push Technology Players**

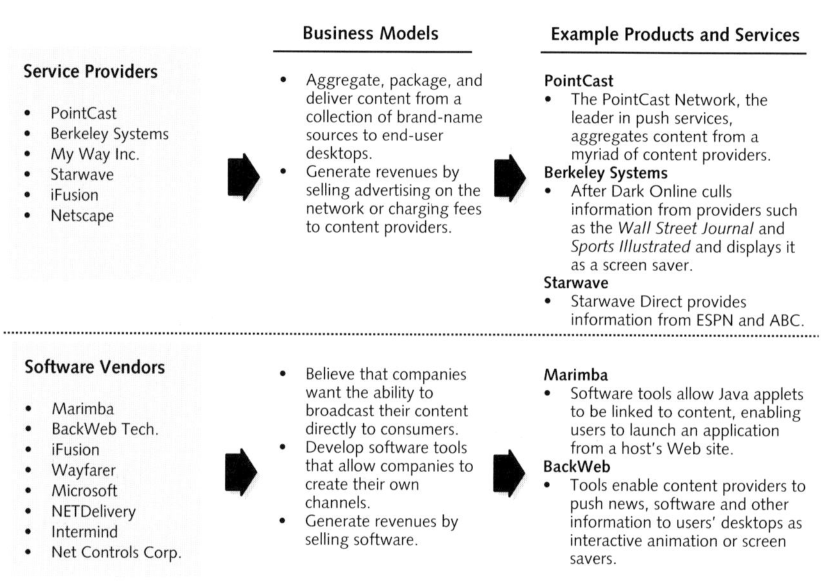

Source: Company Reports; *Business Week; Interactive Age; Digital Media; WebWeek;* Gemini Strategic Research Group.

Push technologies use both client- and server-based applications to deliver information, making them an effective means of helping to manage the plethora of information on the World Wide Web, and offering a more efficient model for obtaining information. Client software is loaded onto a PC where it records a profile of the end user, describing the types of information that person wishes to receive. Server applications monitor and select content based on the user's profile, and deliver it to the user's PC. Some vendors provide a subscription service in which they customise, package, and deliver information for the user from a variety of sources.

Catalogue Software

Catalogue software packages often incorporate a comprehensive set of network commerce features. Software developers are creating applications for publishing catalogues on the Internet and on intranets to streamline internal sales and marketing procedures. While several firms offer stand-alone, catalogue-based network commerce solutions, others have chosen to partner with vendors to create more flexible electronic commerce solutions. Some basic catalogue software functionality is already being built into browsers or simple Web publishing tools.

A number of vendors are offering catalogue applications targeting the Internet commerce marketplace (Exhibit 7.22). These catalogue software products range in capability from static listings to dynamic features integrating back-end functions.

Exhibit 7.22 **Selected Internet Catalogue Software Vendors and Products**

Vendor	Products and Services	Partners and Alliances	EC Applications
Trilogy	• Enterprise software applications for sales and marketing, including catalogue software. • Products designed to streamline internal processes.	• Currently seeking partners to provide professional services and consulting, computer hardware, and software.	• Companies utilising applications for sales chain management functions. • Customers include AT&T, Boeing, Chrysler, DEC, GE, IBM, HP, NEX, Siemens, and Lucent.
SAQQARA	• Software for catalogue authoring and dynamic database publishing. • Services to help customers identify and customise solutions to bring product catalogues on-line.	• Licenses Open Market's software, integrating transaction technology into SAQQARA's StepSearch product. • StepSearch is built into AMP's eMerce Internet Solution offering.	• Enables companies to begin selling and buying online.
Vicom	• Catalogue software and services including systems integration and training.	• Partnership with QuickResponse to develop multimedia standards. • DZGN Advertising licenses Vicom's SmartCatalog software. • DataCat employs SmartCatalog software in its procurement solution.	• SmartCatalog is being used in both transaction- and non transaction-enabled Web sites. • Targeting MRO procurement functions.
iCat	• Browser-based catalogue creation and management software. • Allows for integration of back-office components such as shipping and inventory.	• Business partner program with Web development and Internet hosting companies that use iCat to develop/host sites for customers. • Technology and marketing relationships with Open Market, CyberCash, Compaq, and LitleNet.	• Can be used to create and maintain product catalogues as well as centralised purchasing databases.
Elcom	• Enterprise software applications for sales and marketing, including catalogue software. • Products designed to streamline internal processes.	• Currently seeking partners to provide professional services and consulting, computer hardware, and software.	• N/A
Dataware	• Software for catalogue authoring and dynamic database publishing. • Services to help customers identify and customise solutions to bring product catalogues online.	• N/A	• N/A

Source: Company Reports; Gemini Strategic Research Group.

As the functionality of catalogue software packages is incorporated into other network applications, stand-alone catalogue software is likely to disappear.

Streaming Media

Streaming is a technique that allows data to be transferred as a steady and continuous stream. With streaming, the client browser or plug-in[12] can start displaying the data before the entire file has been transferred. Streaming technologies have played a major role in the evolution of the Internet from a static environment with text-only information to a real-time environment offering multimedia content. These technologies will become ubiquitous as they become integrated into client and host software applications (e.g. Netscape and Microsoft are incorporating streaming functionality directly into their browsers, using their respective LiveAudo and Active Movie technologies). Using Java, content developers are able to embed streaming functionality directly into Web sites, eliminating the need for plug-ins. In the meantime, millions of end users have downloaded free vendor plug-ins to access streaming audio and video content on the Internet (Exhibit 7.23).

Exhibit 7.23 **Selected Streaming Media Technologies**

	Capabilities		Sample Products		
Vendor	**Audio**	**Video**	**Encoder**	**Server**	**Player**
Progressive Networks (RealMedia Partner)	√	√	• RealAudio Encoder • RealVideo Encoder	• RealAudio Server • RealVideo Server	• Real Player • Real Player Plus
Macromedia	√	√	• Flash • Director 6 Multimedia Studio • Authorware		• Shockwave Player
Liquid Audio	√		• Liquifer Pro	• Liquid Music Server	• Liquid Music Player
AudioActive	√		• AudioActive Internet Audio Encoder	• AudioActive Audio Server	• AudioActive Player
VDOnet	√	√	• VDOLive Capture • VDO Broadcast Station	• VDO On-Demand Server • Lite VDO	• VDOLive Player
Xing Technologies	√	√	• Streamworks Transmitter	• Streamworks Server	• Streamworks Player
Digigami	√	√	• Movie Screamer		• CineWeb
Iterated Systems (RealMedia Partner)	√	√	• ClearVideo		• CoolFusion
Vosaic Inc.	√	√	• Media Tools	• Vosaic Server	• Vosaic Browser
DSP Group	√		• True Speech Encoder		• TrueSpeech Player • Beatnik Plug-in
Headspace	√		• Beatnik Editor		• Headspace Audio Engine
LiveUpdate (RealMedia Partner)	√			• Crescendo Streamsite	• Crescendo Plus

Shaded: RealMedia Partners

Source: Company Reports.

Improving core technologies are enhancing the quality of streaming audio and video applications. Streaming products rely on complex core technologies that enable bandwidth negotiation, dynamic connection management, error mitigation, and buffering to deliver a smooth, continuous data flow.

Advanced compression algorithms enable sizeable audio and video files to be reduced to bit rates, enabling data streams to be transmitted without breaks or interruptions. Product offerings are becoming more functional, as formerly audio-only products have incorporated video capabilities as well. Both Progressive Networks and Xing Technologies offer software that enables end users to access both audio and video streams with a single application. Streaming technologies are becoming increasingly complex as developers begin to integrate 3-D and interactive capabilities into their products to create new types of Internet content.

Streaming technologies will profoundly affect the way content developers reach audiences by allowing providers to convey more information, create more compelling and engaging sites, and thus evoke a greater user response. End users have embraced the technologies because they allow users to absorb information "passively." Commerce sites can develop multimedia product catalogues; educational sites can deliver video-based training; and consumers can watch film or music video clips at an entertainment site. Scaleable audio and video streaming technologies provide the foundation for a wide range of on-demand entertainment and information services.

Current streaming technology does not make efficient use of network resources. IP multicasting, the process of sending out data to distributed servers on the Multicast Backbone (Mbone), a special network of routers and software designed to distribute streaming media more efficiently to end users, promises to improve media streaming efficiency. For large quantities of data, IP multicasting is more efficient because the server can broadcast to many recipients simultaneously (Exhibit 7.24).

Multicast transmission is actually well-suited to a range of data-intensive Internet applications, including multiparty videoconferencing, real-time stock quotes, network ticker tapes, and shared whiteboard applications. According to Vint Cerf of the US long-distance telephone carrier MCI Corp., "Internet broadcasting and multicasting are the next chapters in the evolution of the Internet as a revolutionary catalyst for the Information Age."[13]

Exhibit 7.24 **Comparison of Point-to-Point Unicast and Multicast Data Flow**

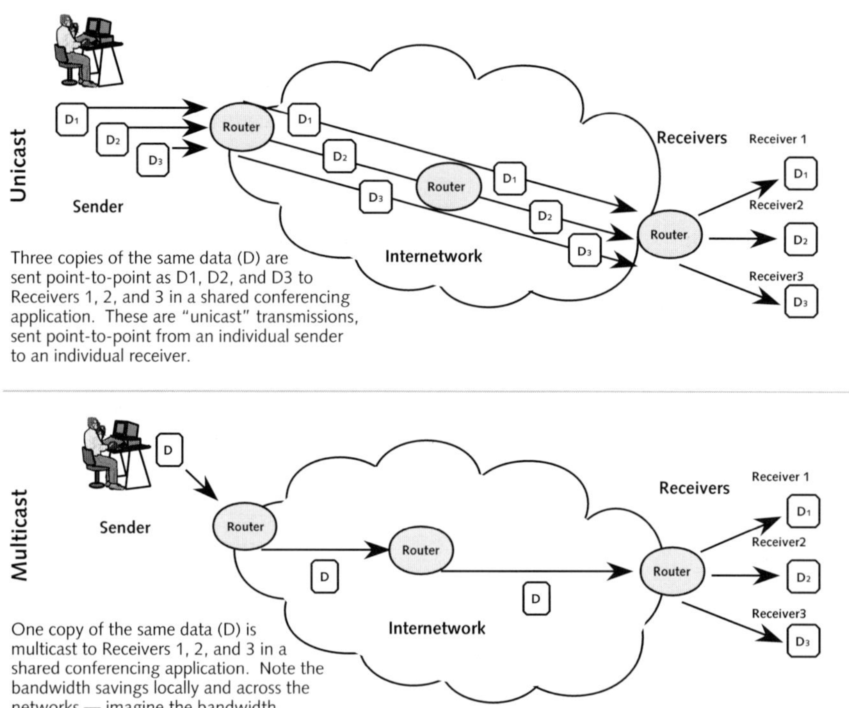
Unicast
Sender
D1
D2
D3
Router
Router
Router
Internetwork
Receivers
Receiver 1
Receiver2
Receiver3
Three copies of the same data (D) are sent point-to-point as D1, D2, and D3 to Receivers 1, 2, and 3 in a shared conferencing application. These are "unicast" transmissions, sent point-to-point from an individual sender to an individual receiver.
Multicast
Sender
D
Router
Router
Router
Internetwork
Receivers
Receiver 1
Receiver2
Receiver3
One copy of the same data (D) is multicast to Receivers 1, 2, and 3 in a shared conferencing application. Note the bandwidth savings locally and across the networks — imagine the bandwidth savings for hundreds of recipients.

Source: Johnson, Vicki and Johnson, Marjory, "IP Multicast Backgrounder," 1996.

Digital Video

The streaming media technologies discussed above are the most important digital video technologies on the network today. Additionally, however, important digital video technologies are also emerging in the consumer electronics and broadcasting arenas. MPEG-2, a digital television compression standard prepared by SC29/WG11, also known as the Motion Pictures Experts Group (MPEG), has emerged as the most important digital media standard for commercial broadcast. Most direct broadcast satellite (DBS) operators around the world have already adopted it in various forms. As cable network operators upgrade to digital networks, they too are adopting MPEG-2. MPEG-2 was formally accepted as an International Standards Organization (ISO) standard in November 1994. It aims at providing CCIR/ITU-R quality for NTSC, PAL, and SECAM (Exhibit 7.25), and also at supporting high-definition television (HDTV). Both European Digital Video Broadcast (DVB) and US Digital Television (DTV) standards are build upon the MPEG-2 compression standard, meaning that regardless of the broadcast standard, the encoding and decoding hardware and software at the core of receiving and production equipment are the same.

Exhibit 7.25 **Major Families of Analogue Television Standards**

NTSC	Analogue US and Japanese format.
PAL	Analogue format used in much of Western Europe.
SECAM	Analogue format used in France and Eastern Europe.

Source: Video Dialtone Technology.

Work on this standard is driven by the desire to globally unify digital television program creation, editing, storage, retrieval, transport, and display. Encryption and scrambling for conditional access are supported by MPEG-2 data stream definitions, but the standard does not specify the actual conditional access mechanisms. A number of different conditional access systems, such as that of the News Corp. subsidiary, News Digital Systems, have been implemented to control programming access to subscribers. Many media firms believe that control of conditional access systems will be an important advantage in the evolution of advanced television systems.

The systems that we now think of as advanced television systems are build upon the MPEG-2 compression standard. Advanced television, however, potentially encompasses a wide range of concepts. The terms advanced television (ATV), digital television (DTV), and high-definition television (HDTV) entered the vocabularies of the consumer electronics and computer industries in the early 1990s.

Today, ATV and DTV are really terms for the same types of technology. Advanced television is typically equated with digital technology. When consumer electronics executives talk about advanced television equipment, they are referring to the television sets, monitors, and set-top boxes that consumers will need to buy in order to receive digital transmissions and view the new DVD films which have recently appeared on the market. Broadcasters, on the other hand, often use the term digital television to refer to the digital broadcast transmissions that will ultimately replace traditional analogue transmissions.

Currently, both the terms ATV and DTV encompass a wide range of new and emerging television formats and systems, including interactive television, which allows viewers to order programs, engage in multiple-user games, and buy products via their television sets and telecomputing, which combines Internet access with television programming.

HDTV is a special type of digital television in which the scan rate of the picture is twice or three times that of today's television images. HDTV provides movie-quality pictures and the added advantage of multiple layers or multiple sources of sound. Within the 6 MHz bandwidth that has been allocated to it, HDTV technology promises to give consumers all of the audio and video features they now receive when they go to a surround-sound film in a movie theatre.

Europe. Europe has a chequered history in terms of bringing advanced television to consumers.[14] In the 1980s, fearful that the Japanese would impose their own HDTV standard on an embattled European consumer electronics industry, Europe embarked on a grand plan to bring about its own HDTV standard. The European Commission steered a development consortium called EUREKA EU-95 that aimed at bringing in fully-fledged HDTV through a transitional phase of widescreen standard-definition television (SDTV). In September 1993, the industry, with the support of the European Commission, launched an initiative for a pan-European digital TV strategy. As part of this initiative, the European Launching Group on Digital Video Broadcasting was formed, and eighty-four European broadcasters, manufacturers, telecommunications companies and regulatory authorities signed a memorandum of understanding (MoU) to tackle the issue of standardisation. This group has defined a set of digital European standards for satellite, cable, MMDS, and terrestrial broadcasting, using MPEG-2 compression, known collectively as DVB.

The DVB standard does not yet specify an HDTV format, and the EU continues to progress through the SDTV stage laid out by EUREKA EU-95. The Action Plan for the Introduction of Advanced Television Services in Europe (the Action Plan) was established on July 22, 1993, with the objective of ensuring the accelerated development of the market for advanced television services in Europe using the widescreen 16:9 format.

The approach is based on stimulating the broadcasting and program production elements in the value chain so that all the different actors and elements necessary to deliver 16:9 services to the home fall into place. The Action Plan lays down two targets to be achieved during its life: (1) a critical mass of advanced television services in the 16:9 format; and (2) an increasing volume of programming in the 16:9 format and with high technical quality both in picture and sound and of such a nature as to facilitate an optimum audience rating.

To achieve these targets, 220 million euro in public funds were allocated for the period from mid-1993 to mid-1997. The Action Plan paid up to 50 percent of the so-called flat rates (reflecting the extra costs associated with each hour of 16:9 broadcasting and production). However, 66 million euro were reserved for so-called "late-starting" markets — those with no widescreen services in 1995. Broadcasters and producers in these countries received 80 percent of the flat rates. The intention was to provide an additional incentive to help them catch up.

By the end of its implementation in December 1998 — when the final allocation of funding will have been spent by the recipients — the Action Plan will have funded the transmission of over 60,000 hours of widescreen material by some sixty broadcasters and aided in the production of 23,000 hours of new or remastered programs.[15]

United States. In contrast to the situation in Europe, standard resolution widescreen TV has not been embraced in the US as an interim step towards HDTV. Instead, the broadcast and cable industries have chosen to wait for the Grand Alliance's digital HDTV system to be finalised and accepted as a standard. Though widescreen TV sets were introduced in the US market more than two years ago, consumers have shown little interest in purchasing these high-priced sets in the absence of a widescreen broadcast service.

Once the Advanced Television System Committee (ATSC) endorsed the digital TV standard worked out by the Grand Alliance earlier this year, the US broadcasting community was firmly put on the digital HDTV rail. Viewers in the ten largest US TV markets should be able to watch broadcast HDTV signals by end of 1998, with another twenty markets coming online the following year. In late March 1998, twenty-six stations, including eleven network-owned and operated stations, committed to this aggressive timetable.

The ATSC has developed a digital television broadcast standard known as DTV which has been formally adopted in the US, where an aggressive implementation process is now underway. In addition, it has been formally adopted in Canada and South Korea, and is actively being considered in Mexico and many other countries outside of Europe.

To ensure that the timetable does not slip too much, the FCC issued rules requiring all major network affiliates in the top ten markets to have a digital signal on air by May 1, 1999, with affiliates in markets eleven through thirty required to follow by November 1 of that year. Of the twenty-six early launches, eight will be by ABC affiliates, seven by NBC affiliates, five by CBS affiliates and three by Fox affiliates.

Meeting the voluntary and FCC-mandated deadlines is likely to require a concerted effort on the part of stations, equipment suppliers and the industry as a whole. Broadcasters are required to carry at least half of the analogue channel's programming on the digital channel four years before surrendering the former. This increases to 75 percent three years before the analogue channel is to be returned and 100 percent during the last two years both channels are in operation. The FCC also set a target of 2006 for the end of NTSC service and return of analogue spectrum. It will, however, reconsider this sensitive issue every two years.

To prepare for digital broadcast, local television stations in the US will spend between 7 and 8.8 million euro each over the next five years. Stations will have to replace most of their equipment, including cameras, switchers, tape machines, amplifiers, transmitters, and towers. In addition, stations will have to rebuild many of their sets because the higher resolution of digital television will no longer mask many of the flaws that were previously hidden by the lower-resolution analogue format.[16]

At a minimum, local television broadcasters will have to spend roughly 880,000 euro to pass through a network digital TV feed and between 4.4 million and 8.8 million euro more to originate their own digital programming.[17]

7.3.3 Network Technologies

As we have discussed elsewhere,[18] the telecommunications industry is in the midst of a period of dramatic change. A number of network technologies are playing key roles in this transformation.

In this section, we will examine in greater detail the technologies affecting the two physical layers of the telecommunications industry, the local access network, and the long-haul network.

Local Access

A number of competing technologies are emerging as local access carriers attempt to meet demand for greater bandwidth. Some of these technologies leverage existing networks, while others require the deployment of entirely new infrastructures. Physical network alternatives include plain old telephone service (POTS), ISDN, cable modems, and xDSL, while wireless solutions are composed of both terrestrial wireless and satellite-based technologies.

The local access network is evolving towards a mix of wireline and wireless technologies that will allow a seamless fabric of high-bandwidth network access from almost any point on the globe (Exhibit 7.26).

Exhibit 7.26 **Emerging Telecommunications Industry Structure**

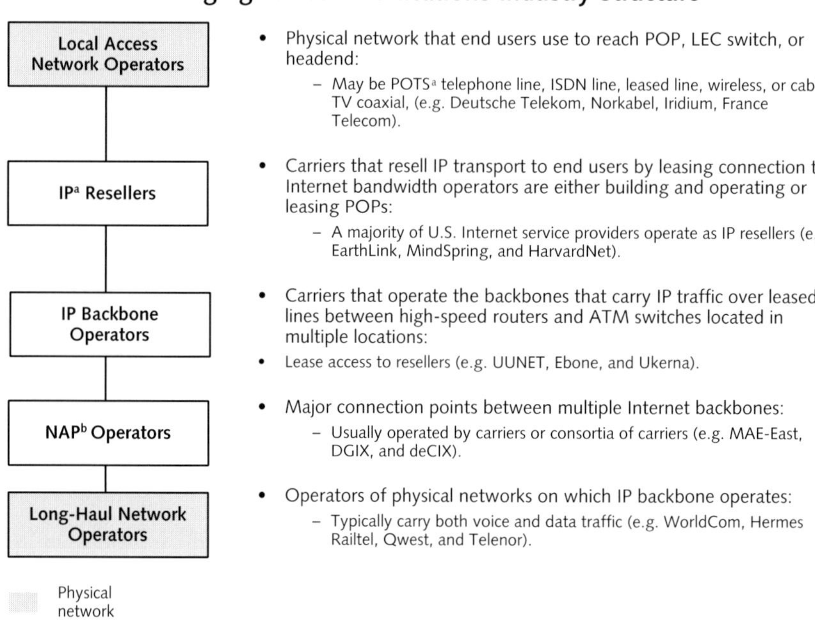

Local Access Network Operators
IP[a] Resellers
IP Backbone Operators
NAP[b] Operators
Long-Haul Network Operators
Physical network
• Physical network that end users use to reach POP, LEC switch, or headend:
– May be POTS[a] telephone line, ISDN line, leased line, wireless, or cable TV coaxial, (e.g. Deutsche Telekom, Norkabel, Iridium, France Telecom).
• Carriers that resell IP transport to end users by leasing connection to Internet bandwidth operators are either building and operating or leasing POPs:
– A majority of U.S. Internet service providers operate as IP resellers (e.g. EarthLink, MindSpring, and HarvardNet).
• Carriers that operate the backbones that carry IP traffic over leased lines between high-speed routers and ATM switches located in multiple locations:
• Lease access to resellers (e.g. UUNET, Ebone, and Ukerna).
• Major connection points between multiple Internet backbones:
– Usually operated by carriers or consortia of carriers (e.g. MAE-East, DGIX, and deCIX).
• Operators of physical networks on which IP backbone operates:
– Typically carry both voice and data traffic (e.g. WorldCom, Hermes Railtel, Qwest, and Telenor).

a. Plain Old Telephone Service.
b. Network Access Point.
Source: Gemini Strategic Research Group.

The wireline infrastructure of choice will eventually be fibre-to-the-home (FTTH), offering multi-gigabit-per-second network access. The wireless technologies of choice will likely be high-frequency terrestrial wireless technologies, using spread-spectrum encoding schemes like code division multiple access (CDMA) to offer symmetrical multi-megabit-per-second access, and broadband satellite systems like Teledesic offering symmetrical access in the Ka-band spectrum of between 2 Mbps and 155 Mbps (Exhibit 7.27).

Exhibit 7.27 **Local Access Network Evolution**

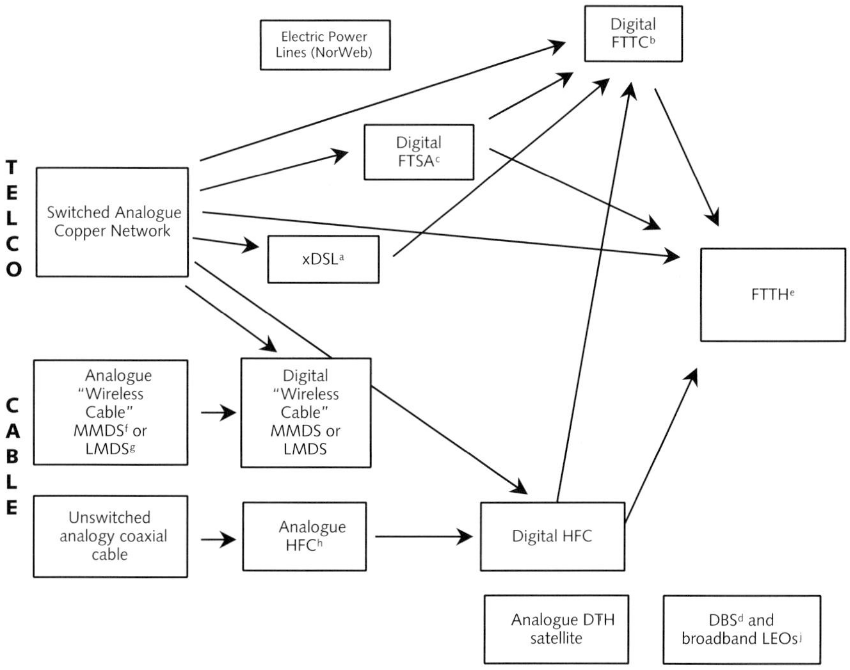

Sources: CED; *Telephony*; International Engineering Consortium; Gemini Strategic Research Group Analysis.

a. Digital Subscriber Line technologies.
b. Fibre to the curb.
c. Fibre to the service area.
d. Direct broadcast satellite.
e. Fibre to the home.
f. Multichannel multipoint distribution service.
g. Local multipoint distribution service.
h. Hybrid fibre/coax.
i. Direct-to-Home.
j. Low-Earth-Orbit Satellites.

Dial-up access is likely to remain the most common means of Internet access over the next five years, with 56-kbps modem access becoming the predominant means for consumers to reach the Internet (Exhibit 7.28).

Exhibit 7.28 **Consumer Internet Access Technologies (Millions of US Internet Service Subscribers)**

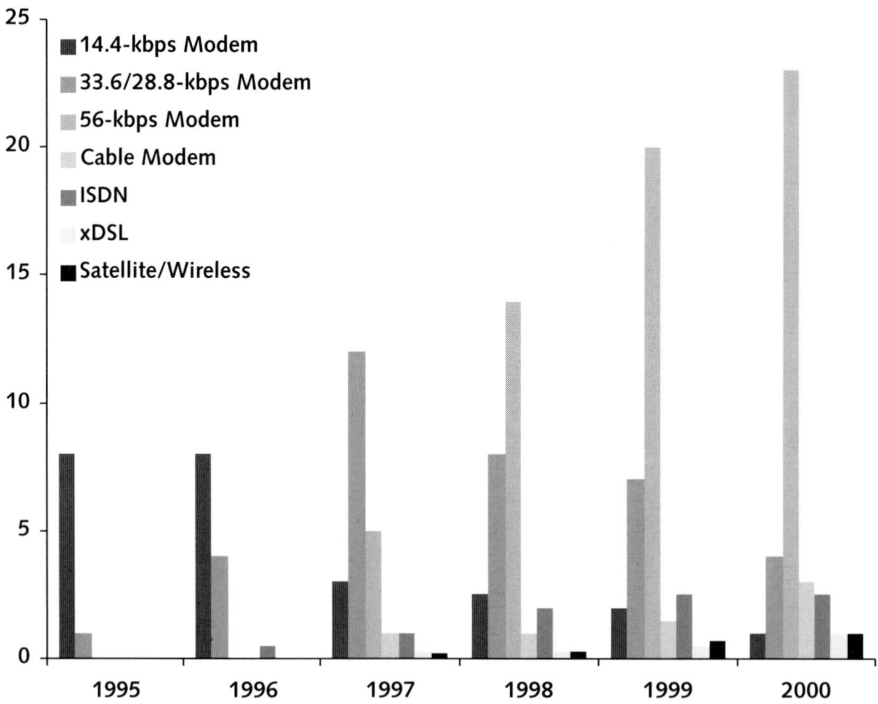

Source: Jupiter Communications.

True broadband access technologies will provide a wide range of capabilities and, depending on location, are likely to have widely varying costs (Exhibit 7.29).

Exhibit 7.29 **Comparison of Selected Network Access Technologies**

Type	Maximum Bandwidth Downstream	Maximum Bandwidth Upstream	Network Deployment Cost per Subscriber	End-User Equipment Cost[d]
POTS and Modem	Downstream 56kbps[a]	Upstream 56kbps	0 euro	90 euro
ISDN	64kbps-2Mbps	64kbps-2Mbps	90 euro	220 euro
xDSL	768kbps-10Mbps	64kbps-1Mbps	270 euro	270 euro
Cable	500kbps-38Mbps	33.6kbps-2Mbps	180 euro	270 euro
LMDS	500kbps-8Mbps	28.8kbps-56kbps[b]	440 euro[c]	900 euro
GEO Satellite	200kbps-400kbps	28.8kbps-56kbps[b]	440 euro[c]	900 euro
LEO Satellite	2Mbps-155Mbps	2Mbps-155Mbps	700 euro[c]	1,300 euro
FTTH	2.488Gbps	2.488Gbps	1,300 euro	440 euro[e]

Source: Gemini Strategic Research Group.

a. Assures digital line from POP to central office.

b. Requires POTS line and modem for upstream.

c. Variable depending on take-up.

d. May be paid by end user or provider.

e. Estimated introduction cost of optical network interface.

Today, integrated Services Digital Network (ISDN) technology is the most widely available broadband access technology in many parts of the world. The most common type of ISDN is known as basic rate interface (BRI), providing 128 kbps of data throughput. Primary-rate interface (PRI) ISDN groups multiple communications channels to offer up to 2.0 Mbps of bandwidth.[19] Because of installation costs, difficulties determining optimum pricing, and complexity, ISDN has not been widely adopted in most markets. The majority of ISDN installations today are in a handful of Western European countries like Germany and France.

One important component of the network convergence between television and other telecommunications media is the cable modem. Cable modems will become an important conduit for residential broadband access. Cable-based Internet access services promise downstream transmission rates between 10 and 38 Mbps and upstream bandwidth between 33.6 kbps and 2 Mbps. Because neighbourhood nodes share network capacity, actual bandwidth to the individual depends on the number of users and their usage habits. Initial deployment has not occurred as rapidly as originally expected due to the high cost of upgrading the existing cable plant in many locations. However, we believe that as cable operators gain experience offering access services and complete the necessary infrastructure upgrades, cable modem access will capture a significant portion of the access market in those areas where it is available.

Digital subscriber line (DSL) technologies offer a variety of methods for upgrading the existing copper twisted pair POTS infrastructure to support high-speed network access. Asymmetric DSL (ADSL) offers at least 7 Mbps downstream and 1 Mbps upstream, while symmetric DSL (SDSL) offers about 768 kbps in both directions. Most incumbent local exchange carriers have been slow to deploy DSL technologies because of high costs and concerns about pricing and cannibalisation of other high-speed data services. The most aggressive DSL players remain new competitive access providers such as Covad Communications in the Silicon Valley in the US, which in December 1997 began offering 1.5 Mbps ADSL services to corporate telecommuters for 172 euro per month, and Harvard.Net, a Boston-based ISP that has been offering SDSL service since 1997.

Terrestrial wireless technologies offer another alternative for broadband network access. Members of Europe's communications industry, for example, have agreed on a standard for third-generation mobile communications known as Universal Mobile Telecommunications System (UMTS). Projected to be available in 2001, this technology will offer transmission speeds of up to 2 Mbps for stationary systems and 144 kbps to 384 kbps for mobile systems. Local Multipoint Distribution Service (LMDS) and Multichannel Multipoint Distribution Service (MMDS) are other terrestrial wireless technologies that may provide alternatives for broadband network access. MMDS has been used for years to deliver analogue television service, and trials are now underway to test MMDS as a possible network access technology. LMDS is currently being used in limited trials in the US, Canada, Japan, and Korea, and may become a more significant access technology after US LMDS spectrum license auctions are completed that began in February 1998. LMDS requires a clear line-of-site between antennas, and large buildings, trees, and even heavy rain showers can block the signal and limit service availability. One system, Cellularvision USA, is currently offering 1.5 Mbps downstream Internet access to consumers in New York City for 44 euro per month, although the service also requires dial-up modem access as an upstream channel.

Satellite service providers offer another alternative for high-speed network access. Some satellite operators have already entered the broadband market using existing geostationary satellites. For example, Tele2 recently launched a GEO-satellite-based service in Scandinavia, and Hughes Network Systems has been operating a high-speed, asymmetric Internet access service in the US that offers downstream bandwidth of up to 400 kbps.

Next-generation satellite systems using both advanced geostationary and low earth orbit satellites will offer wider access, with the LEO services offering symmetrical broadband access. Building upon experience gained from narrowband satellite ventures (e.g. Iridium, Globalstar), firms such as Teledesic, Hughes, and Alcatel are proposing to launch constellations of satellites ranging in number from one dozen to several hundred satellites that are capable of providing multi-megabit, symmetrical communications services. The first of the services is likely to come online before 2003, offering high-speed network access to areas of the globe otherwise unserved by broadband network connectivity (Exhibit 7.30).

Exhibit 7.30 **Proposed Broadband Satellite Systems**

System	Operator	Applications	Altitude	Spectrum	Bandwidth	System Cost (euro)	# of Satellites	Operational
Cyberstar	Loral Space & Communications	Data, video	GEO	Ku, Ka	400 kbps (Ku), 30 Mbps (Ka)	926 million	3 Ka	1998
Astrolink	Lockheed Martin	Data, video, rural telephone	GEO	Ka	Up to 9.6 Mbps	3.5 billion	9	2003
Teledesic	Gates, McCaw, Boeing, Motorola	Video, data video conferencing	LEO (435 mi.)	Ka	16 kbps-64 Mbps (E1 for symmetric links)	7.9 billion	288	2002
Spaceway	Hughes	Data, multimedia	GEO	Ku	Up to 6 Mbps	3 billion	64	2001
Skybridge	Alcatel/Loral	Voice, data, video conferencing	LEO (911 mi.)	Ku	16 kbps-2 Mbps to satellites; 16 kbps - 60 Mbps to user	3 billion	64	2001

Source: Company Reports; Gemini Strategic Research Group.

Digital satellite broadcasting systems offer another example of the growing convergence between television broadcasting and other forms of data communications. Direct broadcast satellite (DBS) was the first and is the most widely deployed digital television access technology. Multiple DBS systems are currently operating in Europe, North and South America, Asia, Africa, and the Middle East. Several of these systems offer more than 100 channels of programming and near-video-on-demand capabilities for pay-per-view programming. In addition, these same DBS satellites can be used for datacasting. To offer digital television services, DBS satellites deliver anywhere from 25 to 34 megabits per second on each transponder, representing an abundance of bandwidth. Chips are now being used to make a card that will slip into a personal computer so that computers can handle this type of data. Broadcasters can push multimedia data to personal computers that have these cards. Firms like New Digital Systems are pushing this technology in the hope that it will motivate consumers to pay for digital content.

Digital terrestrial broadcast is about to begin in many locations as well. In the US, the FCC recently reaffirmed its service rules for the conversion of all US broadcasters to digital broadcasting services (DTV). These rules include build-out construction schedules, NTSC and DTV channel simulcasting, and the surrender of spectrum currently used for analogue transmission to the government in 2006 so that it can be auctioned for other uses.[20] Specifically, twenty-four broadcast stations located in the ten largest broadcast markets have committed to building DTV facilities by 1 November 1998. All commercial stations are to have built DTV facilities by 1 May 2001, and all non-commercial stations by 1 May 2003. This aggressive schedule means that by 2006, all US television viewers will have had to have purchased digital televisions or set-top boxes capable of converting digital television signals for viewing on existing analogue television sets.

Other important access technologies include the free-to-air television broadcast spectrum freed up by the transition to digital television, which may be used for data, as well as Intercast, which enables personal computers equipped with broadcast tuners and special software to receive content simultaneously with television broadcasts. The digital television signal format recently established in the US will allow television broadcasters to transmit variable streams of data alongside video, opening up many intriguing possibilities for interactive media. One example of a firm using Intercast is WavePhone, a US data broadcaster that has announced an agreement to create a branded channel known as "WaveTop" that will allow PC users to receive free access to Time Warner's Internet content over the vertical blanking interval of the TV broadcast signal. To receive the WaveTop service, users will need to obtain the free WaveTop software and use a computer with a TV tuner.

Finally, the most exotic potential access technologies involve the use of high-altitude balloons and aircraft to provide similar broadband access to that envisioned by the backers of the LEO satellite networks. One firm, Sky Station International (SSI) has received approval from the US FCC to offer high-speed telephone and Internet access in the 47 GHz frequency band using at least 250 helium balloons floating in the stratosphere. SSI anticipates that its terminal equipment will cost only about 90 euro. Fixed users would be able to connect at speeds ranging from 64 kbps to 155 Mbps, while portable users would be able to connect at between 64 kbps and 2.04 Mbps.[21]

Long-Haul

Long-haul network operators own and operate the physical networks upon which the IP backbone network is built. These operators include interexchange telephone carriers, Post, Telephone and Telegraph (PTT) organisations, and new entrants owning rights of way and other infrastructure (e.g. railways, electric and gas utilities). Long-haul network operators traditionally faced limited competition due to the prohibitive costs of constructing physical networks, but many new long-haul networks are now being constructed. Most new long-haul networks are being built specifically for IP traffic, and existing long-haul network operators are rapidly upgrading their network capacity.

Fibre-optics are transforming the long-haul network infrastructure. One of the most significant technologies of the last decade is wave division multiplexing (WDM). WDM allows carriers to dramatically increase the capacity of their networks. As illustrated in Exhibit 7.31, WDM works by combining multiple wavelengths of light for transport over a single strand of fibre-optic cable.

Exhibit 7.31 **Illustration of Wave Division Multiplexing Technology**

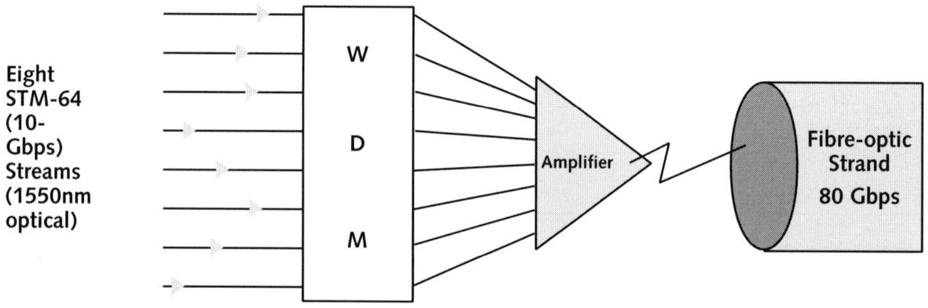

Source: CTR Group Ltd.

Since each wave-length of light can carry at least a 10 Gbps stream of data, this means that the capacity of a strand of fibre-optic cable can be multiplied by as many wavelengths of light as can be multiplexed onto it. Current state-of-the-art WDM technologies allow eight or sixteen streams of data to be multiplexed onto a single strand, but much larger numbers of streams have been successfully multiplexed under laboratory conditions, suggesting that this technology will continue to decrease the cost of long-haul transport for some time to come (Exhibit 7.32). Long-haul network operators like WorldCom/MCI and Sprint have embarked on annual backbone network upgrades as new WDM technologies go to market, with each cycle tripling or quadrupling available bandwidth on key routes.

Carriers around the world are building new fibre-optic networks and using WDM to create a tremendous amount of backbone capacity. Carriers that already operate fibre-optic networks are installing WDM technologies to expand existing network capacity dramatically. WDM means that despite the tremendous growth in Internet-driven data traffic, backbone capacity will grow to keep pace with this traffic and will ensure cheap long-haul transport of rich multimedia data.

Exhibit 7.32 **Comparison of Transmission Speeds**

Network Technology	Bits per Second	No. of Telephone Conversations
Twisted Pair (copper)	7,680,000	120
Fibre	45,000,000	703
Fibre with DWDM[a] (1996)	40,000,000,000	625,000
Improved Fibre with DWDM (1997)	100,000,000,000	1,562,500

Source: Alex Brown; *Telephony*; Schroder Wertheim & Co.

a. Dense wave division multiplexing.

While WDM is being deployed on numerous existing terrestrial and submarine networks, a number of new long-haul networks are being built all over the world. One of the most ambitious of these infrastructure projects is Project OXYGEN (Exhibit 7.33). CTR Group has proposed the construction of this global network by 2003. It will include a 275,000-km network of undersea and overland fibre-optic cables, connecting 175 countries with 265 landing points. Each segment of the network will have a minimum transmission capacity of 320 Gbps and a maximum of 1,000 Gbps. OXYGEN is the largest universal network ever planned. The backers of Project OXYGEN envision it as primarily a transport vehicle for digital video, projecting that the network will be able to allow access to all of the video programming in the world from any other location in the world. Voice traffic will be such a small part of the traffic on this network that it may become a free rider.

Exhibit 7.33 **Map of Proposed Project OXYGEN Network, January 1998**

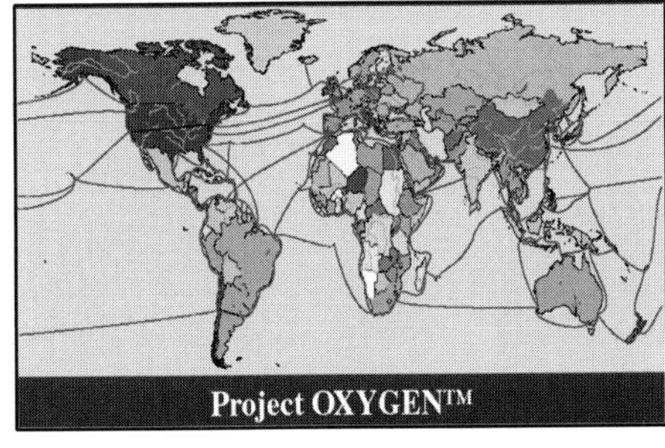

Source: CTR Group Ltd., January 1998.

Global infrastructure projects like Project OXYGEN and Teledesic promise to radically alter the costs of accessing network content and conducting network commerce. As illustrated in Exhibit 7.34, new technologies and economies of scale achieved by a global fibre-optic network have the potential to undercut dramatically the costs of current long-haul transport networks. Many traditional bottlenecks to network access will disappear once these projects are completed.

Exhibit 7.34 **1998 Cost Comparison of Planned and Existing Submarine Cables, Annual Cost in Euro of One 64 kbps Voice Circuit**

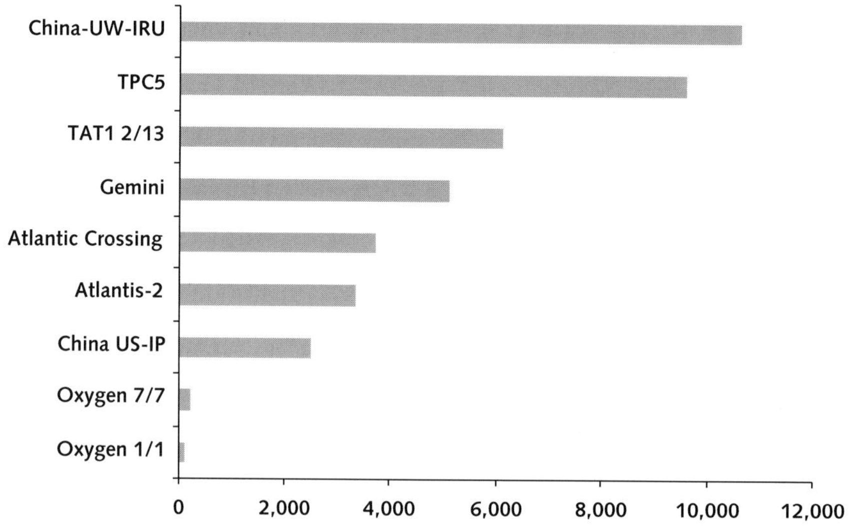

China-UW-IRU
TPC5
TAT1 2/13
Gemini
Atlantic Crossing
Atlantis-2
China US-IP
Oxygen 7/7
Oxygen 1/1
0 2,000 4,000 6,000 8,000 10,000 12,000

Source: CTR Group Ltd.

The potential effect of global networks that offer low-cost access to the rest of the world cannot be overstated. The Internet has offered the first real taste of borderless global communications and commerce, and these global infrastructure projects based on fibre-optics and broadband satellites will tremendously expand the quantity, quality, and functionality of these borderless activities.

7.3.4 Hosting Technologies

Hosting technologies consist of both hardware (computer and networking equipment) and software (server software) that enable many of the core capabilities of network platforms. Hosting technologies include two components, hardware and software. Here we will focus on developments in the server software arena. Several types of core Internet server technologies function as the platform on which all Internet applications operate. A number of the leading Web servers in widespread use are free or shareware products. As the demand for more functionality leads to increased Web site complexity, leading vendors are beginning to bundle server technologies into integrated product suites. An important related group of software applications is "middleware." Middleware enables the integration of Internet applications with legacy systems and supports dynamic content generation, dramatically increasing the value of Web sites to end users.

Server Software

Server software resides at the heart of most networks. A wide range of server applications are required to build a successful network commerce platform (Exhibit 7.35).

Exhibit 7.35 **Types of Internet Servers in 1998**

Type	Description
Web server	• Listens for HTTP requests • Sends HTTP/HTML-based content • Processes CGI/API commands
Commerce server	• Supports transactions • Provides database connectivity
Mail server	• Forwards incoming e-mail to appropriate box • Enables outward messaging of e-mail • Typically uses SMTP or POP3 standards
FTP server	• Listens for FTP requests ("Gopher") • Sends requested files
News server	• Accepts and maintains newsgroup postings • May or may not include HTTP • Typically uses NNTP standard
Proxy server	• Stores frequently accessed documents locally • Reduces demand on network capacity
Chat server	• Supports real-time text-based interaction between users.

Source: Gemini Strategic Research Group.

Exhibit 7.36 **Leading Web Server Operating Systems and Software**

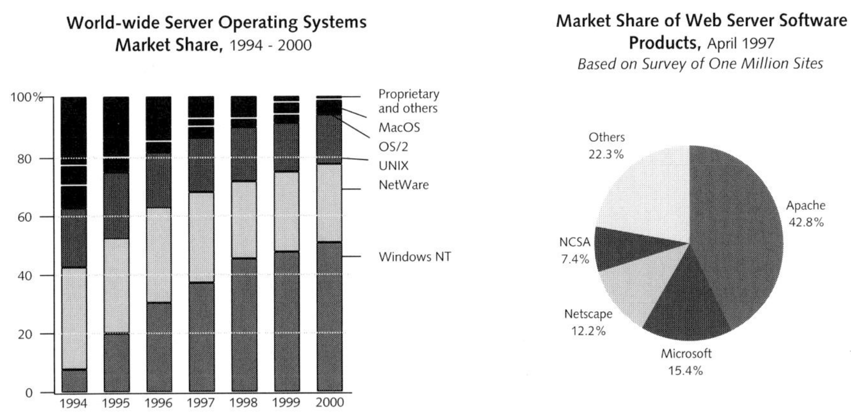

Source: *Business Week*, 10 February, 1997; Dataquest, 1996; Intranet Security Customer Survey, June, 1997; IDC, 1995; Netcraft.

Commerce server vendors are competing aggressively to become the industry standard (Exhibit 7.37). This industry has been highly competitive, with participants making large research and development investments and waiting years to receive any return on this investment. Firms like Open Market, Broadvision, and Connect Inc. have been the market leaders, but Microsoft and Oracle, as well as Netscape, are in hot pursuit. Many of the vendors in this segment have refocused their efforts on the business-to-business market, believing now that it holds the greatest potential.

Exhibit 7.37 **Feature Comparison of the Major Commerce Server Products**

Company	Product(s)	Server-Side Platforms	Server-Side Processing	ORB Support	Database Connectivity	Encryption	Electronic Currency	EDI
Open Market	OM-Transact	HP-UX, IRIX, Stratus, SunOS	CGI, Fast CGI	-	Oracle, Sybase	SSL	-	Yes
Broadvision	One-to-One	HP-UX, IRIX, Sun, Solaris, Windows NT, AIX	CGI, RPCs	Iona, CORBA	Oracle, Sybase, MS SQL Server, ODBC	SSL	CyberCash, Verifone	Yes
Connect Inc.	One Server OrderStream Purchase Stream	HP-UX, Sun Solaris	CGI	-	NA	SSL	NA	NA
Actra	CrossCommerce	HP-UX, IRIX, AIX, SNI, Sun Solaris	CGI	-	Informix, Oracle, Sybase, ODBC	SSL	-	Yes
Microsoft	Merchant Server Commerce Server	Windows NT	CGI, Proprietary	COM	MS SQL Server, ODBC	SSL, Microsoft CryptoAPI	CyberCash, Cybercharge, Tellan, Trintech, Verifon, SET	3rd Party
IBM	Domino.Merchant Net.Commerce	AIX, Windows NT	CGI	-	DB2	SSL	-	-
Oracle	Oracle Merchant Server 1.0	Sun Solaris, Windows NT	CGI, Proprietary	CORBA, Proprietary	Informix, Oracle, Sybase, MS SQL Server, ODBC	SSL	CyberCash, Digicash, First Virtual, Verifon, SET	-
Mercantec	Mercantec Softcart 2.23	AIX, BSDI, Digital UNIX, HP-UX, IRIX, Linux, SCO, Solaris, SunOS	CGI, Fast CGI	-	Informix, Oracle, Sybase, MS SQL Server, ODBC	PGP	CyberCash, Digicash, E-Cash, and most others.	Yes

Source: Company Reports; Gemini Strategic Research Group.

The winners in this segment will play an important role in establishing the standards on which future electronic commerce applications are built.

7.3.5 Security

The growth of the Internet and network commerce activities has placed increasing importance on security. Making commerce secure on a network that was not originally designed with security issues in mind has led to a wide range of security initiatives. Balancing security concerns with ease-of-use is one of the critical challenges facing firms implementing security solutions. Many proposed security solutions have quickly failed due to excessive complexity.

The dramatic increases in computing power described elsewhere in this chapter have placed in the hands of many users the power to break encryption once considered unbreakable. Encryption has become as much a political issue as a technical issue, with many governments expressing concerns about the use of encryption to protect illicit activities. Europe has played an important role in setting internationally recognised standards for security, while attention in the US has focused on government control of encryption and key escrow systems.

Encryption
Encryption is the use of mathematical techniques to manipulate and scramble data so that is cannot be restored to its original form by anyone but its intended recipient. It plays a central role in security systems, providing a solution for authentication, integrity, confidentiality, and nonrepudiation.

Encryption export policies are currently an important political issue. With US restrictions on the export of strong encryption technologies, many US-based software manufacturers that are component suppliers for network commerce infrastructure are prohibited from exporting their products with robust encryption. To demonstrate the need for use of encryption technologies, the Business Software Alliance sponsored research to determine what capabilities were required to crack the forty-bit DES-based encryption that is most commonly used today in financial applications (Exhibit 7.38).[22] This work suggested that forty-bit encryption is inadequate, and most experts now agree that keys of at least ninety bits are necessary to ensure adequate protection.

Exhibit 7.38 **Estimated Time Required to Crack DES Encryption Key**

		Key Length	
Type of Attacker	**Budget**	**40 Bits**	**56 Bits**
Casual hacker	350 euro	5 hours	38 years
Small business	9,000 euro	12 minutes	556 days
Corporate department	265,000 euro	24 seconds	19 days
Large firm	9,000,000 euro	7 seconds	13 hours
Intelligence agency	265,000,000 euro	.0002 seconds	12 seconds

Source: Business Software Alliance, 1996.

There are two common types of encryption: shared single-key and public key. DES is the leading single-key encryption technique. This method works by having the parties share a common encryption key. Since this single encryption key must be kept secret in order to keep the information secure, a separate shared key is necessary for every pair of communication partners. Public-key encryption is based on two keys, a public key to encrypt the data and a private key to decrypt the data. Anyone wishing to receive encrypted data can make their public key available to others, typically through a directory, and then others can encrypt data using that public key and the communication can only be decrypted by the holder of the corresponding private key. These public key encryption systems are slower than symmetric-key systems, but they are much easier to administer.

Trusted Third Parties and Certificate Authorities

A public key infrastructure is required to support a strong public key encryption effort. One means of ensuring the integrity of communications is to have a trusted third party vouch for the authenticity of a public key, usually by distributing the public key with a certificate. The certificate binds the identity of the key holder with the public key value. This trusted third party is known as a Certificate Authority. Commercial Certificate Authorities such as VeriSign and GTE are trying to fill the need for trusted third-party services by issuing digital certificates. These digital IDs can also be used with secure Web servers such as those based on the Secure Sockets Layer (SSL) and Secure Hypertext Transport Protocol (S-HTTP). Other activities of trusted third parties include key generation, key distribution, certificate revocation, key escrow, document escrow, nonrepudiation services, and trusted time stamping. These types of services support applications like secure e-mail, payment protocols, electronic checks, EDI, electronic forms, and digitally signed documents.

SSL and S-HTTP

SSL is the most widely used security technology on the World Wide Web. It has become the standard for encryption between browsers and servers. SSL provides end-to-end channel security between browsers and servers, authenticating the server and optionally authenticating clients. After a simple handshake, it creates a private and reliable channel between the user and server. Secure HTTP extends the basic HTTP protocol that is the primary protocol used between Web servers and clients. S-HTTP supports a variety of security mechanisms for HTTP clients and servers, allowing the appropriate option to be chosen for a range of potential uses.

Secure Electronic Transactions (SET)

The SET standard issued by Visa and MasterCard leverages public-key cryptography to provide a secure standard for credit card payments on the Internet. SET is designed to ensure that credit card account numbers are kept private from anyone who intercepts the transaction, to provide message integrity, and to verify the identities of the parties to the transaction. To date SET has not been widely adopted and it is not clear whether it will be widely used. Most shoppers on the Internet seem to be growing comfortable with the level of security provided by SSL and S-HTTP technologies.

Firewalls

Network firewalls are dedicated hardware and software systems that block unauthorised access to data and applications. The firewall provides both a perimeter defence and a means of monitoring access to services. With private networks and systems connected to public networks like the Internet, firewalls are an essential security feature. Many providers of content on the Internet use simple firewalls to control access.

Digital Content Copy Protection

DVD disc producers use several different techniques to protect against illegal copying of DVDs. For example, most DVD players are equipped with the APS (Analogue Protection System) which blocks analogue videotape copying. In addition, many DVD discs use a serialisation technique known as CGMS (Copy Generation Management System), which embeds the outgoing video signal of a DVD disc with information that specifies whether the contents can be copied. Data encryption and digital watermarks are also being used to protect against DVD piracy. For example, the CSS (Content Scrambling System) used with DVD-video only, prevents the display of unscrambled digital output until a secure digital connection is established. DVD players and DVD-ROM drives generally contain a decryption circuit that decodes the data before displaying it. Digital watermarks (in the form of invisible marks or inaudible noises) signal new equipment to refuse to play the DVD-video or DVD-audio copy.

Another set of security features consists of regional or country codes or zone locks, which are used only with DVD-video. These are being used to prevent the playback of certain discs in certain geographic areas. These electronic geographic restrictions give motion-picture studios the ability to control the release of movies in different countries and to protect the exclusivity rights granted to foreign distributors.[23]

Intel Corp., Sony Corp., Matsushita Electric Industrial Co., Toshiba Corp. and Hitachi Ltd. announced in February 1998 an agreement on a copy protection system for digital content on multiple platforms. The proposed technology would have no effect on television sets, VCRs and computers already in people's homes. But it would be an important component of newer, digital versions of those devices. According to terms of the proposal, high-definition television sets, personal computers, digital video-disc players, digital VCRs, stereos, and set-top boxes would all be equipped with technology that requires a digital "handshake" before a protected piece of work can be transferred from one device to another. Further, it means that someone who buys movies or music over satellite services, cable networks or even the Internet would not be able to make copies — at least not high-quality digital ones — without permission.

The "handshaking" technology at the heart of the system is an encryption technique in which content is basically scrambled by one device and can't be descrambled by another without the correct software key. Computer and electronics executives envision consumers linking all their devices together using cables and a new IEEE 1394 standard interface. The copy protection system adds a layer of software to control what these devices can send to one another and sets ground rules for what can be done with copies that are sent. Without such safeguards, entertainment executives would be reluctant to deliver any of their most valuable content.

Chris Cookson, executive vice president of Warner Bros., called it "one of the most important steps in making it possible to bring the highest quality digital pictures and sound to consumers."[24]

7.3.6 Transaction and Payment Systems

A variety of payment systems are emerging, largely driven by business-to-consumer activity. Emerging electronic payment systems are competing for market acceptance, but credit cards are by far the most important network payment system. As with many of the more elaborate encryption schemes, most alternative payment methods have, to date, proven too complex to gain widespread acceptance.

The techniques that have been developed for making payments on the Internet are essentially electronic versions of the payment systems already in everyday use, credit cards, checks, and cash (Exhibit 7.39).

Exhibit 7.39 **Electronic Payment Models**

Model	Description	Leading Players
Credit Card	• Enables consumers to make purchases based on credit. • Provides secure mechanism for transmitting credit card account numbers over the Internet.	**CyberCash**: Online credit card payment system using an electronic wallet. **First Virtual Holdings:** Offline credit card authorisation system that confirms user purchases via e-mail. **Visa/Mastercard Consortium:** Developed Secure Electronic Transaction (SET) as an open standard to enable secure credit card transactions. **Portland Software:** ZipLock payment system performs credit card authorisation and transactions over a private network.
Electronic Checking	• Authorises the transfer of money from customer checking accounts to merchant accounts. • Replaces paper checks with electronic instruments employing encryption technology.	**BankNet :** UK-based venture that offers ECheque, an electronic checking service using secure encrypted signatures. **CyberCash:** Piloting PayNow electronic checking service which directly debits a customer's checking account. **NetChex:** Provides secure electronic checking technology using public key encryption.
Digital Cash	• Essentially the equivalent of hard currency, makes anonymous transactions of any denomination feasible.	**Digicash:** Ecash is a software-only solution for secure and anonymous payments on the Internet. **CyberCash:** CyberCoin is an electronic cash system that will enable micropayments. **Digital Equipment Corp.:** Millicent is a micropayment system that will enable merchants to create their own micro-currency.

Source: Gemini Strategic Research Group.

Many of these systems have primarily been implemented on personal computers to date, but they are also now being implemented in smart cards and other technologies.

We have already discussed the SET standard and protocol that uses digital certificates and encryption to ensure the security of credit card transactions over the Internet. Another important standard is the Joint Electronic Payments initiative led by the World Wide Web Consortium and CommerceNet. JEPI is an interface between the network and transport protocols that is designed to standardise payment negotiations. On the client side JEPI exists as an interface that enables a Web browser and wallets to use a variety of payment protocols. On the server side JEPI acts between the network and transport layers to pass the incoming transaction to the proper transport protocol, such as e-mail or HTTP, and proper payment protocol, such as SET.

One potentially important new type of payment enabled by new technology is the micropayment. Digital cash can be divided into denominations much smaller than would be practical with physical currency. Because of low transaction costs and the extremely small denominations, merchants can theoretically charge for small amounts of information. Micropayments could be used to purchase small amounts of digital content, such as stock quotes or news stories, or small amounts of time, such as in networked games. Because such small amounts of currency are involved, these micropayment systems can rely upon less robust security systems than those required for larger transactions. While micropayment systems like Digital Equipment's "Millicent" system have been used on a trial basis, there is no indication to date that such systems will achieve wide-scale adoption.

7.3.7 Production and Management Tools

The successful development and operation of a Web site requires a wide range of production and management tools. In this section, we will examine two sets of these tools, content authoring and management software and usage measurement software and services (Exhibit 7.40).

Content Authoring and Management Software

As Web sites become more complex, better design and management tools are required. While many firms are offering Web authoring tools, Microsoft, IBM/NetObjects, and Netscape have captured the largest market share.

Web Site Measurement and Analysis Software

Web site measurement and analysis tools provide firms with useful marketing information. Most of the analysis software products, such as net.Genesis's net.Analysis Pro and Interse's MarketFocus, rely on HTTP server log files. High-end tools provide not only hit counts and visit duration information, but may also attach IDs to users to track subsequent visits to the site and trace their paths through the site. The detailed information produced by these applications helps firms to evaluate how sites are being used and to refine content, navigation, and advertising strategies. Many of the more complex commerce software applications, such as the Open Market servers and the SAQQARA catalogue publishing software, are packaged with sophisticated measurement and analysis tools (Exhibit 7.41).

Exhibit 7.40 **Selected Web Site Authoring and Management Tools**

Vendor	Products and Services	Partners and Alliances	EC Applications
Fusion *NetObjects*	• Provides site creation, management, and data access tools. • Helps manage content more effectively and easily.	• IBM purchased a majority stake and may offer NetObjects. • Alliance agreement with UUNET to package *Fusion* with its ISP hosting services.	• Provides the Web authoring component to IBM's EC offering. • Scalable and highly functional.
FrontPage *Microsoft*	• Web site creation and management software tools. • Primary focus is basic content sites for small businesses and home users.	• Is sold as a product offering separate from Microsoft Office, but offers Office '97 users a discount. • Acquired technology from Vermeer.	• Helps to complete Microsoft's end-to-end product offering for businesses and consumers. • Provides basic EC capabilities.
Navigator Gold *Netscape*	• Web site creation and editing software. • Capabilities for less sophisticated Web sites.	• This separate product offering targets home users and small businesses. • Is currently available for free for a ninety-day trial period.	• Simple, general Web site development application.
QuickSite *DeltaPoint*	• Quicksite is available in several editions for the creation of basic sites or sites supporting corporate Internet and intranet applications.	• Software demos can be downloaded from company Web site. • Partnership agreements with IBM, Sony, Netcom, and Earthlink to license, bundle, or distribute product to customers.	• Focus on building EC-enabled sites and intranets for internal applications.
Sappire Web *Bluestone*	• Web site development and management software. • Supports database-driven content and database applications.	• NA	• Database integration allows customers to receive responses to bid and other information requests quickly.

Source: Company Reports; Gemini Strategic Research Group.

Web site measurement and analysis tools affect network commerce directly with advertising applications and indirectly through its in-depth user profiling capability. Various departments in an organisation can benefit from Web measurement reports. Marketing departments use information to cater content based on popular interest areas. Sales departments can identify markets where efforts need to be strengthened by viewing demographic information by person, organisation, or geographic location. Executives can justify cost of investment or measure responses from marketing campaigns. Basic Web site measurement and analysis tools or features may be bundled with servers in the future. Some analysts predict that site management suite products that incorporate Web analysis tools will emerge similarly to the consolidation of desktop functions into desktop software suites.

Exhibit 7.41 **Selected Measurement and Analysis Vendors and Products**

Vendor	Products and Services	Partners and Alliances	EC Applications
net.genesis *net.Genesis Corp*	• Web site measurement and analysis software.	• *Verisign* to integrate authentication technology (digital certificates) into net.Analysis products. • *IBM* to incorporate net.Analysis Pro into Surf-Aid solution to enable companies to cater advertising and content to individual users.	• Creates in-depth user profiles accessible through database querying. • Can be used with digital certificate technologies to provide robust trading.
Intersé *Microsoft*	• Web site measurement and analysis software.	• Acquired by Microsoft.	• Creates in-depth user profiles accessible through database querying.
NetCount	• Web site measurement and analysis service.	• Partners with several Web site design, development, and hosting companies.	• A third-party service, NetCount is primarily a product offering for advertiser sites.
I/PRO	• Web verification, analysis, and research services. • Business consulting and strategy services are also available.	• Alliances with Nielsen Media, Verifone, NetGravity, and DoubleClick. • Service can complement Web analysis products by providing third-party verifications for ad generating purposes.	• Provides verified user information for advertising-supported sites.
Andromedia	• Web site measurement software, real-time, server-based.	• Sold as a stand-alone product geared for entry-level marketing-focused Web sites.	• Targeted toward small businesses and does not provide in-depth analysis capabilities.
Marketwave	• Web site measurement and analysis software.	• Recently entered the market, no known partners or alliances.	• Three-tiered product offering ranging from low-end for basic info to high-end for sites designed for more than marketing purposes.

Source: Company Reports; Gemini Strategic Research Group.

7.3.7 Service Bureaus

For those firms unable or unwilling to invest in electronic commerce technology, a number of outsourcing options are emerging (Exhibit 7.42). While we deal with marketplace organisers and other types of intermediaries in greater detail elsewhere (see chapter 5), it is important for firms to remember that many of these intermediaries offer important substitutes for investment in technology platforms. These service bureaux offer full electronic commerce solutions customised to meet the needs of particular types of businesses.

Marketplaces function as forums to exchange information and conduct transactions. Three types of marketplaces have emerged: trading communities for buyers and sellers; distributor-centric marketplaces where a company can link its distributors to its site marketplaces for inventory management; and vendor-centric marketplaces where a vendor links with its suppliers to negotiate prices for products. Marketplace organisers typically market their services directly to business end users. Marketplace operators generally set up services around a vertical industry or a specific function, such as maintenance, repair, and operations (MRO) procurement (i.e. purchases of goods and services that are not included as part of the cost of goods sold). These marketplace organisers have developed partnerships and alliances with other network commerce infrastructure providers in order to offer full end-to-end services. Marketplace organisers operate their own marketplaces and act also as middlemen. In an effort to provide comprehensive solutions, companies have been partnering with other e-commerce providers to develop complete offerings. Professional services, specifically systems integration, is a key component in implementing comprehensive solutions.

Exhibit 7.42 **Selected Service Bureau Offerings**

Vendor	Products and Services	Partners and Alliances	EC Applications
IBM World Distributor	• World Distributor is a marketplace and a suite of e-commerce products which companies can purchase to build their own marketplaces. • Operates the Energy Network Exchange marketplace where utilities can buy and sell electric transmission power. • Plans to establish additional vertical industry marketplaces for the insurance and petroleum industries.	• Partnership with Siemens Power Systems Control to co-develop and operate the Energy Network Exchange. • Several partnerships with Web design firms to help customers maximise capabilities. • ISSC, a wholly owned subsidiary of IBM, provides systems integration services.	• Pacific Gas and Electric has signed onto the Energy Network Exchange service. • The World Distributor Marketplace has approximately fifty-five customers. • McLeans, the nation's largest convenience store distributor, uses World Distributor services to link its network of customers and streamline inventory.
TPN Register	• TPN Register operates two marketplaces: – TPN Mart provides MRO procurement services. – TPN Post supports bidding and negotiation for goods and services contracts. • Transaction capabilities are being developed for both services. • Network hosting, Web site design, system integration, and business consulting services are available through TPN Register.	• TPN Register is a joint venture between GEIS and Thomas Register. • The partnership has few outside technology alliances. • GEIS' experience with e-commerce and its deep pockets, coupled with Thomas's extensive database of suppliers, creates a comprehensive product for companies looking to outsource certain functions.	• TPN Mart is still in a beta-testing phase, but TPN Post has signed several customers, including eight GE units. • GE hoped to source approximately 1.8 billion euro worth of goods and services through the TPN Register service in 1997. • EC Cubed is one partner who is helping to design and develop the transaction component.

Source: Company Reports.

A service bureau allows businesses to outsource end-to-end electronic commerce services by joining marketplaces or participating in virtual malls. Generally, marketplace organisers build services around specific functions, such as MRO procurement, or around specific industries such as energy. Marketplace organisers typically are only now beginning to integrate transaction capabilities into their marketplaces. The 1997 bankruptcy of one of the highest-profile marketplace organisers, Nets Inc., highlights the need for these firms to tighten their focus on serving vertical industries or providing specific business functions.

7.4 Looking into the Technology Future

Finally, much can be said about the future of network technology. Here, we wish only to briefly highlight a couple of key issues.

7.4.1 Where It May Lead: Plug-and-Play Commerce

As firms organise to capture network opportunities, they must begin to think beyond the bounds of their own organisations. Many of the most innovative network commerce possibilities involve firms integrating their supply chains more closely with those of their trading partners. Ultimately, to achieve the kind of mass customisation that many firms dream of, systems must be linked from the consumer all the way to the suppliers of raw materials. As this occurs, we are beginning to see a fundamental shift in business strategy focus from the firm to the supply chain (Exhibit 7.43).

Exhibit 7.43 **Shifting Information Technology (IT) Strategy Paradigm**

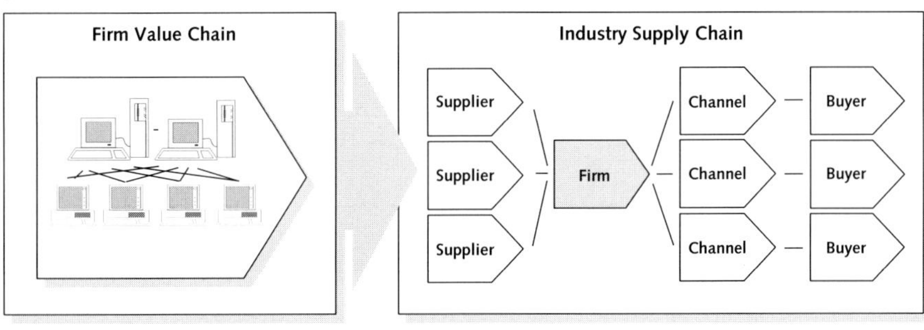

Source: Gemini Strategic Research Group.

Managers are faced with a whole new level of complexity co-ordinating strategy with trading partners that do not completely share the same goals and may even be competitors in other arenas.

7.4.2 Technology Possibilities

We have focused largely on describing state-of-the-art technology. So what does the future hold? We emphasise again that there will be abundant, inexpensive bandwidth, and processing power will continue to increase. At some point between ten and twenty years into the future, we will likely reach the limits of Moore's Law and make a leap to some vastly superior processing technology, probably quantum computing (see Chapter 2). Inexpensive, high-definition "electronic ink" displays are likely to be widely available within 10 years, allowing users to download personalised copies of the news to a device that resembles a traditional newspaper or to store and read the text of hundreds of books on a device that looks and feels like a traditional book (only with moving pictures). Nanotechnology[25] will allow the creation of microscopic computing and storage devices and enable radically new manufacturing processes, perhaps within 20 to 30 years, decentralising many manufacturing processes to an extent similar to the decentralisation of information creation and processing enabled by PCs and the Internet. Holographic storage devices capable of storing terabytes of information in spaces smaller than today's smallest hard drives will be available. Rich, full-immersion, high definition virtual reality experiences will be available to those with multi-gigabit-per-second fibre-optic networks connected directly to their homes or businesses. Even in the remotest corners of the world, 100-megabit-per-second symmetrical data streams delivered by LEO satellite networks will be available to ordinary people. This will likely happen in less than 7 years. These networks will bring connectivity to those parts of the world that cannot be reached by the ever-expanding multi-terabit fibre-optic networks that deliver all of the video programming in the world to anyone anywhere who has access to the Internet (or its successor).

Barring war, disease, asteroid collisions, or economic disaster, this world awaits us. Except for robust nanotechnology, all of these technologies exist today in the laboratory. Their emergence requires only market acceptance, financial capital, and in some instances the political will to make them happen.

7.5 Summary

In this chapter we have reviewed several categories of network technologies, focusing on identifying key technologies and key trends. Technology enables an increasing array of network capabilities, and open-standards-based Internet technologies have unleashed an explosion of service innovations. We began by discussing the differences between "sustaining technologies," such as the incrementally improving public switched telephone network that has evolved for nearly 125 years, and "disruptive technologies," such as Internet Protocol (IP) networking, which has transformed the telecommunications industry in less than a decade of wide-scale use. We then suggested a framework for thinking about network technologies and proceeded to systematically examine each of the technology components in the framework. We closed by briefly examining some of the longer-term implications and possibilities of network technologies.

RECOMMENDATIONS

Businesses and government tend to be fairly comfortable managing the evolutionary development and exploitation of "sustaining technologies." "Disruptive technologies," like the Internet, present huge management challenges to all participants in the marketplace. Several key lessons are emerging from the experiences of firms that have successfully managed to use these disruptive technologies to build new markets and create new opportunities.

Businesses

- Develop a thorough understanding of the capabilities and limitations of the key technologies used in the network economy. The best way to do this is to actively experiment with new technologies to truly understand their capabilities. Many firms have developed internal research groups dedicated to following and working with new technologies. Firms need to encourage experimentation with new technologies, while at the same time exploring how to share the lessons of these experiments effectively throughout the organisation.
- Count on the continued improvement of network-related hardware and software capabilities. Many current technological constraints will be minimised as software and hardware rapidly continues to develop. In other words, "bet on Moore's Law." We have moved into a period in the history of microprocessor development where every doubling of processing power brings huge increases in computing capabilities. Planners need to keep this in mind as they explore potential market developments over multi-year periods.
- Use technologies based on open standards. Do not try to lock in customers or partners through proprietary technology; open standards eventually prevail.
- Participate in standards development. A good way to ensure that a firm is investing in the right standards and that it is taking a leadership role in the market is to actively participate in standards development processes. Do not leave it to your competitors to create the standards.

Content Firms

- Digitise content and treat it as the primary product rather than the secondary product. Firms should organise their production and distribution processes around digital content. By reengineering content development processes (e.g. create common databases of digital content), firms will increase flexibility, enable the creation of new types of products, and cut costs over time by capturing the improvements in price/performance generated by Moore's Law.
- Explore how interactivity enhances content and changes its nature and value. Many interactive content products are new to the world, so the only way to understand the real market potential is to experiment with them and learn from user response. Businesses should experiment with a wide range of interactive products and continuously track how technology can enhance these products.

Governments

- Support businesses in the creation of open and common technological standards, without restricting the development of technology. Government should, at all costs, avoid legislating narrow, inflexible standards. However, governments can play an important role in facilitating industry efforts to create standards and in efforts to build consensus around international standards.

- Improve processes for commercialisation of government-funded research (e.g. through public-private partnerships). Government can play an important role in funding and pursuing technology research that is too expensive or risky for most businesses to pursue on their own. Government should work together with businesses to form partnerships and develop other methods of ensuring that new developments are rapidly commercialised by business.

Notes

1. Clayton M. Christensen, *The Innovator's Dilemma: When New Technologies Cause Great Firms to Fail*, Boston, Massachusetts: Harvard Business School Press, 1997.
2. See chapter 2.
3. *Television Business International*, October 1997.
4. Consumer Electronics Manufacturers Association.
5. *Video Magazine*, October 1997.
6. Consumer Electronics Manufacturers Association.
7. *Video Magazine*, October 1997.
8. See chapter 6 for a discussion of where end users access the Internet. Note that European users are much more likely to access the Internet from the workplace.
9. http://www.eink.com.
10. In-Stat, "DVD Players Are Finally Here," November 1997.
11. See chapters 3 and 5 for a more detailed discussion of the role of end users as content creators.
12. A "plug-in" is a modular software add-on to a browser that enables it to support additional functions.
13. "Progressive Networks and MCI Debut 'Netcast' Infrastructure," *ProSound Europe*, November 1997.
14. For a detailed discussion, see *Telecommunications* (International Edition), September 1997.
15. *Television Business International*, October 1997.
16. *Greensboro News & Record*, 15 February 1998.
17. *Video Magazine*, October 1997.
18. See chapter 4 for a discussion of the connectivity in the context of industry structure.
19. The maximum is 1.5 Mbps in the US and 2.0 Mbps in Europe.
20. Memorandum Opinion and Order in Reconsideration of the Fifth Report and Order, 17 February 1998 (FCC 98-23).

21. *International Multimedia Investor*, 13 May 1997.

22. Data Encryption Standard.

23. Multimedia & Web Strategist, January 1998.

24. Greg Miller, "Firms Agree on Anti-Piracy Technology," *Los Angeles Times*, 19 February 1998.

25. Technology of constructing mechanical devices at the nanometer level, i.e., by manipulating individual atoms. See K. Eric Drexler, *Engines of Creation*, London: Doubleday Anchor Press, 1986; Ed Regis, *Nano: The Emerging Science of Nanotechnology,* London: Little, Brown and Company, 1995.

Framing Legal and Regulatory Issues

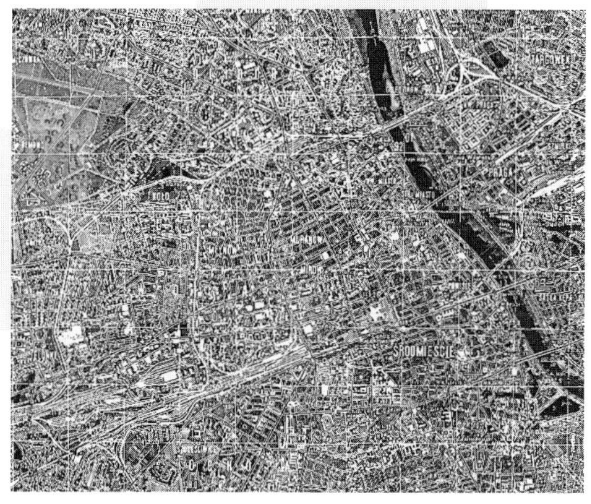

Network commerce presents many challenges to existing legal and regulatory systems. In this chapter, we examine several of the areas most critically affected by network commerce and offer an overview of the key laws and regulations that at the same time are helping to shape the network economy.

Europe's legal and regulatory framework creates a number of preconditions for the successful development of network commerce. Many legal and regulatory issues are particularly relevant to content creators and aggregators and challenge some of the fundamental premises on which these industries have traditionally been based.

8.1 Overview of Legal Issues Related to Network Commerce

Regulatory conflicts and loopholes may hinder the development of network commerce. As Sir Leon Brittan, EU External Trade Commissioner, explained recently, "The explosion of the Internet is unstoppable; the only question is whether this will be accompanied by over-regulation [with conflicting national rules] or confusion [where no rules apply]."[1]

Network commerce is at odds with an economic assumption governing much of the modern system of nation states — that all income streams, production, sales, loans, and so forth take place in specific geographic locations. Regulatory and taxation systems are based on the premise that it is possible to determine whose law or regulation applies and in which national market or jurisdiction the transaction takes place. If a computer programmer sitting at a terminal in Bangalor is upgrading code in real-time over the Internet on computer servers located in Frankfurt, London, and New York, where is the "transaction" taking place? In the network economy, distinctions between "domestic" and "foreign" are losing meaning.

The question of the nationality of a firm, product, or technology may be irrelevant in the integrated global network economy. The Internet exists simultaneously in many places and in no place. Individual services and physical network components can be identified precisely in geographic space, but they do not constitute "the Internet" they are only pieces of it. The Internet creates, as one commentator has aptly described, the "nightmare scenario of every government censor" with "no physical existence and [recognising] no national barriers."[2]

The transborder nature of network commerce leads to uncertainty about which laws apply to a given transaction. Without common rules, individual countries are likely to fill in the gaps with differing rules on encryption technology, data privacy, intellectual property rights, liability for illegal transmissions, fiscal treatment of products and services sold electronically, and so on, thus segmenting the global market for network commerce. Failure to legislate may also hinder the development of network commerce by undermining its credibility in the eyes of consumers and businesses. The EU and governments everywhere are challenged to find the balance between legislation and market forces.

8.2 Networks and Commercial Law

The network-enabled transaction process raises many basic legal issues. A network business must define its market in terms of competition, taking all existing distribution networks into consideration. It must then take into account the coexistence of information concerning the product (which can be advertising) and the offer of sale, in that order. In most cases, the transactional contract is unwritten, which means that applicable laws and regulations must be determined by the parties to the transaction. In some cases, parties agree on the conditions to be applied to their transaction ahead of time, potentially leading to legal challenges in contracts between businesses and consumers. Reference to code and common practices will be useful for completing the sales process. If litigation does arise, the parties must determine the applicable laws and the courts having jurisdiction.

8.2.1 Competition and Fair Trade Practices

The first legal challenge for network commerce is in examining the relationship between this new form of distribution and the previously existing distribution networks and determining which rules of fair trade are applicable. The trans-border nature of the Internet makes the concepts of "market" and "territory" difficult to define.

Traditionally, each nation has the power to sanction unfair trade practices that occur within its jurisdiction. Consequently, any unfair trade practice taking place in the EU is subject either to national law (if the violation occurs within the territory of a member state) or to community law (if the violation occurs in the territories of several member states). The national legislation of the member states are aligned and the community law resulting from the Treaty of Rome has precedence over any national law that runs counter to it.[3] Similarly, US federal law dictates that unfair trade practices within US territory are subject to US federal anti-trust law.[4]

Network-based firms around the world are competing with each other in a single market, even though subject to highly disparate rules and attitudes concerning competition. In traditional commerce, products must not only be adapted to targeted markets, but also be distributed in compliance with local fair trade laws. In the case of commercial exchanges over networks, a new problem exists: a marketing effort targeting a certain market or a certain territory may now be in direct confrontation with a market which potentially covers the entire globe.

Can two companies be considered competitors in the same territory solely because consumers are able to order services online, without checking whether the service-provider intended to serve a given territory? Can a distributor selling over the network venture outside of its own territory? These key questions remain unresolved.

Regulators and businesses must determine whether online goods or services should be treated as being provided in the country from which they are transmitted or in the country where they are received. Transmission and reception locations can be subject to different, and sometimes even contradictory, regulations. This is especially true for legal, medical fields, or other regulated professions which have traditionally enforced their own standards and regulations. In addition to the obvious question of regulatory compliance, an escalating problem of fair trade among practitioners of these services also exists. In certain European countries, for example, lawyers do not have the right to solicit clients, while this is permitted in other countries.

8.2.2 Advertising and Promotion

Even prior to selling, concerns arise surrounding the legal treatment of product or service descriptions, advertising, and offers of sale. The capacity for order processing online gives advertising a crucial role in the selling process on open networks. Through hypertext "links," the solicited consumer can place an order quickly and easily. This growing importance of advertising creates problems which may significantly hinder the development of network commerce.

Internet advertising is world-wide. Thus, ads are subject to distinct regulations in each country (within the EU, some efforts to address this problem through standardisation are underway).

Most advertising legislation falls into a category that is subject to criminal law (in the sense that advertising legislation's purpose is to protect local consumers). A single ad will be subject to the laws of all the countries in which it can be seen. The definition of online advertising, special regulated items, comparative and false advertising, and self-regulatory efforts by the advertising industry must all be taken into consideration in terms of standardisation across borders.

Definition of Advertising
Regulators must determine at what moment a message transmitted on a network legally qualifies as advertising, and thus becomes subject to regulation. In fact, no uniform and precise definition of advertising currently exists, and one needs to be formulated. Now an ad deemed acceptable by legal standards in one country can be unacceptable in another.

Businesses and regulators must also differentiate advertising from simple information, which does not incur the same liabilities for the author of the message. Unlike advertising, an offer of a contract contains all the elements needed for drawing up the contract, with acceptance by the consumer providing the link between the two parties. Since the conditions for such an offer vary from country to country, an advertisement could be considered an offer of this type. To prevent such confusion, the conditions for offers must be standardised, especially for network commerce.

It is also necessary to distinguish the concept of advertising from that of information in the strictest sense. While no one doubts that a banner placed on a Web page can constitute an advertising message, the question is less obvious for Web sites. Here, the question is whether the entire site is subject to regulations concerning advertising, even though the site may contain offers and pure information as well as advertising. The International Chamber of Commerce (ICC) recommends that a distinction be made, with advertising being clearly identified and distinguished from purely informational content.[5]

Advertising on the Internet makes use of new forms. Networks can transmit a message either globally (to all connected parties) or individually (personalised mail). For example, advertising on the Internet appears in advertising banners and other hypertext links, Web sites, e-mail, newsgroups, and discussion or mailing lists. Specific difficulties can arise from the cumulative nature of the medium; setting up a mailing list on a Web site requires a special effort, which can itself be subject to legal advertising regulations.

Special Regulated Items
Certain ads are regulated because of the nature of the merchandise or service advertised (e.g. weapons, pharmaceuticals, alcoholic beverages). Specific regulations can ban such ads or require them to bear legal notices or use a particular language (national language of the country of destination). Most such regulations are national and not standardised.

Comparative and False Advertising
Regulations concerning comparative and false advertising should not be considered an obstacle to the development of network commerce, in that standardisation is currently underway in Europe, the US, and Japan. In the meantime, consumer protection legislation will help to establish a more secure environment for network commerce growth.

Today, laws governing comparative advertising differ from country to country. Among the EU member states, the Netherlands and Germany prohibit comparative advertising in all cases, France and Spain impose strict conditions, and the UK permits it widely as long as the comparative advertising does not constitute an unfair trade practice. These disparities should disappear by 2000 within the EU because the European Commission and Parliament have adopted a directive to standardise the legal status of comparative advertising.[6] In the US, comparative advertising is permitted under conditions similar to provisions concerning false advertising, but the doctrine of substantiation, which is applicable to comparative advertising, obliges advertisers and advertising agencies to represent their goods or services factually and objectively (i.e. claims must have a "reasonable basis").[7]

False advertising is prohibited by law in all EU nations, the US, and Japan. While defining exactly what constitutes false advertising and the liabilities incurred in all these different areas of the world, none of the laws seems an obstacle to the development of network commerce.

Many similarities exist between US legislation and that of the EU member states. For example, the doctrine of substantiation has legal equivalencies with the provisions of the EU member states. The laws of the member states were standardised by the Commission Directive of 10 September 1984 concerning false advertising.[8] The US federal government has also enacted laws banning false advertising, with the Federal Trade Commission Act[9] and the Lanham Act[10] being chief among these.

Self-Regulatory Efforts
Globally, the advertising industry has tended to pursue self-regulatory efforts that seem especially well-adapted to advertising on open networks. The EU, like the US and Japan, has expressly encouraged the development of self-regulatory systems for advertising on networks, with legislation providing only a framework.

8.2.3 Network Transactions

Two major difficulties affecting network transactions consist of determining the national and supra-national laws applicable to formal or informal contracts and verifying the identity of the contracting parties.

A distinction exists between business-to-business relations and business-to-consumer relations, since the latter are generally protected by specific national and international regulations. All of these transactions are contractual in nature and are thus subject to regulation by law, and even without a formal contract, contractual clauses can be offered online. Once the contract, formal or informal, is finalised, it must be fulfilled according to common practice. If difficulties arise for which there are no pertinent contractual clauses, the parties must determine the applicable law and the court having jurisdiction.

Offers
For business-to-business transactions, the parties have considerable freedom to negotiate contracts and clarify legal inconsistencies between jurisdictions. According to the Vienna Convention, no condition or form is required for the sale of goods between businesses.[11] The offer can therefore be written, oral, or electronic (e.g. e-mail). However, this particular convention applies only to goods and not to services.

Businesses must meet three basic conditions:

- The offer must be addressed to specifically designated parties.
- It must reflect the author's desire to accept the transaction as binding in case of acceptance.
- The offer must indicate a set or determinable price for a set item.

For sales to consumers, all the laws of the EU, the US, and Japan create special disclosure obligations for network business operators selling to consumers (remote sale). As might be expected, these laws, too, vary from country to country. For example, in a remote sale in Spain, the offer must mention the address of the supplier, the characteristics of the product, its price and delivery costs, the mode of payment, the methods for fulfilling the contract, and how long the offer is valid. In France, the offer must be written in French, specify the nature of the contract, designate unequivocally the proposed product or service, and indicate the price and the period of validity for the offer. Given such disparities among national laws, which laws, then, are applicable for a given contract?

In the EU, the Distance Selling Directive requires member states to standardise their legislation by 2000.[12] Further, this directive will require all online merchants to display trading terms and conditions clearly on screen. Vendors will have to ensure that consumers receive a copy of these terms and conditions by proving that they have been downloaded or by sending a hard copy by post.

Right to Revoke an Offer

Revocability of an offer is essential, especially in a digital environment that favours instantaneous transactions. In transactions between businesses, customarily an offer is in principle revocable as long as one party has not expressly accepted it. According to the Vienna Convention, the offer is in principle revocable unless the circumstances imply the contrary.[13] It can become irrevocable when it expressly indicates a validity period or sets a deadline for acceptance. For offers to consumers, each nation requires the selling party to uphold the offer for a certain time that varies from country to country.

Object of the Transaction

Competition to sell certain goods is regulated. In all the EU countries, Japan, and the US, it is unanimously agreed that merchandise can be marketed only if it is indeed available for sale in a legal sense. This is a matter of state control for the purpose of upholding law and order and ethical practices in commerce, especially in network commerce. The problem is that national laws do not perceive the concepts of "merchandise available for sale" and "law and order" in the same way.

Price

In a commercial transaction, the main obligation of the purchasing party is to pay the price of the goods delivered. The price must be set or determinable in the contract. However, in the absence of such precision, the laws vary. In the absence of a price or determinable price, the transaction could be considered void under the laws of such countries as France, Belgium, or Spain, while in countries such as the UK, Italy, Germany, or the Netherlands, a "reasonable" price could still be enforced.

Capacity and Identity of the Parties

A major difficulty encountered by network businesses is how to know that the contracting party has the capacity to enter into the contract. A contract concluded with an "incapacitated party,"[14] in the legal sense of the term, is void. This difficulty should be significantly diminished with the development of certifying third parties (e.g. banks, government agencies, other trusted parties). It will persist, however, for so-called "informal" contracts (especially for micropayments).

Form of Contract

In each of the EU countries, the US, and Japan, no specific contractual form is required for many business contracts. Acceptance can be written or oral, but cannot result from silence or inaction (unless common practice dictates otherwise). As soon as business operators establish "customary commercial relations" with each other, it will be useful to formally agree on the means for making and accepting offers to clarify the form their online transactions will take.

On closed networks, this is already done through electronic data interchange (EDI) contracts that rely on legal and technical standards adopted at the national or supra-national level. On open networks, EDI-type exchanges correspond to the needs of the many companies that have not invested in EDI but need to formalise their habitual network relations. Current EDI standards cannot be directly transposed, and standardisation efforts are under way. In business-to-business relations, a trend exists toward interchange contracts that resemble common network transactions, and which are both less secure and more affordable. For example, standard contracts for common commercial exchanges between network businesses have already been developed by the United Nations Commission on International Trade Law (UNCITRAL). Nonetheless, work is continuing in this field.[15]

Currently, no simple and secure means exists to ensure that a message sent by a consumer has indeed been received by a business. Certain consumer laws (in France, Greece, Belgium, and the US) require a written contract, and exchanges of electronic messages have generally not been considered to meet these requirements. Some laws are in the process of modification, raising the thresholds for which written specification is required and recognising the validity and of digital signatures. For contracts solely between businesses, no written specification is required unless common practice dictates otherwise.

In its model law, the UNCITRAL has suggested the adoption of the proposal according to which "when the law requires that an information be written, a message will fulfil this requirement if the information contained in it can be accessed and read at a later time."[16]

Digital Signatures

A signature means the application of a distinctive sign, intended to identify the signer, declare the signer's acceptance of the contract, and prove the identification and declaration of desire. The technical solution for network commerce consists of the use of electronic "keys" as a "signature" and a third-party certification authority in possession of verified information concerning the identity of the holder of these keys. From a legal point of view, national laws should uphold digital signatures as a valid means of proof in the same way as written signatures and should set up standardised certifying third parties to guarantee the contract's security.

Online Contractual Clauses

The parties should insert in each contract (whether online or on paper) a clause concerning the applicable law and a clause naming the court of jurisdiction.

Still, such clauses are not valid in all cases. For business-to-business contracts, there is great freedom of choice, and businesses often rely on arbitration.

For contracts between businesses, the choice of jurisdiction is broad; however, the validity of such applicable law/court of jurisdiction clauses varies from one country to another. In the US, this choice must be neither "unreasonable" nor "unjust." In Japan, the jurisdiction can be chosen only if no other court has exclusive jurisdiction and if the case is within the sphere of competence of the chosen court.[17] In Europe, according the Brussels Convention (applicable in the signatory countries, which are all European), "if the parties, at least one of which has its domicile in the territory of a Signatory State, have agreed upon a court or courts of a Signatory State to hear any contentions arising from or to arise from the execution of the terms of the contract, the court or courts of that State have exclusive jurisdiction."[18]

The jurisdiction clause is valid according to this Convention if it is specified: "(a) in writing or verbally with written confirmation, or (b) in a form which complies with the usual practices that the parties have established with each other, or (c) in international commerce, in a form which complies with a practice of which the parties have knowledge or can be supposed to have knowledge and which is widely recognised and regularly occurring in this type of commerce for parties under contracts of the same type in the field of commerce in question."[19]

The only limits on the choice of applicable law between businesses are those imposed by the theory of fraudulent evasion (the clause must not be intended to circumvent the application of the mandatory provisions of the normally applicable law) and that of the protection of law and order.

For business-to-consumer transactions, choice of jurisdiction clauses vary in validity. In Japan, there are no specific provisions for contracts concluded with consumers. Therefore, the rules defined for business operators seem to apply. This is not the case in other countries.

For clauses designating the court as having jurisdiction, the Brussels Convention eliminates the possibility of such a clause in the following types of contracts, except under specific circumstances:

- The sale on instalments of tangible movable articles (credit transactions);
- Instalment loans or other credit operations concerning the financing of the sale of such articles;
- The supply of services or tangible movable articles if on the one hand, the conclusion of the contract was preceded in the State of the consumer's domicile by a specially formulated proposal or an advertisement and if, on the other hand, the consumer has completed in that State the operations necessary for the conclusion of the contract.[20]

Such a clause would nonetheless be valid in these contracts if it is concluded after the dispute that it enables the consumer to refer the case to courts other than those designated by the Convention, and upon the conclusion of the contract both parties have their domicile or their habitual residence in the same signatory nation, the clause designates the courts of that nation and the law of this nation does not prohibit such a clause.

In the US, jurisdiction clauses are valid as long as they are justified either by the risks incurred by a business operator faced with several co-contracting parties of different nationalities, or by the fact that the choice of jurisdiction in the domicile of one of the parties is reasonable.[21]

In Europe, this choice of applicable law is circumscribed. Article 5 of the Rome Convention addresses the problem of the applicable law "for contracts for the purpose of supplying tangible movable articles or services to a consumer, for a usage which can be considered unrelated to his/her professional activity, as well as contracts for the purpose of financing such a transaction."[22]

According to Article 5, "the choice by the parties of the applicable law cannot result in depriving the consumer of the protection provided by the mandatory provisions of the law of his/her country of habitual residence:

- If the conclusion of the contract was preceded in that country by a specially formulated proposal or an advertisement, and if the consumer has completed in that country the actions necessary for the conclusion of the contract, or
- If the consumer's co-contracting party or his/her representative has received the order from the consumer in that country, or
- If the contract concerns the sale of merchandise and the consumer has gone from that country to another country and has placed the order there, upon the condition that the travel was arranged by the selling party for the purpose of inciting the consumer to conclude a sale."[23]

In the US, according to Article 2B-107 of the proposed amendment to the Uniform Commercial Code, parties can choose freely the applicable law for their contract. In a contract concluded with a consumer, this choice cannot prevent the consumer from enjoying the protection of the law which would normally be applicable if no such clause were specified.[24] This provision codifies the jurisprudence currently applied by US courts.

Unfair Clauses

In the US, Japan, and Europe, laws concerning unfair clauses are mainly intended to protect the consumer. Generally speaking, a clause is considered unfair if it has not been subject to individual negotiation and if it creates a significant imbalance between the rights and liabilities of the consumer and the business. This concept is perceived differently from country to country. For example, in the EU, the directive of 5 April 1995 was adopted by the various member states.[25] Because they had the possibility to adopt more protective provisions, disparities arose within the EU. As a result, the consumer is able to demand the application of the law of their own country. This means that any business operator or service provider who wishes to add a particular clause in its contracts with its online clients no longer has the legal capacity to assess whether a given clause is unfair.

Reservation of Ownership

Reservation of ownership is a contractual provision enabling a business operator to retain ownership of the merchandise until full payment. For transfers of goods on networks, this clause constitutes an especially effective way to guarantee payment. In fact, for digital products it is possible to insert a technical "lock" in a digital message that makes its use impossible after the payment deadline unless the business operator gives the appropriate "key." The validity of such a clause is generally recognised, even though there are differences from one legal system to another.

Waiver of Liability

For all transactions, either between businesses or involving consumers, the validity of the clauses that limit a business's liability is analysed in terms of the national law that applies to the contract. The main points in common between the different legislation are the following:

- When the co-contracting party is a consumer, clauses limiting or waiving liability are generally discouraged by the national laws.
- For contracts concluded between business operators, the waiving of liability for wilful misconduct is not accepted. However, the concept of "wilful misconduct" is interpreted broadly from one state to another.
- Finally, such clauses are generally not admitted for latent defects or defective products.

8.2.4 Reference to Codes and Common Practice

The national governments of the US, Europe, and Japan have all insisted on the need to develop principles of self-regulation in network commerce. Self-regulation entails the acceptance by business operators of rules codified in conventions called "codes of conduct" or "codes of ethics," which they are committed to follow in their commercial transactions.

For self-regulatory codes to work, they must meet certain criteria:

- The codes must contain substantive rules and not just general principles.
- Consumers must be sufficiently informed of the content of the codes.
- Sanctions must be possible.

Currently, codes specific to network commerce — although much needed to regulate this new form of commerce — are few and not well known.

The OECD has drafted recommendations, to be made public in the autumn of 1998, for the protection of consumers which make express reference to the implementation by businesses of principles of loyalty resulting from self-regulatory codes.

We have observed that most of the current codes are adopted at the national level, which means that for a single profession, the codes will be different in each country. There are also a few supra-national codes, but these are currently minimal and do not contain the criteria that would give them real value.

Common practice is an extremely important legal concept in national and international commerce requiring us to refer to it in an examination of the specific characteristics of network commerce. "Common practices" are habitual, widespread practices that are regularly followed over time and are considered to have the force of obligations. Practices that meet the above criteria are widely taken into account by the courts. Historically, common practice made up the first set of rules regulating business conducted on the Internet, as codified in the famous Requests for Comments (RFCs).[26] Today, it is still difficult to speak of "common practice in network commerce," since the practices observed do not yet meet all the criteria defined above. In the future, the considerable importance of network commerce will surely generate common practices that will be accepted as standards on an international scale. It should be noted, however, that common practice will come from those who use online commerce most, which means the English-speaking world. Ignorance of common practice will represent a new risk in transactions. A great effort must therefore be made to collect and possibly codify common practice in order to ensure its more widespread acceptance. We could also note the currently growing number of groups monitoring practices in network commerce in Europe, Japan, and the US.

8.2.5 Completion of a Sale

Once a sale is concluded, payment must be ensured and the possibility of retraction by the consumer and any liabilities incurred must be taken into account.

Payment

Determining the payment deadline is essential. The deadline corresponds to the point in time when the selling party delivers the merchandise to the buyer, but payment can also be due before (advance payment) or after (credit) the delivery. Businesses must be aware of the different consumer protection laws concerning credit sales. As we have seen, the use of contractual reservation of ownership clauses should offer a workable solution for many network-based transactions.

Bank card payment has emerged as the most common method of payment for many network transactions. However, its implementation poses a number of problems. First, purchasers must have a certain degree of confidence in the business to which they transmit personal financial information. This implies that the identification mechanism must be protected from interception by ill-intentioned third parties during transmission. In addition, the online consumer often provides only the bank card number without the personal identification number (PIN). In certain countries, including France and Spain, payment by card number alone can at any moment be revoked by the customer within a time period which varies from country to country. The risk of fraud by dishonest customers is therefore high, and payment is not secure. Finally, it should be noted that a bank card cannot normally be used for amounts of less than ten to twenty euro (depending on the country and the bank card issuer). To solve this problem, software and financial services firms are working on a number of applications that will enable consumers to create "electronic purses" (methods of storing value on a computer hard-drive or "smart card").

Sales Administration

In all EU member states and in Japan, consumers have the right to retract an order that they have placed. Unfortunately, the deadline for retraction is different in each country. In Europe, the consumer generally has a grace period of at least seven business days to retract an order without penalty and without indicating the reason.[27] Japan's Home Sales Law specifies a deadline of eight days.[28]

This right to retract raises two difficulties: the concept of the "business day," which varies from one nation to another, and the immediate consumption of intangible goods such as software or information directly accessible via the network. The European Distance Selling Directive tends to limit the consumer's right to retract for intangible goods.[29]

Delivery Deadline

Between business operators, it is generally accepted that the delivery must take place on the date agreed upon between the parties, or, if no such indication is provided, within a reasonable period of time. For delivery to consumers, the laws are stricter and more disparate. Within the EU, unless the parties have agreed otherwise, the supplier must fulfil the order at the latest within a period of thirty days starting on the day after the consumer placed the order.[30] If this is not possible, the supplier must inform the consumer and reimburse the purchase price as soon as possible, within a limit of thirty days. The member states are in the process of standardising regulations on this point.

Transfer of Risk

The risk of the merchandise being lost in transport or arriving in a damaged state is as much a concern for network businesses as it is for other businesses. In international commerce, the transfer of risk in the sale of tangible goods (merchandise) is nearly always specified in contractual clauses. Many contracts refer to a set of standard contractual terms promulgated by the International Chamber of Commerce, called Incoterms.[31] The Incoterms do not apply to intangible transactions or to consumers. Therefore, for risks concerning intangible goods and services, there are neither standardised rules nor specific rules for online transactions. Here again, the solutions will be contractual in nature.

Product Liability

In the EU member states, as in the US and Japan, the quality of saleable merchandise is subject to increasingly restrictive regulations covering a growing number of products. These now include children's toys, automobile parts, clothing labels, medicinal drugs, and several others. While in the EU certain directives concerning the general safety of products have been adopted in Germany, Belgium, Spain, France, Italy, the Netherlands, and the UK, there is no single comparable law on the international level. A firm wishing to sell goods online must comply with all the regulations in effect. Moreover, the business operator must guarantee that the merchandise not only complies with the terms of the contract, but, in particular, that it is covered by the "legal guarantee" required by the domestic law governing the co-contracting consumer. The Vienna Convention establishes a balance between the liabilities of the selling party and the buyer for goods sold between business operators: the selling party must deliver a product which complies with the contract and is adapted to common usage; the buyer must inspect the goods upon reception and declare any defects found within a reasonable period of time.[32]

For sales to consumers, national laws are not standardised, which is a source of legal uncertainty for the business operator on the Internet. In the EU, it is possible to specify more extensive contractual guarantees than the national legislation governing the consumer, but it is not possible to restrict the field of application, even contractually.

8.2.6 Settlement of Litigation

If there is no contract and no other specification, the applicable law must be determined as well as the court having jurisdiction for the settlement of any litigation. Sometimes the parties prefer to submit their dispute to arbitration. In all cases, the decision must then be carried out. Most legal rules do not specifically address network commerce. However, as we have seen, the multinational nature of the transactions considerably increases the importance of determining the applicable law and the methods for settling disputes.

Applicable Law and Court Having Jurisdiction
In the absence of any supra-national law, it is the international private law of each country which settles problems of legal conflicts and conflicts of jurisdiction. Consequently, the solutions vary from one country to another.

The two main international conventions concern only the EU. For conflicts of personal jurisdiction, legal jurisdiction, and execution of decisions, the Brussels Convention is the main convention besides those that apply specifically to transport contracts. For conflicts between laws, the Rome Convention of 19 June 1980 upholds the principle of contractual freedom and the possibility for the consumer to choose the application of the mandatory regulations of their country. This Convention is universal in character, which means that the law designated by the convention applies even if it concerns the law of a country that has not signed the Convention.[33]

Outside Europe, the international private law is far from unified. Currently, in the US, the National Conference of Commissioners on Uniform State Laws is completing an effort to draft Article 2B to the Uniform Commercial Code that addresses several key network commerce issues.[34] This article includes provisions to settle problems of applicable law and the court having jurisdiction.[35]

For business-to-business transactions, if the parties have not agreed otherwise, the Brussels Convention specifies that as long as the defendant is domiciled in one of the EU member states, the plaintiff has the choice of referring the case to the court of the defendant's domicile or head office or to the court "of the place where the obligation which forms the basis of the petition was or must be fulfilled."[36] If the defendant is not in Europe, the rules of international private law of the countries in question will apply. Traditionally the legislation designates jurisdiction in the defendant's domicile or the place of fulfilment of the obligation.

If the parties have not expressed a choice, it is a traditional principle of international private law that the applicable law is the one that has the closest links with the contract. But the criteria for determining this law vary from one country to another. According to the Rome Convention, the applicable law is presumed to be that of the country where the business operator who is to supply the characteristic service has its principle establishment (or, if according to the contract the service is to be supplied by an establishment other than the principle establishment, the country where this other establishment is located).[37] In Japan, it is the law of the country in which the contract was signed which will apply. For remote contracting, the contract is considered to be signed at the place from which the communication was sent. If this place is unknown to the recipient of the offer, the contract is considered to be signed at the place of the domicile of the offering party.[38] In the US, the principle is defined in Article 1-105 of the Uniform Commercial Code which establishes the criterion of a "reasonable link."[39] As previously noted, a proposal to add a new section to the UCC establishing specific rules for network commerce is currently under consideration by the National Conference of Commissioners on Uniform State Laws and the American Law Institute.[40]

Court Having Jurisdicition

The Brussels Convention grants the consumer the choice to sue the selling party either in the court of the nation of the selling party's domicile or in the court of the nation of the consumer's domicile. The only option for the selling party is to refer the case to the court of the consumer's domicile.[41] If the defendant is domiciled in a nation not bound by this Convention, for example Japan or the US, Article 4 of the Convention specifies that "in each State bound by the Convention, the jurisdiction is determined by the law of that State."[42] In Japan and the US, the regulations for contracts between businesses operators will apply.

Under the Rome Convention, "the law of the country in which the consumer has his/her habitual residence" will apply if the conclusion of the contract was preceded in that country by a specially formulated proposal or advertisement, and the consumer completed in that country the actions necessary for the conclusion of the contract; the selling party or its representative received the order in that country; or the contract concerns the sale of merchandise and the consumer has gone to another country to place the order, upon the condition that the travel was arranged by the business operator for the purpose of inciting the consumer to conclude the sale.[43]

In all other cases, the applicable law is presumed to be that of the habitual residence of the selling party. In the US, the applicable law is determined in the same way as for contracts between businesses (i.e. there must be a "reasonable link"). Finally, one must not forget to mention common practice, which increasingly creates a set of rules for the resolution of litigation, whether in or out of court. The observers who monitor, compile, and publish reports on Internet practices will be reference sources, not only for the resolution of litigation, but also simply for the practices of the operators of network services.

Arbitration
A significant trend in network commerce is the establishment of extra-judicial systems which can provide quick litigation settlement. Such systems offer the double advantage of international scope and technical specificity. Currently, the extra-judicial methods of settling conflicts remain voluntary — the parties can defer to them if they so wish (where their national laws authorise arbitration). Moreover, the systems for extra-judicial settlement of conflicts which are specific to online services and the digitisation of works do not protect the end user any better than the traditional systems. Consumers remain quite vulnerable in the case of litigation.

Consumer-accessible systems should be established for settling litigation while taking into account the restrictions specific to the network (duration, comity, identification, applicable law). In a recommendation dated 30 March 1998, the European Community has advocated the establishment of effective methods for settling litigation which are easily and conveniently accessible to the consumer.[44] Such methods are considered to be key elements in content industry development.

These current systems include the InterNIC Charter, arbitration boards created by WIPO, and extra-judicial systems for direct marketing and advertising. The InterNic Charter proposes and implements rules to resolve litigation involving domain names. The arbitration boards created by the World Intellectual Property Organisation (WIPO), have established an extra-judicial system for settling litigation involving intellectual property. However, it is too early to know whether it will be able to solve litigation specifically concerning the networks. Extra-judicial systems for direct marketing and advertising have already been implemented. Such is the case in the UK and France. These extra-judicial solutions retain a strong territorial aspect; they produce few joint solutions on the international level which take trans-border exchanges into account.

For certain audiotext-type online services, independent self-regulatory bodies exist to facilitate effective settlement of conflicts. Moreover, the courts give great importance to recommendations made by these specialised bodies.

Comity
Finally, when a court hands down a decision, it still has to be carried out. Its enforcement in a foreign country is subject to the rules of comity.[45] In Europe, the Brussels Convention makes comity quasi-automatic ("quasi" because of the possibility of invoking considerations of law and order).[46] Outside of Europe, problems concerning comity are likely to be more frequent. For example, the Supreme Court of Japan, in a case decided 11 July 1997, ruled against enforcement of punitive damages awarded by a US court against Japanese machinery maker Mansei Co., holding that the award violated "public order and standards of decency."[47]

8.3 Content Control and Regulation

Legal control over content is important for network-based content firms. For them, this content can be sold online directly to an international clientele. However, control of content is also important for other firms that create online content in order to sell goods or merchandise. As we have noted elsewhere in this study, more and more companies are becoming online content providers. Their main concern will be the management of the complex body of intellectual property rights associated with the content thus offered.

The second aspect of control over content necessary for companies in this sector is the legal control of personal client and potential client data collected online or for use in online commerce

8.3.1 Managing Intellectual Property Rights

Historically, new technologies have repeatedly created uncertainty about what is and is not copyrightable. When radio launched, music companies worried their works would be stolen. When copy machines became generally available, publishers worried that people would use them to illegally copy books. Inexpensive videocassette recorders created great fear in the movie industry. In this sense, the Internet is the latest technology to threaten intellectual property holders. While new technologies have inevitably altered industries in the past, new business models and opportunities have led to even greater growth; there is no reason why the cycle will be any different this time.

The management and licensing of intellectual property rights constitutes a key element for content industries and for other industries that do business on open networks. As we have discussed elsewhere, content can be understood either as a medium that makes network commerce possible or as the object of the transaction. Legal control over content will increasingly be based on the use of technologies that protect the works and the management of authors' rights. Smaller firms that do not have the means to invest in these technologies should be able to access them either directly or through collective management bodies.

8.3.2 Copyright

It is now generally accepted that we need only adapt traditional copyright laws to the new digital environment and standardise the rules at the international level. For the EU countries, rather than creating new copyright laws specifically for open networks, it is more a question of responding to the situation using existing legislation. Since copyright laws have a territorial application, whenever an intellectual work is "present" in a territory — displayed, reproduced, or used — the applicable law in that territory should prevail.

On 10 December 1997, the European Commission adopted a Directive on Copyright and Related Rights in the Information Society.[48] This bill aims to harmonise the rules on copyright, specifically concerning the transmission of works on networks, in order to counteract any inequalities of competition among the various countries of the EU. By so doing, the European Commission hopes to give content suppliers a legal framework which will enable them to profit from their investments. This bill is part of the extension of the treaties negotiated in December 1996 at the Geneva Diplomatic Conference of the World Intellectual Property Organisation (WIPO) (the two treaties are the "WIPO Copyright Treaty" and "WIPO Performances and Phonograms Treaty").[49] It gives a broad definition of the two main rights which need to be applied on the networks (reproduction right and right of communication to the public) and subsequently establishes a list of exceptions to these rights.

One of the essential aspects of the bill is that it requires the member states to adopt measures for sanctioning circumvention of technical measures for protection and marking of intellectual property, thus upholding the provisions of the WIPO Treaties. The European Community has thus established a base of protective rules, which each country may build upon to some extent.

A concerted effort is also possible at the international level, as shown by the global efforts to respond to the two WIPO Treaties.[50] These provisions mark a decisive step in the process of updating the Berne Convention by upholding the protection of literary and artistic works that are used, created, and transmitted online. All fifteen member states of the EU and the US have signed these treaties, but Japan has not. This genuine effort toward alignment has led to an extension of the field of protection for creative works to include their digital form or mode and the online transfer of content.

Network businesses must accurately identify all actions which require authorisation from the holders of the rights and the situations in which the creative works digitised on open networks can be freely used. Reproduction rights and the right of communication to the public are the two main rights which raise specific problems on networks.

Reproduction Right

Within the EU there are disparities among the legislation of the different member states concerning reproduction rights, their limits and the level of protection offered. Most of these laws do not specifically cover the digital use of creative works, thus jurisprudence must decide whether and how to sanction unlawful reproduction on the networks. In its proposed directive of 1997, the European Commission strengthened the harmonisation of reproduction rights by adopting an extensive concept which includes direct or indirect reproduction, temporary or permanent, by any means, in any form, in whole or in part. Today there is no doubt that the digitisation of a creative work, its presence on a network, or its storage on a computer hard disk (for example) constitute acts of reproduction.

Right of Communication to the Public

Once more, the proposed directive of December 1997 upholds a very broad conception of the right of communication which responds to the question of using digitised works on a network. The act of making a creative work accessible to other previously unidentified persons via the network calls the right of communication to the public into question.

In practice, since two distinct persons can hold the rights of reproduction and communication to the public, it is up to companies online to be vigilant when negotiating transfers of rights in order to avoid fraud in the future.

Private Copying and "Fair Use"

The WIPO Copyright Treaty calls for restrictions to the author's monopoly in special cases where there is neither infringement upon the normal use of the creative work, nor any unjustified damage to the legitimate interests of the author.[51] In the EU, under the proposed directive of December 1997, the exceptions and limits are applicable only in certain special cases that do not conflict with a normal exploitation of the work and do not unreasonably prejudice the legitimate interests of the author.[52]

The bill establishes a list of exceptions to the rights of reproduction and communication to the public, making a distinction between those which the states are committed to adopt (temporary reproductions) and those whose adoption is optional (which will lead to "customised," and therefore imperfect, standardisation of the regulations). The bill gives a long list of exceptional cases including quotation, uses for scientific research or education, etc.

In the US, the main variance to copyright concerns "fair use." This is a very broad concept and its field of application is defined by jurisprudence. It therefore applies to various uses of digitised works on networks. The United States Conference on Fair Use (CONFU) was set up to bring together copyright owners and users to discuss fair use issues and to develop guidelines for fair use of copyrighted works by libraries and schools.[53] It attempted to set up codes of conduct applicable in the information society. It is therefore up to the content industry to comply with these practices,[54] although the protection of a contract is still advised.

"Fair use" includes the exception of copying for private use, which is admitted in those countries that recognise copyright protections, including European countries and Japan. This exception grants the user of a protected work the freedom to make a copy for his or her exclusive personal use. Making a private copy of a work for the purpose of broadcasting it on an open network does not come under the exception of private copying. Once this reproduction is broadcast on an Internet-type open network, any connected third party can access it. In this case, there is the presumption of collective use.

Allowing an exception for private digital copies is a delicate question. Many companies (especially in multimedia publishing) hope that such an exception will be eliminated or limited in scope.

During the WIPO Conference in Geneva, the differences of opinion on this point were such that no agreement could be reached. The Commission Directive on copyright also fails to address this point, under the pretext that the making of digital private copies will not become a widespread practice and will have no great economic effect. Today, this point poses a major obstacle to the optimal growth of the content industry.

Moral Rights

The very technique of reproducing works by digitisation represents a major source of infringement of the author's moral rights because it entails the reprocessing of the work, which could enable any number of modifications and manipulations. The 1995 Green Paper on Copyright and Related Rights in the Information Society took the position that moral rights do not constitute a legal problem that requires global intervention.[55] The European Commission, which considered that this question did not have sufficient economic impact, did not see fit to harmonise the provisions on moral rights in its proposed Commission Directive on copyright.[56] However, the question of moral rights must not be underestimated in practice. In fact, there are very few fraudulent acts that infringe on moral rights. Still, network businesses cannot ignore the various "moral" prerogatives of the author (including the right to choose to divulge the work for the first time, the right to claim authorship, and the right to respect for the integrity of the work), that are by principle inalienable.

Marking the Work

An effective way of ensuring protection for copyright holders is to set up international technical systems of identification and marking. Article 12 of the WIPO Copyright Treaty requires the states to establish appropriate legal sanctions against any infringement upon information "used to identify the work, the author of the work, the holder of any rights to the work or...to the conditions and methods of using the work, including any number or code representing this information...."[57]

Article 7 of the proposed Commission Directive on copyright codifies this point and offers greater protection than that proposed by the WIPO Treaties.[58] Harmonisation at the European Community level is being sought for the legal protection of the integrity of the technical systems for identifying and protecting works. The identification of the works and the necessary related information are not specified, since the commission preferred to allow the industries concerned to reach an agreement on standards.

Collective Rights Management

The appearance of new techniques, and the accompanying increase in the number of users of the works, has made it more difficult for authors to manage their rights individually and for users to identify the holders of the rights and obtain their authorisation.

Collective management (non-mandatory) is often presented as the most suitable solution for safeguarding the exclusive rights of the author. Under such a system, the rights holders authorise collective management bodies to administer their rights, which means negotiating with the users for permission to use the works under certain conditions and in consideration of payment of a fee, monitoring the use of the works, and collecting the fees and distributing them accordingly.

The multimedia world (online and offline) is currently giving rise to a new form of collective management. We are seeing the establishment of single systems (particularly in France, with the SESAM experiment, and in Switzerland) grouping together the various bodies managing so-called "electronic" rights, and thus helping users to identify the holders of the rights and obtain authorisation.

Given the fast-growing use of the networks, such systems should be established on an international scale through increased co-operation among collective management bodies worldwide. Reliance on fewer intermediaries can only be beneficial for members of the information society, in which the speed of operations is of utmost importance.

8.3.3 Sales of Content over the Network

An effective way to ensure copyright protection is to set up international technical systems to control the use of works. The WIPO Treaties addressed this question. Article 11 of the WIPO Copyright Treaty concerning authors' rights specifies that the signatory parties must provide legal protection for, and sanctions against, the circumvention of technical measures that protect the use of works.[59] According to Article 6 of the proposed Commission Directive on copyright, which conforms to the provisions of the WIPO Treaties, member states must set up "appropriate legal protection against all activities, including the manufacture or distribution of mechanisms or the supply of services whose commercial value or use is limited to the neutralisation of technical protection mechanisms, if the person concerned acts knowingly or having valid reasons to think that they will enable or facilitate the unauthorised neutralisation of any effective technical measure designed to protect copyright, or neighbouring rights, as specified by the law or the autonomous right as defined in Chapter III of Directive 96/9/EC...."[60] Similarly, the Digital Millennium Copyright Act, nearing final approval by the US federal legislature, makes it a crime in the US to create or sell any technology that would be used to break copyright protection devices such as encryption and digital watermarks. However, the House of Representatives version of the bill permits cracking of copyright protection devices to conduct encryption research.[61]

Prohibiting the circumvention of technical protective systems raises two problems. First, such a system could effectively prevent private copying in all cases. This questions whether private copying is a right or is simply tolerated. The general position among legal experts leans toward the latter. The other problem is in determining when liability should accrue for circumventing copy protection systems. It is a question of either sanctioning the circumvention itself (regardless of whether authors' rights were violated) or sanctioning only in cases of demonstrable infringement on authors' rights.

Several systems for preventing copying and managing intellectual property rights are currently in development. These include the EU programs COPICAT and COPYSMART. In the case of rights management, for several years the EU has been developing a program called "IMPRIMATUR" for the purpose of setting up an Electronic Copyright Management System within the member states. It is therefore up to the market to develop the technology and up to the legislatures to provide legal protection. The degrees of security, compatibility, and inter-operability will be deciding factors in the future.

Companies whose main business is the marketing of content must manage the intellectual property rights related to that content. Consequently, they must have control over the technologies that make possible the use of the content and the management of authors' rights.

These technologies are used both to identify the rights holders by marking their works and to limit the uses of the work which are offered to various users. Currently, the major rights-holding firms are investing heavily and collectively in the development of such technologies.

In this context, smaller content industry players should also have access to such technologies, either directly or through collective management bodies, without which they will be forced out of business. In the EU, a project is already underway to attempt to develop an alternative to the privately funded technologies which are currently being developed in the US. The conditions for access to these technologies in Europe are not yet clearly defined.

8.3.4 Commercial Use of Databases

The WIPO Diplomatic Conference adopted a recommendation concerning databases which aims to lay the groundwork for a future treaty on this subject.

An examination of the protection granted by law to databases entails making a prior distinction between the content and the container. According to Article 2.5 of the Berne Convention for the protection of literary and artistic works, "collections of literary and artistic works... which by the choice or the disposition of the materials constitute intellectual creations are protected as such, without copyright infringement for each of the works which are included in such a collection."[62] According to Article 5 of the WIPO Copyright Treaty, "compilations of data or other elements, regardless of their form, which by the choice or the disposition of the materials constitute intellectual creations, are protected as such. This protection does not extend to the data or elements themselves, and it does not infringe on the existing author's rights for the data or elements contained in the compilation."[63]

The Database Directive protects the database as "a collection of works of data or other independent elements made available systematically or methodically and individually accessible by electronic or other means." Non-electronic databases are therefore included in the field of protection. The directive decides that"...databases which, through the choice or disposition of the materials, constitute a creation which is original to their author are protected as such by copyright." Therefore, the originality is the result of only the choice or disposition of the materials. These criteria alone will be used to determine whether the database can or cannot be protected.[64]

Most copyright laws contain express provisions on the protection of copyright for collections of literary and artistic works (encyclopaedias, anthologies). This is true in the US, Japan, and nearly all the EU member states. However, US law provides little if any protection for compilations of information that are not literary or artistic works.[65]

To prevent data from being taken from one database to create another that is identical in content, a new form of protection was needed. It aims to protect the investments made by operators of databases, even if the content of the databank is not original. To this day, there is no international standard on the protection of databases by an autonomous right. The Database Directive protects, for fifteen years starting on 1 January of the year following its completion, the autonomous right of databases whose maker proves that "obtaining, verifying, or formatting the content...entailed a substantial qualitative or quantitative investment."[66] Consequently, the producer or manufacturer of a database (including electronic databases) has the right to prohibit the extraction or re-use of the totality or a substantial part (to be evaluated quantitatively or qualitatively) of the content of the database. The difficulty is in distinguishing what constitutes a "substantial part" of a database. The directive also lists exceptions and limits to the autonomous right that include the extraction of substantial parts of databases for purposes of research and education. Member states are free to decide whether to include this exception or not in their national legislation. Given the growing number of academics using the Internet, the adoption of such an exception would substantially narrow the scope of the protection granted under autonomous right.

This concept of autonomous right is recognised only in the countries of the EU. Many laws are in the process of being drafted at the European Community level. France, Germany, Sweden, the UK, Austria, and Spain have already enacted legislation pursuant to the Database Directive.

8.3.5 Industrial Property Protection

In addition to copyright protection, it is possible to protect the presentation of content by enforcing the rights to industrial drawings. In fact, the icons which enable users to navigate within the content are protected by authors' rights, which prohibit their identical reproduction. On the other hand, these icons can benefit from a protection which is shorter in duration (maximum ten years) but more extensive in definition, because the registration of an icon as an industrial drawing can be used to protect the general features of an icon, thus extending the protection to different variants of the same basic icon. However, this relatively new possibility of protecting icons as industrial drawings is not recognised in all countries. In any case, it does not protect icons whose presentations are governed only by their utilitarian function.

8.3.6 Trademarks

Trademarks are important for two reasons. Traditionally, trademarks constituted extra protection in addition to authors' rights, similar to the protection offered by industrial drawings described above. Trademarks on electronic networks can also protect the electronic address through which the content is accessible. This is the problem of domain names on the Internet. Last but not least, trademarks are used simply in the conventional way to identify the products or services offered. They constitute one of the essential assets of businesses. As we shall see, trademark law proves to be especially ill-adapted to commerce on networks. We will see that, in fact, this type of commerce forces companies to register and defend their brand names in territories that extend beyond their traditional geographic markets, a process which can be quite costly for smaller companies.

General Issues

While companies traditionally register trademarks only in their home countries (or in a group of countries in which they operate), networks bring them in contact with an international market. Companies therefore face the problem of registering their trademarks in all countries which can potentially become markets in the future. The regulation of trademarks is not consistent on the international level. Moreover, the cost incurred can be considerable.

Generally speaking, trademarks are divided into forty-two classes recognised by many countries and are acquired through the registration of a distinctive sign for different products and services. The protection of the trademark is limited to the products or services designated in the registration. Certain trademarks which have very strong recognition are not required to register. In common law countries, trademark law is strongly influenced by the concept of their usage.

Within a single country, totally different products can be covered by a single trademark. On the international level, this problem is necessarily intensified due to the multiplication of possible combinations. While this problem is not recent, it has been exacerbated by the Internet. In fact, two business operators can be the legitimate owners of the same trademark in each of their home countries. Legislation on the acquisition of the rights to a trademark and the extent of the protection granted varies from one country to another, despite standardisation attempts at the European level (creation of the European Community trademark) and the international level.[67]

The current systems for registering trademarks specify time limits during which trademark holders can protect their rights in other territories and other trademark holders can dispute these rights. All of these time limits, which seem to be reasonable in traditional commerce, seem very long in network commerce because of the possibility of instantaneous access to new markets. Finally, before an existing trademark can be registered in all of its potential markets, the necessary analysis procedures alone (the classic example being the search for precedents) entail significant costs.

Generally speaking, the owner of a trademark must exert constant vigilance for its protection (to fight against counterfeiting, etc.). In English-speaking countries, counterfeiters must be pursued in the courts, incurring considerable legal expenses which are often beyond the means of smaller companies.

A trademark holder can lose trademark protection if the trademark is not used for a certain period or if the proper measures are not taken to preserve its distinctive character. In certain countries, a trademark can be forfeited if the holder tolerates the use of an identical or similar brand for a certain period. Only Japan seems to recognise its use to promote goods as being effective without requiring that the goods be backed by marketing efforts. On the other hand, the use of a trademark by third parties could be detrimental to its legal holder, in the sense that this use could render the trademark "generic" and thus lead to the loss of protection. For this reason, technological monitoring systems have recently been implemented on the Internet to enable trademark holders to check use of their trademarks, and when possible to control the consequences.

The question is raised as to whether the circulation of products and services on a network is considered to be effective circulation, and thus whether the rule of exhaustion of rights is applicable. This theory, developed in the EU, considers that merchandise in circulation in one of the EU member countries with the consent of the trademark holder makes possible the free circulation of this product throughout all the member countries, in order to prevent the trademark holder from compartmentalising the market for the product.[68]

Metatags, Frames, and Links

Apart from conventional counterfeiting (when a trademark is copied without the authorisation of its holder), new forms of infringement have recently appeared on the Internet. The first type consists of integrating a trademark into a "metatag." A metatag is a device by which the trademark of a competitor is embedded within a Web site in a manner that is invisible when someone views the Web site. However, the metatag is visible to Internet browsing software. Therefore, if someone performs an Internet search using the competitor's trademark, both the Web site belonging to the trademark owner and the site with the metatag will be retrieved for the user to view. Another practice, called "framing," consists of displaying on one site pages from another site and creating hypertext links between them. US courts have decided that the use of these links constitutes an infringement of any trademark reproduced in the links.[69]

The use of a metatag was enjoined recently by a US federal court.[70] The court based its holding on traditional unfair-competition principals that the defendant could not use metatags referring to Playboy magazine that resulted in the defendants' Web site being retrieved when searches for "Playboy" and "Playmate" were conducted.

Hyperlinking one Web site to another has led to some interesting litigation by trademark owners attempting to prevent use of their mark on the Web sites of others. Hyperlinks are addresses for other Web sites appearing in the text on another Web page. A viewer clicks on the address and immediately is transferred to the hyperlinked Web site.

Hyperlinking will direct users to a lower level portion of the hyperlinked Web site. This allows users to bypass the entrance to the Web site as well as the usual advertisements and other information on the trademark owners' products. In a recent case, Ticketmaster (a major broker of tickets to sporting and entertainment events in the US) sued Microsoft alleging improper use of

Ticketmaster's name and logo on Microsoft's "Seattle Sidewalk" Web page.[71] Microsoft had included hyperlinks that brought users directly to Ticketmaster's list of events, bypassing all policies and service information on the home page. Ticketmaster alleges numerous causes of action including an anti-dilution claims, misrepresentation, unfair competition, and unfair business practices.

Although the Ticketmaster case is not yet resolved, a decision by another US federal judge may have injected the US Constitution's First Amendment (protecting free speech and freedom of the press) into this and other hyperlink disputes.[72] The court upheld a challenge to a state criminal statute that prohibited certain activities on computer networks. One of the issues raised in the case was the effect of the statute's prohibition on the unauthorised use of trade names or trademarks in hyperlinks. The court specifically addressed the plaintiff's concern that the prohibition of the use of trademarks in conjunction with hyperlinks would impinge on free speech rights. Although the court attempted to limit its holding to non-commercial speech, the court struck down the statute's prohibition on the unauthorised use of trademarks as overbroad on First Amendment grounds. It still remains to be seen what will happen in a case of hyperlinks that involve commercial speech.

Trademarks and Domain Names

Trademark holders are having difficulty ensuring that their rights are respected in the attribution of Internet domain names. In order for the network to function properly, it is important that corporations be able to use their registered trademarks online to identify their products and services and prevent third parties from using their trademarks. Given that trademark protection is by nature territorial and special, due to the choices of products or services for which the trademark is to be protected, it is inevitable that different companies are able to adopt the same name, as long as they are not operating in the same business sector or in the same countries.

Internet domain names, although they can be distinguished as generic or geographic names, are unique in that they are directly connected to a digital address that identifies the site. The addition of suffixes which make it possible to identify a larger aggregation to which a site belongs (.fr, .uk, .it, .com, etc.), have no power to prevent counterfeiting arising from the illegal use of a trademark.

The proposed rules are essentially criteria for caution to be observed by the various national organisations which handle the registration of domain names. These include checking the rights submitted to them by the registering parties. The creation of seven new generic domain names, which proportionately extend the use of identical denominations, plus the creation of twenty-eight registration offices in charge of applying uniform regulations, should make it possible to improve the functioning of the naming system. The second type of measure concerns the prevention of litigation by the implementation of an extra-legal procedure for handling and resolving complaints. Both in the US and internationally, this system calls for a period of one month during which any interested third parties can request suspension and examination of complaints arising from the registration of a new domain name. If it is implemented by truly independent commissions, such a procedure will have the advantage of avoiding the need to settle all conflicts in court and would provide a rapid solution for resolving potential litigation online. Naturally, this leads to the question of the real value of these arbitrated decisions.

Trademark-holding corporations wishing to register a domain name corresponding to their trademark would be well advised to register in the classes covering telematic products and services. In the case of litigation, the holders of these trademarks will have a greater chance of winning the right to keep the corresponding domain name.

8.4 Protection of Personal Data

Technically speaking, networks facilitate the circulation and processing of public domain financial data and information, personal data, and data protected by copyright. Legally speaking, access to and use of the last two types of data is regulated. Therefore, before any operation, one must know the laws of the countries of transmission and reception concerning the protection of such data, and sometimes even the laws of the countries of transit. However, these protection systems vary from country to country.

The problem today for operators in network commerce is determining the conditions that must be met when processing personal data via a computer network (intranet or Internet).[73] This question concerns not only the protection of data on open networks, but also cross-border data flows, since these networks are global and "borderless."

8.4.1 Protection of Personal Data on Open Networks

Consumers would likely use networks even more if given a technical and/or legal guarantee that their personal data would not be used without their authorisation. All business operators must therefore understand the dangers posed to personal privacy created by network usage and other guarantees of privacy where the law does not offer them.[74]

Dangers
There are many techniques that can be used for processing the information available on the networks concerning a given person. These include the use of "cookies," which are text files that enable service providers to identify a user and compile a log of his/her online actions; the use of sites such as "*déjà-news*," which can be used to trace all of a user's submissions to Usenet newsgroups based on e-mail addresses; and the use of log files kept by access providers, which record all the connections made by their clients as well as all the files and Web pages read or downloaded.

Legal and Contractual Solutions
EC Directive 97/66 of 15 December 1997 requires a minimum level of protection for subscribers and users of the telecommunications networks (natural persons or legal entities) whose personal data is processed.[75] One of the proposed solutions is the possibility for users to remain anonymous. The problem here is that although all individuals are free to express their opinions and convictions, it is also accepted that persons who exercise this freedom must be held respon-

sible for their acts. This implies that they can be subject to legal recourse, and therefore that their identities can be known. Moreover, in services involving buying and selling, total anonymity is not easily maintained because the payment is usually done by credit card. Therefore the business must have ways to check the data received. One way to preserve anonymity would be to institute an electronic exchange currency comparable to cash, which would allow completely anonymous transactions (e.g. DigiCash).

8.4.2 Cross-border Flows of Personal Data

Under many international and national regulations, the circulation of personal data across national borders constitutes a cross-border data flow. For example, there is a cross-border flow of data when data is collected in France from a computer located in the US or when a personal database is transferred by a party in charge of processing located in Spain to a receiving party located in Japan. It makes no difference if the transferring party is the parent company and the receiving party is its subsidiary.

The main problem is that there are restrictive rules at the European level[76] but none at the international level.[77] In order not to impede commercial operations on networks, countries outside the EU must adapt. This adaptation can take the form of legislation, or the companies concerned can sign contracts for each data flow. How can the cross-border flow of personal data be organised between a EU country and other countries such as the US and Japan?

According to Article 25 of the European Privacy Directive, there is no limit on the transfer of data between member states because of the principle of "free circulation of data." However, the Directive prohibits transfers to "non-EU countries," except "if the latter ensures an adequate level of protection."[78]

Several dispensations to this prohibition are specified. The Directive specifies that the member states can decide whether the protection offered by the non-EU country is adequate and can grant, in the absence of adequate protection, the necessary authorisations to parties in charge of the processing who offer sufficient guarantees, provided that the European Commission and the member states are duly informed.[79] Currently, only Italy and Greece have enacted legislation pursuant to the Directive of 1995. Most other European countries have bills in preparation, since they must act on the Directive by 1 October 1998.

The European Commission considers that for certain sectors of the economy, an "adequate" level of protection is provided by the codes and laws already in force. This includes the sectors of banking and telecommunications. However, it considers that codes of conduct and technical facilities alone are not sufficient for providing "adequate protection." The data protection system in the US falls short because (i) it lacks sanctions and compensatory damages in the case of privacy violation, (ii) individuals lack the right to access or rectify their personal data, and (iii) no supervisory authority exists which could receive and handle complaints from Europeans in the case of violation of their privacy by American entities or assume the role of mediator and privileged correspondent with the European Commission or the supervisory authorities of the member states.

The US Secretary of Commerce has asked companies to establish effective self-regulation before the end of 1998, after which time the government could react by enacting restrictive legislation. Given such pressure, on 22 June 1998 thirty-nine US firms and twelve business associations announced the creation of a group to protect online privacy, the Online Privacy Alliance. [80] Members are from the computer industry, advertising and financial services firms, database providers, telecommunications companies, retail marketers, and ISPs. Members of the "Online Privacy Alliance" said they would "respond to concerns about privacy online" by working to protect consumers from unethical business practices and to stop companies from pitching products to children. Those members, who include among their number Time Warner, Walt Disney, AOL, and IBM, undertake to publish their privacy policy online, to disclose any third-party use of data, to require consent, to ensure data security and quality, and to enable consumers to gain access to data about themselves. The Alliance also endorses the system of "Privacy Approved" seals proposed by TrustE and BBBOnline.

In the absence of a pertinent law in Japan (the only applicable law, in effect since 1 October 1989, concerns the public sector only) and supervisory authority for the private sector, Japan does not have adequate protection for the importation and processing of data from Europe.

In fact, for the private sector, the protection of personal data is provided not by legislation but by codes of good conduct.

For non-EU countries which do not seem to provide adequate protection of data, member states can authorise the application of Article 26.2 of the Privacy Directive, which specifies that a Member State can authorise a transfer of personal data to a non-EU country which does not provide an adequate level of protection if the party in charge of the processing offers sufficient guarantees for the protection of privacy and the fundamental rights and liberties of the persons concerned.

It will therefore be "sufficient" to codify the commitment of the receiver of the data in a contract. The supervisory authority concerned must then be notified. (The supervisory authority in Germany thus approved such a contract between Citibank and the Deutsche Bundesbahn in 1997).

The Council of Europe, the European Commission, and the International Chamber of Commerce have jointly drafted a "model contract for the purpose of providing equivalent protection of data in the cross-border flow of data." In the absence of a contract, and given the declarations of the European Commission, personal data can be transferred to countries which have ratified the Convention, provided that the receiving country has an independent supervisory authority and is the final destination of the transfer (and not merely a transit country for the data).

Personal data can be transferred to countries which have not ratified Convention only in the following three cases: (i) If the personal data is transferred by a party in charge of processing established in the EU to a party in charge of processing established in a non-EU country; (ii) if the transfer is carried out by a party in charge of processing established in a country of the EU to a subcontractor acting on his behalf established in a non-EU country; or (iii) if the transfer is carried out by the person concerned located in a country of the EU to a party in charge of processing established in a non-EU country.

The principle obstacle to the cross-border flow of personal data is in the differences between the European and EU legislation and the US and Japanese legislation. The most suitable solution in the short term may be a contractual solution, in which the party in charge of the file undertakes to provide protection equivalent to that provided in the country where the data is collected so that the rights of the persons on file are not violated. In the long term, minimum but restrictive international standards — which do not exist today — must be established.

8.5 Summary

In this chapter we have examined a number of key legal and regulatory issues either impacting or impacted by network commerce. Most of these issues are complicated by the transborder nature of the global Internet. Questions of choice of law and jurisdiction create many uncertainties about the conduct of many Web-based activities. Our discussion begins with an examination of the legal treatment of the online sales process, moving from regulations on fair trade practices and other aspects of the offer through payment, delivery of the good or service, and the conduct of litigation and enforcement of judgements in instances where transactions go awry. We then examine various aspects of content regulation, ranging from copyright protection to the relationship between domain names and trademarks. Finally, we look at the ongoing debate over how to protect the privacy of individual data collected by or maintained by marketers on the network.

RECOMMENDATIONS

Existing legal and regulatory regimes create many problems for the development of network commerce — many arising from its global nature. Businesses must act to fill some of the legal and regulatory gaps created by network commerce, or risk overzealous regulators filling these gaps in ways that may not be conducive to the development of network commerce. Governments must strike a delicate balance between not acting and taking sufficient action to ensure that rights are protected and orderly markets evolve. Governments are exploring ways to work together on a bilateral and multilateral basis to ensure that differences between national laws do not hinder network commerce development or damage national competitiveness.

Businesses

- *Self-regulate where practical, with an eye toward developing broad, transparent guidelines that can be enforced in a meaningful way.* If businesses can successfully build guidelines for businesses on the network, governments are not compelled to intervene. Successful self-regulation requires effective guidelines. Businesses should create and participate in self-regulatory organisations as serious alternatives to government regulation.
- *Ask governments to address key business issues, but also seek opportunities to partner with them to resolve these issues.* Governments can only do so much, so businesses should explore what they can do in partnership to address these issues.

Content Firms

- *Embrace alternatives to government content regulation, such as rating and filtering systems that allow parents to protect children from harmful content.* One of the most contentious legal regulatory issues for content firms is the control of offensive or putatively harmful content, such as hate speech and pornography. By embracing rating and filtering systems and other technological methods that put content control in the hands of consumers, content firms can defuse this potentially explosive issue and help to strike a balance between freedom of speech and concerns over harmful content.
- *Work with and push governments to address content-critical issues (e.g. intellectual property protection, censorship, universal access).* Content firms should act to ensure that the legal and regulatory issues critical to their success in the network economy are resolved quickly and effectively.
- *Explore how technologies such as Intertrust and digital watermarks can be used to protect intellectual property rights.* The ability of existing intellectual property rights to adequately protect many forms of content in the network marketplace is limited. Technologies exist that could provide a valuable complement to new intellectual property laws. The challenge for content businesses and technology vendors is to find a solution that is simple, inexpensive, effective, and can quickly become ubiquitous. Such a solution may emerge, but content firms will have to work closely with technology vendors and users to find the best solution.

Governments

- *Ensure that data privacy regulation protects the privacy of citizens while remaining flexible enough to accommodate personalisation of services.* The balance between protection of personal privacy and the ability to investigate consumers' preferences and deliver personalised goods and services is delicate. Governments should adopt a cautious and flexible approach to determining how to balance these interests instead of rushing to regulate and hindering the development of potentially valuable services.

- *Re-evaluate the impact of competition laws on firms' ability to compete in the global marketplace (e.g. restrictions on media cross-ownership, media concentration limits).* As we have noted elsewhere, market boundaries are blurring and firms are increasingly competing in a global marketplace. Competition and cross-ownership laws, developed to ensure competitiveness and openness in national markets, may hinder the ability of firms in those smaller markets to compete in the global marketplace.
- *Facilitate self-regulation among businesses, especially on a global basis.* Governments can play a critical role in ensuring that businesses that they represent are able to participate equitably in global self-regulation efforts. They can also ensure that the interests of their citizens and businesses are represented in these processes.
- *Play a strong role in global organisations in order to smooth differences between national laws and regulations.* It is imperative that governments participate in global efforts to harmonise relevant laws and regulations. This ensures that the interests of citizens and businesses are protected and that equitable ground rules for competition are developed.

Notes

1. Elizabeth de Bony, "Regulating Electronic Commerce," *EIU European Policy Analyst*, 16 February 1998.

2. George Cole, "Censorship in Cyberspace," *Financial Times*, 21 March 1996.

3. Treaty Establishing EEC, Mar. 25, 1957, 298 U.N.T.S. 3, arts. 85-86 (known as the Treaty of Rome).

4. Sherman Act, 15 U.S.C. 1 (1994); Clayton Act, 15 U.S.C. 18 (1994).

5. International Chamber of Commerce Marketing Codes, including International Code of Advertising Practices, Paris, 1987. Most countries have adapted and expanded the International Chamber of Commerce's International Code of Advertising Practice first created in 1937, later updated in 1987, for their own use. The International Association of Advertisers has recently taken on self-regulation as part of its mandate and is promoting it worldwide.

6. Commission Directive of 6 October 1997.

7. The Federal Trade Commission's Advertising Substantiation Statement is appended to Thomson Medical Co., Inc., 104 F.T.C. 648, at 839-842 (1984). Whether the basis for a claim is "reasonable" or not depends on a subjective case-by-case determination similar to that required to apply the "reasonable person" standard in tort law.

8. Commission Directive 84/450 of 10 September 1984.

9. Federal Trade Commission Act, 15 U.S.C. § 45 (1994).

10. Lanham Act, 15 U.S.C § 1125 (1994).

11. United Nations Convention on International Sales of Goods (known as the Vienna Convention), published in 1980 by the United Nations Commission on International Trade Law. The Vienna Convention has been since adopted by the US and thirty-eight other nations.

12. Commission Directive 97/7 of 20 May 1997 on the Protection of Consumers in Respect of Distance Contracts. Member states must enact legislation to harmonise their laws pursuant to this Directive by 4 June 2000.

13. Vienna Convention, *supra*.

14. Party that does not meet legal criteria to conclude a specific type of contract (e.g. child, mentally ill adult, corporate agent without adequate authorisation).

15. The UN Commission on International Trade Law (UNCITRAL) has been continuing its pioneering work of harmonising and codifying commercial principles applicable to selected fields of traditional law. It adopted in 1996 a Model Law on Electronic Commerce applicable to exchange of information in the shape of data message for commercial activities. The Model Law is expected to play a significant role in facilitating network transactions.

16. Report of the United Nations Commission on International Trade Law on the work of its twenty-ninth session, 28 May-14 June 1996, U.N. GAOR, 51st Sess., Supp. No. 17, U.N. Doc. A/51/17 Annex I (1996) reprinted in 36 I.L.M. 200 (1997) (hereinafter UNCITRAL Model Law).

17. See Zentaro Kitagawa, *Doing Business in Japan*, Matthew Bender & Co., 1996.

18. Convention on Jurisdiction and Enforcement of Judgement in Civil and Commercial Matters, 27 September 1968, 8 I.L.M. 229 (known as the Brussels Convention) art. 17.

19. Ibid.

20. Ibid. arts. 13-15.

21. *Carnival Cruise Lines Inc. v. Shute*, 499 U.S. 585, 111 S.Ct. 1522 (1991) (holding that a forum-selection clause that was included among three pages of terms attached to a cruise ship ticket was enforceable).

22. Convention on the Law Applicable to Contractual Obligations ("Rome Convention") Rome, 19 June 1980. art. 5.

23. Ibid.

24. U.C.C. art. 2B-107.

25. Commission Directive of 5 April 1995.

26. RFCs are at the core of the process developed by the loosely organised Internet Engineering Task Force (IETF), the chief Internet standard-setting body. Since February 1987, the IETF has developed Internet specifications using the Internet itself as the medium. Most work is done on e-mail discussion lists, while physical meetings only occur three times per year. Anyone can propose changes to Internet standards through the RFC process.

27. Consumer Code art. L 121-16.

28. Home Sales Law art. 6.

29. Commission Directive 97/7 of 20 May 1997 on the Protection of Consumers in Respect of Distance Contracts.

30. Ibid.

31. Incoterms are a codification of international customs regulating carriage of goods by sea. These terms prepared by the International Chamber of Commerce (ICC) are the most widely used of published trade terms. By use of an Incoterm, the seller and buyer incorporate the obligations spelled out in the ICC's Incoterm publication.

32. Vienna Convention, *supra*.

33. Convention on the Law Applicable to Contractual Obligations ("Rome Convention") Rome, 19 June 1980. art. 2.

34. U.C.C. art. 2B (proposed). Adoption of U.C.C. provisions by the states is voluntary. Individual states are free to enact some or all amendments to the U.C.C. into legislation.

35. U.C.C. arts. 2B-107 and 2B-108 (proposed).

36. Brussels Convention, *supra*.

37. Rome Convention, art. 4-2.

38. Act concerning the Application of Laws - Horei.

39. U.C.C. art. 1-105.

40. U.C.C. art. 2B (proposed).

41. Brussels Convention art. 14.

42. Brussels Convention art. 4.

43. Rome Convention art. 5 § 3.

44. European Commission Recommendation of 30 March 1998.

45. "Comity" is the principle by which courts in one nation agree to honour judgements handed down by courts in other jurisdictions. Comparable to the French legal concept of exequator.

46. Brussels Convention arts. 27 and 34.

47. *North Con I v. Mansei Co.*, Japanese Supreme Court Petty Bench, 11 July 1997. Jiji Press Ticker Service, 11 July 1997.

48. Commission Directive of 10 December 1997 on Copyright and Related Rights in the Information Society [see MEMO: 97/108].

49. A Diplomatic Conference, hosted by the World Intellectual Property Organisation (WIPO), an organisation of the United Nations, was convened in Geneva to consider adoption of three treaties to update the Berne and Rome Conventions, and bring international copyright law into the digital era. The Berne Convention for the Protection of Literary and Artistic Works, drawn up in 1886, is the oldest international copyright treaty, although the US did not become a Member of it until 1989. The

International Convention for the Protection of Performers, Producers of Phonograms, and Broadcasting Organisations was adopted in 1961 in Rome. From 2 through 20 December 1996, representatives from over 150 countries and from over seventy-five non-governmental organisations debated and negotiated the provisions of the treaties released by WIPO in draft form last August. The treaties proposed at the Conference were: the Treaty on Certain Questions Concerning the Protection of Literary and Artistic Works (the "Copyright Treaty"), the Treaty for the Protection of the Rights of Performers and Producers of Phonograms (the "Performances and Phonograms Treaty"), and the Treaty on Intellectual Property in Respect of Databases (the "Database Treaty"). The Database Treaty ultimately was tabled for further discussion and analysis.

50. Ibid.

51. Ibid.

52. Commission Directive of 10 December 1997 on Copyright and Related Rights in the Information Society [see MEMO: 97/108].

53. See Notice of First Meeting of Conference on "Fair Use" and National Information Infrastructure (NII), 59 Fed. Reg. 46,823 (1994). A final report for the first phase of CONFU was released in September 1997. Report to the Commissioner on the Conclusion of the First Phase of the Conference on Fair Use, September 1997. Available at http://www.uspto.gov/web/offices/dcom/olia/confu/conclutoc.html. A second phase of CONFU commenced in 1998.

54. See Report to the Commissioner on the Conclusion of the First Phase of the Conference on Fair Use, September 1997.

55. European Commission, Green Paper, Copyright and Related Rights in the Information Society, COM (95) 382 final (arguing that European intellectual property rights need to be enhanced and harmonised for the digital environment) (see IP/95/798) which resulted in a Communication by the Commission of 20 November 1996 announcing the issues to be contained in the initiative (see IP/96/1042).

56. Commission Directive of 10 December 1997 on Copyright and Related Rights in the Information Society [see MEMO: 97/108].

57. WIPO Copyright Treaty art. 12.

58. Commission Directive of 10 December 1997 art. 7.

59. WIPO Copyright Treaty art. 11.

60. Commission Directive of 10 December 1997 art. 6.

61. Courtney Macavinta, "Congress Clears Copyright Act," CNET NEWS.COM, 4 August 1998.

62. Berne Convention art. 2.5.

63. WIPO Copyright Treaty art. 5.

64. Directive 96/9/EC of the European Parliament and the Council of the EU of 11 March 1996 on the legal protection of databases, 1996 O.G. (L77/20) (the Database Directive).

65. See *Feist Publications, Inc. v. Rural Tel. Serv. Co.*, 499 U.S. 340 (1991).

66. European Community Database Directive of 11 March 1996.

67. E.g. the *Convention d'Union de Paris* of 1883; the Arrangement of Madrid.

68. Directive of 21 December 1988, art.7.

69. *Hasbro v. Internet Entertainment Corp.*, C96-130 W.D., 40 USPQ 2d 1479 (W.D. Wash. 1996) (permanent injunction in favour of Hasbro, manufacturer of children's game "Candyland," against use of domain name CANDYLAND.COM by an Internet adult entertainment company).

70. *Playboy Enterprises, Inc. v. Calvin Design Label*, Docket No. 97-3704.

71. *Ticketmaster Corp. v. Microsoft Corp.*, No. 97-3055 DDP (C.D. Calif., filed 28 April 1997).

72. *American Civil Liberties Union of Georgia v. Miller*, 1997 U.S. LEXIS 14995, * 13-14, 43 U.S.P.Q.2d1356 (1997) (finding state statute prohibiting unauthorised computerised transmission of trademarks unconstitutionally vague and overbroad because it could "prevent . . . the use of trade names or logos innon-commercial educational speech, news, and commentary") (The court cited the Act and Congress' intentional limitation of the scope of the Act, in support of its ruling.).

73. The term "processing" encompasses operations such as the "collection, recording, organisation, conservation, adaptation or modification, extraction, consultation, use, communication by transmission, broadcasting or any other type of distribution, combination or interconnection, as well as locking, erasure or deletion." Commission Directive 95/46 of 24 October 1995.

74. According to the US Federal Trade Commission, 90 percent of all commercial sites on the Web collect personal data on their visitors, but fewer than 15 percent warn them.

75. European Commission Directive 97/66 of 15 December 1997. See also Directive 95/46/EC.

76. Convention of 28 January 1981 concerning the protection of natural persons in relation to the processing of data of a personal nature (Convention no108) of the European Council; Directive 95/46 of 24 October 1995 concerning the protection of natural persons in relation to the processing of data of a personal nature and the free circulation of this data; Directive 97/66EC concerning the processing of data of a personal nature and the protection of privacy in the telecommunications field,

15 December 1997; this text is an application of the first Directive specifically for the telecommunications sector (the Telecoms Data Protection Directive).

77. The Guidelines governing the protection of privacy and the transborder flow of data of a personal nature drafted by the Council of the OECD (Recommendation of 23 September 1980) are the minimum standards, but are not mandatory.

78. EC Data Protection Directive (95/46/EC). Directive of 24 October 1995. Council Directive 95/46 of the European Parliament and of the Council on the protection of individuals with regard to the processing of personal data and on the free movement of such data, 1995 O.J. (L 281) 31 (hereinafter European Privacy Directive) (attempting to harmonise the protection of personal information within the European Union).

79. Ibid.

80. Online Privacy Coalition, http://www.privacyalliance.com/.

Identifying Key Financial Drivers and Constraints

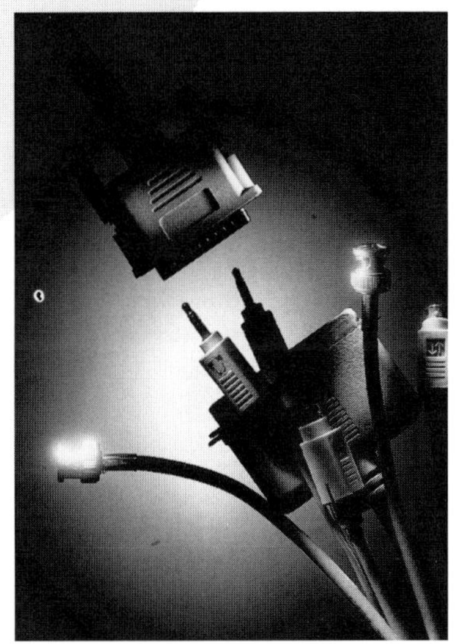

Network commerce has emerged more rapidly in some markets than others and has had a greater impact in some markets than others. In this chapter, we seek to identify the key financial drivers and constraints that have helped network commerce to bloom in some markets while causing it to founder in others.

When asked why he robbed banks, the notorious American bank robber Willie Sutton replied, "because that's where the money is." An observer of the developing technology market might give the same reply when asked why so much of the entrepreneurial activity in this area is taking place in the US. Tax policy and the venture capital environment play a central role in determining "where the money is" to fund the development of these industries. In this chapter, we will discuss the impact of tax policies on the emerging network economy, as well as the potential impact of the network economy on tax policy. We will then discuss the impact of the venture capital environment in Europe on new business formation in the content and network commerce sectors. Another emerging financial consideration in the European Union (EU) is the European Monetary Union (EMU). EMU has the potential both to drive network commerce adoption and to hinder it. In fact, EMU will make tax and product price disparities more apparent to consumers and businesses by providing consistent pricing. It is also likely to play a critical role in creating larger and more flexible capital markets to fund European firms. In the final section of this chapter, we will provide a brief overview of EMU and examine its potential role in shaping network commerce evolution.

9.1 Overview and Context

Before turning to the specific discussion, however, we should remember that the question of "where the money is" to build the rapidly evolving network economy must be addressed. We must also take into account the important differences in capitalism as it is practised in various European countries, the US, and Japan. These differences are highlighted by the great concern in Europe about the spread of the aggressive "new world capitalism" practised in the US and a growing fear that this spells the end of Europe's business civilisation. Stated most starkly, many Europeans foresee "an American maelstrom of atomistic competition, job insecurity, and social division"[1] brought about by the relentless spread of Anglo-American capitalism.

Important differences do exist between capitalism as it is practised in Continental Europe and in the US. To date, many of these differences have played an important role in the development of the network economy in these regions.[2] The Anglo-American model of capitalism — most prominently practised in the US, the UK, New Zealand, Australia, and Canada — places the interests of the shareholder at the centre. The state-led social market capitalism practised in Continental European nations such as Germany, Sweden, Austria, Denmark, and the Netherlands focuses on co-operation and consensus building. The social compact between citizens and the government plays a central role in most activities. Japan's brand of capitalism is based on values of communitarianism, with management of the firm controlled by a variety of disciplining mechanisms in an effort to serve a plurality of stakeholders. Shareholders, employees, but also suppliers, customers, members of the business group or keiretsu, and local government make up these stakeholders.

In general, the Anglo-American system provides short-term flexibility. Clear management objectives and differing disciplining mechanisms allow the system to stimulate dynamism, job rotation, and entry and exit of firms. In the model, prices stimulate entry of firms in promising industries. Competition stimulates innovations especially rapidly. For firms, investment in research and development is driven primarily by market forces and availability of venture capital financing. In this system, knowledge that is relatively easily codified will be produced and exchanged. By contrast, European-style state-led capitalism has traditionally proven to excel at guiding complicated technology projects in which research, production, and commercialisation can be isolated from the international market (e.g. weapons systems, public transport, nuclear energy). This type of capitalism is weak in sectors that have to react flexibly to market signals because of the relative short-term rigidity and dependence on personal relationships.

The differences in the nature of capitalism in Continental Europe and the US lead to important differences in tax policies and the venture capital environment. We believe that the transition to a network economy exacerbates these differences and may lead either to significant differences in the evolution of network content and commerce businesses in Continental Europe, or to significant and perhaps unwelcome shifts in the nature of capitalism as practised in Continental Europe.

9.2 Taxation

Tax policy both affects and is affected by the evolution of the network economy. First, tax policy plays a critical role in creating an environment that can foster the development of network commerce. Second, the borderless nature of network commerce creates serious problems for administration and enforcement of tax laws. These issues converge where the network economy eases the way for network businesses to move to jurisdictions with the most favourable tax policies. In this manner, the network economy magnifies the impact of local and national tax policies on decisions about where to locate businesses due to the ease of moving business activities to jurisdictions with the most favourable tax treatment. High taxes suck away badly needed cash flow and put off investors (why risk everything if half the proceeds go to the government?). Tax policy plays a critical role in determining "where the money is" and where it is likely to be in the future.

Taxation also can hurt demand for new services by limiting the amount of disposable income available to purchase these services and by inflating their prices. For example, in a survey published in January 1998, the French multimedia department store FNAC found that French consumers would be more eager to "get wired" if it were not for a 20.6-percent value added tax on computers and programs.[3]

Regulation imposes another form of taxation on businesses, and both regulation and taxation disproportionately affect the small firms that tend to drive innovation. Many Europeans believe that excessive regulation has hurt the development of new businesses, especially technology-related businesses in Europe. German President Roman Herzog joked in his now famous "Berlin

Address" of April 1997, that "Bill Gates started in a garage, and while still a young man turned Microsoft into a world-wide company, but if he tried that in Germany, the factory inspector would close down the garage."[4] Regulation throttles small firms that cannot afford to devote resources to complying with complex rules and procedures. A 1995 study by the European Network for SME Research (ENSR) placed the total annual administrative burden of regulatory compliance on business in the EU at 180 billion to 230 billion ECUs, or between 3 percent and 4 percent of the EU's GDP.[5]

9.2.1 Overview

The network economy is a double-edged sword for tax authorities. The new technologies enabling the network economy create opportunities for tax administrators to improve the efficiency and administration of the tax system; however, the same technologies create dramatic new opportunities for tax evasion and avoidance, and in some cases undermine the fundamental principles upon which certain tax concepts are built.

Even relatively small differences in taxation can have a significant impact on business decisions to invest in a specific country or region. The network economy magnifies these effects by making it easier to shift business activities to jurisdictions with lower taxes and fewer regulations. It is now a well-known observation about the Internet that packets travelling this vast internetwork interpret attempts at censorship and regulatory control as damage and bypass them on the way to their ultimate destinations. Many libertarians and other foes of government interference have relished this aspect of the Internet and attempted to elevate this principle to the level of national or international policy. In some sense, the proposal in the Clinton administration's White Paper on Electronic Commerce[6] to create a "free trade zone" for transactions in digital content on the Internet flows from this conception.

An article in the London Times rather succinctly summed up the potential impact of the global network economy on the tax policies of individual nations:

> In the next century, separate national systems of taxation may become as obsolete as the separate taxing powers which once existed in Antwerp or Padua. As there is not going to be a single world government, countries will have to compete in low taxation if they are to attract business. It will be easy for large taxpayers, corporate or individual, to use the Internet to locate their transactions in low-tax countries.... The erosion of the world's tax base will be one of the greatest forces for social and political change in the first half of the next century, far more important than the euro.[7]

Disparate levels of taxation and regulation between jurisdictions will likely lead to the creation of "data havens," where network enterprises can set up operations under the most favourable regulatory and tax regimes.[8] Today we already see the emergence of data havens in some of the same countries that have traditionally been known as tax havens. Some of these data havens are simply countries with lower tax rates, like Switzerland, which has a VAT rate of 6.5 percent, much lower than any of the EU countries. Other data havens, such as Costa Rica or the island nation of Anguilla, can offer high-speed Internet access to the world over a fibre-optic backbone, while providing a tax-free environment and a veil of financial privacy that is extremely difficult for other governments' tax authorities to pierce.

Exhibit 9.1 **Comparison of Conventional Payment System and Network Economy**

Current Payment System	Electronic Payment System
• High degree of central bank control • Highly structured supervision/regulation • Large legal and policy literature • Body of examining and Customs mechanisms • Physical means of payment-checks, currency • Huge infrastructure established world-wide • Relatively labour intensive • High value infrastructure - brick and mortar • Bank-dominated wire transfers • Clearing mechanism required • Transportation - courier, land, sea, air • World-wide use of US currency • Serial numbers and bank records • Significant statistical data collection • Economic national borders • Defined jurisdictions • Generally non-refutable, standard methods of validation • Authentication, established structure to verify authenticity	• Various national views about control • Highly technical, yet to be designed • Little current literature • Monitoring technology unavailable • Intangible electronic analogues • Downsized, computer-based • Relatively capital intensive • Low-cost decentralised facilities • Personal computer transfers • Clearing requirement reduced • Telecommunications • Easy currency exchange/one currency • Encrypted messages • No borders, effectively • Overlapping, unknown jurisdictions • Evolving methods of transaction verification • Undetermined, system specific may involve third party

Source: OECD (1997).

The privacy afforded by encryption and digital currency has enabled businesses and individuals to remove themselves from government "radar screens." Technology has the potential to make each individual semi-sovereign and increasingly free of all government control except that for which he/she voluntarily contracts. Governments will bid for network citizens the way many smart governments now bid to attract employers.[9]

Tax compliance has traditionally been facilitated by identifying key "taxing points," such as financial institutions, employers, and retail outlets, that are relatively easy to monitor. Network commerce may eliminate one or more of these intermediating institutions or allow the movement of the intermediary "offshore." From an economic perspective, this friction-free capitalism is a huge advantage, but it poses a huge problem for tax authorities.

Network commerce fosters greater national and international mobility for economic operators and world-wide integration of their markets. Tax-base mobility is more advantageous for production than for consumption, and is greater for software, marketing, financial services, manufacturing, and communications than for activities such as real estate and labour trading.[10]

Major controversy among tax authorities centres on whether network commerce should be taxed according to traditional principles or whether a complete reformulation of all tax principles is required. Difficulties lie in demarcation of a jurisdiction's tax system. It is practically impossible to tax network commerce according to territory.

9.2.2 Taxable Activities

In considering the network commerce activities that may potentially be taxed, it is unclear how many candidates should be treated by authorities.

Merchants that Use the Network
Businesses that use the network for marketing and sales.

Network Access Providers
Providers may be taxed as regular businesses or may be subject to communications and other special taxes like those paid by public switched telecommunications network (PSTN) operators.

Sales of Digital Content over the Network
Network-based content delivered electronically to the consumer may be subject to different tax treatment than tangible media (e.g. CD-ROMs, videocassettes).

Network Advertising
Taxation of revenue generated by online advertising.

Real-time Multimedia Communications
The Internet has emerged as an alternative to the PSTN network for real-time communications.[11] Authorities must consider whether or not to tax it as such.

9.2.3 Tax Administration and Compliance Issues

The network economy will create a number of specific tax administration and compliance problems. In a working paper prepared for a Round Table discussion at the December 1997 OECD summit in Turku, Finland, the OECD laid out a number of these critical administration and compliance issues:[12]

Establishing Identity

The identities of parties to an online business transaction may be difficult to determine. Similarly, it may be impossible to trace the identity of a Web-based business owner. Identification and registration requirements will be difficult to enforce with the increasing number of "offshore" Web sites being established, and with the use of strong encryption making it virtually impossible to access transaction records.

Establishing Location

Internet addresses can be established by anyone in almost any taxing jurisdiction. As illustrated in Exhibit 9.2, a consumer electronics retailer in Malaysia might sell a DVD player to a German citizen via the Internet making use of network and hosting facilities located in several other jurisdictions. The Malaysian retailer might operate a Web site hosted in the US with a mirror site hosted in Ireland. The financial transaction might be processed using a server located in Costa Rica, and the product itself might be shipped from a plant in Thailand. Typically in OECD countries, the physical existence of technical equipment does not constitute a permanent establishment for taxation purposes, nor does network access provision.

Exhibit 9.2 **Example of Transaction in Multiple Jurisdictions**

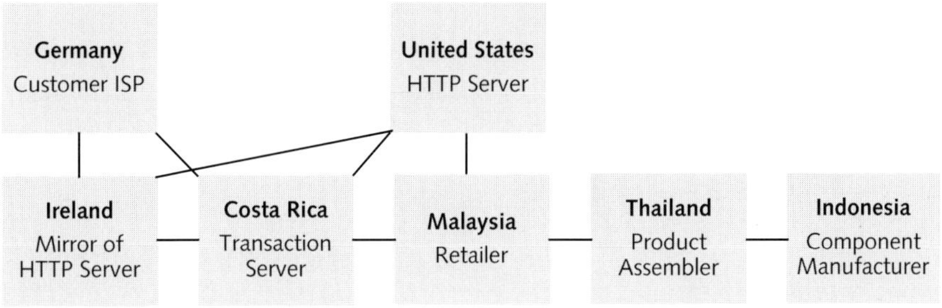

Germany
Customer ISP

United States
HTTP Server

Ireland
Mirror of HTTP Server

Costa Rica
Transaction Server

Malaysia
Retailer

Thailand
Product Assembler

Indonesia
Component Manufacturer

Source: Gemini Strategic Research Group.

Obtaining Documentation

Tax authorities within a given jurisdiction typically possess extensive powers to obtain information from taxpayers. These powers are relatively easy to enforce. Obtaining such information in other jurisdictions, however, requires the use of bilateral tax treaties between nations. In light of this, tax authorities may have difficulty accessing books and records maintained in tax havens. Domestic disclosure requirements may become difficult to enforce. It is also unclear whether evidence of network transactions would meet the documentation standards established by many tax codes and courts.

Disappearance of Taxing Points

The elimination of certain types of intermediaries will force tax administrations to collect smaller revenues from a larger number of taxpayers, and will increase administrative and compliance costs. Traditional banking systems, characterised today by a small number of large banks, may be transformed by the large number of banking facilities operating over the network from offshore environments. If this happens, tax authorities will no longer be able to enforce compliance-based reporting requirements.

Growing Access to Tax Havens and Offshore Banking

The Internet is making it increasingly easy for taxpayers to use offshore banking centres. Traditional tax havens are already offering numbered and coded bank accounts combined with international wire transfers online and other electronic payment options. While the principles that govern offshore banking are similar to those that govern traditional banking, future operational procedures will significantly affect tax authorities' ability to counteract international tax evasion. Internet banking will offer an ease of access, low transaction costs, a degree of anonymity, and a fluidity of funds which is not available today. Well-run offshore institutions that provide these attributes in a secure environment will attract a much wider customer base.

Special Challenges to the Value-Added Tax

Consumption or value-added taxes account for an average of 30 percent of tax revenues in the twenty-nine OECD[13] nations. The growth of network commerce poses special problems for the traditional concepts underlying VAT systems.

Place of Supply. All value-added tax systems include a set of rules that determine the geographical jurisdiction where taxes will be imposed. Place of supply rules fall into two broad categories, those which depend on the identification of the relevant establishment (belonging to either the supplier or the customer) and those based on the place of performance or enjoyment (irrespective of the location of the supplier or customer). Many services can now be provided without the supplier having a physical presence where the services are consumed. This creates challenges to tax authorities in VAT regimes.

Goods versus Services. Most value-added tax systems make important distinctions between goods and services. For VAT purposes, goods are generally classified as physical objects. Content, which was traditionally sold in the form of goods, such as newspapers, books, and packaged software, can now be delivered over networks, raising important questions about the viability of these distinctions. In Europe, exports of physical goods are not subject to VAT. Services, however, are treated as products delivered in the vendor's home country and subject to VAT regardless of where they are delivered. This distinction becomes distorted when digital goods are sold. For example, the sale of a music CD over the Internet by a British company to a French consumer will be exempt from VAT, but if that same consumer purchases digital files of the music and downloads them over the Internet, the British retailer will be subject to a seventeen percent VAT on the sale.[14]

9.2.4 Role of Government

Governments have responded cautiously to tax issues raised by the growth of the network economy. According to the OECD[15], to date, no government has issued new laws, regulations, or instructions on how to apply existing concepts to Internet-based activities. Governments have generally waited to learn more about the network economy's likely evolution. At least twelve OECD member nations have dedicated groups examining the tax implications of the Internet. The US and Australia have issued discussion papers. Several jurisdictions view the Internet as a source of revenue. Taxes on Internet usage, modems, and access have been suggested, and, in some cases, implemented, in some jurisdictions. In some German states, authorities have imposed television license fees on the owners of personal computers connected to the Internet because those computers are capable of receiving audio and video programming.[16]

Despite their caution, European governments are deeply concerned by the potential impact of the network economy on their tax bases. Many government leaders share the concern voiced by Oklahoma Governor Frank Keating when he said that, "Many states fund local government, roads and highways, law enforcement, and education by sales tax revenues. If people begin to buy goods and services via the Internet and not at the local grocery store, small businesses in local America will be paying the taxes that big businesses in catalogue America won't be paying."[17]

Tax law development will require considerable reflection and care. In setting out proposals on issues raised by network commerce, the OECD has recently enumerated a number of criteria that governments should consider as they respond to the network economy.[18]

Equitable
Taxpayers in similar situations who carry out similar transactions should be taxed in the same way across jurisdictions.

Simple
Administrative costs for the tax authorities and compliance costs for taxpayers should be minimised as far as possible. Compliance costs are a form of taxation that benefits no one.

Certain
A taxpayer should be able to pre-determine the tax consequences of a given transaction. Taxpayers should know what is to be taxed and when and where the tax is to be accounted for.

Economic Distortions Avoided. Corporate decision-makers should be motivated by commercial rather than tax considerations. This applies to both domestic and international transactions.

Flexible
A sufficiently flexible and dynamic system will ensure that tax rules keep pace with technological and commercial developments.

Burden Shared between Nations
Domestic and international tax arrangements should be structured to ensure a fair sharing of the Internet tax base between countries.

Built upon Existing Laws
Initially existing tax arrangements should be adapted to the Internet, rather than abandoned in favour of implementing a new structure.

Effective
It should produce the right amount of tax at the right time, minimising the potential for evasion and avoidance.

If governments are to successfully amend their tax systems in order to meet the challenges of the network economy, they will have to work together to an unprecedented degree. The Internet and the network economy are a global phenomenon that cannot be effectively controlled or regulated by any one country. Tax authorities must reach globally consistent approaches to taxing these activities. Inconsistent approaches to taxation will rapidly drive this emerging economic sector toward jurisdictions with the most favourable policies.

The European Commission has generally endorsed a policy of tax neutrality for network commerce, seeking to treat all business transactions in the same way and subjecting online transactions to the same VAT as conventional purchases.[19]

In the US, the Clinton administration has long argued against the imposition of new taxes on network commerce activities, saying that such taxes would stifle growth and would likely prove counter-productive in the long-term. In February 1998, President Clinton called for a moratorium on new taxation of goods and services sold over the Internet. In addition, he has announced his intention to back legislation, one of several versions of the so-called "Internet Tax Freedom Act" being considered by the US Congress in mid-1998, that would put a moratorium on new taxes that discriminate against the Internet and electronic commerce. While versions of this bill vary somewhat, all versions would place a multi-year ban on imposition by states or localities of new taxes on the electronic sale of goods and services. These announcements followed the adoption of a resolution by the National Governors' Association urging Congress to pass legislation that would prohibit taxation of Internet access but would allow states to impose taxes on electronic commerce. Many US governors and other local authorities worry that network commerce could erode their tax base by drawing business away from local vendors. They believe that businesses operating by traditional methods would be at a disadvantage against online firms that do not have to pay sales taxes.[20]

The various proposed network commerce tax moratoriums being considered by the US Congress have recently raised a new concern. Because users of the Internet are disproportionately located in upper income brackets and very few poor people have Internet access, there is a growing concern that use of the Internet will disproportionately shift the burden of paying sales taxes to the poor.[21]

In December 1997, the US and the EU issued a joint statement on electronic commerce that included agreements that "taxes on electronic commerce should be clear, consistent, neutral, and non-discriminatory," and that unnecessary existing legal and regulatory barriers should be eliminated and the emergence of new ones should be prevented."[22]

9.3 Investment Funding

The availability of venture capital is equally critical in deciding where and how to bring innovative technologies and services to market. In this section, we describe the role of venture capital firms, survey the European venture capital environment, and assess its strengths and weaknesses.

Despite massive government intervention, Europe's information technology industry has been in a state of decline for thirty years relative to the US and Japan.[23] Software firms like SAP, Business Objects, and Micro Focus, are among the few European technology firms to have achieved success in niche markets; however, they are not yet household names like Microsoft and Lotus. The hardware industry has been dominated by a few government-backed national champions like Groupe Bull, Olivetti, Siemens, and ICL.

Venture capital is critical to the development of successful new businesses and their ability to build the infrastructure and services that constitute the network economy.[24] As Alan Shugart, founder of both the disk drive manufacturer Seagate Technology and the venture capital firm Shugart Associates says, only half jokingly, "Cash is more important than your mother."[25]

Firms building the infrastructure for the network economy are particularly dependent on venture capital. Firms in the software and network commerce sectors often display what is sometimes described as increasing returns to scale. Put simply, this means that the company that establishes a standard in a given market will become dominant. After reaching a certain inflection point in the growth of market share, the firm will actually become increasingly dominant as opposed to suffering the decreasing returns to scale experienced by firms in traditional markets.[26] This is a common characteristic of network businesses. For example, individuals often choose a software because their colleagues and business partners do, which reinforces the product's dominance. This means that investment performance is highly variable, and start-ups in these sectors require risk capital, which conventional investors such as mutual funds are constrained in providing. Enter the venture capitalist. Tim Draper of the US venture capital firm Draper Fisher Associates, anticipates that his latest fund will contain five losers, five winners, and fifteen middling performers.[27]

While we will address employment issues in greater detail in Chapter 10, recent analysis suggests that a lack of venture capital may play a significant role in Europe's weak employment growth levels. In 1997, economists Paul Krueger and Jorn-Steffen Pischke[28] argued that instead of seeking supply-side explanations to the weak labour market performance, we should examine instead the possibility that it represents demand-side constraints. The rigidities that exist in

Cash Multimedia

Saga of a European Start-Up

Cash Multimedia is a Paris-based company specialising in online content. Its clients are mainly ISPs such as Microsoft Network, Infonie, America Online, and France Télécom. The aim of Cash Multimedia's founders and directors, Jean-Christophe Despres and Christophe Sailly, is to promote this medium as a field of experimentation for information and entertainment services. In their view, interactivity is a means to renew and strengthen customer relationships, not just the latest marketing fashion.

Faced with limited budgets, they have set up a team of more than twenty developers, graphic designers, and writers, who work for free on new projects. In exchange, those professionals, mainly freelancers, are priority choice on Cash Multimedia's paid projects. The company's expected revenues for 1998, its first year of existence, will not exceed 100,000 euro.

A Cross-Channel Partnership

In 1996, Cash Multimedia partnered with Artewisdom, an established, UK-based technology start-up firm. Artewisdom brought technology, start-up funds, and project management, while Cash Multimedia came with expertise in designing scenarios and content.

The concept of the interactive sitcom is to let the user build his or her own story, to interact with the players, all within the technical parameters of the Internet. In the initial stage, the project consisted of developing turnkey entertainment programs for major Internet sites (ISPs, online boutiques, etc.). Later, the programs could be used to create a Web-based entertainment channel, financed by advertising.

The product was very well received by market observers. It was sponsored by Sir Clive Sinclair, the inventor of the ZX81 (one of the first personal computers), and received strong media exposure in England and France. Lacking the development to support such a service, the Internet's immature advertising market hindered the projects. Although many prospects called the product interesting and full of promise, the partners found it difficult to sell. The product was too expensive given that most of the prominent Internet sites were still operating on a not-for-profit basis.

The Challenge: Finding Money and the Right Partners Quickly Enough

Cash Multimedia and Artewisdom had difficulty meeting investors and approaching potential partners to finance the development of their product. They had minimal knowledge of the venture capital world and its rules.

Cash Multimedia suffers from the usual chicken-and-egg problem: It needs funding to finance its development before the market takes off, but has difficulty finding money if the product does not sell. In June 1998, Artewisdom's founders sold their shares to a bigger company, setting aside interactive sitcoms and their partnership with Cash Multimedia, "for the time being."

Companies like Cash Multimedia and Artewisdom are able to self-finance new developments for only very short windows of time, just long enough to search for clients and partners (four months in this case). They need to meet with the right partners and quickly, those who will be receptive to innovation, able to assist them in making the right business decisions, and willing to take risks.

The Quest of a European Market... and for Investors

"The European market is far from being homogeneous, and it does not seem to offer any opportunity for content producers," says Despres. "As every local market has its specificities, only a few Web sites do not require a specific sales and marketing strategy." Therefore, the lack of European funding structures (private or public) has major consequences in terms of transnational co-operation. The Artewisdom and Cash Multimedia's experience reveal the limited attraction produced by their across-the-Channel partnership for potential investors. It even highlights the danger that such partnerships create for small companies given the unaffordable expenses it generates.

Start-ups like Cash Multimedia wish they could work in an environment such as the Silicon Alley in New York. On the contrary, they observe that big media groups are obsessed with adapting their own content rather than supporting and funding new, original content projects. "Big corporations are more likely to pay for an Internet programme than any media company or even ISPs," says Despres.

Managing Director Jean-Christophe Despres expresses no doubt about his ability to keep the company alive at this stage, but he thinks that new media firms at large will find it hard to be profitable until some major but hypothetical changes occur. Therefore, Cash Multimedia is currently looking for strong technological partners in order to deliver one-to-one content to specific segments. As the market is global, Cash Multimedia does not want to focus only on the European market, which doesn't seem open to new ideas in their view, but on the American one which gives more opportunities to start-ups. Cash Multimedia founders say that being European is more of a handicap in the US market and that they will have to offer a very strong business model. But to them, there is no real alternative to develop their project.

www.peripateticiens.com/cashma.htm

the European economy may not, in fact, be in the labour market at all. Fundamental economic conditions that depress demand in product or capital markets could be responsible for weak employment growth.

The authors cite one or two possibilities that seem to make intuitive sense. Most significantly, the US has well-developed, highly liquid, deep capital markets that have, especially in the last decade, become extremely efficient at channelling capital efficiently to the right start-up businesses, which have in turn become highly successful job-producers. When there is a shortage of capital for entrepreneurs, demand for labour becomes much less sensitive to the level of wages, since no matter how low wages drop, entrepreneurs will not be able to create business in the first place.

9.3.1 Defining Venture Capital

Venture capital is risk financing for privately held companies, generally in the form of equity and/or long-term convertible debt. Firms seek venture capital when funding from banks, financial institutions, or public debt or equity markets is either inappropriate or unavailable. Venture capitalists usually provide funding without collateral or guarantees in the private equity market. In 1994, the venture capital industry represented about 79 billion ecus in financing world-wide.[29]

The venture capital community is part of the investment community. It is analogous to commercial banking in that the venture capitalist, like the banker, serves as an intermediary between the investors (or lenders) and the entrepreneurs (or borrowers). Venture capitalists, like mutual fund managers, raise capital from investors in order to manage a portfolio of privately held investments.

In much of the world, venture capital funds concentrate on expansion or buy-out stages. The key exceptions are in the US and Canada, where venture capital funds make available significant capital for early-stage financing of new ventures.

Traditionally, in the US, venture capital has been (and remains, to a large extent) "early stage" (which does not necessarily mean "start-up") financing for emerging growth, privately held businesses. Such investments differ from investments in publicly held companies in that they are generally provided for newer companies with little operating history; for smaller companies in which the venture capital firm and the entrepreneurial company have a high degree of personal involvement; illiquid in the short term, that is, until the company goes public or is acquired by another company — a process that generally takes three to seven years; difficult to value, as there is no public market for such securities; and going to require future financing.

9.3.2 Types of Venture Capital

In a broad sense, venture capital is funding for businesses in various phases of development, from the "idea" stage to just before the initial public offering (IPO), or before the company is acquired by a larger corporation. Administered in stages, the first round of financing is generally the most expensive for borrowers, in that entrepreneurs might give up half of their equity in a venture.[30] The next round might provide a further dilution of 10 percent to 20 percent of equity, as will the following round of financing. Thus, after the initial public offering, the entrepreneurs might own 20 percent of the company, the venture investors might own 60 percent, and the public might own 20 percent.

Multiple financing rounds are quite common for high-tech businesses that invest heavily in research and development (R&D). Consequently, the process of raising capital becomes a constant activity for early-stage ventures.

Types of venture capital can be grouped into three broad categories: early stage, expansion financing, and financing for mature firms.

Early Stages

There are three types of early-stage venture capital funding:

Seed Financing. Capital provided at the "idea" stage. The capital, usually less than 45,000 euro, is often spent on product development and market research.

Start-up Financing. Capital used in product development and initial marketing. This is generally for companies that have been in operation for under a year but that have not sold their products or services commercially.

First-stage Financing. Capital provided to initiate commercial manufacturing and sales.

The venture capital industry finances only a very small percentage of the seed and start-up operations in the US, although it does finance a much higher percentage of these then do European venture capitalists. This affords the "informal investor" an attractive opportunity to fund companies at these early stages of development.

Expansion

There are also three stages of expansion financing:

Second-stage Financing. Capital used for initial expansion of a company that has already been producing and selling a product. The company might not be profitable at this time.

Third-stage Financing. Capital provided to fund major expansion, such as plant expansion, product improvement, or marketing.

Mezzanine (or Bridge) Financing. Capital provided for a company that expects to go public within approximately one year.

Mature Firms

Finally, there are two "special cases" of venture financing targeted at mature firms:

Turnarounds. Capital provided to restructure or revitalise a troubled company that is generally at a more established stage of development.

Leveraged Buyouts (LBOs)/Management Buyouts (MBOs). Capital provided to fund a management team or a group of outside investors attempting to purchase a company or a subsidiary from a major corporation; in an LBO (which is a type of "asset-based lending"), the company's assets are generally used as collateral for loans.

9.3.3 Sources of Venture Capital Funds

There are three main types of venture capital investment funds:

Captive Funds
Subsidiaries of corporations involved in other activities, such as manufacturing or finance, and are financed by the parent company.

Public Sector Funds
Financed by government institutions.

Independent Funds
Receive more varied financing, ranging from private individuals and institutional investors to corporations, governments, and foreign investors.

9.3.4 Other Aspects of Venture Capital

The venture capital process, as much as the capital itself, fuels the growth of the venture and often enables the entrepreneurial idea to become a reality. In essence, the venture capital process makes entrepreneurship better. As Neil Weintraut of 21st Century Venture Partners puts it, "You are everything from top recruiter, top salesman, top worrier, top nanny."[31]

First, the process forces the entrepreneur to recruit a management team. In return for providing funding, venture capitalists take a role in the management of the firms they fund. Typically, the venture capital firm takes at least one seat on the board of directors. In addition, the venture capital firm typically helps recruit and select top managers. Venture capital firms build networks of contacts in related firms and are able to find experienced managers to come in and assist entrepreneurs in the development of their firms. An entrepreneur who approaches a venture capital firm for funding will not typically have the management expertise to take the company public. "If you hire a good CEO, the business will take care of itself; but usually an entrepreneur has no network and no idea who to hire," says Tim Draper of Draper Fisher Associates. So, the venture capitalist usually takes on the role of matchmaker, leavening the visionaries with some seasoned executives. John Doerr of Kleiner Perkins, which brought in Jim Barksdale as chief executive officer of Netscape and in the 1980s, supplied one of its own partners to help run computer-maker Tandem, says: "My main job from 7 a.m. to 9 p.m. is to recruit people. I am a glorified recruiter."[32]

The process also forces entrepreneurs to prepare a business plan to delineate their objectives and to specify their financial projections. For example, Nolan Bushnell, the founder of Atari and several other ventures, says that, "Every time you prepare a business plan, you become a better entrepreneur."[33] Accel Partners has a program for entrepreneurs-in-residence, to whom it gives office space and time to develop business plans. For inexperienced entrepreneurs, venture capitalists are mentors, too. "We are professional coaches," says Ann Winblad, co-founder of Hummer Winblad.[34]

An active venture capitalist refers the companies in which it invests to professional services firms such as lawyers and accountants with practices specialising in information technology. Start-ups backed by a well-known venture capital firm can often obtain legal and other professional advice at a discounted rate, until they have the revenues to cover full fees.

Venture capitalists are boosters for the companies in their portfolio. The backing of a leading venture capital firm that has predicted technology trends correctly in the past brings credibility with commentators and the start-up firm's potential customers. "Far from just providing money, the venture industry brings contacts and confidence," says Weintraut. "We create markets as much as we create companies."[35] The most ambitious venture capitalists act as boosters, not just of a few companies, but of the entire category into which an investment falls. They attempt to create a buzz of excitement around a particular concept, such as the Java computer language, which will validate it as a business.

The venture capital firm as well as the entrepreneurial team should benefit as a result of the venture capital process, often a long-term process lasting five to ten years. And the benefit should be significantly more than financial. This is one of the most important differences between venture capital and conventional financing — venture capital is more than investing and more than building personal wealth, it is building companies.

9.3.5 Venture Capital and the Internet

Nowhere can the importance of venture capital be seen more clearly than in the birth and development of a series of Internet-related businesses in the US during the mid-1990s.

Exhibit 9.3 **US Internet-Related Venture Capital Deals and Average Funding per Deal, First Quarter 1995 – Second Quarter 1997**

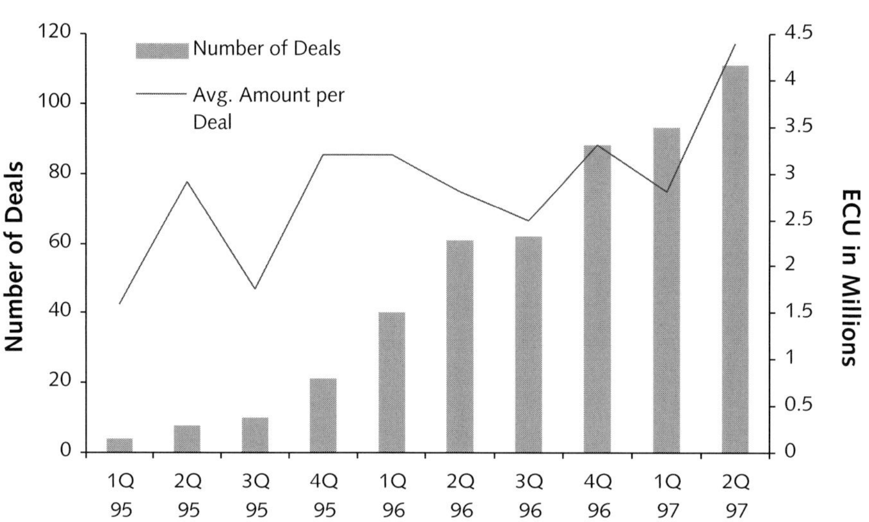

Source: Price Waterhouse Venture Capital Survey 1997; *Interactive Multimedia Investor.*

As Exhibit 9.3 indicates, the number of Internet-related venture capital deals has continued to rise steadily while the average funding per deal has recently begun to climb after a decline in late 1995 and the first half of 1996. Much of the fluctuation in the amount of funding per deal is attributable to the stock performance of Internet-related firms that have already completed initial public offerings. Exhibit 9.4 illustrates the range of Internet content firms receiving funding from venture capital firms and the amount and nature of the funding.

Exhibit 9.4 **Funding Raised by Private Internet Content Companies, Second Quarter, 1997**

Company	Content Category	Investor	Capital Raised (Mil. Euro)	Round
Abaton.com *www.abaton.com*	Health care	Acacia Venture Partners, Accel Partners, Humana Venture Capital	3.1	First
AutoWeb Interactive *www.autoweb.com*	Automotive	Geocapital Partners	5.4	First
cBooks *www.cbooks.com*	Computer books	APV Technology Partners, Sierra Ventures, Trinity Ventures	2.2	Second
Cybersmith *www.cybersmith.com*	Publishing	Applied Technology	1.0	Follow-on
Ebay *www.ebay.com*	Commerce	Benchmark Capital	4.0	First
Farcast *www.farcast.com*	News	Altos Ventures, Doll Technology & Venture Fund, Draper Richards, UOB Venture Capital, Vertex Management	3.5	Second
GardenEscape *www.garden.com*	Gardening	Austin Ventures, Oak Investment Partners, Phillips-Smith Specialty Retail Group, Scripps Ventures	4.7	Second
GolfWeb *www.golfweb.com*	Golf	Institutional Venture Partners, Trinity	7.1	Third
Greet Street *www.greetst.com*	Digital postcards	Altos Ventures, Robertson Stephens Venture Capital	0.8	Fourth
ImproveNet *www.improvenet.com*	Home improvement	Alta Partners/Burr, Egan, Deleage	0.2	Mezzanine
Internet Broadcasting Sys. *www.ibsys.com*	Local content	Brightstone Capital	0.3	Second
Internet Health *www.health-library.com*	Health care	Atlas Ventures, Firepond Partners	0.0	Seed
Internet Travel Network *www.itn.com*	Travel	Brentwood Venture Capital, Charter Venture Capital, Norwest Venture Capital, Robertson Stephens Venture Capital, U.S. Venture Partners	5.3	Second
JuniorNet *www.juniornet.com*	Children	Dominion Ventures	4.4	First
Lightspan Partnership *www.lightspan.com*	Education	Accel Partners, Institutional Venture Partners, JAFCo Americas Ventures, Kleiner Perkins Caufield & Byers, Microsoft, State of Michigan, Tribune	23.1	Follow-on
NetChannel *www.netchannel.net*	Information	Mercator Investments, Technology Partners, Tellnor Ventures	1.6	Second
Online Resources & Comm. *www.orcc.com*	Banking	Apex Investment Partners, Dominion Ventures, East River Ventures, Geocapital Partners	15.9	Third
Pacific Information Exch. *www.pixi.com*	Internet services	HMS Hawaii Management Partners	0.4	First
Picture Network Int'l *www.publishersdepot.com*	Image database	Marquette Venture Partners	0.2	N/A
Product Partners *www.productpartners.com*	Commerce	Telecom Partners, Wolf Ventures	0.5	Second
Sandbox Entertainment *www.sandbox.net*	Entertainment	Newtek Ventures, Sundance Venture Partners, Wasatch Venture	0.3	Mezzanine
Tripod *www.tripod.com*	Publishing	Berkshire Fund, Cowen, Interpublic Benefit Protection Trust, Massachusetts Capital Resource, New Enterprise Associates, Rho Management, Gabelli Multimedia Fund	8.8	Second
Virtual Vineyards *www.virtualvin.com*	Wine	Alpine Technology Ventures, Applied Technology, Robertson Stephens Venture Capital	2.0	Second
Wire Networks *www.women.com*	Women's content	RVI Capital	0.5	Mezzanine
Women's Connection Online *www.womenconnect.com*	Women's content	Mid-Atlantic Venture Funds	0.8	Seed

Source: Price Waterhouse Venture Capital Survey, 1997.

9.3.6 The Venture Capital Environment

The seeds of technology innovation come primarily from private business initiatives. The venture capital financing of high-technology start-ups plays an essential role in fostering this innovation. Europe possesses many elements that would support the successful commercial exploitation of technology and network media: 380 million customers, good infrastructure, multiple global financial centres, an excellent education system with fine universities, and numerous pockets of high-tech activity.

With few notable exceptions, the staffs of European banks, venture capital firms, stock brokers, market analysts, support agencies, and government policy makers do not embrace the level of necessary technology/market understanding which is evident within the US financial markets. Until such competencies have a much wider dissemination, European venture capital will not be able to provide the type of support to European entrepreneurs that the US venture capitalists have been able to provide to their technology entrepreneurs. One reporter quotes a European venture capitalist as saying, albeit facetiously: "If it has a plug or coloured wires, we won't touch it." Government incentives won't help to overcome such prejudice. What is required is a Silicon Valley standard of technological expertise, where many venture capitalists have experience in high-tech businesses themselves and are often the best-informed people on the sector as a whole.[36]

As one venture capitalist said at the *Red Herring's* annual Venture Capital Roundtable in 1997, "It's not just the talent and access to capital that make it so much easier to start a company in Silicon Valley. It's the whole infrastructure. The lawyers know what they are doing, the accountants know what they are doing, and the outsourcing resources are readily available."[37] One key distinction between the venture capital environment in Europe and that in the US is that the entrepreneurs and venture capitalists in the US, particularly in the Silicon Valley, seem more inclined than the rest of the world to take risks and accept failure in the business of creating technology companies.

The technical proficiency of the venture capitalists has improved. Partners now typically focus on specific areas such as enterprise software or networking equipment. Firms specialise, too. Hummer Winblad invests exclusively in software companies, and 21st Century Venture Partners only in Internet companies. "People are much more knowledgeable than they were fifteen years ago," says Dick Kramlich of NEA.

Venture capitalists believe their broad perspective on the IT industry gives them better returns than other investors would be able to achieve. "We probably have more insight than anyone else," says Geoffrey Yang of Institutional Venture Partners. "We know what has been funded and so we can tell what the market will look like in three years' time."[38]

Prompted by heightened competition for the most promising investment opportunities, venture capitalists have become more active in seeking out companies and individuals with potential. In 1990, about 60 percent of NEA's investment ideas came from within the firm rather than from outside entrepreneurs; now about 85 percent come from within.[39]

The European Venture Capital Association reports that in 1996 European venture capital and private equity firms disbursed nearly 6.8 billion ECUs, up nearly 22 percent from 1995. Despite this growth in venture capital funding, many firms still report that it is difficult to raise funding, especially early-stage funding. In 1997, the amount of venture funding in Europe more than doubled, with nearly 19.4 billion ECUs of investment. While the bulk of this investment was still concentrated in the UK, there was a 650 percent increase in Germany and a phenomenal 2,000 percent increase in Sweden. Moreover, venture investment in early-stage firms rose by 60 percent.[40]

Exhibit 9.5 **European Venture Capital Investments by Country, 1995 – 1996, Millions of ECU**

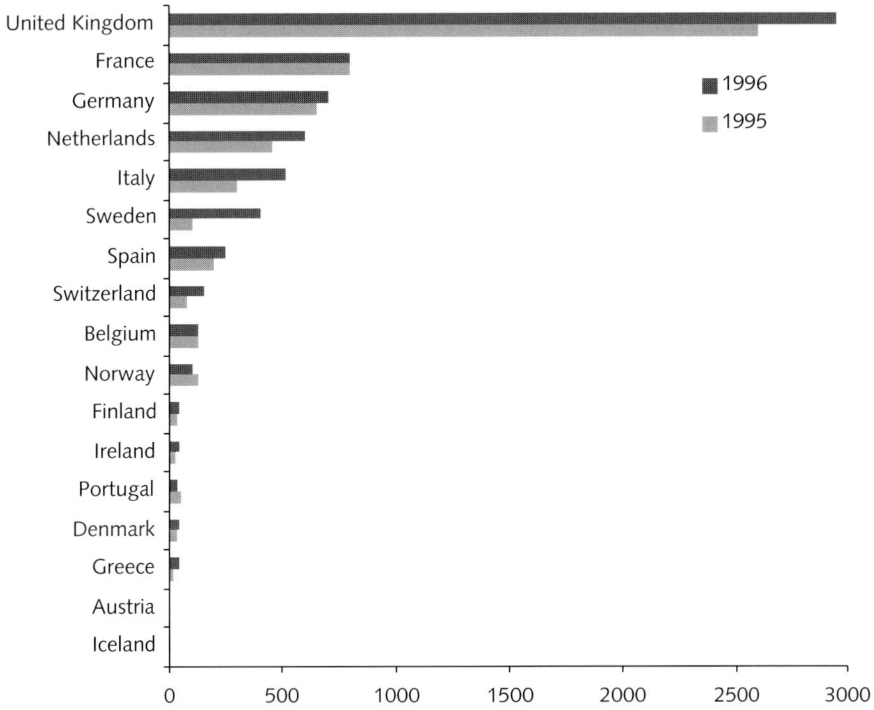

Source: European Venture Capital Association.

As Exhibit 9.5 indicates, venture capital activity in the UK far exceeds that of any other European nation, representing about half of European venture capital investment. There are several reasons for this. Most significantly, the venture capital community in the UK is more mature than that of many other European countries. Many argue that the wave of deregulation and privatisation that the Conservative Party unleashed on the UK in the 1980s created an environment more friendly to entrepreneurial activity and capital formation than that found in many other European countries. However, to put this into perspective, California and Massachusetts alone have bigger venture-capital industries than the whole of Europe.

The venture capital that is available in Europe, usually goes to firms in later stages of development.

Exhibit 9.6 **Distribution of Investment in Europe by Stage, 1996**

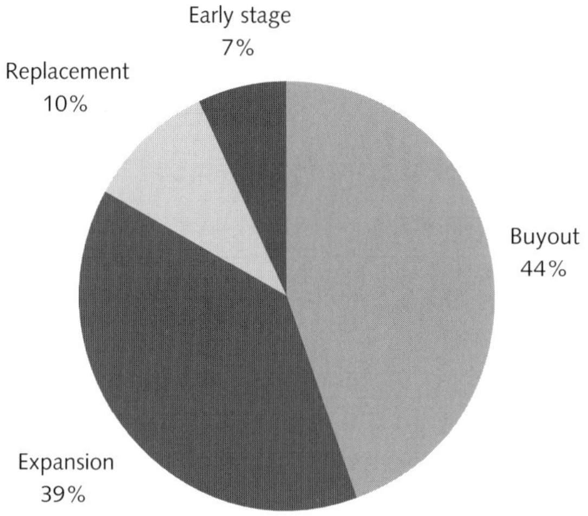

Early stage 7%

Replacement 10%

Buyout 44%

Expansion 39%

Source: European Venture Capital Association.

As Exhibit 9.6 shows, only about 7 percent of European venture capital goes to firms in the start-up phase. European venture capitalists seem less inclined to risk investing in start-ups. One observer notes that Europe "suffers from the lack of true venture capital — risk capital" and the tendency to think in national, or, at best, European terms. "That means when we do invest, we've got to put in enough capital to think globally, which Americans do."[41]

Britain's venture capital industry invests a similar proportion of gross domestic product to its US equivalent, about 0.8 percent a year. But just 40 percent of the British finance went into high-tech companies in 1995 compared with 78 percent in the US.

Hermann Hauser, who has founded or backed about twenty start-ups in Britain, explains how difficult it was to raise finance for one venture: "The recommendation of UK venture capitalists was to go to the US and find US investors alongside whom they would be prepared to invest."

In fact, US venture capitalists have already begun to arrive in Europe, attracted by the success of investments such as that in 1993 by General Atlantic Partners in Baan, a Dutch business that develops software used by companies such as Boeing and Hitachi to control stock and project sales. Baan's market capitalisation has since risen thirtyfold.

Venture capital firms such as Advent, Warburg Pincus, New Enterprise Associates, and Oak Investment Partners have brought not just money to Europe but also the networking skills that have helped small start-ups in the US find managers, publicity, and customers. Additionally, several West Coast investment banks such as Robertson Stephens arrived in 1996 offering to take European information technology companies to NASDAQ, New York's exchange for growing businesses.

According to Marcus Lovell Smith of Ramar, a European maker of chips that read electricity meters, "The issue is the sheer size of the US market." Ramar had to tailor its product to satisfy differing regulations in each European country; US competitors can address a huge home market with one standard product.[42]

For the moment, observers at US firms such as Hambrecht & Quist believe there are profits to be made in European IT investment. "We are seeing a resurgence of European entrepreneurialism and good technical skills," says Rafner, "and we are here to finance them."[43]

9.3.7 Role of Stock Exchanges

Efficient exit mechanisms are critical for the development of the venture capital industry. Investors and entrepreneurs require exit routes for mature investments. Exit mechanisms include trade sales, private placements, initial public offerings, and repurchases (buy-outs and buy-ins). Trade sales are the main exit route in Western Europe, while IPOs tend to be the preferred route in the US, the UK, and Japan. Second-tier or parallel markets for IPOs constitute efficient exit vehicles in the US (NASDAQ) and Japan (JASDAQ).

As the managing director of a UK-based venture capital firm told us, "Exit is easier in the US, for example, through flotation. Europe is a split market. There is little co-operation between venture capital firms and exit strategies are more difficult because the various markets are distinct, regionally focused. This financial market makes it difficult to spot the right companies."[44]

A large number of Internet-related IPOs on the NASDAQ exchange in the US in 1996 and 1997 have played an important role in spurring further investment (Exhibit 9.7).

Exhibit 9.7 **Internet-Related IPOs, 1996 – 1997**

Company	Symbol	Product or Service	Date Complete	Capital Raised (Mil. Euro)
Objective Comm.	OCOM	Video Conferencing	4-4-97	6.98
Yahoo!	YHOO	Content/Search	4-12-96	29.80
Netscape	NSCP	Internet Software/Content	8-8-96	91.70
Mindspring	MSPG	ISP	3-13-96	13.76
E*Trade	EGRP	Online Trading	8-16-96	52.45
Take2 Interactive	TTWO	Video Conferencing	4-16-97	7.76
ClNet	CNWK	Content	7-2-96	28.22
Sterling Commerce	SE	Electronic Commerce	2-13-96	222.21
@Home	ATHM	Cable Modem Service Provider	7-11-97	83.33
ONSALE	ONSL	Web Retailing	4-17-97	13.23
Check Point Software	CHKPF	Internet Security/Firewalls	6-28-96	51.85
Lycos	LCOS	Content/Search	4-1-96	42.33
Amazon.com	AMZN	Web Retailing	5-15-97	47.62
MEMCO	MEMCF	Info. Security Software	10-15-96	44.51
Fine.com	FDOT	Site Developer	8-13-97	5.73
UOL Publishing	UOLP	Training/Education Software	11-25-96	16.39
Excite	XCIT	Content/Search	4-4-96	29.98
CyberCash	CYCH	Electronic Commerce	2-15-96	35.98
Spyglass	SPYG	Internet Software	6-26-95	26.98
Navidec	NVDC	Intranet Solutions	2-11-97	5.29
Object Design	ODIS	Database Management Tools	7-24-96	18.52
Concentric	CNCX	ISP	8-1-97	45.50
Net. B@nk	NTBK	Web Retailing	7-29-97	37.04
ObjectSoft	OSFT	Info. Transactions Software	11-26-96	5.51
V-One	VONE	Internet Security/Firewalls	10-24-96	13.23
NetSpeak	NSPK	Net Telephony	5-29-97	15.43
IAT Multimedia	IATA	High-end Video Conferencing	3-26-97	17.72
Multimedia Access	MMAC	Video Conferencing	2-5-97	5.56
SCOOP	SCPI	Content/Business Info.	4-9-97	5.73
Earthlink Network	ELNK	ISP	1-22-97	22.93
Trusted Information	TISX	Internet Security/Firewalls	10-10-96	38.98
PC411	PCFR	Internet Directory	5-16-97	5.07
GO2NET	GNET	Content/Metasearch	4-24-97	11.29
Broadvision	BVSN	Web Marketing	6-21-96	18.52
Sec. 1st Ntwk. Bank	SFNB	Internet Banking	5-23-96	43.03
Vocaltec	VOCLF	Net Telephony	2-16-96	41.89
XLConnect	XLCT	Internetworking Connectivity	10-17-96	44.05
Talx Inc.	TALX	Net Telephony	10-16-96	15.87
HomeCom Comm.	HCOM	Info. Transactions Software	5-12-97	5.29
Open Market	OMKT	Electronic Commerce	5-23-96	63.49
Allpin Comm.	ALLN	ITV Digital Imaging	11-1-96	26.45
Peapod	PPOD	Net Grocery Shopping	6-11-97	56.44
Infoseek	SEEK	Content/Search	6-11-96	36.45
CompuServe	CSRV	Online Service Provider	4-22-96	423.27
Connect	CNKT	Electronic Commerce	8-15-96	12.70
Individual	INDV	Content/Info Delivery	3-15-96	30.86
e-NET	ETEL	Secure Internet Voice	4-8-97	6.61
OneWave	OWAV	Info. Transactions Software	7-2-96	52.91
Multicom Publishing	MNET	Interactive Publishing	6-25-96	6.30
			TOTAL	**1982.74**

Source: Interactive Media Investor.

The success of the NASDAQ has encouraged the creation of other such markets around the world. Except for JASDAQ, however, this first generation of second-tier markets has failed. In Western Europe, a new generation of second-tier markets has recently been created, including EASDAQ, AIM, METIM, Nouveau Marché, and Neue Markt.

Exhibit 9.8 **Europe's New Stock Markets**

Name	Location	Date Created
Alternative Investment Market (AIM)	London	June 1995
EASDAQ	Brussels	November 1996
Nouveau Marché	Paris	1996
Neuer Markt	Frankfurt	March 1997
Euro NM	Brussels	March 1997
NMAX	Amsterdam	March 1997

Source: *Business Week.*

As of mid-1997, some 178 companies had gone public on these exchanges, raising nearly 2.5 billion euro in equity. An additional 170 IPOs were expected by the end of 1997.

The money raised in Europe may be minimal compared with the 22 billion ECU the NASDAQ raised in 1996, but the trend marks a dramatic shift in Europe's equity culture. For the first time ever, young tech companies can turn to local bourses to fuel growth. Europe's tech start-ups are responding, showing signs of competitive vigour and global reach. However imperfect, fledgling markets are granting them the element for global success they always lacked: capital to match the speed at which US rivals grow. "We are finally seeing the infrastructure to support high-growth technology companies," says Robert Hook, managing director of Prelude, an investment company based in Cambridge, England.[45]

Going public also improves a company's credibility in global markets, as public trading gives a company greater visibility to investors and customers. For instance, ActivCard, a 7.3 million-euro French company making smart-card systems for the Internet and corporate intranets, raised 9.7 million ECU on EASDAQ in December. It plans to use the proceeds to fund expansion in the US and Asia, but founder Yves Audebert says the real boost from the listing has been increased confidence among potential buyers of his systems. "It is much easier to sell now," he says.[46]

US investment banks spotted the first opportunities in Europe and helped take companies public on NASDAQ. Now, the second phase of the revolution has begun. US small-cap specialists such as Cowen, Hambrecht & Quist, Robertson

Stephens, and Goldman Sachs are supporting EASDAQ and screening European tech start-ups for IPOs. "We see incredible opportunities for investing here," says Jerrold B. Newman, managing director of investment banking at Cowen & Co. DRAWBACKS. Shares of online service company Infonie, the first listing on France's Nouveau Marché, plummeted 66 percent over the first twelve months. Both AIM and the Nouveau Marché, hit by a handful of shaky offerings, recently tightened their listing criteria. Lack of liquidity is a major drawback. EASDAQ companies with dual listings on NASDAQ find their bankers tend to do most of the trading in the US, where the big institutional money is, leaving EASDAQ with minimal turnover.[47]

One of the most interesting exchanges is an independent stock exchange in Sweden called Innovations Marknaden (Innovation Market). Innovation Market was founded in July 1994 by Swedish economist Lennart Ohlsson on the assumption that Swedish investors would be willing to provide risk capital in a country where the banks and venture capitalists were unwilling to invest in risky start-ups. Innovation Market's ability to circumvent the old guard and to create an efficient electronic exchange has made it a model in its field. In three years, Innovation Market has established itself as an active market for start-up firms. With the structure of a stock exchange and the due diligence process of a venture capital firm, as of mid-1997 the firm listed sixteen companies, about half of which are developing technology products and services today. All sixteen of Innovation Market's first offerings were oversubscribed; as a result, it has developed a lottery system to determine who can invest in a given offering.

Buoyed by its success in Sweden, Innovation Market is moving to establish affiliate markets in other countries. Its founders plan to organise a network of Innovation Markets in Northern Europe, with the first scheduled to have opened in Norway in late 1997. If regulatory approval is granted, it hopes to open up cross-border investment opportunities in the Nordic countries.[48]

9.3.8 Role of Academia

In the US, there is a close relationship between the academic community and the entrepreneurial community, with universities, especially the science and technology departments, servings as hotbeds of entrepreneurial activity across the US. For example, a 1996 study found that graduates of the Massachusetts Institute of Technology in Cambridge, Massachusetts, were responsible for the creation of 4,000 firms that employed 1.1 million people and created 205 billion ECUs in sales in 1994 alone.[49] Perhaps no other university can match MIT in the shear number of jobs created, but the dynamic at work there is at work in universities throughout the US. Klaas Bruman of Disc Direct, a German start-up, says that German universities lack the kind of entrepreneurialism that is so common in US schools. "German universities spend a lot of money, but they're slow-moving organisations with industry and venture capital. It's not that there are no results at all, but there aren't enough for a country that needs to be competitive."[50]

In general, European university graduates, especially engineers, are less willing to gamble on risky start-ups than their US counterparts. The educational system has fostered a certain reliance upon large institutions; it is easier to take a prestigious job at a large corporation than to endure hard work for little money (as is often the case when launching a small start-up firm). European engineers and scientists aren't likely to rush off to emulate their US counterparts until they see some of their colleagues successfully following that path. Nothing breeds success like success.

Opportunities such as these are changing the European IT business culture. Managers at large companies have been previously unwilling to risk their careers on start-up firms, while technologists have been reluctant to forfeit control for expansion finance. "The image of start-ups is a problem," one German venture capitalist told us. "Most of the time in Europe, becoming an entrepreneur is the last choice."[51] He also told us that, "The problem is that the value system in Europe is different. People prefer to live a risk-free life and prepare their pension plan! What we need to do is show to people what the opportunities are."[52]

Some European leaders are now trying to foster this kind of environment. For example, German Chancellor Helmut Kohl attempted to spur this new attitude among young Germans by promoting the example of nineteen-year-old technology millionaire Lars Windhorst as the "German Bill Gates."[53]

In part, this is a matter of culture. For science graduates from MIT or Stanford, business success carries as much prestige as the academic career which tends to attract their counterparts in Europe. Moreover, they know the rules of the venture capital game; visionaries such as Marc Andreessen of Netscape become wealthy but rarely maintain control. "The model is so well-known by everybody that the issue of control is academic," says George Still of Norwest Venture Partners.[54]

Risk-taking, even if it results in failure, is genuinely lauded. "If someone has tried a venture and failed, there is still great respect for that person," says Jim Breyer, managing general partner at Accel Partners. As an example, he cites Bill Campbell, who survived the failure of Go Computing, the pen computing company, to emerge as one of the key managers at Intuit, the personal finance software house.[55]

9.3.9 Role of Government

Governments have been extremely active in attempting to foster technology innovation and new business creation across Europe. Because of its potential for job creation, European governments have kept a close eye on information technology for decades. Governments have invested billions of euro into research and technological development. The EU has backed more than 7,000 joint projects through its Framework programs.[56]

Many European governments are making efforts to fund Internet activities. In January 1998, France, a laggard in the information-technology race, unveiled a 225 million-euro plan to get in step with the Internet era. According to France's President Lionel Jospin, part of the effort includes doubling the amount France spends on adding computers to its schools to more than 75 million euro. Equal amounts will be earmarked as risk capital for high-technology firms and for several dozen programs to be offered by various government ministries. Jospin encouraged a public debate on Internet-related issues, saying that, "In this sector, solutions cannot be imposed on society by the public authorities. By the summer, every school will organise a dialogue, when the school councils meet, to discuss choices for networks and equipment." Other target sectors for the government include catch-up in electronic commerce, cultural policy, and industrial innovation.[57]

Nevertheless, most technology industries are moving so fast that extra bureaucracy will have an unacceptable time-cost. Start-ups with good prospects will not wish to waste a year or more on meetings and memos in order to obtain subsidies. If they do, opportunities might well evaporate by the time required money becomes available.

A UK-based venture capitalist told us that because of the lack of business skills among many would-be entrepreneurs in Europe, one useful government function would be to help improve management education. "Regional development agencies could help to teach how to make a business plan, how to get capital."[58]

9.3.10 European Technology Centres

Europe still has no cluster of high-tech companies that compares with that of Silicon Valley — or even Israel — although Ireland, the self-proclaimed "software capital" of Europe, ships more than 60 percent of all packaged PC software sold in Europe. In hardware, too, Intel Ireland is the group's sole manufacturing centre for Europe. It produced the world's first eight-inch wafers of pure silicon and is the largest supplier of Pentium chips in the world.[59]

Several European governments have worked to further the development of technology centres like the Silicon Valley to encourage clusters of expertise. The oldest of these initiatives in Europe are the Sophia Antipolis, founded in France in 1969, and the Cambridge Science Park, founded in the UK in 1970 and inspired by Stanford University's industrial park in Palo Alto in Silicon Valley. Conceived as part of the UK's response to a perceived "brain drain" of its top technological talents to the US in the late 1960s, today the Cambridge Science Park houses approximately seventy-five companies employing 4,350 people. More importantly, the Park and the university have created the critical mass for one of Europe's greatest concentrations of high-tech firms, with more than 1,000 of such firms employing more than 35,000 people in the Cambridge area. Sophia Antipolis in the south of France is now host to more than 1,000 firms employing about 17,000 people. It was the inspiration of French senator, Pierre Laffitte, who wanted to build an "international city of wisdom, science, and technology."[60]

Several other countries are attempting to emulate the success of Cambridge and Sophia Antipolis. Luxembourg has created Mediaport Village to capitalise upon its role as home to Astra, and CLT/UFA, and other important pan-

European media firms. Spain has created the Parc Tecnologic del Valle near Barcelona. The State of Saxony in the former East Germany launched Saxony Telematics Development. The Silicon Glen in Scotland has firms employing more than 52,000 and produces 12 percent of Europe's semiconductors and 38 percent of the branded personal computers sold in Europe.[61]

9.4 European Monetary Union

EMU is an important event. "European monetary union has the potential to create the largest single financial market in the world," says Bronwyn Curtis, the London-based economist of Nomura Securities. Europe's total capital market, if all the stocks, bonds, and bank deposits of the EU's fifteen countries are added together, is already larger than that of the US — 24 trillion euro for Europe, 20 trillion euro for the US.[62] The eleven countries coming together in this first round of EMU are Austria, Belgium, Finland, France, Germany, Ireland, Italy, Luxembourg, the Netherlands, Portugal, and Spain. They will create a euro-zone with nearly 300 million inhabitants, accounting for 19.4 percent of the world's gross domestic product (GDP) and 18.6 percent of world trade. That compares with 19.6 percent of world GDP and 16.6 percent of world trade for the US.[63]

Adoption of the euro is likely to have a significant impact on the development of network commerce across Europe. It will also speed up the process of price rationalisation that is sure to take place as easily comparable prices are attached to goods and services across Europe. While the long-term implications of EMU for network commerce are almost certain to be positive, it is difficult to determine whether EMU will ultimately speed or slow network commerce development. In this section we will examine the background and timetable for euro conversion before discussing the impact of EMU on business in general and on network commerce in particular.

9.4.1 Background and Timetable

The 1957 Treaty of Rome began the European integration process with the formation of the European Economic Community (EEC).[64] In 1986, the Treaty of Rome was amended by the Single European Act (SEA), which established the internal market with free movement of goods, persons, services, and capital within the EEC.[65] The Maastricht Treaty, signed in 1992, established the EU in which members agreed to co-operate on political and economic policy without surrendering their sovereignty.[66]

Even before the Maastricht Treaty, European nations took steps to co-ordinate economic policy and eventually converge their currencies of Europe. In 1979, the EEC adopted the European Monetary System (EMS), which includes the Exchange Rate Mechanism (ERM) and the European Currency Unit (ECU).[67] The ERM was created to maintain exchange rates of currencies of EU member countries within certain limits when valued against the Deutschmark. The ECU is a weighted composite of the currencies of EU member countries that functions as a benchmark and is used as a unit of account by EU central banks and institutions. Although many financial contracts are denominated in the euro, it is not a currency in the traditional sense.

A practical plan for a three-stage introduction of economic and monetary union (EMU) was presented in the Delors Report of 1989. With the plan approved by the EU Council, Stage I of EMU began in 1990, focusing on removing remaining barriers on capital movements, increasing co-ordination of national economic policies, and intensifying co-operation between central banks.

The Maastricht Treaty significantly advanced EMU by providing a plan for conversion to a single currency. The Maastricht Treaty endorsed Stages II and III of EMU, as established in the Delors plan. Stage II began in early 1994 with the establishment of the European Monetary Institute (EMI), created to monitor and guide ongoing convergence of member countries and to prepare the ground for the independent European Central Bank based in Frankfurt and a system of regional Central Banks analogous to the US Federal Reserve system. "Such a system will demand that monetary policy be aligned for all countries and perhaps tax policy too," says economist Bill Montague of Transatlantic Futures, a Washington-based research organisation.[68] This bank, which will be independent of any national government, will set monetary policy for all countries participating in EMU, wielding enormous power over the economic fate of each country. The bank itself was established 1 June 1998, in Frankfurt, the current home of the Bundesbank.[69]

The Maastricht Treaty details many aspects of how and when EMU is to be achieved. At its Brussels summit in April 1998, the EU Council decided to allow eleven EU nations to participate in EMU, based on a report released earlier in the year by the European Monetary Institute. The report found that Greece failed to meet the criteria for a variety of reasons. Denmark, Sweden, and the UK had previously chosen not to participate, at least in the first stages of monetary union. At the summit, the heads of state also named the first president of the bank, Wim F. Duisenberg of the Netherlands, and executive directors of the European Central Bank. These eleven countries may participate in the conversion to the euro beginning on January 1, 1999. The Maastricht Treaty lists five criteria an EU member country must meet before it may convert to the euro:

- **Exchange Rate Stability.** The national currency of the member country must have remained within the fluctuation margin of the European Monetary System during the two preceding years, without a unilateral devaluation.
- **Price Stability.** Inflation in the member country may not have exceeded by more than 1.5 percentage points the average rate of inflation of the three member countries with lowest inflation.
- **National Deficit.** The member country must be in a "sustainable fiscal position," which is defined as having a budget deficit no larger than 3 percent of the gross domestic product (GDP).
- **Public Debt.** The member country's gross debt may not exceed 60 percent of its GDP.

- **Long-Term Interest Rates.** The member country's long-term interest rates over the preceding year may not have exceeded those of the three best-performing member countries by more than 2 percent.

These criteria are intended to safeguard the economies of the other member countries by ensuring that all participating countries share a commitment to monetary stability. Already efforts to bring national economies in line with the requirements have had considerable national political significance in France and Germany, where budget tightening has been required.[70] Recent activity in the bond markets indicates that investors expect the move to a single currency to proceed as scheduled, with a large number of countries, but not all, participating from the start.[71] The European Council has prepared two regulations to govern implementation of the EMU conversion process, one of which was finalised in June 1997.[72] Implementation will occur in two phases.

Prior to the Phase 1 implementation date of 1 January 1999, the exchange rates between each of the participating countries' currencies[73] and the euro will be fixed. At the time of this writing, it is not yet known exactly how and when these rates will be set. While euro conversion rates probably will not be fixed until late 1998, it was agreed in September 1997 that bilateral exchange rates for existing currencies would be announced in the middle of 1998 at the same time as the participating countries were announced.[74] This move was intended to forestall market speculation against EMU. On 1 January 1999, the euro will become the unit of account for the European Central Bank and all participating country central banks. (Non-participating countries' central banks will continue to use their own currencies for monetary policy, but will have to use the euro in those situations where they currently use the ECU). The euro will replace the euro on a one-to-one basis. However, this may cause difficulties because not all countries with currencies included in the ECU will move to the euro at that time.[75]

Phase 1 will continue for no more than three years. During this time, legacy currencies will continue to exist and bank notes and coins denominated in legacy currencies will remain legal tender, since euro notes and coins will not yet be in circulation. The principle of "no prohibition, no compulsion" will apply, meaning that payments will be allowed in either the euro or the relevant legacy currency.

Phase 2 of Conversion will begin no later than 1 January 2002. During Phase 2, euro notes and cents will become available for use in retail transactions. From the beginning of Phase 2, both the euro and the legacy currencies will be in circulation; however, by 1 July 2002, legacy currencies will cease to be legal tender. The euro will become the exclusive currency of the participating countries, and conversion will be complete. By 1 July 2002, any reference to a legacy currency in a legal instrument will be deemed a reference to the euro.

9.4.2 General Implications

Introduction of the euro is already having several important general impacts on European businesses.[76] Euro conversion has already required significant spending to upgrade information technology (IT) systems and will continue to do so. National participation guidelines for EMU have forced governments to tighten spending in an effort to improve the business climates in participating countries. In general there are four sets of implications of EMU that will effect most commercial activity across the EU: efficient capital markets, simplification, transparent prices, and competition and consolidation.

Efficient Capital Markets

A larger, unified capital market will give Europe's people and businesses the kind of financial capabilities that US companies and individuals take for granted. For example, mortgages will be more abundantly available increasing home ownership. The US mortgage market has expanded to its present 4.4 trillion-euro scale thanks in part to the development of mortgage-backed securities thirty years ago. European societies, with smaller, national financial markets, lack such innovations and have lower home ownership. On a grander scale, European companies will get the financing they need to operate globally. European companies are already combining forces, and the single currency will facilitate cross-border mergers.

Businesses will no longer need to hold large capital reserves against currency changes among countries when the euro eliminates those differences. Capital will be freed up. Pension investments in the larger capital market will move money around and stimulate business.

The perceived importance of large financial markets with abundant capital is so great that more than 1,000 foreign companies, ranging from Daimler-Benz of Germany and L.M. Ericsson of Sweden to Toyota, Honda, and Nissan of Japan, list their stocks on US exchanges, even though they have had to reconcile their accounting with US principles and accept the exacting regulations of the US Securities and Exchange Commission.

A large market offers big capital. In the *Financial Times* list of the world's largest companies based on value of their stock, thirty-four of the top fifty are US firms. Only twelve are European.

Many factors have contributed to the entrepreneurial surge that produced US leaders in those fields, but among the most crucial are abundant venture capital and markets for risk-taking investors.

Simplification

For individuals travelling among European countries, it will mean no longer having to grapple with a variety of currencies and fluctuating conversion rates. In these eleven countries, there will be only one currency — the euro. For businesses, a single currency means the end of currency conversion and a savings of millions of dollars. Officials at the US Mission to the EU in Brussels point out, for example, that a US-based firm like Motorola would save nearly 14 million euro per year - 880,000 euro by eliminating the paperwork and staff required to deal with different currencies and 13.2 million euro the company loses annually on currency conversions.[77]

Transparent Prices

For the first time, Europeans will be able to compare prices throughout Europe, something that up to now has been either difficult or impossible. In the US, the ability to know what a car or computer costs in Massachusetts as compared to New Mexico is taken for granted. But it is only possible because the US States share a common currency. For Europeans, this will be a revolutionary concept. Prices frequently vary widely from one country to another. For example, a Volkswagen may sell in Italy for as much as 4,400 euro less than in Germany, due to currency and tax differences. These differences will now be easier for consumers to identify and will almost certainly result in lower prices throughout Europe.[78] The price consistency that will result from using a single currency across national borders is likely to affect all kinds of businesses for the better. "Companies that manufacture commodity items like copper wire are always juggling where they produce their products to take advantage of currency fluctuations and material costs," says Nick Jones of the IT consultancy Gartner Group. "With the euro, that won't be necessary anymore."[79]

Competition and Consolidation

Price transparency will lead to greater competition. Companies will need to change the way they do business and how they think about competition. National firms will need to become more European. Firms will need to develop new strategies for pricing, distribution, purchasing, and financing. As competition increases, we can also expect a rapid wave of consolidation and mergers.[80]

9.4.3 Implications for Network Commerce

The introduction of the euro will have several network commerce implications. It will provide a critical opportunity for implementation of network commerce activities. However, preparing for EMU will draw valuable attention and resources away from network commerce activities.

The euro could also be a boost to electronic commerce. The convenience of a single currency will encourage many people will compare prices and shop on the Internet.

The cost of preparing for EMU is expected to be substantial. Industry wide, software conversion costs in Europe alone will top 88 billion euro, estimates Gartner Group. This estimate includes the costs of upgrading larger corporate systems, but not PCs or the software that will also need to support the euro. Combined with mounting year 2000 conversion efforts, EMU will create an even greater strain on already tight IT resources and could extend the current IT labour shortage to 2004.

The adoption of the euro will affect a multitude of systems and applications, including general ledger, accounts payable and receivable, taxation, price lists, payroll, expense accounts, and historical databases. It will also affect EDI and other electronic-commerce systems. Additionally, the euro symbol will need to be incorporated in computer keyboards, screen and printer fonts, and applications.[81]

"At the same time [euro-conversion and Year 2000 projects] may stimulate awareness of the need for best practices in IT system procurement, development, and deployment that can benefit industry and other organisations in the longer term," one industry analyst.

"For the euro in particular, the need for change should prompt enterprises to undertake a more fundamental reappraisal of the way in which they do business. This, in turn, can lead to longer term competitive advantage."

When many IT executives think of the impending changeover to a single European currency, they think of the disruption it will cause to their international operations; however, some vendors and managers are looking beyond the hurdles to new electronic-commerce opportunities.

Price transparency will be a benefit to IT when purchasing services and equipment in Europe. "If you're shopping for hardware today, you have to deal with different currencies and tax policies, so it's very hard to compare prices," says Denis Haensler, a network engineer at 8.8 billion-euro pharmaceutical conglomerate Hoffman-LaRoche in Basel, Switzerland.

"With the euro, vendors will have to price their products consistently, which will make procurement much easier and probably increase the competitive pressures on pricing," he says.

Potentially, the euro's greatest benefit for IT will be its boost to network commerce. Users will be able to identify prices without calculating exchange rates.

The currency change is also likely to bring consolidation of European operations, since presence in each national market will become less of an economic and logistical necessity. That means fewer WAN nodes, fewer offices, lower overhead, and less remote support headaches.[82]

The bottom line is that EMU will clearly be a long-term stimulant for network commerce activity and is likely to drive a significant amount of revenues for various content industry players who provide information and services related to EMU. In the short-term, however, the cost of converting systems to EMU may lead to a reduction in spending on other network commerce activities and divert attention from development of network commerce capabilities and strategies. Incumbent firms may be particularly vulnerable in some areas as new competitors who are not faced with the costs of EMU conversion move quickly to exploit the combined opportunities presented by network commerce and EMU.

Savvy European firms will consider how to take advantage of EMU and Year 2000 implementation processes to implement innovative network commerce strategies. In the longer run, firms will be able to sell more effectively and less expensively across Europe due to the reach of network commerce and the consistency created by a common currency. Growing pan-European capital markets may at last help to funnel much-needed capital to innovative network commerce and infrastructure firms in Europe, helping them to compete more effectively with their well-funded American competitors.

9.5 Summary

In Chapter 9 we examined three sets of key financial drivers and constraints to the evolution of network commerce. The first of these is taxation. We discussed the impact of tax policies on the emerging network economy, as well as the potential impact of the network economy on tax policy. We then discussed the impact of the venture capital environment in Europe on new business formation in the content and network commerce sectors. Finally, we provided a brief overview of EMU and examined its potential role in shaping network commerce evolution. EMU has the potential both to drive network commerce adoption and to hinder it. In fact, EMU will make tax disparities more apparent to consumers and businesses by providing consistent pricing and it is likely to play a critical role in creating larger and more flexible capital markets to fund European firms.

RECOMMENDATIONS

Both businesses and governments can play a role in making sure that funding is available to build the new economy.

Businesses

- Work with and press governments to reform laws and regulations that impact new business formation and competitiveness (e.g. lower taxes, streamlined regulations, capital gains tax reform). Keep government leaders' attention focused on these critical issues and look for ways to work with governments to address them.
- Combine preparation for the European Monetary Union (EMU) and Year 2000 (Y2K) with network commerce development. Most European businesses are already focused on these important business and IT issues. Businesses can use the focus on these IT issues as a catalyst for developing a business-wide network commerce strategy and infrastructure. By the same token, firms must be careful not to invest all of their IT resources and attention in EMU and Y2K to the exclusion of network commerce.
- Create internal corporate venture funds. These funds can achieve two important goals: First, they provide an important vehicle for firms to pursue organised experimentation in risky new network commerce markets. Second, they increase the pool of venture capital and create local opportunities for entrepreneurs to pursue their ideas and create value.

Governments

- Support the development of a pan-European small-cap market. Investment capital does not flow as efficiently among technology firms in Europe as it does in the US. In addition, this capital is spread among a number of small markets. A pan-European small-capital market would help to concentrate capital and investment opportunities and provide greater liquidity for venture investors and entrepreneurs in Europe.
- Aid entrepreneurial ventures. In the early stages, much of the innovation in the network economy is being driven by entrepreneurial start-ups. Governments can take several actions to aid these activities. They can help to educate entrepreneurs through business outreach programs and through formal education. They can create opportunities to facilitate meetings between entrepreneurs and venture capitalists and develop other methods of matching venture capital with venture opportunities. Governments can improve the tax treatment of stock options granted to employees in entrepreneurial firms. They can remove red tape around new business formation and ameliorate draconian bankruptcy laws that exist in many jurisdictions.
- Place a moratorium on taxation of network commerce activity until the market has evolved sufficiently to understand how best to tax it. It is not at all clear how best to tax network commerce activity today. Governments should wait until the market has evolved instead of enacting taxes today that may distort or hinder market development. In addition, this provides another valuable incentive for network commerce development.

Notes

1. "Showing Europe's Firms the Way," *The Economist*, 13 July 1996.

2. For an excellent analysis of the different forms of capitalism and their implications, see John Groenewegen, "Institutions of Capitalisms: American, European, and Japanese systems compared," *Journal of Economic Issues*, June 1997.

3. *Agence France Presse*, 16 January 1998.

4. Ruth Walker, "Germans' Conscience Wants to Be a Guide," *The Christian Science Monitor*, 23 July 1997. President Herzog has evidently confused Gates, who did not found Microsoft in a garage, with Steve Jobs of Apple Computer, who did found that firm in his garage.

5. Study by European Network for SME Research. Reported in "Please Dare to Fail," *The Economist*, 28 September 1996.

6. The White House's *Framework for Global Electronic Commerce*, written by Ira Magaziner, proclaims that "The Internet [should] be declared a tariff-free environment whenever it is used to deliver goods or services.

7. William Rees-Mogg, "Tax Exiles on the Web," *The Times* of London, 26 February 1998.

8. In the 1984 science fiction novel *Neuromancer*, author William Gibson presented the concept of a "data haven," a country that provided complete privacy to parties transacting business under its jurisdiction.

9. Robert J. Posch, "Keep Privacy Laws Out of Cyberspace," *Direct Marketing*, January 1997.

10. See, e.g., "L. Hinnekens, "New Age International taxation in the Digital Economy of the Global Society," *Intertax: International Tax Review*, 1997.

11. Some estimates suggest that 30 percent or more of all voice traffic will be transported over the Internet by 2000.

12. "Electronic Commerce: The Challenges to Tax Authorities and Taxpayers," an informal Round Table discussion between business and government held in Turku, Finland, 18 November 1997 (the Turku Conference Round Table).

13. Ibid.

14. *The Electronic Commerce Briefing,* 1 January 1998.

15. Turku Conference Round Table, *supra*.

16. *The Electronic Commerce Briefing*, 1 January 1998.

17. Reuters, 26 February 1998.

18. Turku Conference Round Table, *supra*.

19. *European Report*, 12 July 1997.

20. Reuters, 26 February 1998.

21. Center on Budget and Policy Priorities, "A Federal 'Moratorium' on Internet Commerce Taxes Would Erode State and Local Revenues and Shift Burdens to Lower-Income Households," Washington, DC: May 1998.

22. Joint Statement of the United States and the European Union on Electronic Commerce, Washington, DC, 5 December 1997.

23. *European Information Technology Observatory* 1997, European Information Technology Observatory, Frankfurt-am-Main, Germany, 1997.

24. The importance of risk capital was recently highlighted in a Communication of the European Commission, "Risk Capital: A Key to Job Creation in the European Union," April 1998. The findings reported in the Communication largely agree with our findings reported in this section.

25. W. Keith Schilit, "Venture Catalysts or Vulture Capitalists," *The Journal of Investing*, 1996 Fall, vol. 5, no. 3, p. 86.

26. See Paul Romer, "Increasing Returns and Long-Run Growth," *Journal of Political Economy*, vol. 94, no. 5 (October 1986), pp. 1002-37.

27. Nicholas Denton, "Venture Capital, Catalyst of the High-Tech Boom," *Financial Times*, 4 June 1997.

28. Observations and Conjectures on the US Employment Miracle, A. Krueger & J. Pischke, Working Paper 6146, National Bureau of Economic Research, Cambridge, MA, August 1997.

29. Schilit, *supra*.

30. These are very general guidelines. There are numerous factors that can affect the equity positions of the entrepreneurs and the venture investors, such as past success of the venture, expected returns for investors, proprietary position, quality of management, experience in marketing, or prior investment in the venture by the entrepreneurial team.

31. Denton, *supra*.

32. Ibid.

33. Timmons, J.A., and L.E. Smollen, and A.L.M. Dingee. *New Venture Creation*, 2nd edition. Homewood, IL: Richard D. Irwin,1985, p. 32.

34. Denton, *supra*.

35. Ibid.

36. Ibid.

37. *Red Herring* European Outlook.

38. Denton, *supra*.

39. Ibid.

40. "Europe's Great Experiment," *The Economist*, 13 June 1998.

41. *Red Herring* European Outlook.

42. Nicholas Denton, "Drive to Plug the Gap," *Financial Times*, 3 February 1997.

43. Ibid.

44. Gemini Consulting interview.

45. Gail Edmonson and Heidi Dawley, "Europe Finally Wakes Up to High-Tech Startups," *Business Week*, 26 May 1997.

46. Ibid.

47. Ibid.

48. For more information on the Innovation Market, see *Red Herring* European Outlook.

49. Study by Bank of Boston Corporation and the Massachusetts Institute of Technology. Reported in "Study Finds MIT Affiliates Create 4,000 Jobs," *The Patriot Ledger*, 5 March 1997.

50. *Red Herring* European Outlook.

51. Gemini Consulting interview.

52. Ibid.

53. *London Observer*, 27 October 1996. The subsequent fall of Windhorst due to financial problems shook the German public.

54. Denton, *supra*.

55. Ibid.

56. Ibid.

57. *Agence France Presse*, 16 January 1998.

58. Gemini Consulting interview.

59. Nicholas Denton, "Drive to Plug the Gap," *The Irish Times*, 10 February 1997.

60. *Red Herring* European Outlook.

61. Ibid.

62. James Flanigan, "Euro's Value Promises to be More than Monetary," *Los Angeles Times*, 1 February 1998.

63. Paul Tooher, "Europe Counts on Currency for Clout," *The Providence Journal-Bulletin*, 27 April 1998.

64. Treaty Establishing EEC, 25 March 1957, 298 U.N.T.S. 3 (known as the Treaty of Rome).

65. 3 Single European Act, 1986 O.J. (L169).

66. For background on the Treaties of Rome and Maastricht see Edwards, "Fearing Federalism's Failure: Subsidiarity in the European Union," *44 Am. J. Comp. L.* 537 (1996); O'Keeffe, "Blaine Sloan Lecture: Current Issues in European Integration," *7 Pace Int'l L. Rev.* (1995); Note, "The Ramification of the Exchange Rate Collapse in Europe: Implications for Monetary Union," *B.U. Int'l L. J.* 263 (1995).

67. For a discussion of the EMS see Works, "The European Currency Unit: The Increasing Significance of the European Monetary System's Currency Cocktail," 41 Bus. Law. 483 (1986).

68. James Flanigan, "Euro's Value Promises to be More than Monetary," *Los Angeles Times*, 1 February 1998.

69. Paul Tooher, "Europe Counts on Currency for Clout," *The Providence Journal-Bulletin*, 27 April 1998.

70. See Barber, "France and Germany firm on EMU," *Financial Times*, 8 July 1997, at 14; TOWARD EMU, Kicking and screaming into 1999, *The Economist*, 17 June 1997, at 19.

71. Bray, "Bond Markets Bet That EMU Will Begin On Schedule, But They Could Be Wrong," *Wall Street Journal*, 28 July 1997, at A-9B.

72. Proposal for a Council Regulation[ ] on some provisions relating to the introduction of the euro, 96/0249 (CNS); Council Regulation 1103/97 (Council Regulation on the introduction of the euro). Proposals for Council regulations are self-implementing, that is, they are legally binding upon all EU member countries and do not require the enactment of enabling legislation by any country or international body. The following discussion is based on this regulation and proposed regulation.

73. The term "legacy currencies" refers to the existing national currencies of the participating EU member countries for periods after 31 December 1998.

74. "EU sticks to EMU timing," *Financial Times*, 15 September 1997, at 1.

75. See "Zigzag path to the euro," *Euromoney*, July 1997, at 5.

76. James Flanigan, "Euro's Value Promises to be More than Monetary," *Los Angeles Times*, 1 February 1998.

77. Paul Tooher, "Europe Counts on Currency for Clout," *The Providence Journal-Bulletin*, 27 April 1998.

78. Ibid.

79. Lenny Liebmann, " Finding Euro Opportunities — Many firms see currency unification spurring E-commerce efforts," *InternetWeek*, 12 January 1998.

80. Paul Tooher, "Europe Counts on Currency for Clout," *The Providence Journal-Bulletin*, 27 April 1998.

81. Bob Violino, The Euro: Are You Ready Yet?" *InformationWeek*, 26 January 1998.

82. Lenny Liebmann, " Finding Euro Opportunities — Many firms see currency unification spurring E-commerce efforts," *InternetWeek*, 12 January 1998.

Exploring the Broader Implications

Network commerce will not only have a huge impact on the content and communications businesses, it will also impact all segments of commerce and society. In this chapter, we explore the broader implications of network commerce, in particular its potential impact on employment, education, politics, culture, competitiveness, and national sovereignty.

Technological innovations have been quickly changing the nature of communication, allowing greater connectivity among individuals, businesses, and communities and driving many economic changes. Today a gap exists between network-enabled capabilities and society's ability to exploit these capabilities. Changes in employment, education, political processes, and culture will occur as people incorporate the network into their lives. Many of the network revolution's broader implications remain unknown; still, we must consider the potential changes and prepare to address them.

10.1 A Revolutionary Change

We believe that many of the attributes of the network environment will eventually be reflected in society. The network revolution has been gaining momentum as communications media develop and achieve strength via global interactive networks. The network's ultimate impact on politics, economics, and society cannot be predicted, but we may have some clues today. The network environment encourages decentralisation of control, pushes decision-making power to the individual, and encompasses growth of an efficient or "friction-less" connection. By applying these ideas to economies, politics, and societal relationships, we can begin to envision what is to come. As in other revolutions, societal structure will change and things will never again be as they were.

10.2 Education and Employment

The network economy is creating new jobs today and will continue to create many new jobs across Europe. At the same time, it will likely destroy many jobs, significantly affecting large European firms. The net effect of the Internet on employment is likely to speed up the creation of increasingly global and efficient labour markets. In light of this, education and re-training of the workforce are two pressing macro-economic issues. The ability of economies to rapidly adjust their workforces and create new jobs will play a large role in their long-term success.

While the industrial revolution created the need for factory workers, engineers, mechanics, and production managers, many labourers were displaced as machines took over many of their functions. The network revolution has created a demand for information technology (IT) specialists, software developers, Webmasters, and content creators, and has led to a greater focus on knowledge workers (e.g. health care professionals and educators). However, because the basic technology for the network economy has developed very quickly, society's transition is lagging, especially in terms of re-training and educating the workforce. Although the European Union's unemployment rate was about 10.2 percent in May 1998, roughly 10 percent of all IT jobs remained unfilled.[1] In Germany, the unemployment rate was just under 10 percent while 50,000 IT jobs remained unfilled.[2] There is a shortage of workers with the skills necessary to support the network economy, a problem which could become more severe as network commerce, Year 2000, and European Monetary Union issues become more pressing.

Exhibit 10.1 **Projected Change in Employment, 1996 – 2006, Thousands of Jobs**

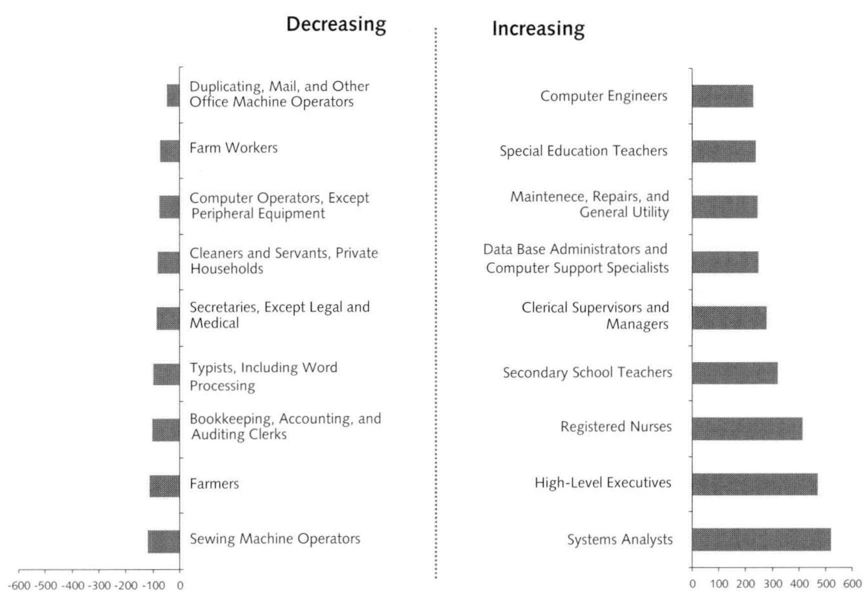

Source: US Bureau of Labor Statistics.

As network commerce takes a more prominent role in the economy, there will be a negative impact on employment in some sectors. As with many other intermediary services, the travel ticketing industry may see a significant reduction in the number of travel agencies as more people obtain tickets and other travel services directly over the Internet. Bureaucracies will become smaller as information transfer is performed automatically by machines, and labour-intensive information processing jobs may migrate to areas like Bangalor, India, where an abundance of skilled and inexpensive labour can be utilised to write computer code and perform data entry.

10.2.1 New Job Creation

Network Economy Companies

The network economy, particularly the growth in computers and Internet usage, has created thousands of new firms such as Microsoft, SAP, and Cap Gemini. More recently it has created markets for America Online, Dell, and DoubleClick. These companies are leading a new generation of firms that are all involved in network commerce. In their paper, "A First Approximation of Internet's Economic Impact" (1997), Takuma Amano and Robert Blohm calculated that more than 760,000 Internet-related jobs were created in the US in

1996, about half the total number of jobs created in the US during that year. This number does not include a multiplier effect, ignoring the secondary impact of the Internet on employment in the economy (i.e. employment in companies that do business with Internet-related companies). Several macro-economic factors such as taxes, availability of investment capital (see Chapter 9), and the legal and regulatory environment (see Chapter 8), affect the attractiveness for investment for any particular nation, thereby affecting the potential growth of businesses creating jobs.

Bertlesmann's joint venture with America Online to create AOL Europe has created 1,200 new jobs since November 1995. Microsoft's alliance with Britain's ICL in early 1998 is expected to create 1,000 jobs across Europe, and Xerox announced in June 1998 that it will invest $270 million in Ireland, creating 2,200 jobs over the next three years. The Institut der Deutschen Wirstschaft estimates that by the year 2000 there will be 50,000 new jobs in multimedia production in Germany alone.

Ireland has had particular success in creating jobs. It has lowered its corporate tax rate to 10 percent for some industries[3] and made many efforts to create a flexible workforce, leading to many investments by companies such as IBM, Microsoft, Intel, and many others. Over 150,000 jobs[4] were added in the three years ending April 1998, with a total of 49,000 new jobs expected in 1998.[5] This strong growth has reduced Ireland's unemployment rate dramatically (Exhibit 10.2).

Exhibit 10.2 **Unemployment Rate in Ireland versus EU15, 1993 – 1998**

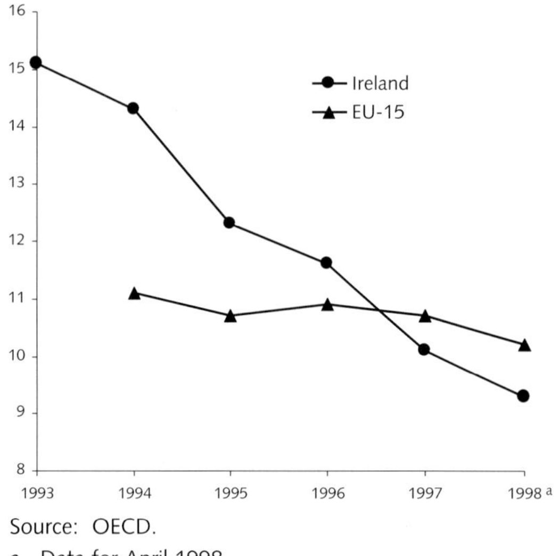

Source: OECD.

a. Data for April 1998.

Small and Medium-Sized Enterprises (SMEs)

SMEs are playing a larger role in employment for many countries. A study of 500 SMEs in Europe conducted by IP Strategies, showed that those companies added 183,000 jobs from 1991–1996 (Exhibit 10.3) while 290 of Europe's biggest firms cut over 500,000 jobs from their payrolls. The network economy continues to fuel this trend by eliminating many business process inefficiencies, allowing smaller companies to reach a world market.

Exhibit 10.3 **Selected SMEs' Growth and Job Creation, 1991 – 1996**

Company Name	Country	Revenue Growth[a]	Revenue[b] ($ Millions)	Net Jobs Created[a]
ITE Group	Britain	13,567%	30.2	153
Firm Security Group	Britain	8,679	25.8	765
Software Warehouse	Britain	7,714	23.0	204
Euro-Med	Germany	6,567	20.2	166
Paco Retail	Britain	5,457	21.6	234
Business Objects	France	4,659	65.9	527
Cofiman	Spain	3,681	38.6	68
Poundland	Britain	3,404	83.5	998
Costcutter Supermarkets	Britain	3,143	220.9	267
IKM Group	Norway	2,849	35.8	386
DX Communications	Britain	2,678	36.9	150
Advance Risk Machines	Britain	2,219	24.6	143
Teles	Germany	2,100	33.4	255
Merceron MDG MCCR	France	1,951	27.9	91
Berger Bau	Germany	1,847	35.6	184
Lintec Computer Germany	Germany	1,762	73.5	162
Altec Information Systems	Greece	1,413	53.5	135
Telepizza	Spain	1,364	163.6	5,787
Afinsa Bienes Tangibles	Spain	1,348	83.9	163
Caves de Landiras	France	1,239	63.2	135
Faulds Advertising	Britain	1,239	35.5	72
Elcoteq Network	Finland	1,200	166.0	1,178
Elemaster Technologie	Italy	1,183	21.6	80
Casa Diamani	Italy	1,119	78.7	82
Lernout and Hauspie Speech	Belgium	1,068	20.8	66

Source: IP Strategies; Europe's 500 1997 Honorary Listing; *Business Week*, March 23, 1998.
a. 1991 – 1996.
b. 1996.

Continued growth of, and employment driven by SMEs, largely depends on the availability of venture and investment capital (See Chapter 9). In the US, companies with fewer than five employees were responsible for the creation of 450,000 jobs in 1995, 35 percent of the total new employment that year.[6] Companies with fewer than 100 employees accounted for 33 percent of the net new jobs created in 1996; the 5,500 firms on the NASDAQ market, many of which are SMEs, employ around 9 million people.[7]

10.2.2 A Flexible Workforce

Jobs are also being created by existing companies that require workers with new skills. While many of these jobs are creating employment opportunities, unfortunately, many cannot be filled by the current pool of workers. In the US, roughly 350,000 IT positions were unfilled during the first half of 1998. Europe too is suffering a shortage of available IT workers, and as the network economy continues to grow, the situation could become as bad as that in the US, if not worse. Because the supply of skilled workers is below demand, a "balancing" period must take place. Workforce flexibility will play a large role in the success and timeliness of this adjustment. A network of governments, businesses, and individuals dedicated to retraining and educating the workforce for a changing environment is beginning to create just such flexibility.

Re-Training

Re-training is the near-term solution to the European Union's shortage of skilled technology workers. For example, in Belgium, Unisys was having trouble recruiting skilled technology workers. The company hired educated people to take part in a special IT skills training program. An opera tenor, a former hockey player, and an actress[8] were among the new hires, all of whom learned the requisite new skills and became valued Unisys employees. Similarly, government initiatives such as Spain's "employability action" programs are targeting workers and unemployed people who require new skills in order to become employable. The implications of re-training are significant: Companies that retrain employees will have greater workforce flexibility; countries can create job security and address workforce adjustment issues through effective retraining and relocation programs; and individuals will gain a greater adaptability to new job and career options (Exhibit 10.4).

Exhibit 10.4 **Projected Job Openings by Most Significant Source of Education or Training, 1996 – 2006, Millions of Jobs**

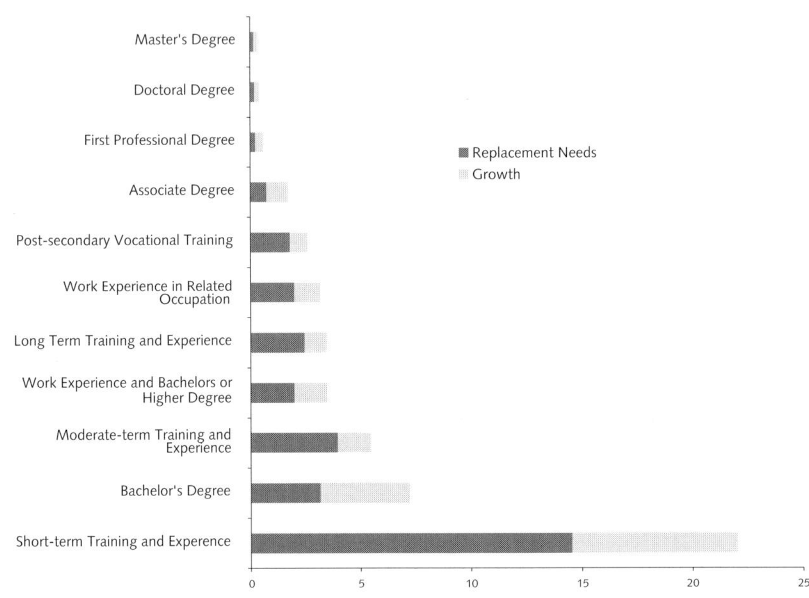

Source: US Bureau of Labor Statistics.

Re-training programs can greatly reduce the number of open positions, as in the case of Unisys and other firms throughout the world. Firms are able to eliminate or reposition jobs without losing experienced and loyal workers, thereby increasing loyalty, retaining employees, and improving morale. The network economy is demanding a more flexible workforce, enabling change in business models and processes, industry structures, and skill requirements.

In many countries, employment flexibility is crucial to a nation's future competitiveness. Governments that actively retrain the unemployed provide a social service and increase their economies' competitiveness. A lack of properly trained individuals is straining the US labour market. Europe's labour market is also under strain, although unemployment is over 10 percent. At the semi-annual EU summit in Luxembourg in November 1997, countries agreed to emphasise "active" measures for putting the unemployed back to work rather than to continue "passive" measures such as income support.[9] For many years, Ireland has been following active labour-market policies (ALMPs) by providing training programs, job-search counselling, and job brokerage services while strictly limiting increases in unemployment benefits. These ALMPs, along with other macro-economic initiatives, such as lowering corporate tax rates, have reduced Ireland's unemployment rate from over 15 percent in 1993 to 9.3 percent in April 1998.

The Confederation of British Industry recently surveyed employment trends in 5,000 organisations and found that 41 percent of those organisations are using more contract staff, 47 percent are using more temporary staff, and 38 percent are offering more flexible working hours (Exhibit 10.5). Additionally, one-third of these organisations believe that job security has decreased over the past three years. These trends suggest that individuals must create their own long-term job security by acquiring skills that various employers can leverage. In light of this, individuals must view re-training as an opportunity as well as a necessity. Adair Turner, Director of the Confederation of British Industry, said, "Ultimately, it is individuals who are employable. An employable individual has the qualities and competencies that employers need — and these are likely to change several times during a person's lifetime... Individuals' confidence in their employability is the key antidote to job insecurity, enabling them to see labour market flexibility as liberating rather than threatening."[10] Businesses and governments can add significantly to that confidence by creating the proper infrastructure for retraining and education. Individuals must work to obtain transferable skills, taking advantage of all available training.

Education

The current shortage of IT workers is fuelling an increase in the number of jobs that require more education and training (Exhibit 10.6). However, studies show that the number of students pursuing education aimed at the needs of the network economy is not high enough. In the US, engineering schools are turning out only one-fourth of the computer specialists required over the next ten years.[11] In Germany, only 8,000 students began courses in mechanical engineering in 1996 – 1997, compared with 16,000 in 1990 – 1991. By contrast, India is turning out 55,000 computer specialists per year, and Bangalor has the highest concentration of computer specialists in the world.[12]

Elemond

Creating Opportunities for Content Firms

Elemond, an Italian publisher of educational products, is part of the Mondadori Group. It is working actively to develop the education market, which is still in its infancy. In Italy today, 3,500 schools have Internet connections and 400 of them have Web sites. The Ministry of Education has provided some hardware but no software, nor any support — schools still have limited budgets. "From a cultural point of view, it is still too early for electronic commerce. It is still a territory for techno-enthusiasts," says Spiro Coutsoucos, Director of Operations and New Initiatives at Elemond.

Elemond has taken the initiative. In 1997, it created an informational Web site providing teachers with free services (e.g. information about schools from the Ministry of Education, didactic information, links to other schools' Web sites). "The budget allocated to this project is a business development budget. About 2,000 teachers visit the Elemond site every day. In collaboration with Microsoft, Elemond has also been organising half-day training seminars for teachers in more than twenty Italian cities. More than 4,500 teachers have already attended those seminars."

The school market can be used to cross-fertilise the family segment. "Educational electronic products are used both at school and at home. The ideal is to have products which combine three characteristics: A traditional paper format, interactivity brought by multimedia, and communication capabilities provided by the Internet," Coutscoucos explains.

For example, Elemond made an English manual combined with a CD-ROM with hyperlinks to various Web sites. They are also preparing a similar product to teach Italian to emigrants in Australia. The product will be promoted via the Internet, instead of creating a new distribution system. "The product would not be viable otherwise," says Coutsoucos.

Elemond is considering many scenarios, but a new principle seems to be emerging, according to Coutsoucos. "There should not be one book for one course. Teaching materials must become more modular, more flexible, and more differentiated. Schools want more autonomy in the selection of the teaching material," he explains. "Today, teachers push families to buy a comprehensive book but families argue that they are too expensive. Tomorrow, one could imagine a basic book plus modules to be bought online," he adds.

Elemond also considers that a market for remote learning could develop. It could target eighteen-to-twenty-year-old graduates seeking two years of complementary education while they work.

www.elemond.it

Exhibit 10.5 **Part-time Employment as a Percentage of Total Employment, 1986 and 1996**

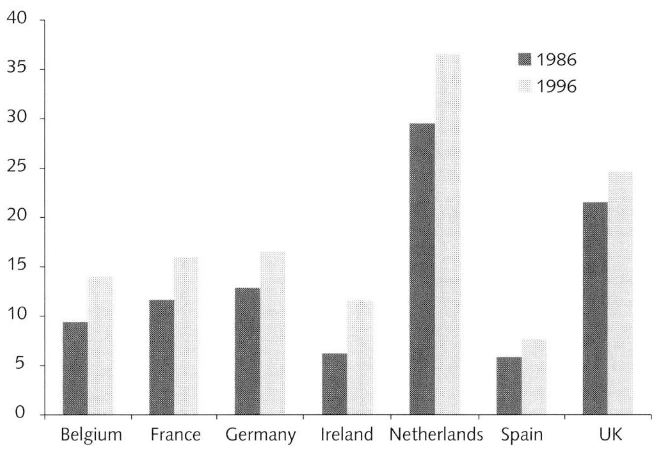

1986
1996
Belgium France Germany Ireland Netherlands Spain UK

Source: OECD.

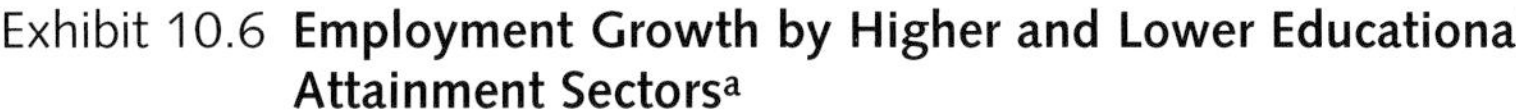

Exhibit 10.6 **Employment Growth by Higher and Lower Educational Attainment Sectors[a]**

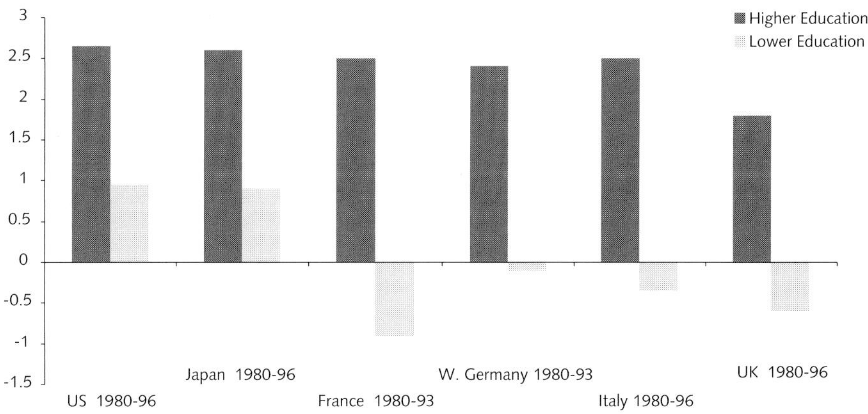

Source: OECD and US Bureau of Labor Statistics.

a. Higher education sectors are those sectors in the US in which 30 percent or more of full-time workers have college degrees.

Not surprisingly, there will be more job growth for workers with higher levels of education (e.g. Bachelor's degree) over the next several years than for jobs requiring less education (Exhibit 10.7). As this shift in employment continues, education plays a much larger role in individual, business, and national competitiveness. Education is another tool for achieving workforce flexibility, and a solution for the European Union's long-term need for skilled technology workers.

Exhibit 10.7 **Projected Change in Job Growth Rates by Most Significant Source of Education and Training, 1996 – 2006**

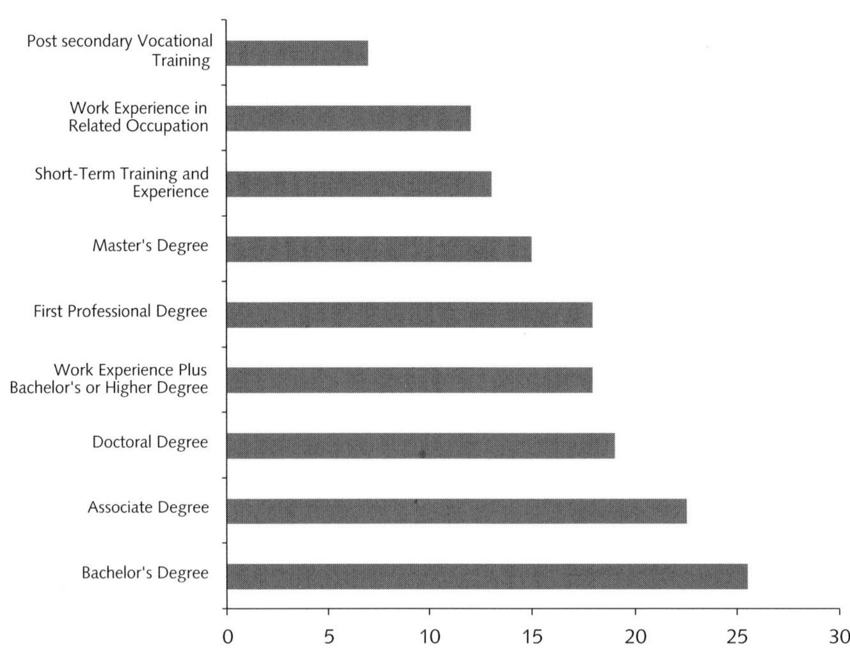

Source: US Bureau of Labor Statistics.

In the UK, Prime Minister Tony Blair has unveiled a plan — the National Grid for Learning — to link 32,000 schools to the Internet. The plan is aimed at increasing Internet awareness and developing the skills required for the network economy. These skills include computer literacy and Internet comprehension. Students with these basic skills will be better prepared to work in a network environment.

Along with governments, many businesses have seen the importance of becoming involved in education. Businesses need to ensure that students entering the workforce possess the skills needed by companies. Some high-tech firms believe that by investing in education today they will reap the rewards in the future by ensuring a better workforce and increasing demand for network products. Intel Corporation is providing many schools with Internet access technology. It also sponsors an international science and engineering fair and offers prepared computer-related educational curriculum and projects. In Ireland, Intel employees are encouraged to volunteer their time to local school systems. For every volunteer who donates 100 hours, the local school receives IR£500 from Intel. Unisys Corporation has developed the Science Learning Network (SLN), a global consortium of leading science museums, collaborating to provide online resources, experiences, and interaction that support science learning. For the past three years, six museums in the United States have provided schools with telecomputing technology, Web resources, teacher training, and interactive online forums. The SLN program has expanded to include partner museums in France, the United Kingdom, the Netherlands, Finland, Japan, Singapore, and Mexico.

Additionally, many businesses are joining together to try to address educational issues. A CEO Summit titled "The Corporate Imperative: Results and Benefits of Business Involvement in Education," scheduled for September 1998 in New York, has attracted 100 of the top CEOs in the US, including the heads of Price Waterhouse, Prudential, and Mattel. This meeting, along with others like it, shows that businesses are taking some responsibility for the education of the workforce.

Regulations
While re-training and education will enable a flexible workforce, regulations can be a constraint to workforce flexibility. Regulations on when and how long employees can work, layoffs, and immigration all constrain adjustments in labour. Many countries are trying to balance the social benefits of regulated employment with the economic benefits of workforce flexibility.

By limiting job protection regulations, nations increase flexibility by reducing restrictions to eliminate unneeded jobs and eliminating disincentives to hiring new employees. In Spain in the 1980s, restrictions to, and high costs of, dismissal were partially responsible for many companies greatly reducing the number of new hires and driving unemployment rates to over 20 percent. Even though many steps have been taken to reduce regulations, in 1998, the average cost of laying off permanent employees was two years of full salary.[13]

The European Union has created a unified labour market, greatly adding to workforce flexibility. In addition, the European Employment Service (EURES) is facilitating worker mobility by helping labourers work or be recruited from abroad. EURES is made up of the European Commission along with the public employment services of seventeen European countries. This service has succeeded in placing over 1 million workers in positions throughout Europe and has between 50,000 and 100,000 jobs available daily.[14] However, as the need for skilled technology workers continuous to grow, additional workers will be needed to fill many openings. In the US, where 350,000 IT jobs are open, an additional 30,000 H-1B visas — those for highly skilled foreign workers — were made available in May 1998 in addition to the annual allotment of 65,000 such visas. Preventing skilled workers from entering an economy may force companies to migrate many of their functions internationally or compete without the necessary human resources.

10.3 Network Communities

Interactive networks such as the Internet are connecting people from a variety of cultures and are becoming catalysts for social and cultural change. On the Internet, location is no longer a barrier to instant communication among many people. Although communities of language and interest have existed for thousands of years, supported by magazines, newsletters, and television, the network's interactive nature allows members of these communities to become more actively connected, having a greater influence on many established cultures around the world.

Two phenomena are occurring simultaneously: A "global" culture is slowly emerging as news, entertainment, ideas, etc. from all cultures are shared on a global network; at the same time, bonds among groups or cultures are being strengthened by linking people. For example, if an Italian in Rome has a strong interest in woodworking, she can use the Web to exchange ideas and tips about woodworking with people in Milan, Chicago, Buenos Aires, and Cairo. Many distinctive styles and techniques will converge as the woodworking "community" becomes connected. After spending time at the woodworking Web site, she might go to an Italian newspaper site attracting Italians who wish to exchange ideas about their common heritage, strengthening their connection.

10.3.1 Language

Language allows people on the network to communicate. In the example used above, the woodworker in Rome would not be able to exchange ideas with other people throughout the world without using a common language. The need for a common language on the network is affecting cultures throughout the world, leading us toward a "global" culture by enabling communication across all cultures. While it will be unrealistic to expect that a lingua franca will dominate the network environment, the common language requirement may be satisfied by emerging translation technologies. As these technologies improve, communication will not be restricted by language; and ideas and information will flow freely among cultures.

As of the first quarter of 1998, roughly 70 percent of all Internet users in OECD nations lived in countries where English is the primary language (Exhibit 10.8), and about 80 percent of all content on the Internet was in English.[15] This is quickly changing as more and more people from Latin America, France, Germany, India, China, and many other countries connect to the Internet. To account for the growing user-diversity, Web sites, particularly in Europe, are increasingly becoming available in multiple languages. Many of the major Web portals (e.g. Yahoo!, Altavista, Lycos) are now available in Spanish, German, and French, as well as a growing number of other languages.

Yahoo! launched the Spanish version of its popular Web site in early 1998. The site is aimed at a growing number of Spanish-speaking Internet users, including 8.5 million in Latin America, 1.3 million in Spain, and hundreds of thousands of others throughout the world; it serves as an example of how communities of language will arise on the network. The site will aggregate Spanish-language Web sites and users from around the world, allowing them to share ideas and information. Similarly, French-language Web sites attract people from France, Canada, Martinique, Vietnam, etc., creating another network community. Countries trying to maintain cultural identity through control of language will have a hard time doing so since broader, language-based communities will encompass a variety of cultures. Countries will be able to promote their cultural assets through the network to a variety of network communities.

Exhibit 10.8 **Distribution of Global Internet Users by Language, First Quarter 1998, OECD Nations**

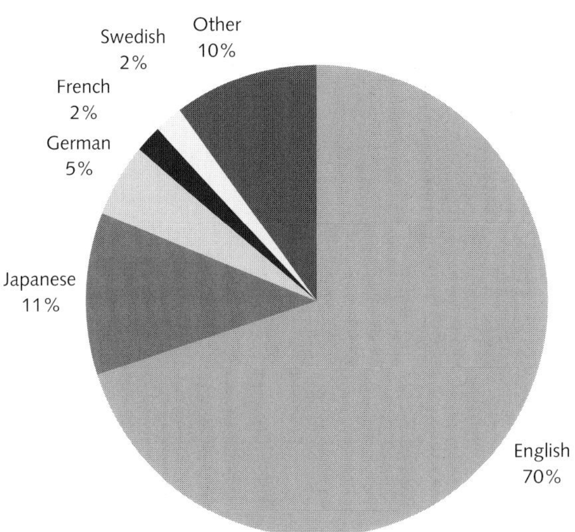

Source: NUA Internet; OECD.

10.3.2 Interest

Communities of interest are playing a large role in the emerging network economy. GeoCities allows Internet users to set up free Web sites providing individually-created content. GeoCities organises the millions of Web sites its users have developed by areas of interest such as soccer, opera, or cooking, creating a variety of network communities. On a larger scale, users world-wide can interact on a variety of Web sites dedicated to specific interest areas. This exchange of information also plays a role in creating a more global culture, blurring the lines of cultural identity. In the case that the common interest is a culture, network communities can reinforce the bonds and uniqueness of that culture and promote its cultural assets.

10.4 Government and Politics

The network revolution reflects a sense that the institutions of today — including governments and nations — aren't necessarily best structured to satisfy society's evolving needs. The many issues discussed in this report point to substantive changes occurring in both the economy and in social relationships. Business and commerce changes caused by the network economy are happening swiftly, being widely felt and easily observed, but political and governmental changes will be much slower, and therefore harder to detect.

Some issues are emerging that call the roles of today's governments into question. The emergence of a global economy and a global network that blur the concepts of geography and product also confuse the issue of national sovereignty and political jurisdiction. The availability of fast and free information empowers individuals to make informed decisions, not just on buying products, but on political issues. Finally, the emergence of a network such as the Internet enables fast and easy interaction among citizens or organisations promoting political agendas.

As more economic activity moves to the network, geographic boundaries become less significant and issues of jurisdiction and tax collection call into question the effectiveness of current geographically-based governing systems. The network economy's legal and tax implications have been closely examined in Chapters 8 and 9; while those issues are being addressed under the current government infrastructure, ideas about business self-regulation and reduced government involvement seem to be more prevalent than in the past. Additionally, creation of multinational governing bodies such as the European Union and the World Trade Organisation provides initial evidence of governments adapting to a more global economy. The network economy will fuel the need for co-ordination and some form of global governance as economies become connected.

At the same time, people and organisations are becoming more closely connected to governments and the political process through improved communications technologies. The global network is providing access to much more information by putting many government resources at their fingertips. EUROPE DIRECT is part of the European Union's effort to provide citizens with information about rights and opportunities in a single market, job listings, free advice from experts, and a mechanism to provide feedback or ask questions to the European Commission. The European Union also plans on placing all existing legislation on its EUROPA Web site, making it freely available to all Internet users.

At the local level, city governments such as those in Barcelona or Bologna have moved aggressively into the network economy with efforts to connect their governments and citizens more closely. In Barcelona, the city council will place an abundance of public information and pending issues on the Internet for review and reaction from citizens. Citizens will be able give their opinions through polls, contribute ideas and suggestions, and have discussions with other online citizens, experts, or municipal officials. Similarly, the IPERBOLE project, started in 1995 in Bologna, connects citizens with over 240 municipal offices, discussion groups on relevant issues, and even free Internet access to some individuals (in an effort to educate people about the Internet). IPERBOLE boasts 13,000 citizen users and roughly 15,000 visitors per day.[16] The projects in both cities aim to empower the citizens in the democratic process as well as create a transparent government system that gains the support and trust of its citizens.

Citizens and organisations are also using the network to exchange information, and to enable the organisation of political and social groups. In the UK, the UK Citizens Online Democracy (UKCOD) was established in 1996 by citizens to provide political information and democratic discussion about many issues. During the 1997 election, UKCOD ran discussion forums on major policy areas that received limited attention from mainstream media, and more recently is involved in a forum aimed at informing citizens and involving them in the discussions surrounding the UK's Freedom of Information Bill. The discussions and feedback about the Freedom of Information White Paper are publicly available, allowing citizens to be informed and connected to the process. Another example of how the network economy is spurring change by giving citizens and organisations a stronger voice in government through the ability to come together is the emergence of a coalition of business executives, journalists, and members of parliaments throughout Europe called InterParle. This group has set up a Web site called Virtual InterParle, intended to facilitate dialogue among Europe's 4,818 nationally elected politicians, in an effort to provide information and open dialogue about European issues.

10.5 European Competitiveness

The rapid growth of the network economy raises serious competitive concerns for European businesses. The network economy promises to alter competition among regions. Many issues discussed so far, such as workforce flexibility, network commerce infrastructure development, tax policies, availability of capital, and many others affect regional ability to attract and build new businesses and to compete successfully with established ones. With the proper environment, businesses and workers will seek more fertile ground in which to grow. The network economy is fuelling the growth of a global business environment in which all players can connect in order to be most successful.

The network revolution is occurring. This time of change and uncertainty presents the opportunity for success and the threat of failure. Everyone involved in the network economy is striving to understand the possibilities, and while some governments such as Singapore's are attempting to use the Internet as a springboard into economic strength, other governments are taking a more passive approach and letting businesses take the lead. Either way, a complete effort by citizens, businesses, and governments will be needed for regional success. The key to the network economy lies in embracing change but working hard to make it lead to a healthier society.

Singapore ONE

National Competitiveness

Singapore ONE (One Network for Everyone) is the world's first nation-wide broadband network. Promoted by the government of Singapore, it is part of a greater design to build an "intelligent island," or a hub for network commerce. It comprises two main elements:

- A 155 Mbps backbone operated by the 1-Net Singapore Pte Ltd. Consortium.
- More than fifty services offered by public and private entities to over 5,000 users.

End users connect to the backbone either using ADSL technology through Singapore Telecom or by cable modem through Singapore Cable Vision. Government, information, learning, entertainment, financial, business, and shopping services are available to individuals, businesses, and schools.

Singapore ONE is only one element in a strategy to transform the island into a network commerce hub. This strategy relies on the development of a mature market, an adequate regulatory environment, and the necessary infrastructure. Singapore's government, business, and technical constituencies arrived quickly at this proactive approach, while other countries are still sorting out the issues.

Since 1981, Singapore's government has striven to computerise its administration. Today, there is one PC for every two government employees in Singapore. In households, PC penetration has reached 41 percent and 300,000 in a population of 3 million are Internet users (10 percent penetration). Already, 100,000 people have filed their income taxes via the Internet.

In order to support companies trying to make business online and to make the infrastructure more cost-competitive, a second telecom operator has been awarded a license. Singapore also boasts strong logistics and fulfilment capabilities. For example, it takes only six hours for a container boat to turn around. Already a major financial centre in Asia, Singapore has built data houses and call centres, and wants, ultimately, to host network commerce platforms.

The policy and regulatory environment are also being upgraded to accommodate network commerce activities. An "e-transaction bill" has recently been integrated into the commercial code, in particular to set up a public key infrastructure (rules regarding electronic signatures and certification authorities, etc.). Certification authorities have been set up and smart card schemes (e.g. for home banking) have been rolled out.

A seller of physical goods could build a warehouse, make transactions, and ship its products from Singapore. This would be all the more the case with digital goods. In fact, given that network commerce transcends borders, various locations throughout the world will likely strive to accommodate network merchants. Network commerce in Singapore is seen as "the next engine for growth."

s-one.net.sg

10.6 Summary

In this chapter we have explored the broader social arena to consider the potential impact of the network revolution on work, culture, society, and politics. The ultimate impact on these aspects of our lives is likely to be great, but it is much too early to discuss with certainty the dimensions or timing of these changes. Many jobs have already been created by the network economy, but many national workforces are not properly skilled to build the network economy. Job training and new educational emphases will be necessary to create skilled workers and to ease the transition of those whose jobs will be destroyed. Finally, new global cultural and interest groups are emerging and political power is being further diffused by the ability of citizens and others to organise on the network.

RECOMMENDATIONS

While the broader social impact of the network revolution will not be felt as rapidly as its impact on business, it will, nonetheless, affect virtually every aspect of society. Some effects of the network revolution are already apparent; other potential implications are beginning to come into focus. Many of these broader implications are relevant to businesses, and many have deeper implications for governments. While it is too early to know the significance of these changes, there are many important trends that governments and businesses should track.

Businesses

- *Actively retrain and move current employees to higher-value jobs.* Improve employee skills and create employee incentives to pursue continued formal education, such as in-house training programs, subsidies for continuing education, and sabbaticals for employees to upgrade skills. Invest in training programs and actively partner with educational institutions.
- *Provide globally competitive salaries and incentives in order to attract and retain skilled workers.* The network economy is de facto a global marketplace for talent. Skilled workers, especially knowledge workers, can sell their skills across geographic and political boundaries with relative ease. Firms must evaluate the salaries and benefits they offer against those offered in other countries around the world.
- *Recognise that relationships between governments and businesses are shifting, creating greater opportunities for businesses to participate in governance, but also challenging businesses to take on greater responsibilities.* Government power is becoming more diffuse as governments choose to play more selective roles in society and as bilateral and multilateral organisations play greater roles in influencing (or even directly regulating) various spheres of government activity (especially trade activities). Businesses must responsibly act upon self-regulation opportunities and work with governments world-wide to create a global business environment that fosters network commerce.
- *Target communities of interest as well as communities of geography.* As we have noted elsewhere, geographical boundaries are blurring, creating opportunities for savvy firms to effectively target markets built around global communities of interest and cultural groups.

Content Firms

- *Ensure that all employees are technology-literate and that they develop skills to complement their traditional content skills.* Content firms are technology firms. Employees should be technology-literate. Most content firms are likely to employ a substantial number of information technology professionals (e.g. software developers, programmers).
- *Seek opportunities to market to global populations with common language.* Recognise that the global population of users speaking a given language may already be large enough to support a network business even if the local market is relatively undeveloped.
- *Develop educational products and services to help improve skills.* Education is a huge market for content; by providing for this market, firms can both generate additional revenues and contribute to the training of better skilled workers. Training and education programs will continue to be a rapidly growing market for content.

Governments

- *Evaluate and, where appropriate, remove limits on employment flexibility (e.g. contracting regulations, "red tape" around hiring and dismissal of employees).* This is a delicate issue, but many European businesses have found that limits on their ability to add and remove employees place significant strains on their ability to respond to changing market conditions. Network-enabled firms tend to be leaner, more flexible organisations, relying on communications technology to take the place of middle-layer employees. It is difficult for incumbent firms to adopt network-enabled organisational structures because of their inability to remove or replace labour.
- *Develop subsidies to help redundant workers cope with change.* Employees will inevitably be dislocated by the development of the network economy. Governments can play an important role helping these employees retrain and find new or better jobs.
- *Promote education and training initiatives to address the need for skilled, flexible workers.* This includes, developing life-long learning programs, promoting changes in curricula to reflect new skills needed by graduating students, and partnering with businesses to develop education and training programs that focus on real-world needs and employability. To this end, governments can facilitate interaction between businesses and educational institutions to improve relevance and quality of education.
- *Provide funding to connect schools to network.* Schools are a key arena for introducing the population to network technologies. In addition, the network provides access to a tremendous wealth of educational and cultural resources.
- *Use networks to more effectively communicate with citizens, and move government activities to networks.* Facilitate interaction between governments and constituents. Reconsider the role of government in various sectors. Migrate political processes to the network (e.g. voting, interaction with citizens and businesses on policy issues).
- *Promote national culture by placing cultural assets on the network.* Governments must recognise that the global network is a cultural as well as business marketplace. Government can play an important role in making sure that national and regional cultures are well represented in this marketplace. In addition, governments can partner with businesses to exploit cultural assets in the global marketplace (e.g. digitising public-domain information and making it available to businesses).
- *Help to create social acceptance of change (e.g. create interest and enthusiasm in the new economy, explain the social and economic costs of not changing).* The network revolution means change, and many people are afraid of change. Much fear of change arises from uncertainty about how it will affect people's lives. At their best, governments can help to demystify change and provide a positive vision of the future.

Notes

1. Giga Information Group.

2. Andrew Craig, "Tech-Skills Shortage Threatens Europe," *TechWeb News*, 10 March 1998.

3. Joan Warner, "Lessons from the European Tigers," *Business Week*, 6 July 1998.

4. John Burgess, "Sons and Daughters of Ireland, Come Home," *International Herald Tribune*, 18 March 1998.

5. OECD, 1998 Employment Outlook.

6. Sergio Arzeni, "Entrepreneurship and Job Creation," The OECD Observer, December 1997/January 1998.

7. OECD; Silvio Scaglia, "Europe Has the Capital to Create Jobs, if It Chooses To," *International Herald Tribune,* 16 June 1998.

8. Paul Floren, "Euro-Techies: Scarce and Valuable," *International Herald Tribune*, 6 April 1998.

9. Michael Smith, "Signs of Progress in EU Campaign for More Jobs," *Financial Times*, 12 June 1998.

10. Andrew Bogler, "Insecurity at Work on the Increase Says CBI," *Financial Times* (London), 4 June 1998.

11. William Tucker, "Biting the Hand that Feeds Us," *The American Spectator*, May 1998.

12. Ibid.

13. Gail Edmonson, "Spain's Success," *Business Week,* 3 August 1998.

14. "EURES: Developing the European Labour Market," *RAPID*, 9 July 1998.

15. Jim Erickson, "Cyberspeak: The Death of Diversity," *Asiaweek*, 3 July 1998.

16. Democracy and Government OnLine Services - Contributions from Public Administrations around the World, G7 GOL.

Appendix A
European Commission Directorate General XIII/E

Our thanks to the European Commission Directorate General XIII/E for the opportunity to undertake this study and for its support as we brought this project to completion.

EUROPEAN COMMISSION
Directorate General XIII/E
Telecommunications, information market and exploitation of research

Mr. R. Frans de Bruïne, Director
Mr. Wolfgang Huber
Dr. Massimo Garribba

Appendix B
Steering Committee Members

We would like to thank the members of the CONDRINET Steering Committee for their valuable comments and assistance in the completion of the study.

Gianni Bellisario
Director, RAI Educational
Via Ettore Romagnoli 20
00137 Rome
Italy
Fax: +39 06 36 86 86 92
Bellisa3@aol.com

Eric Blot-Lefèvre
Trésorier, Thomson CSF
President, ECE
173, boulevard Hausmann
75415 Paris Cedex 08
France
Fax: +33 1 53 77 81 71
Eric.blot-lefevre@ec-europe.org

Dr. Brian Blunden
President, AIRTO
Chairman & CEO, IEPRC
Pira House, Randalls Road
Leatherhead
Surrey, KT22 7RU
UK
Fax: +44 1372 802 242
Blunden@pira.co.uk

Dr. Margot Blunden-Willms
Company Secretary, IEPRC
admin.ieprc@pira.co.uk

Dr. Stéphane Boudon
Directeur de la Production, Masson - Havas
Publication Edition
120, Boulevard St. Germain
F-75006 Paris
France
Fax: +33 (0) 1 40 46 60 01
S.boudon@masson.fr

Stig Carlson
Directeur Général, EAAA
Rue Saint-Quentin 5
B-1000 Bruxelles
Belgium
Fax: +32 2 230 09 66
stig.carlson@eaaa.be

Dr. Marcel Coderch Collell
Director of R&D, Grupo Anaya
Calle Juan Ignacio
Luca de Tena 15
28027 Madrid
Spain
Fax: +34 1 742 6631
mcoderch@anya.es

Johan Hjelm
Consultant (previously with The Bonnier Group)
Tomtebogatan 46
113 38 Stockholm
Sweden
Fax: +46 8 30 40 77

Dr. Erik Hupkens van der Elst
Director Business Development & Analysis, VNU
Ceylonpoort 5-25
P.O. Box 4028
2003 Haarlem
The Netherlands
Fax: +31 23 546 39 04
e.van.der.elst@hq.vnu.com

Reinhold Schulzki
Head of Digital Media, Siemens Nixdorf
Servicesall 11
Ruhrallee 165
45136 Essen
Germany
Fax: +49 201 266 1501
reinhold.schulzki@rw.sni.de

Appendix C
Participants in Interviews and Round Tables

Round Table Participants

Chem Assayag
Sales Manager
Open TV (France)

Robert Bense
Business Architect, New Products
Philips (The Netherlands)

Ad Latjes
Chairman
European Travel Network (The Netherlands)

Jean-Etienne Bouédec
Project Manager
La Française des Jeux (France)

Laurent Carozzi
Financial Analyst/Media
Paribas (UK)

Pieter Casneuf
Business Development Director
AdValvas (Belgium)

Fernando Cortiñas Luquez
Marketing Director
Via Digital (Spain)

Andrew Doe
Business Development Director
Line One (UK)

Ralf Heublein
Head of Network Management
Premiere (Germany)

Patrick Kerven
Marketing Director
Fridayware (France)

Gert Köhler
Managing Director
Technologieholding VC (Germany)

Paul-Louis Meunier
Manager, Advanced Marketing & New Products
Thomson Multimedia (France)

Michael Simmons
VP Marketing, Sales & Customer Service
A2000 (The Netherlands)

Amaury Simon
Multimedia Services Manager
Eutelsat (France)

Alain Staron
Director of New Services
TPS (France)

Caroline Vincent
Business Development
Planète Livre (France)

David Windsor-Clive
Chairman
IMVS (UK)

Interviewees

Stefan Andersson
Business Area Director for Commerce
Scandanavia Online (Sweden)

Catherine Barba
Director
DDB Interactive France (France)

Joel Berger
Manager New Media
Sony Music (Germany)

Jean-Michel Billaut
Director
L'Atelier de Paribas (France)

Stéphane Boudon
Director of Production
Masson-Havas Publication Edition (France)

Michele Castegnaro
Marketing Manager Europe
3COM (France)

Spiro Coutsoucos
Director of Operations and New Initiatives
Elemond Mondadori (Italy)

Françoise Crausse-Saugier
Head of Electronic Publishing
L'Expansion (France)

Erhard Engelmann
Director of Electronic Banking
Deutsche Bank (Germany)

Alain Fages
Product Manger ADSL
France Télécom (France)

Sam Gazal
Digital Business Development Manager
British Sky Broadcasting Ltd. (UK)

Steffan Hillberg
CEO
Bonnier Online (Sweden)

Thomas Kirchenkamp
Managing Director
Ravensburger Interactive Media GmbH (Germany)

Timo Koskinen
Digital Media Specialist
Nokia (Finland)

Marie-Christine Lepany
Director of Media
Carat Multimedia (France)

Paolo Parlavecchia
Head of Rizzoli New Media
RCS Libri & Grandi Opere (Italy)

Joël Poix
Director of Multimedia
Infogrames (France)

Paul-Dominique Pomart
Electronic Publishing and Documentation
Bayard Presse (France)

Hans-Peter Rohner
Senior Vice President
Publigroupe (Switzerland)

Participants in Interviews and Round Tables

Emmanuelle Rosenfeld
Montparnasse Multimédia (France)

Reiner Schmitt
Managing Director
Mediacom (Germany)

Benedict Tompkins
Managing Director
Broadview Associates (UK)

Agnès Touraine
CEO
Havas Interactive (France)

Jean-Pascal Tranié
Director of Multimedia
Cegetel (France)

Hans Wachtel
Managing Director
G&J Electronic Media Service GmbH (Germany)

Alan Williams
Partner
Denton Hall (UK)

Kei-Ishiro Yoshida
Senior Producer, Program Production Department
NHK (Japan)

Appendix D
Additional Case Studies

AdValvas

www.advalvas.be

Founded in Belgium in 1995, AdValvas maintains secure directories for consumers and businesses. In three years, AdValvas has generated a critical mass of users and is being courted by some of Belgium's biggest firms.

AdValvas has integrated a number of security technologies in order to protect the availability, integrity, and confidentiality of information. It provides physical infrastructures and a number of services and technologies, including identification and authentication, privilege definition, encryption, and audit capabilities. Directories (white and yellow pages) provide search facilities, direct connectivity to the registered users, sophisticated information such as video and sound, as well as a natural front end for network commerce. AdValvas also maintains a registry, by linking directories to databases of certificates. It has partnerships with Belsign (which uses Verisign technology) and with Trusted Third Parties (TTPs). It also keeps track electronically of service provision proofs (integrity, confidentiality). Its aim is to provide a public key infrastructure (PKI) for secure, trusted network computing applications.

A light, flexible, and co-operative business model, AdValvas has developed a wide range of activities:

- Person-to-person messaging: white and yellow pages, email, SMS (short messages to GSM phones).
- Person-to-multiperson messaging: online chat, customised newsletter (push).
- Publishing or content-based services: news, TV listings, job postings, concert listings.
- Network commerce: magazine subscriptions, classified ads, coupons, music, books, fast food.

AdValvas has developed a light, flexible, and co-operative business model meeting three objectives:

- Combine all possible revenue streams.
- Serve narrow communities while keeping up with technological innovation.
- Avoid double investments and obtain higher returns on technology investments.

According to AdValvas, pragmatism and opportunism should prevail in the rapidly evolving network commerce environment. No revenue stream should be ignored.

AdValvas strives to a have a focused marketing strategy. Its core competence is to manage online communities by leveraging directories and communication services. It is challenged to target narrow communities and, at the same time, to foster a critical mass of users. This formula is critical to ensuring quality service. To resolve this dilemma, AdValvas has created a decentralised and modular organisation. AdValvas is composed of a dozen companies, some concentrating on technology-driven services, others delivering content and communications services directly to end users (as described above).

A hub for online communities

AdValvas aims to be a hub for online communities, centred around professions or regions, either open or closed. Through direct relationships with customers, the company has the power to "control the value chain and thus the business." It plays an intermediary role as a technology "integrator." "Each subsidiary is such an integrator, developing its own value chain and teaming up with a specific set of technology suppliers."

This organisation enables on-going technological innovation by sharing expensive resources between the various companies, while each of them serve a specific market or community. All the subsidiaries are placed under a holding company, as well as under a unique front end, a strong brand, and franchising rules. The capital structure is kept flexible as well (options for share transfers, share swaps, or share acquisitions). Still, AdValvas tries to ensure that "the glue is strong enough to keep the units together into one broad initiative."

As its business model and activity constantly evolve, AdValvas is naturally moving toward providing a network commerce platform. For example, it takes part in the deployment of the Proton micropayment facility, based on smart cards. Its partners in this endeavour are among the leading international and Belgian firms: Microsoft, Banksys, Netvision, EUnet Belgium, and PING.

Scandinavia Online

www.scandinavia-online.se

SOL is an online service owned by Telia (40 percent), Shipsetdt (40 percent) and Telenor (20 percent). SOL markets various products and services: tickets for events, travel, online shopping (through the electronic marketplace Passagen), financial services, online gaming, information services, and advertising services. SOL's mission is to "create and operate leading Internet services helping the individual to live a more effective and stimulating life. SOL believes in the Internet and its money-making potential on the B-to-C market," said Stefan Andersson, Business Area Manager for Trade.

SOL has undergone a learning process. Inevitably, it made mistakes in the beginning:

- SOL did not understand the importance of having detailed trade knowledge (especially competitive dynamics).
- SOL overestimated market and customer maturity. As a result, it invested too much too soon.
- SOL did not understand the importance of having (and gathering) intimate knowledge of end-user habits and needs.

After two years, Stefan Andersson sees two main key success factors:

- Having strong industry knowledge (value chains, competitive dynamics).
- Having the right resources (both financial and human). "It is very important to have the right technology competence within the company," Andersson noted.

In order to learn continuously, SOL also watched the US market closely. It sought to identify companies likely to enter the European, Scandinavian or Swedish markets — to determine how it could beat them — as well as companies unlikely to enter those markets, to determine what could be learned and "borrowed" from them.

SOL would not disclose how much its owners had invested in it. It is publicly known that Telia, for example, has invested about 400 million Swedish Kronor in developing Passagen, its electronic marketplace. According to Andersson, the pay-back time, product by product, service by service, is going to be lengthy. Given that network commerce is still emerging and changing continuously, SOL knows that revenue sources will have to evolve over time. Today's advertising-based model will evolve, and as a result, transactions will become much more prevalent.

Revenue Sources	Today	Over Time
Advertising	90%	50%
Subscriptions	5%	5%
Transactions	5 %	30%
New sources	-	15%

The sale of demographic and sociographic information about the end users will generate new sources of revenue. "We intend to sell this information for a high price!" said Andersson. Transactions and other "new sources" are expected to become the driving revenue sources long-term. The business model also implies indirect revenues. Passagen, the online mall, generates a lot of traffic for Telia. From that perspective it is profitable.

Sony Music Germany

www.sonymusic.de

Currently, music companies are unable to exploit fully the potential of interactive networks. "Because of copyright, it [Sony Music Germany] is not allowed to aggregate songs from different artists. And the choice was made not to allow the sale of single tracks. Therefore, the idea to provide a service by which consumers would be able to make their own pot-pourri is not possible," explained Joel Berger, Manager New Media at Sony Music Germany. "The pre-packaged goods (someone picks the songs for you, as is the case with usual discs) will prevail," he added.

"What we try to do at the moment is to provide services around the product. But even if we keep it only to promotion, there is a huge field which we have not tapped into yet. It would be perfect if we could design, for example, the Jean-Jacques Goldman site. We could bundle music with content, ticketing, selling tee-shirts, etc," Berger added.

Sony Music has created one big database containing content from its various European units. An approval process has been designed to make that content available for listening via the Web (in RealAudio). Sony Music notifies a producer when it wants to put an music sample online. The producer then contacts the artist, and if the artist approves, the excerpt is put online. The standard sample is thirty seconds in length, and is played using streaming media to prevent digital copying.

For example, a site called Net Noize incorporates excerpts of new releases into ten-minute broadcasts, similar to radio shows. Production costs limit the length of each broadcast to ten minutes. Subscribers who complete a questionnaire receive a newsletter on new releases.

Sony plans to enhance its database to include images, text, and video in addition to music. The music is already digitally formatted, and Sony Music plans to remaster, and consequently digitise the old analogue content.

"We thought of a juke box, whereby people would buy by the piece. But we will probably not do it because of the legal issues. A "radio" Web site would be hard to control. Sony Music only has the right to distribute content, not to provide it," Berger said.

Appendix E
Quotes From Interviews and Round Tables

"Having the Content Is a Huge Comparative Advantage"

"Newspapers and magazines have a very important potential on digital networks, on the condition that they provide real usage value on their sites and that they are able to provide to advertisers sophisticated tools to measure and qualify their audience. The capacity to provide audience data of high quality and with maximum availability is a key differentiating factor."
Head of a French online advertising purchasing agency.

"Now Microsoft says: "Give me the content." Companies like Microsoft are world-wide organisations; they already have partnerships with IBM, Sony, Philips, Lockheed, etc. This does not mean a company like ours will disappear, this just means that we are not in the AAA category. We are just a content provider. We are too small, except for very specific local needs. Even world-wide companies now have Italian versions of their sites. In the online world, we might even lose distribution, which we had as broadcasters."
Director of the educational division of a television production firm.

"We have a network and calculation systems, which we manage and monitor, spanning over 100 countries. We have customers, whom we know intimately. But to sell content, we need editorial, design, and marketing skills. Therefore, we will still need content providers. All players should concentrate on their core competencies and make the relevant partnerships."
Head of electronic banking for a German bank.

"In this new strategic context, there are two key success factors for content providers:

- First, the ability to continuously adapt content to modes of consumption and to deliver it over any relevant platform at any given time (owning rights without having this capacity is worthless)
- Second, the ability to associate strong brands and characters to this multimedia know-how in an international setting
- In this context, Infogrames's strategy is to create assets which can be exploited fast through the relevant distribution networks on a given time. The same approach will apply to interactive networks."

French publisher of electronic games.

"Content creation and distribution are two different competencies. Content creators now have the possibility to distribute their content directly and/or to leverage content to sell, but I am not quite sure that they should do it. On the contrary, there will obviously be an impact on the distribution industry because of dematerialisation, but this does not mean that distributors will disappear."
CEO of a French interactive publishing firm.

"It is all a matter of content, whatever the media. Having the content is a huge comparative advantage."
Managing Director of a multimedia subsidiary of a board games publisher.

"A huge transformation of editorial processes."

"The true revolution is occurring in content production. Content should be digital from the upstream side and all the way down, structured in databases in a platform-neutral format, and distributable on various delivery channels to accommodate for the various end-user contexts. Therefore, content creators must learn how to structure their content. However, this does not necessarily apply to all markets (some markets may not need that). We are working on this structuring of content with a publisher of encyclopedias."
CEO of a French interactive publishing firm.

"Today, e-publishing develops on the fringe of the core processes. The next challenge will be a huge transformation of editorial processes in the organisation. The objective is to create more value by leveraging brands, the customer base and the portfolio of authors, with a global perspective. In the future, authors will not see a final copy anymore. Authors will have to finalise a semi-finished product (instead of a finished one, to allow for multiformat packaging). Publishers will be in charge of packaging this content in several formats. Printers will have to return digital versions for further reprint. Gains are important in the area of production costs. In the professional media, comparative costs for one page are 12 euro for a magazine, 0,15 euro for a book and 0,07 euro for the Web."
Director of Production for a scientific and professional publishing group.

"Our Web site lets buyers of our encyclopedia download updates on the 15th of each month. About 3,500 people download the update (500kb) every month on average. In fact, they are 5,000 or 6,000 of the same customers who make all the downloads. Maybe some of them give the diskette to friends, but still this number is much less than the 210,000 buyers of the encyclopedia. We also provide extra exercises and links to resources online to users of *Speak Up!*, a monthly magazine used to learn English. The magazine was already on cassettes, in video and on CD-ROM. Online components come in three forms:

1. Updates allow consumers to make their product anew. They must not change the index in order to keep a consistent product.
2. Chats and virtual communities, although they do not work very well.
3. Complementary material. For example, exercises and articles for *Speak up!* linked to the CD-ROM are available online, along with tutoring services (correction of exams)."

Director of the offline multimedia subsidiary of a publishing group.

"Who will be able to capture the value of customer relationships?"

"There is a traditional physical value chain and an "information value chain." The question is: where will value be created in the latter and who is going to capture it? What really is at stake is the B-to-C market because that is where one-to-one marketing will be used. The challenge is to develop customer relationships and to capture this relationship's value. The customer (with whom you have established a relationship) has a quantifiable value. This value is not the same whether, for example, it is a France Loisirs or a Canal+ customer. At the same time, multi-channel distribution strategies will develop. End users will assemble the content components they need. One must bear in mind that one-to-one marketing is very nice but it requires specific competencies."
CEO of a French interactive publishing firm.

"We tested Firefly-like tools in Germany, but they are difficult to implement. I am not sure the results of the searches correspond to the actual tastes of the consumers. The risk is then that people get disappointed and do not come back."
Manager of an online music store.

"New media makes publishers enter in a direct marketing logic, which is new to them, because of the possibility to have permanent direct contact with the customers. It brings up a difficult question: How to fully integrate into the marketing strategy the exploitation of the precious information received from the field? How to sell directly to the public using the direct marketing tools on the network? The need for good Web site management is one of the unexpected implications of the development of the Internet. The management of the customer interface requires a lot of people, who have a very important role. On the Internet, the quality of the answers sent to clients is a critical element of the publisher's offering."
Head of Electronic Publishing at a major French economic news magazine.

"You can imagine competition coming from anywhere."

"In the specific healthcare area, pharmaceutical laboratories are prevented by law to propose free services to doctors. This protects publishers. But in other areas, you can imagine competition coming from anywhere. For example, lawyers can use their specific knowledge and case law to propose (by themselves, therefore bypassing publishers) very effective information to corporate lawyers or to specific targets. Banks can become genuine competitors for the financial print media."
Director of Production for a scientific and professional publishing firm.

"Entry into the digital information market implies the positioning on a new value chain, and that creates new competition between publishers and software publishers. The software publishers are in fact one of the most dangerous new

entrants in the content market: Microsoft's market share of digital encyclopedias (70 percent) brings evidence to it."
Head of Electronic Publishing at a major French economic news magazine.

"Service corporations are seeing competition coming from content providers. Look for example at the alliance that Deutsche Telekom made with AOL."
Head of Electronic Banking for a German bank.

"Of course Nokia could also be a possible partner, but since they own an interface to the end user, in the shape of their mobile phones, and since they work more and more toward software developing, as well as a mix of content and distribution of content, you'd better watch out."
Business Area Manager (Trade) of an online directory and community.

"The window of opportunity is still open for new entrants."

"I do not believe that small start-ups will be able to compete massively against big companies. Big companies still have the possibility to come back and be present when it is time, because they have financial means and they have the content."
Head of Electronic Publishing at a major French economic news magazine.

"Big companies have access to capital but they are inflexible. Therefore, there will always be room for new companies. For example, Philips was beaten by Ubisoft. Ubisoft will remain independent if it performs well. It could become difficult if growth happened to slow down. As long as the share price is high, it should be OK. Actually, the game is just starting. The window of opportunity will remain open for some time."
Managing Director of an M&A and venture capital firm in the UK.

"Employees in big incumbent firms are not computer-literate (e.g. Belgacom). They are not tough competitors. They are still invoice-driven instead of community-driven. In the latter case, there can be no revenues on the first day. Nobody knows how revenues will be made. People do not want to change. The window of opportunity is still open. Nobody understands how this new economy works."
Head of Business Development for an online community/commerce site.

"Barnes & Noble would never have done what they are doing without Amazon.com."
Commercial Director of a UK-based online service.

"People in start-ups accept reduced wages in exchange for a carott (stocks). Start-ups incur half the costs compared to multinationals. It is difficult for

incumbents to develop network commerce internally. Internal politics kill enterprise."
Chairman of an online music shop in the UK.

"We provided capital to the founder of Intershop (publisher of a very successful software used to create virtual shops), a twenty-four-year-old German. Everybody thought he would fail. When we took him to the Silicon Valley to set up his operations there, we realised that it was his first time in the US! Three months later, he had succeeded in hiring thirty Internet specialists, while people thought he would never hire anyone at salaries of $40,000 a year. One of the secrets for this success was that he allowed people to smoke at the office! This was only one sign that he had a new behaviour, a new spirit."
Managing Director of a German venture capital firm.

"The problems with start-ups is the lack of business skills."

"The problem with start-ups in Europe is the lack of management education of the entrepreneurs, of business skills. We see thirty to forty start-ups every week, among which only one or two are well thought out. The money exists but the market is not efficient. Regional development agencies could help to teach how to make a business plan, how to get capital. By contrast, the Americans are more entrepreneurial, have more MBAs."
Managing Director of an M&A and venture capital firm in the UK.

"(We) do some internal financing, but also some external financing. For example, we bought a game company and we made an IPO in Sweden. Even though we do some venture capital financing (for outside companies), we cannot do everything. Entrepreneurs usually bring an idea, eighty-hour weeks and enthusiasm. But most often, they never ran a company. Therefore, we bring capital (seed money and at later stages too) and management capabilities. We are also psychologists."
CEO of an online publishing firm.

"As a venture capitalist, what I am looking for is the thinking behind, not the figures. I need to know what is the vision, who are the people and what is their strategy. That is the business concept. A business plan with five pages of concept and fifty pages of figures is ridiculous. I know it is the right company primarily by intuition."
Managing Director of a German venture capital firm.

"In order to succeed, you also need to be in the Top 10 sites on Alta-Vista. And last, you need to put yourself in your customer's position, which is not often what is on traditional retailers' minds."
Chairman of an online music shop in the UK.

"Start-ups need visibility. It is expensive to advertise as the Internet creates monopolies, for example search engines. Sooner or later, there will be a limited number of sites (in a given sector) able to survive."
Chairman of a Dutch virtual travel agency.

"The key success factors are to gather a critical mass of users, to build a strong community, to get visibility and to get the good people."
A French entrepreneur who founded a chat service on the Internet.

"In start-up companies, you can pay people less in exchange for stock options. But in Europe, we are not so used to that."
Commercial Director of a UK-based online service.

"Start-ups need access to capital."

"The USA is a large, homogeneous market. It also has a sophisticated financial market and a large venture capital community, which is more specialised, with a large number of venture capital companies in each market. Exit is easier in the US, for example through floatation. Europe is a split market. There is little co-operation between venture capital firms, and exit strategies are more difficult because the various markets are distinct, regionally-focused. This financial market makes it difficult to spot the right companies."
Managing Director of an M&A and venture capital firm in the UK.

"Start-ups need access to capital and creativity."
Chairman of a Dutch virtual travel agency.

"In the US, the NASDAQ has been very patient, in particular given the massive marketing investments which must be made. Still today, everybody is valued as a winner. As far as IMVS is concerned, I worked in the City and I know how finance works and this helps me a lot since raising capital is crucially important. At the same time, some of the well-known failures in the UK were among the most capitalised."
Chairman of an online music shop in the UK.

"It is becoming easier for venture capitalists to exit, mainly by listing the company either in Europe or the US. The main criteria for an exit strategy are price, liquidity, lower volatility and the emergence of new capital markets (a.k.a. the *Nouveau Marché* in France). Also, the image of start-ups is a problem. Most of the time in Europe, becoming an entrepreneur is always the last choice. But an entrepreneur can earn more than an employee. Those who dare are actually motivated by money."
Managing Director of a German venture capital firm.

"Being an entrepreneur is a state of mind. Some people who already made money are ready to put it back (business angels). This is especially true in the US."
Commercial Director of a UK-based online service.

"We have a lot cash in our subsidiaries (about ten of them, each with their own business model). Cross participations in Belgium are limited to 10 percent. Therefore, when cash flows in one subsidiary, we capitalise it."
Head of Business Development for an online community/commercial Web site.

"There is not one revenue model."

"There is not one revenue model, it is early to say. You have to try them, you should understand all of them. You will need to mix them anyway. Banner advertising is hopeless. If it works, fine, otherwise, too bad. But you cannot build a business on it. People are willing to pay subscriptions, even in the B-to-C market. (We) have products which are very focused, others which are for a wide audience. Those products have different revenue models."
CEO of an online publishing firm.

"The business models based on transactions have the most potential. As for subscriptions, people are not used to paying for content."
Managing Director of an M&A and venture capital firm in the UK.

"We sell sales leads, about 3 euro each, to travel agencies. This provides us with 80 percent of our revenues."
Chairman of a Dutch virtual travel agency.

"We derive most of our revenues from transactions (80 percent books, 18 percent music), plus advertising and the sale of data about consumers."
Business Development Executive for a French firm specialising in building online bookshops.

"Ninety-nine percent of our revenues comes from transactions. Advertising is mostly used internally, between our various services. We have not decided whether advertising was relevant to us. We also market our customer database."
Chairman of an online music shop in the UK.

"Selling services to businesses (for example Web site development) is a new and important source of revenues for start-ups. As far as we are concerned, subscriptions make up 90 percent of our revenues. We get most of the rest from advertising, and we try to personalise it by tracking and building profiles.

We sell this advertising with a 25 percent premium although the goal is still to make volume."
Commercial Director of a UK-based online service.

"You can also imagine to get commissions from telcos on the traffic you generate on telecommunication networks. Generating traffic is a very important motivation for telcos to move into network commerce. In addition, this kind of traffic is often generated off-peak, and because of fixed costs you can valuate it with a factor of five to ten."
Managing Director of a German venture capital firm.

"(We) have another original source of revenues: we rent chat software tools, for example for one month."
A French entrepreneur who founded a chat service on the Internet.

"It is too early to have a rate of return."

"We are still in a phase of experimentation. In this context, it is crucial to have a portfolio of products to diversify the risk. We cannot pour too much money into these experiments. The level of investment must stay reasonable. We try to determine how much money to spend in exchange for learning, which means: "We are ready to lose that much." Finding the right amount is not easy. Only when we have a budget, we define priorities and we make a business plan. If we need more money, it is possible but a business plan is always needed. It is too early to have a rate of return. We try to reach the break-even point now and we plan to become profitable in three to five years. If we could, we should also measure the intangible benefits of the experiments."
CEO of an online publishing firm.

"We are experimenting, not making money yet. We are still in the midst of developing the infrastructure for those new services. We need to be faster in terms of delivery, in terms of providing satisfaction to customers. We use periods like the Christmas season to test and boost this new business."
Managing Director of the multimedia subsidiary of a board games publisher.

"Our strategy in new media today is to learn and experiment, while keeping ourselves abreast of new market developments. We are betting on our capacity to react to those developments (i.e. to transfer our products on new, promising platforms) and to gather first-hand information about the market (i.e. to be the first to identify those new platforms). We are developing relationships with platform operators such as TPS, Canalsatellite, telcos, etc. The objective of those partnerships is to share with them the results of some experiments. We know we must keep an open mind and be ready to adopt new, innovative means of communication. For example, we could create an interactive gaming TV channel on the model of MTV, based on a community of players and complemented by an Internet site."
French publisher of electronic games.

"Partners need to be complementary."

"As an 'intrapreneur,' I can do things which are not usually allowed inside our parent company, for example co-operate with competitors, choose a competitor for a joint venture when he is more efficient that an internal business unit, as well as fail a lot of times. Our parent is a very decentralised group. When we need to partner with someone inside the group, we select the potential partners and we make a proposition. When we see that it is not worth our time to fight with them, we just take the next one on the list. We do a lot of networking inside the group and internal marketing. And we take those people for one-week business trips in the US twice a year."
CEO of an online publishing firm.

"We need to adapt our products. For that we need synergies, for example to get technologies and budgets, in order to share the risk with other companies. We have not had good experiences with content partners so far. Partners need to be complementary."
Managing Director of the multimedia subsidiary of a board games publisher.

"Traditional media can make alliances with e-commerce firms just to find users. For example, the trade magazine Miller Freeman (part of United News & Media) made a joint venture with OnDemand simply to find users (i.e. extend the customer base)."
Managing Director of an M&A and venture capital firm in the UK.

"In the future, everybody will belong to a community. The leader of this community will negotiate and choose a partner to get exclusive rights for its content. That way, he will be able to actually squeeze its competitors out. Partners can be gold, silver or bronze partners, depending on the level of exclusivity they grant to you."
Head of Business Development for an online community/commercial Web site.

"We have partnerships with other sites in order to generate traffic between our sites. That way we make the economy a media plan."
Business Development Executive of a French firm specialising in building online bookshops.

"You need as many alliances as possible to spark impulse purchases. People need to hear the music at once. Allies can be ISPs, radios, music companies, or sports sites; content providers, in fact. You cannot sell by your own."
Chairman of an online music shop in the UK.

"Content is used more and more as a selling tool."

"The role of content is changing. As content is used more and more to sell all types of products, content production and the ability to use it to attract view-

ers is a major challenge on the Internet, which goes well beyond the sale of content as a stand-alone product. The challenge is to build the most appealing site to attract viewers, to make them loyal and to generate stable traffic, in order to "lock in" a target and to market advertising and services to that target. As a consequence, production of content on the network is not the monopoly of traditional content firms anymore. New players coming from other sectors provide more and more free information, for example with the sole purpose of creating traffic (e.g. Yahoo!)."
Head of an online advertising space purchasing agency.

"There are two schools of thought. For the first one, the customer should only be provided with the basic information directly related to the product and then buy it. According to the second school of thought, the customer should be provided with a large amount of information, for example recipes in connection to foodstuffs. We take both schools into consideration, since the same customer may have different needs on different occasions."
Business Area Manager (Trade) of an online service.

"You need to put the content in the right context. It must match the consumer's need."
Business Development Executive for a French firm specialising in building online bookshops.

"Books and music are different. A book is a considered purchase, not an impulse purchase. Therefore, is it relevant to link a book site to a music site to get the same consumers? Maybe classical music would be a good match for books."
Chairman of an online music shop in the UK.

"As we are still in the discovery phase, I am wondering whether we will have to pay for content from music companies. Right now, they do not pay for being listed but they do if they want to actively promote their products on our site. Internet budgeting is on the rise in those companies. Besides, consumers buy more music overall because of the Web and that frees up much of the tension that exists with high street retailers."
Chairman of an online music shop in the UK.

"We actually pay for book extracts and for sounds. It is very complicated to advertise because most publishers or authors do not understand. When we ask permission to put a book extract online, they say: 'You are robbing my book.' But the situation is improving."
Business Development Executive for a French firm specialising in building online bookshops.

"The main difference between Europe and the US is the attitude towards risk."

"First of all, the US are not homogeneous and 70 percent of the US are in many respects behind France for example! Secondly, money is not the problem. In Germany, the amount of venture capital invested in the IT industry has gone from DM500 to DM700 three or five years ago to DM3 billion to DM4 billion. The problem is that the value system in Europe is different. People prefer to live a risk-free life and to prepare their pension plan! What we need to do is to show to people what the opportunities are."
Managing Director of a German venture capital firm.

"I see three main problems: the lack of seed capital, the social cost of employing people and the attitude towards risk."
Chairman of an online music shop in the UK.

"A start-up like us is not even thinking about the risk. We have nothing, therefore, we never see the risk. We started with less than 10,000 euro. We run the firm with the cash flowing from operations. There is risk as soon as there is an upfront investment."
Head of Business Development for an online community/commercial Web site.

"Interactive TV is already network commerce."

"The Internet is information-based. TV, in comparison, provides quick information. And for news services, the more local, the more successful. That is where cable has an advantage because it is local."
VP Marketing, Sales & Customer Service of a cable TV operator offering interactive services.

"Interactive TV is already network commerce. There is no black and white situation. There is room for the Internet, TV, netTVs, etc. The user wants service, whatever the delivery means. And the need is different depending on the delivery channel. TV is maybe for people their armchair, when they come back tired from work... Interactive gaming will develop, as well as medical applications."
Manager, Advanced Marketing & New Products for a multimedia publishing group.

"In the US, over 30 percent of WebTV owners also have a PC. Actually, end users may have certain needs in the living-room. And they may want to do other things in the study room or in other places in the house. It is impossible to say to the TV viewer: 'You need to reboot.' It has to be: 'click and see.' There is a shift from being typical broadcasters to being Internet content makers. HTML can now be put into a video signal and that means that new partnerships will need to be set up. In WebTV trials in the US, the two killer apps

are communication (e-mail) and local news. The main technical hurdle is the payment system."
Business Architect, New Products for a consumer electronics firm.

"We provide an interactive weather service. It is simple, but it is a way to start. Interactive services should generate 1 million euro in 1998. We try to promote impulse pay-per-view and we launched a pilot experience with a bank, Caixa Tarasa, to sell tickets. We are also launching an interactive banking service with Banco Bilbao Vizcaya and Telefonica. The main applications in the future should be home banking, teleshopping and download of games."
Head of Market Studies at a digital satellite TV operator in Spain.

"We are considering interactive gambling on TV. We want to get closer to our customers and TV is the best medium to do this. The market is here and we are ready."
Jean-Etienne Bouédec, Project Manager at a national lottery.

"We provide extensive coverage of the Bundesliga and we started to offer some basic interactive services, such as statistics or the name of the scorer. Tomorrow, while watching a match, viewers will be able to buy tickets, for example. There is no way VOD can develop. In Germany, home banking is the killer app."
Head of Network Management for a pay-TV channel.

"Interactive TV has an advantage: The modem line can be encrypted in order to authenticate people. There are two options to pay. Either you need to pay for pay-per-view; it is easy and natural. Or you need to pay for digital goods. It works with electronic tokens, in two separate transactions. First, you must buy tokens with a smart card inserted in the set-top box. And then you use those tokens stored on the smart card to buy products as you go. Plus, there is no hacker with interactive TV. Moreover, unlike with the Internet, we know our customers. Subscriber management gives confidence to consumers. Our brand is on the remote control, and we are responsible for the merchants on our system. Finally, the Internet implies a lot of non-productive time. I wonder how many sites the average Internet surfer has in his bookmarks. A dozen maybe? A few branded sites (CNN, etc.) and a few focusing on specific topics. We propose 200 interactive services free of charge, and there are no communication costs. Some of our subscribers will always want to be able to go everywhere. In fact, well over half of our subscribers today already have access to the Internet."
Director of New Services for a digital satellite TV operator.

"The Minitel in France works because it is cheap, easy and useful. In the UK, the planned British Interactive Broadcasting service will be cheap and simple, offering banking, shopping and e-mail applications. We should actually be looking for the 'boring app'."
Financial Analyst for the Media sector at a French investment bank, in the UK.

"Demos work well, for example for advertising and sponsoring, and interactive gambling. And there is something else which nobody dares mentioning: Sex. Also, sometimes, the need is not where you expect it. For example, many people now use their TV instead of their stereo to listen to music because it is of good quality.
Sales Manager at an electronic programme guide provider.

"It is very hard to explain the benefits of interactive TV services."

"At the beginning of TV, 80 percent of consumers said they would not want it, ever. They were still 60 percent twenty years later. It takes a generation."
Business Architect, New Products for a consumer electronics firm.

"The education process will accelerate. People will be more and more technology savvy."
VP Marketing, Sales & Customer Service for a cable TV operator offering interactive service.

"It will not be that fast, although we see the emergence of the "screenagers." Consumer habits cannot be changed so rapidly. People know nothing about interactive services. According to our studies, 5 million households in Spain (out of 12 million) are resisting those services. On average, those have lower income, lower education and live in rural areas."
Head of Market Studies at a digital satellite TV operator.

"There is competition for the discretionary entertainment dollar: In the upscale segment, it is very spread out (between various types of entertainment). Those with a lower income, on the contrary, are looking for value."
VP Marketing, Sales & Customer Service for a cable TV operator offering interactive service.

"In fact, it is a bimodal distribution. At one end, the upscale segment buy the capacity to select (between various types of entertainment). At the other end, those in the downscale segment are looking for the best fit for the family. Those who resist more are the mothers. The fathers are the buyers, the children are the prescriptors. There is also the 'chocolate effect:' People resist buying because they know the product is addictive and disruptive."
Head of Market Studies at a digital satellite TV operator.

"It is very hard to explain the benefits of interactive services. To sell our service, we do not use the argument of interactive services."
Director of New Services for a digital satellite TV operator.

"There is a business model for free TV, but not yet for interactive TV."

"The bulk of our revenues are made of subscriptions. We sell space (for malls, home banking, interactive advertising, etc.), and we also get revenues from pay-per-view, micro-transactions and sponsoring. Home banking users can look up their bank account for 0.45 euro, for up to ten times per month. Beyond that, it is free. It is the same conditions as on the Internet. In the short term, the model for interactive TV will be based on subscriptions. In the long term, it will be based on direct marketing."
Director of New Services for a digital satellite TV operator.

"We derive 90 percent of our revenues from subscriptions. Most of our subscribers are fed up with advertising; except for travel services. We also use sponsored programming to lower production costs. For example, we had co-sponsored programming in which various manufacturers of golf clubs could describe their products, allowing viewers to compare. Actually, we should introduce the Quality Rating Point to replace the GRP (Gross Rating Point)."
Head of Market Studies at a satellite TV operator.

"The bundling of video with other services (for example Internet access) generates more opportunities to sell pay-per-view."
VP Marketing, Sales & Customer Service for a cable TV operator offering interactive service.

"The increase of the storage capacity on user access platforms such as WebTV could be subsidised by content providers. They could rent space on the hard drive of those boxes to see their content promoted on the start page proposed by the device, which plays a major role in guiding users in their navigation. Those spaces on the hard drive can be updated overnight."
Business Architect, New Products for a consumer electronics firm.

"The fact of adding new, interactive services is a selling argument. The 'bouquet effect' entails an overall increase of revenues. But while there is a business model for free TV, there is not any yet for digital satellite TV. And, for a banker, the valuation of those new interactive services is zero."
Financial Analyst for the Media sector at a French investment bank in the UK.

Appendix F
Euro Exchange Rates

The following exchange rates were used to convert currencies into euro:

BLF	40.5332
DKR	7.4836
DM	1.96438
PTA	165.887
FF	6.61260
IRL	.747516
LIT	1929.30
HFL	2.21081
OS	13.8240
ESC	198.589
FMK	5.88064
SKR	8.65117
UKL	.692304
USD	1.13404
YEN	137.077
SFR	1.644
NKR	8.01861
CAD	1.56920
AUD	1.52813

Glossary

Bold words in definitions have glossary entries

Altair PC Kit
Generally accepted as the first personal computer, the Altair 8800 was introduced in 1975 as a do-it-yourself kit by a firm called MITS. In 1975, Microsoft founders Bill Gates and Paul Allen wrote a Basic Interpreter for the Altair 8800, which was the first programming language for the PC and the **"killer app"** for the Altair.

Analogue
Varying physically (either in frequency or amplitude) rather than by a code. The human voice is analogue, as is the traditional "plain old telephone service" (POTS) network. While it is comparatively simple to transmit analogue signals, they are very difficult to compress or filter for noise. As a result, **digital** technology is rapidly replacing analogue.

Attention Economy
An economic environment in which there is an overabundance of information, and time — or "attention" — is the scarcest resource.

Authoring Tools
Software used to design and construct interactive multimedia applications. Popular authoring tools include Macromedia's Director and Authorware and Aimtech's IconAuthor. Such programs are quickly being upgraded to support **World Wide Web** and interactive television applications. Authoring tools are typically **object-oriented** and do not require sophisticated programming abilities to be used effectively.

Banner Ad
Ads that are usually presented within a rectangular (or banner-shaped) box positioned at the top or bottom of a **World Wide Web** page.

Beta
The final testing stage of a software or service product prior to commercial release.

Broadband (Network)
A general term used to describe high-capacity transmission equipment or systems that use a large portion of the electromagnetic spectrum through fibre-optic and coaxial cabling. Broadband systems can typically deliver multiple video channels and other services. Coaxial cable TV networks are a classic example of broadband services, where numerous video channels (and theoretically, telephony and data services) can be supported simultaneously.

Browser
A software application used to view **HTML** documents. Browsers may be used to display or retrieve HTML documents — such as **World Wide Web** pages — across the **Internet.** Popular browsers include Netscape's Navigator, Microsoft's Internet Explorer, and NCSA's Mosaic.

Cable Modem
Modem is a contraction of *Mo*dulator/*Dem*odulator. A cable modem is used to transmit digital data over an analogue channel on a CATV coaxial cable. Because purely digital transmissions require a higher bandwidth than ordinary coaxial lines can handle, modems are required to modulate carrier signals with data signals and extract data signals from modulated carrier signals, respectively.

Cache
Very fast intermediate memory between a fast **CPU** and a slower **RAM** memory subsystem used to store recently or frequently accessed information. Cache memory retains this information so that the CPU does not have to repeatedly access its slower RAM memory to use it.

CD-ROM
Compact Disk-Read Only Memory. Designed for data storage, these discs hold 650 Megabytes of data.

Chatting
A network-based style of communication that allows people to "chat" by typing messages to each other in real time. Chatting is a text-based simulation of conversing on a party line and has become one of the most popular online activities.

Client/Server
Term used to describe the latest configurations of distributed computing where processing is shared by local and remote computers. With a client/server system, the workload is split between PCs and one or more larger computers on a network. The information resides on the server; the computer used to request or retrieve that information is the client.

Component-Based Commerce
Interconnected standardised business units functioning among a variety of separate companies in order to produce a common product. Each company focuses on its core competencies while outsourcing other functions.

CONDRINET
A contraction for *Con*tent and Commerce *Dri*ven Strategies in Global *Net*works.

Content Firms
Businesses involved in the production, manipulation, or distribution of text, audio, images, or video.

CPU
Central Processing Unit. The primary microprocessing chip that controls and conducts a computer's operations.

Cryptography
Enciphering and deciphering data in code to ensure confidentiality.

Dense Wave Division Multiplexing (DWDM)
Data transmission that simultaneously sends multiple optical signals through a single fibre-optic line employing several light sources and detectors operating at different wavelengths.

Digital
Divided into discrete steps as opposed to an analogue signal, which typically resembles a sine wave. In data communications, digital refers to the binary (off/on) output of a computer or terminal. Modems convert the pulsating digital signals into **analogue** waves for transmission over conventional analogue phone lines.

Digital Subscriber Line (DSL)
Broadband transmission technology using **digital** filtering to remove noise from twisted-pair copper lines. There are several varieties of ADSL (Asymmetric Digital Subscriber Line) using varying hardware, modulation software, and compression techniques.

Digital Television
A television network that transmits **digital,** as opposed to **analogue,** television signals. Digital television enables interactivity and provides improved capacity and picture quality.

Digital Watermark
An invisible identification code permanently embedded into data as a means to prevent piracy or fraud.

Disruptive Technology
Technology that brings to market a very different value proposition than has previously been available. At least initially, disruptive technologies do not provide as high of a level of performance as existing technologies; however, they are less expensive and improve over time.

DRAM
Dynamic Random Access Memory. A computer's short-term memory **(RAM)** enhanced so that information stored in memory is regularly refreshed.

EASDAQ
*E*uropean *A*ssociation of *S*ecurities *D*ealers *A*utomated *Q*uotations. A small-cap pan-European stock exchange based in Brussels.

Electronic Data Interchange (EDI)
Computer-to-computer exchange of structured transactional information between autonomous computers. EDI is often used to connect various parts of a business (such as billing, ordering, and inventory) with common vendors.

Electronic Payment System
Monetary exchanges over **digital** networks.

Encryption
The manipulation and scrambling of data for security purposes to prevent restoration to its original form by anyone but its intended recipient.

End User
An individual, business, or organisation that uses products.

Ethernet Protocol
A protocol used for high-bandwidth local area networks (LANs). Ethernet is a networking standard operating at up to 1 Gbps. Ethernet connections — even

those involving two hosts — require use of T-connectors and terminators for proper operation.

Firewall
Hardware and software systems that block unauthorised access to data and applications.

Frictionless Economy
An economy in which producers' transaction costs tend toward zero.

Gateway
Program or device that passes information between networks or applications.

Hosting Service
A service that provides an electronic repository (usually a computer) for information available to other computers on the network.

HTML
Hypertext Markup Language. Formatting language used on the **World Wide Web.** HTML is viewed using a Web **browser.**

Hypertext
Text containing links to other texts. A core building block for the World Wide Web and much **interactive** media.

Intelligent Agents
Software programs that can act autonomously and with a high degree of flexibility. These applications can be programmed to perform actions, such as locating products according to specified criteria, and make decisions without human involvement. They may operate proactively, initiating a communication or transaction, or reactively, responding to external events and conditions.

Interactive
Two-way electronic communications.

Interactive Content Value Web
A framework developed by Gemini Consulting that helps define various content industry segments and players, maps their relationships, and provides a visual representation of the network media industry.

Interface
Point at which two devices or systems are linked. The shared connection or boundary between two devices or systems.

Internet
The global network of computer networks, based upon TCP/IP (Transmission Control Protocol/**Internet Protocol).**

Internet Protocol (IP)
Common shorthand referring to the suite of transport and application protocols that run over **packet-switched networks.**

Internet Service Provider (ISP)
Public providers of remote access to the **Internet.**

Internet Telephony
Telephone services that use **IP** networks to transmit voice signals.

Internet Time
Refers to the speed of change in the network economy. A year of calendar time has been equated in the industry to about four years in **Internet** time.

Intranet
Private or closed internal company network based on TCP/IP protocol.

Java
A programming language based on the C programming language. Separate Java applications, called "applets," do not have to be compiled for each different operating system. An applet will run identically and without modification in virtually any environment. The first programming language optimised for the **Internet**, Java contains inherent security features and compact code that support the development and delivery of content over narrowband connections.

Killer App
Literally a "must-have" software application that is considered revolutionary or superlative. The phrase also represents technological "must-haves" that are not software related, such as television.

Knowledge Workers
A term coined by Peter Drucker describing workers who are thought to add value through interpretation, analysis, and presentation of information.

Legacy/Sustaining Technology
Existing technology.

Mass-Customisation
An oxymoron describing "individually tailored" products and services cost-effectively offered in large quantities.

Metcalfe's Law
The utility of a network is equal to the square of the sum of its parts. Robert Metcalfe was inventor of the **Ethernet** networking **protocol** and founder of 3Com Corporation.

Microchips
Highly integrated circuit on a single substrate plate — the chip. More specifically, a microchip is an integrated circuit with extensive logic. Microprocessors and **DRAMs** are examples of microchips.

Micropayment
The exchange of small sums of money, including fractions of currency.

Middleware
Software that connects **legacy** systems with servers.

Mirror Site
A second or duplicate **World Wide Web** site that contains the same information as the site it "mirrors." Many software vendors have mirror sites on the

Web to bridge long-distances and to accomodate a high volume of requests for drivers and beta copies of programs.

Moore's Law
A 1964 observation made by Gordon Moore, co-founder of Intel, that the speed of an integrated circuit that can be purchased for a given amount of money was doubling every twelve months and would continue to do so for some decades. Processing power has actually doubled about every eighteen months, but the pattern has been remarkably steady and promises to continue into the next century.

Multimedia
Generic term for applications involving a combination of media forms, such as video, audio, text, and graphics.

Narrowband
Sub-voice channels able to carry data at speeds up to 64 Kbps, up to T-1 rates. Sometimes used to refer to Plain Old Telephone Service (POTS) and non-video-capable systems.

NASDAQ
*N*orth *A*merican *S*ecurities *D*ealers *A*utomated *Q*uotations. Small-cap securities market listing based in New York City. Many technology firms are listed on this exchange.

Network Access Points (NAPs)
A juncture between major **Internet** service providers. Also known as Internet Exchanges (IXs), connection at one or more of these NAPs constitutes connection to the Internet.

Network Commerce
The commercial exchange of goods, services, or information between two or more parties enabled by a **digital** medium.

Network Economy
The emerging economy based on open, **interactive, digita**l networks, such as the **Internet,** and the capabilities that such technology enables.

Network Revolution
Period of transition from the industrial economy to the **network economy.**

Neuer Markt
A small-cap German securities market.

Nouveau Marché
A small-cap French securities market.

Object-Oriented
Modular programming that allows software coding to be reused and interchanged between programs.

Online
State of a computer when it is connected to another.

Open Standard
A technological standard that allows a variety of autonomous electronic terminals to interact together with publicly-accessible specifications.

Operating System
Software that operates close to the hardware level and controls and supervises a computer's operation.

Packet-Switched Networks
Networks over which information is divided into small "packets" and transmitted over multiple routes to arrive and reassemble at a common destination.

Personal Computer (PC)
Term often used to refer to any standard desktop or portable computer.

Platform
Computing or networking hardware, software, and services.

Plug-in
A plug-in is a modular software add-on to a **browser** that enables it to support additional functions, such as audio or video.

Portal
Designation given to Internet sites used as main points of entry to the **World Wide Web.** The Web sites of AOL, Yahoo!, Excite, and Netscape's Netcenter are all portals.

Processing Speed
The amount of time required for a microchip to process a given amount of information.

Public-Switched Telephone Network (PSTN)
The world-wide voice telephone network.

Public-Key Encryption
Public-key encryption is based on two keys, a "public" key to encipher data and a "private" key to decipher data. Anyone wishing to receive such data can make his or her public key available to others, typically through a directory.

Push Technologies
Push software packages automatically deliver **Internet** text, graphics, and audio to a client machine. Push technologies mimic the ease-of-use of television and appeal to "passive" needs of consumers.

RAM
Random Access Memory. A computer memory chip in which data can be directly read from or written on.

Real-time
Transmitting or interacting with no time delay.

Re-Intermediate
To interpose as a new network-enabled intermediary in a direct-to-consumer product or service distribution channel.

Remote Access Server
A computer in a network that provides access to remote users via analogue modem or ISDN connections.

Router
A device that routes data packets from one local area network (LAN) or wide area network (WAN) to another.

Search Engine
An electronic service that scans the **Internet** for **Web** sites related to criteria entered by an end user and returns a list of relevant sites.

Server
A shared computer on a network.

Set-Top Box
A device that sits on top of a television set and acts as an interface to a **broadband network.** Set-top boxes encompass a wide range of technologies. Some are simple boxes that translate CATV frequencies making them compatible with old television sets that are not cable-ready; others are digital, decoding transmissions from advanced networks and demodulating them for viewing on an analogue television set.

Shareware
Software that any user can download for free prior to buying an official version.

Silicon Valley
Area of Northern California stretching from San Jose to San Francisco where many of the leading Internet and technology firms in the United States are located.

Single Key Encryption
Encryption method enabling communication sharing a common encryption key. Since this single encryption key must be kept secret to keep the information confidential, a separate shared key is necessary for every pair of communication partners.

Smart card
A card containing a microchip which can store and transmit information.

SMTP
*S*imple *M*ail *T*ransfer *P*rotocol. The standard e-mail protocol on the **Internet**. It is a TCP/IP protocol that defines the message format and the message transfer agent, which stores and forwards the mail.

Source code
The "raw" or "uncompiled" code in which software programs are written.

Streaming
A technique that allows data to be transferred as a steady and continuous stream. With streaming, the client browser or plug-in can start displaying the data before the entire file has been transferred.

Telecommuting
Working remotely (usually from home) and communicating with the office or colleagues by network.

URL
*U*niform *R*esource *L*ocator. The address that defines the route to a file on the **World Wide Web** or any other Internet facility. URLs are typed into the **browser** to access Web pages, and URLs are embedded within the pages themselves to provide **hypertext** links to other pages.

Value-Added Network (VAN)
A communications network that provides services beyond normal transmission, such as automatic error detection and correction, protocol conversion, and message storing and forwarding.

Video-on-Demand (VOD)
Ability to receive video programming on demand from a broadband network. VOD also implies VCR-like control of video playback.

Viral Uptake
Exponential growth in activity (resembling the spread of a viral infection).

Virtual Community
A group of people sharing a common interest over a network.

Webcasting
"Broadcasting" over the **World Wide Web** using a **streaming** media technology such as RealAudio or RealVideo.

World Wide Web
"Hypermedia" information display medium created for the **Internet.**

Year-2000 Problem
A programming error that will result in many computer systems being unable to recognise dates after midnight on December 31, 1999.

Bibliography

Agarwal, Manoj K., "Forecasting Market Adoption Over Time," School of Management, Binghamton University, Binghamton, New York, November 1997.

"America Online Increases Shelf Space For Barnes & Noble," *Newsbytes,* 17 December 1997.

Armstrong, Larry, "Downloading Their Dream Cars," *Business Week,* 9 March 1998.

Arzeni, Sergio, "Entrepreneurship and Job Creation," *The OECD Observer,* December 1997/January 1998.

Bailey, Steve and Steven Syre, "Its a Bull Market for Web Brokers," *Boston Globe,* 5 May 1998.

Barber, Benjamin, *Jihad vs. McWorld.* Ballantine Books, 1996.

Binary Compass Enterprises, Internet Shopping Report, 1997.

Blankenhorn, Dana, "Marketers Toy with New Ways to Keep Eyes on Site," *Business Marketing,* 1 February 1998.

Bodwin, David and David Kline, "Information publishing enters a post-Web world," *Upside,* February 1998.

Bogler, Andrew, "Insecurity at Work on the Increase Says CBI," *Financial Times* (London), 4 June 1998.

Bunting, Helen, "European Consumer Magazine Publishing: Facing the Electronic Challenge," *Financial Times Media & Telecoms,* 1997.

Burgess, John, "Sons and Daughters of Ireland, Come Home," *International Herald Tribune,* 18 March 1998.

Carvajal, Doreen, "The Other Battle Over Browsers," *The New York Times,* 9 March 1998.

Center on Budget and Policy Priorities, "A Federal 'Moratorium' on Internet Commerce Taxes Would Erode State and Local Revenues and Shift Burdens to Lower-Income Households," Washington, DC: May 1998.

Chisholm, Jim, "Global publishers predict rosy future for newspapers; top European newspapers," *Campaign,* 14 November 1997.

Christensen, Clayton M., *The Innovator's Dilemma: When New Technologies Cause Great Firms to Fail.* Cambridge: Harvard Business School Press, 1997.

Cole, George, "Censorship in Cyberspace," *Financial Times,* 21 March 1996.

Communication of the European Commission, "Risk Capital: A Key to Job Creation in the European Union," April 1998.

Craig, Andrew, "Tech-Skills Shortage Threatens Europe," *TechWeb News,* 10 March 1998.

Davis, Stan, and Christopher Meyer, Blur: *The Speed of Change in the Connected Economy,* Addison-Wesley, Reading, Massachusetts: 1998.

de Bony, Elizabeth. "Regulating Electronic Commerce," *EIU European Policy Analyst,* 16 February 1998.

Denton, Nicholas, "Drive to Plug the Gap," *Financial Times,* 3 February 1997.

Denton, Nicholas, "Venture Capital, Catalyst of the High-Tech Boom," *Financial Times,* 4 June 1997.

Downes, Larry and Chunka Mui, *Unleashing the Killer App.* Cambridge: Harvard Business School Press, 1998.

Dugan, I. Jean, "Boldly Going Where Others Are Bailing Out," *Business Week,* 6 April 1998.

Edmonson, Gail and Heidi Dawley. "Europe Finally Wakes Up to High-Tech Startups," *Business Week,* 26 May 1997.

Edmonson, Gail, "Spain's Success," *Business Week,* 3 August 1998.

"Electronic Commerce: The Challenges to Tax Authorities and Taxpayers," an informal Round Table discussion between business and government held in Turku, Finland, 18 November 1997 (the Turku Conference Round Table).

"English-speaking Nations Ahead in High Tech," Reuters, 28 April 1998.

Erickson, Jim, "Cyberspeak: The Death of Diversity," *Asiaweek,* 3 July 1998.

eStat, 1998. http://www.emarketer.com/estats/net_geogaphy_exp.html.

"EU sticks to EMU timing," *Financial Times,* 15 September 1997.

"EURES: Developing the European Labour Market," *RAPID,* 9 July 1998.

"Europe's Great Experiment," *The Economist,* 13 June 1998.

European Audiovisual Observatory, Statistical Yearbook '98, Council of Europe, 1998.

European Information Technology Observatory, *European Information Technology Observatory 1997,* Frankfurt-am-Main, Germany, 1997.

European Network for SME Research, *Fifth Annual Report of The European Observatory for SMEs,* 1998.

Eurostat, *Eurostat Yearbook '97: A Statistical Eye on Europe 1986-1996.* Luxembourg, Office for Official Publications of the European Communities, 1997.

Eurostat, *Panorama of EU Industry,* Luxmbourg, Office for Official Publications of the European Communities, 1997.

Festa, Paul, "Net Traffic Ratings Debated," CNET NEWS.COM, 12 June 1998.

Find/SVP, *American Internet User Survey 1997,* Find/SVP, 1997.

Flanigan, James, "Euro's Value Promises to be More than Monetary," *Los Angeles Times,* 1 February 1998.

Floren, Paul, "Euro-Techies: Scarce and Valuable," *International Herald Tribune,* 6 April 1998.

Forrester, Jay, *Industrial Dynamics,* Cambridge, MA: MIT Press, 1961.

Forrester, Jay, *Urban Dynamics,* Cambridge, MA: MIT Press, 1969.

Forrester, Jay, "The Counterintuitive Behavior of Social Systems," *Technology Review,* January 1971.

Friedman, Thomas, "The Internet Wars," *New York Times,* 11 April 1998.

G7 - Government On Line, "Democracy and Government OnLine Services - Contributions from Public Administrations around the World," http://www.state.mn.us/gol/democracy/.

"Gates, Buffett a bit bearish," CNET NEWS.COM, 2 July 1998.

Gelmis, Joseph, "New Technology Takes Games into the Mainstream," *Newsday,* 31 December 1997.

Georgia Institute of Technology GVU, Eighth WWW User Survey, http://www.gvu.gatech.edu, 1998.

Green, Heather and Linda Himelstein, "Portal Combat Comes to the Net," *Business Week,* 2 March 1998.

Groenewegen, John, "Institutions of Capitalisms: American, European, and Japanese systems compared," *Journal of Economic Issues,* June 1997.

Hagel, John and Arthur Armstrong, *Net.Gain: Expanding Markets through Virtual Communities.* Cambridge: Harvard Business School Press, 1997.

Hinnekens, L., "New Age International taxation in the Digital Economy of the Global Society," *Intertax: International Tax Review,* 1997.

Hu, Jim, "Net Metrics Inching Along," CNET NEWS.COM, 4 August 1998.

Information Technology Industry Databook, 1960 – 2002, Information Technology Industry, 1997.

International Data Corporation, "The Western European Forecast for Internet Usage and Commerce," 1998.

Johnson, Vicki and Marjory Johnson, "IP Multicast Backgrounder," 1996.

Kagan World Media, *European Television Markets,* 1996.

Kitagawa, Zentaro, *Doing Business in Japan.* Matthew Bender & Co., 1996.

Kotler, Philip, *Marketing Management: Analysis, Planning, Implementation, and Control.* Englewood Cliffs, New Jersey: Prentice Hall, 1988.

Krueger, A. and J. Pischke, "Observations and Conjectures on the US Employment Miracle, Working Paper 6146," National Bureau of Economic Research, Cambridge, MA, August 1997.

La Franco, Robert, "Entertainment and Information," *Forbes,* 12 January 1998.

Laing, Dave and Bob Tyler, "The European Radio Industry," *Financial Times* Telecoms & Media Publishing, London, 1996.

Li, Kenneth, "Cyberspace Calling: US News President Taking Internet Post," Daily News (New York), 16 April 1998.

Liebmann, Lenny, " Finding Euro Opportunities - Many firms see currency unification spurring E-commerce efforts," *InternetWeek,* 12 January 1998.

Macavinta, Courtney, "Congress Clears Copyright Act," CNET NEWS.COM, 4 August 1998.

Mahajan, Vijay and Jerry Wind, "Market Discontinuities and Strategic Planning: A Research Agenda," *Technological Forecasting and Social Change* 36, August 1989, p. 187.

Manchester, Philip, "PC as a Games Platform," *Financial Times,* 3 December 1997.

Miller, Greg, "Firms Agree on Anti-Piracy Technology," *Los Angeles Times,* 19 February 1998.

Morrison, Jeffrey, "How to Use Diffusion Models in New Product Forecasting," *Journal of Business Forecasting Methods & Systems,* Summer 1996.

Mutooni, Philip and David Tennenhouse, "Telecommunications @ Crossroads: Modeling the Communication Network's Transition to a Data-Centric Model," Conference Paper, Harvard Information Infrastructure Project Conference, December 1997.

Net Usage vs. Offline Media, http://www.emarketer.com/estats/usage_net_vs.html, 1998.

NetSmart-Research, "What Makes Women Click," 1997.

Nielsen Media Research, "Number of Internet Users and Shoppers Surges in United States and Canada," 24 August 1998, http://www.nielsenmedia.com/news/commnet2.html.

Organisation for Economic Co-operation and Development, Committee for Information, Computer and Communications Policy, *Measuring Electronic Commerce,* OCDE/GD(97)185, Paris, 1997.

Outing, Steve, "Study: 16% of U.S. Households Read Web Newspapers," *E&P Interactive,* 12 June 1998.

Paul Kagan Associates, "Netmarket — to Be the E-Commerce Leader?" *Interactive Multimedia Investor,* 20 January 1998.

"Please Dare to Fail," *The Economist,* 28 September 1996.

Porter, Michael E., *Competitive Strategy: Techniques for Analyzing Industries and Competitors.* New York: The Free Press, 1980.

Posch, Robert J., "Keep Privacy Laws Out of Cyberspace," *Direct Marketing,* January 1997.

"Progressive Networks and MCI Debut 'Netcast' Infrastructure," *ProSound Europe,* November 1997.

Rees-Mogg, William, "Tax Exiles on the Web," *The Times of London,* 26 February 1998.

Reeve, Simon, "High Phone Prices Threaten Europe's E-Commerce Future," *The European,* 20-26 July 1998.

Romer, Paul, "Increasing Returns and Long-Run Growth," *Journal of Political Economy,* vol. 94, no. 5 (October 1986), pp. 1002-37.

Sandomir, Richard, "Warily, Baseball Prepares to Make Murdoch Owner of the Dodgers," *The New York Times,* 8 March 1998.

"Showing Europe's Firms the Way," *The Economist,* 13 July 1996.

Scaglia, Silvio, "Europe Has the Capital to Create Jobs, if it Chooses To," *International Herald Tribune,* 16 June 1998.

Schilit, W. Keith, "Venture Catalysts or Vulture Capitalists," *The Journal of Investing,* 1996 Fall, vol. 5, no. 3, p. 86.

Schwartz, Evan I., "How Middlemen Can Come Out on Top," *Business Week,* 9 February 1998.

Shakespeare, Tom, "The games people play: Super Mario is now bigger than Mickey Mouse," *The Irish Times,* 18 August 1997.

Shankar, Bhawani, "The brave new world," *Telecommunications*, January 1998.

Simmons, Simmons Teen-Age Research Study (STARS), 1998.

Smith, Michael, "Signs of Progress in EU Campaign for More Jobs," *Financial Times,* 12 June 1998.

Staple, Gregory C., *Telegeography,* Telegeography, Inc., 1997.

"Study Finds MIT Affiliates Create 4,000 Jobs," *The Patriot Ledger,* 5 March 1997.

"Surprise! Surprise! Latin America Internet Use is on the Rise," PR Newswire, 19 November 1997.

"The European Currency Unit: The Increasing Significance of the European Monetary System's Currency Cocktail," 41 *Bus. Law.* 483 (1986).

"The Ramification of the Exchange Rate Collapse in Europe: Implications for Monetary Union," *B.U. Int'l L. J.* 263 (1995).

Timmons, J.A., L.E. Smollen and A.L.M. Dingee, *New Venture Creation,* 2nd edition, Homewood, IL: Richard D. Irwin, 1985.

Tobey, Alan, "Back to the Right Future: The Case for Neo-Intermediation," *The American Banker,* 10 November 1997.

Tooher, Paul, "Europe Counts on Currency for Clout," *The Providence Journal-Bulletin, 27* April 1998.

Towards an Information Society Approach, Green Paper on the convergence of the telecommunications, media and information technology sectors, and the implications for regulation, COM(97)623, Brussels, 03.12.1997.

Trippett, Frank, "Looking for Tomorrow (and Tomorrow)," Time, 26 April 1982.

Tucker, William, "Biting the Hand that Feeds Us," *The American Spectator,* May, 1998.

"UK: Global Music Market Expected To Grow 26 Per Cent By 2003," *AAP Newsfeed,* 14 January 1998.

"User Demographics: Net User Age," http://www.emarketer.com/estats/demo_age.html, 1998.

United States Department of Commerce, *The Emerging Digital Economy,* 1998.

United States Information Infrastructure Taskforce, *Framework for Global Electronic Commerce,* 1997, http://www.iitf.nist.gov/eleccomm/ecomm.htm.

University of Michigan Business School, 1997, via "eCommerce: What's Selling Online, http://www.emarketer.com/estats/ec_sell.html, 1998.

van der Heijden, Kees, Scenarios: *The Art of Strategic Conversation,* Chichester: John Wiley & Sons, 1996.

Veronis Suhler & Associates, *Communications Industry Report 1997,* Veronis Suhler & Associates, Inc. 1997.

Violino, Bob, "The Euro: Are You Ready Yet?" *InformationWeek,* 26 January 1998.

Vogel, Harold L., *Entertainment Industry Economics: A Guide for Financial Analysis.* Cambridge: Cambridge University Press, 1998.

Warwick, Martyn, " The wake up call; Europe's telecommunications industry," *Communications International*, January 1998.

Walker, Ruth, "Germans' Conscience Wants to Be a Guide," *The Christian Science Monitor,* 23 July 1997.

Warner, Joan, "Lessons from the European Tigers," *Business Week,* 6 July 1998.

Wilson, Ron, "Research verifies quantum process - Experiment reveals that data can be encoded in molecular quantum states," *Electronic Engineering Times,* 18 May 1998.

Wysocki, Bernard Jr., "The Outlook: Internet Is Opening a New Era of Pricing," *Wall Street Journal,* 8 June 1998.

"Yahoo starts Speaking Spanish," CNET NEWS.COM, 26 June 1998.

Yankelovich Partners, Inc. via "eCommerce: What's Selling Online," http://www.emarketer.com/estats/ec_sell.html, 1998.

Yankelovich Partners, Inc./Cyber Dialogue, Internet User Survey, 1997.

"Zigzag Path to the Euro," *Euromoney,* July 1997.

Selected Legal Sources

European Community Law

Treaty Establishing EEC, Mar. 25, 1957, 298 U.N.T.S. 3, arts. 85-86 (known as the Treaty of Rome).

Directive 84/450 of 10 September 1984.

Directive of 5 April 1995.

Council Directive 95/46 of the European Parliament and of the Council on the protection of individuals with regard to the processing of personal data and on the free movement of such data, 1995 O.J. (L 281) 31.

Directive 96/9/EC of the European Parliament and the Council of the EU of 11 March 1996 on the legal protection of databases, 1996 O.G. (L77/20) (the Database Directive).

Directive 97/7 of 20 May 1997 on the Protection of Consumers in Respect of Distance Contracts.

Directive of 6 October 1997.

Directive of 10 December 1997 on Copyright and Related Rights in the Information Society [see MEMO: 97/108].

Directive 97/66 of 15 December 1997.

Recommendation of 30 March 1998.

United States Law

American Civil Liberties Union of Georgia v. Miller, 1997 U.S. LEXIS 14995, * 13-14, 43 U.S.P.Q.2d 1356 (1997).

Carnival Cruise Lines Inc. v. Shute, 499 U.S. 585, 111 S.Ct. 1522 (1991).

Clayton Act, 15 U.S.C. 18 (1994).

Federal Trade Commission Act, 15 U.S.C. § 45 (1994).

Hasbro v. Internet Entertainment Corp., C96-130 W.D., 40 USPQ 2d 1479 (W.D. Wash. 1996).

Lanham Act, 15 U.S.C § 1125 (1994).

Notice of First Meeting of Conference on "Fair Use" and National Information Infrastructure (NII), 59 Fed. Reg. 46,823 (1994).

Playboy Enterprises, Inc. v. Calvin Design Label, Docket No. 97-3704.

Report to the Commissioner on the Conclusion of the First Phase of the Conference on Fair Use, September 1997.

Sherman Act, 15 U.S.C. 1 (1994).

Thomson Medical Co., Inc., 104 F.T.C. 648, at 839-842 (1984).

Ticketmaster Corp. v. Microsoft Corp., No. 97-3055 DDP (C.D. Calif., filed April 28, 1997).

Uniform Commercial Code.

Japanese Law

Consumer Code.

Home Sales Law.

North Con I v. Mansei Co., Japanese Supreme Court Petty Bench, 11 July 1997; Jiji Press Ticker Service, 11 July 1997.

International Law

Convention on the Law Applicable to Contractual Obligations ("Rome Convention") Rome, 19 June 1980.

Convention on Jurisdiction and Enforcement of Judgement in Civil and Commercial Matters, 27 September 1968, 8 I.L.M. 229 (known as the Brussels Convention).

International Chamber of Commerce, ICC Marketing Codes, Paris, 1987.

United Nations Convention on International Sales of Goods (known as the Vienna Convention), published in 1980 by the United Nations Commission on International Trade Law.

Report of the United Nations Commission on International Trade Law on the work of its twenty-ninth session, 28 May - 14 June 1996, U.N. GAOR, 51st Sess., Supp. No. 17, U.N. Doc. A/51/17 Annex I (1996) reprinted in 36 I.L.M. 200 (1997)

World Intellectual Property Organisation, Treaty on Certain Questions Concerning the Protection of Literary and Artistic Works (the "Copyright Treaty"), December 1996.

World Intellectual Property Organisation, Treaty for the Protection of the Rights of Performers and Producers of Phonograms (the "Performances and Phonograms Treaty"), December 1996.

World Intellectual Property Organisation, Treaty on Intellectual Property in Respect of Databases (the "Database Treaty"), December 1996.

Gemini Consulting

Gemini Consulting is a global management consulting firm that partners with clients to design and implement strategic change. We are committed to helping clients achieve results that exceed their expectations.

The firm has earned its unique reputation through a simple but powerful belief: people matter. We know that the best consulting solutions are those that the people of an organisation can wholeheartedly embrace. Through the power of people, Gemini helps leading companies around the world and across industries achieve results faster, more sustainably, and with higher impact on performance than they could alone or with anyone else in the world.

Gemini Consulting was formed in early 1991, but the firm is built on a thirty-five-year heritage of consulting expertise through the integration of more than a dozen firms around the world. As new firms have joined the organisation, Gemini has continuously expanded its geographic reach and service offerings. The recent integration of Bossard Consultants has further strengthened Gemini's operations, particularly in Europe, broadening our capabilities and enhancing our global position.

Gemini Consulting is an independent, wholly owned subsidiary of the Cap Gemini Group, Europe's leading systems integration and IT implementation firm.

Gemini Strategic Research Group

The Gemini Strategic Research Group was formed to help clients better understand their rapidly changing markets — providing client-specific, fact-based research and analyses that enable sound strategic business decisions. We aim to provide world-class expertise and insights within a wide range of Digital Age topic areas, including electronic commerce strategies, telecommunications markets, and digital media.

Gemini Strategic Research Group's staff includes strategy consultants, industry experts, research analysts, and information and knowledge specialists who bring together a wide range of capabilities to address today's complex strategic services.

European Commission

Content and Commerce Driven Strategies in Global Networks – Building the Network Economy in Europe

Luxembourg: Office for Official Publications of the European Communities

1998 — 419 pp. — 21 x 29.7 cm

ISBN 92-828-4289-4

Price (excluding VAT) in Luxembourg: ECU 70